Sexuality and the Law

Feminist Engagements

The interaction between legal regulation and the domain of sexuality has been the subject of much academic discussion, particularly in the context of feminist theory and politics. However, feminist understandings of several key issues have become subsumed within broader gender-oriented analyses.

Sexuality and the Law 'rediscovers' the peculiarity of feminist perspectives within this arena. More specifically, and in showcasing a diversity of scholarship that covers crime, the family and child, contract, jurisprudence, public, and international law, it revitalises a conception of sexuality as at the centre of feminist theorising.

Vanessa E Munro is Reader in Law, King's College London.
Carl F Stychin is Pro-Vice-Chancellor and Professor of Law and Social Theory, University of Reading.

Sexuality and the Law

Feminist Engagements

Edited by Vanessa E Munro
and Carl F Stychin

Routledge·Cavendish
Taylor & Francis Group
a GlassHouse book

First published 2007
by Routledge-Cavendish
2 Park Square, Milton Park, Abingdon, Oxon OX14 4RN, UK

Simultaneously published in the USA and Canada
by Routledge-Cavendish
270 Madison Ave, New York, NY 10016

A Glasshouse book
*Routledge-Cavendish is an imprint of the Taylor & Francis Group, an
informa business*

© 2007 Vanessa E Munro and Carl F Stychin

Typeset in Times by
RefineCatch Limited, Bungay, Suffolk
Printed and bound in Great Britain by
TJ International, Padstow, Cornwall

British Library Cataloguing in Publication Data
A catalogue record for this book is available from the British Library

Library of Congress Cataloging-in-Publication Data
A catalog record for this book has been requested

ISBN10: 1–904385–67–2 (hbk)
ISBN10: 1–904385–66–4 (pbk)

ISBN13: 978–1–904385–67–7 (hbk)
ISBN13: 978–1–904385–66–0 (pbk)

Contents

Notes on the contributors

Rosemary Auchmuty is Reader in Law at the University of Westminster and an Associate Director of the AHRC Centre for Law, Gender and Sexuality. Her research interests lie at the intersection of feminist history, law and popular culture, with particular reference to gender, sexuality and property.

Davina Cooper is Professor of Law and Political Theory at the University of Kent and Director of the AHRC Research Centre for Law, Gender and Sexuality. She is the author of *Challenging Diversity* (2004), *Governing Out of Order* (1998), *Power in Struggle* (1995) and *Sexing the City* (1994). In the late 1980s, she chaired the Women's Committee and was vice-chair of the Lesbian and Gay Committee of London's Haringey Council – one of the most controversial British local authorities then developing equality initiatives.

Sharon Cowan is a lecturer in law at the School of Law, Edinburgh University, where she is a member of the Centre for Law and Society. Her teaching responsibilities are in criminal law, medical jurisprudence, gender and justice, and theories of law and society. Her research interests include feminist legal theory, sexuality and the law, criminal law, criminal justice and medical law. She is currently working on a book on feminist perspectives on consent in the criminal law.

Margaret Davies is Professor of Law at Flinders University, South Australia. Her research crosses several fields of legal theory, notably feminist legal theory, legal pluralism, the philosophy of property, postmodernism, and queer theory. She is the author of several books, including *Asking the Law Question* (2nd edition 2002). She is currently working on a book about critical approaches to property.

Ratna Kapur is Director of the Centre for Feminist Legal Research, New Delhi. She has written and published extensively on issues of postcolonial theory, feminist legal studies, human rights and international law. Her latest book *Erotic Justice: Law and the New Politics of Postcolonialism*

(2005) addresses the issues of law, culture and sexuality from a postcolonial and subaltern perspective.

Prabha Kotiswaran is a Lecturer at the School of Law, School of Oriental and African Studies, University of London. She recently graduated with an SJD (doctorate in law) from Harvard Law School where her dissertation was on the economies of illegality in the sex industries of two Indian cities.

Daniel Monk is a Senior Lecturer in Law at Birkbeck, University of London. His research and publications in child/education law have focussed on sex education, school exclusions, home education and children's rights generally. His publications include the following co-edited collections: *Gendered Boundaries and Sexual Movements: legal negotiations of the global and the local* (2005), *Feminist Perspectives on Child Law* (2000), and *Legal Queeries: Lesbian, Gay and Transgender Legal Studies* (1998). He is Assistant Editor of *Child and Family Law Quarterly*.

Surya Monro is a Senior Research Fellow at the Policy Research Institute, Leeds Metropolitan University. She has published substantially in the fields of gender, sexuality and equalities, with a particular focus on trans-gender and bisexuality. She is the author of *Gender Politics: Citizenship, Activism and Sexual Diversity* (2005). Her research interests include gender and sexual diversity, democracy and citizenship, and governance. Surya has been involved in sexual/gender activism for over 15 years.

Vanessa E Munro is a Reader in Law at King's College, University of London. She has published various articles on feminist legal and political theory, which have focussed in particular on contemporary debates surrounding power and gender identity. In addition, she has combined this with empirical projects examining the law's engagement with the parameters of women's consent. With the support of grants from the ESRC, Nuffield Foundation and British Academy, she has conducted, and continues to conduct, research on rape, sex trafficking and prostitution.

Dianne Otto is an Associate Professor and Director of the International Human Rights Law Program of the Institute for International Law and Humanities (IILAH), at the University of Melbourne. She is also the inaugural Convenor of the University's interdisciplinary Human Rights Forum. Her research interests include peace and security issues, inter-national economic and social rights, international 'equality' jurisprudence, the exclusionary effects of legal representations of marginalised groups, gender issues in human rights and development, international human rights non-governmental organisations, and the domestic implementation of international legal obligations. In 2004, she was the Kate Stoneman Endowed Visiting Professor in Law and Democracy at Albany Law School, New York.

Carl F Stychin is Professor of Law and Social Theory at the University of Reading, where he currently serves as a Pro-Vice-Chancellor. He is the author of *Law's Desire: Sexuality and the Limits of Justice* (1995), *A Nation by Rights: National Cultures, Sexual Identity Politics, and the Discourse of Rights* (1998), and *Governing Sexuality: The Changing Politics of Citizenship and Law Reform* (2003). He is the co-editor (with Didi Herman) of *Legal Inversions: Lesbians, Gay Men, and the Politics of Law* (1995) and *Sexuality in the Legal Arena* (2000).

Matthew Weait is Senior Lecturer in Law and Legal Studies at Birkbeck, University of London. He studied law and criminology at the University of Cambridge and gained his DPhil in socio-legal studies from the University of Oxford. His interest in theories of responsibility stems from his voluntary work, and his political commitment to combating discrimination against people living with HIV and AIDS. He is the author of a number of articles on the criminalisation of HIV transmission, and in 2006, was appointed to the UK government's Expert Advisory Group on AIDS. His first book, *Intimacy and Responsibility*, will be published in 2007.

Introduction

Vanessa E Munro, King's College, University of London
Carl F Stychin, University of Reading

The interaction between legal regulation and the domain of sexuality has long been the subject of critical attention, particularly, but by no means exclusively, amongst those within the feminist community. Yet the relationship between feminism, law, and sexuality remains a complex one. Moments of tension, as well as of consensus, mark the engagement between feminist analyses and many of the concepts derived from broader sexuality scholarship. What's more, the role that law has played in constructing norms, systems of power and structures of desire in modern society is still much debated by feminist and sexuality scholars alike; as indeed is the potential that law offers for bringing about meaningful reform thereto.

In developing this collection of essays, our aim is not to impose any kind of strict coherence or over-arching framework on this interaction between feminism, law and sexuality. Rather, it is to present a series of commentaries and perspectives that constructively underscore the complexity and ambiguity of this relationship. As a result, in this introduction, we seek simply to outline in more detail the parameters of this simultaneously troubling and inspiring engagement, before moving on to briefly indicate the key issues addressed in the subsequent chapters.

Feminism and law

For feminist theorists and activists (and we recognise here the great diversity of views encapsulated in that phrase), 'law' has been a contested and contradictory domain of social and political struggle. On the one hand, law has often been viewed as a productive site in which to advance social change. Thus, feminists have embarked on reform strategies that have turned to the law, both as a system of social control and as a symbolic index of social attitudes. Even those commentators who have appeared most staunch in their challenge to liberal law have, at times, adopted this technique (for example MacKinnon, 1982; 1987). And while the success of such strategies has been contested, many feminists are committed to the inevitability of retaining law as a focus of critique and as a medium for reform (see for example Finley, 1989: 906).

On the other hand, however, a number of feminists have also come to reject the law as irredeemably patriarchal. Under this analysis, it is beyond question that 'the analytical frames of patriarchal law are not the spaces within which to create visions of feminist futures' (Wishik, 1985: 77). As a result, it is submitted that reforms secured through the law will be pyrrhic and that the best route to gender equality in fact lies in a decentring of law from feminist analysis (Smart, 1989).

Meanwhile, in the midst of these positions, a third, and arguably more nuanced, position has emerged. This sees law as both potentially productive but also dangerous (and indeed dangerously seductive). As a result, this approach adopts a contextual analysis towards the utility of legal strategies and maintains a permanently unclosed perspective on their benefits and burdens. To the extent that this avoids the double-binds of futile legal reform and constructive paralysis that threaten the previous approaches, this may represent an improvement. That said, however, it does nothing in itself to redress the profound complexity that plagues feminist use of law.

Feminism, sexuality and law

So too it is clear that 'feminism' and 'sexuality' have had a chequered relationship. Years ago, many radical feminists placed sexuality at the fore-front of their critiques of the oppression of women. They rejected claims to biological essentialism which suggested that sexuality was anything other than a product of society. Thus, MacKinnon, for example, isolated women's sexuality as the 'lynchpin' of patriarchal domination and held it up as a fundamentally social and relational construct that had men as its principal authors (MacKinnon, 1982; 1987).

But while this kind of analysis had the benefit of clarity of vision and powerful rhetoric, it also proved, for many, to be a partial and incomplete analysis of what seemed to be a more complex narrative. Indeed, it adopted a blanket hetero-critical perspective that marginalised alternative sexual identities and dismissed as instances of 'false consciousness' heterosexual women's assertions of positive sexual relations.

In more contemporary times, disillusionment with this approach has led many feminists to rethink the relationship between gender, sexuality and domination. This has been reflected, for example, in the work of Gayle Rubin (1984) who asserts that gender and sexuality are in fact distinct modes of oppression. What's more, this kind of analysis has been built upon to high-light the complex ways in which gender and sexual identity also intersect with various other axes of social stratification, such as race, ethnicity, class and age. As a result, it emerges that these factors play distinct and multifaceted roles in the creation and maintenance of any system of social power.

Adding further layers of complexity to this story, moreover, is the lesbian and gay movement, which has come to appropriate both 'sexuality studies' in the academy, and legal activism in the political realm. Within the claims made by lesbians and gay men, the discourse of rights seems to link seamlessly to social struggle, although some have expressed a note of caution as to the seductiveness (and limitations) of rights discourse (Herman, 1994). The achievement of rights claims by the disempowered has often resulted in the 'normalisation' of more radical claims aimed at social transformation. 'Minorities' thus become absorbed and validated in terms of prevailing dominant norms.

To even write of a lesbian and gay movement is, of course, problematic. It often erases, for example, the specificity of radical lesbian feminism, which has long viewed both law and gay male activism with a good deal of suspicion. Nonetheless, it seems that both lesbians and gay men have increasingly turned to law (and rights in particular) as a powerful (and hegemonic) discourse in large parts of the world, which has centred on the institution of marriage. For feminists, many of whom have had an uneasy relationship with marriage, this has been a source of concern, bemusement, or both!

Those engaged in an analysis of gender, sexuality and law have also been increasingly forced (sometimes painfully) to come to terms with the exclusions which have often been wrought in their analyses and politics. In this regard, critical race theory has provided an important and rich source of analysis which has demonstrated, not just that too often feminism and lesbian and gay politics have been dominated by the concerns of the racially dominant, but also that gender and sexual oppression have been constructed and maintained through the deployment of racialised categories (Harris, 1990; Crenshaw, 1994). Likewise, postcolonial feminism and sexuality struggles have provided further complementary insights into the exclusions which 'western' analyses have perpetrated in the past decades (Kapur, 2005).

Finally, transgender and queer analyses have also posed other challenges for both feminist and gay scholars and activists (for example Monro, 2005; Sharpe, 2002; Stychin, 1995). Simultaneously, some have found the complexity of gender and sexual identity politics to be a source of frustration and silencing, for fear that to articulate a theoretical or political claim will necessarily prove exclusionary. Yet, while identity politics by definition is founded on exclusions, it remains a powerful basis for mobilisation through which alliances and coalitions can be formed.

An overview of the collection

In this collection, we have sought to create an intellectual space for engagement across feminism, sexuality and law. We seek not to replay past struggles, but to underscore both continuities and change in the shape of gender and sexual politics in the twenty-first century. We have attempted to provide a forum in which to 'reconnect' feminism, sexuality and law. In so doing, we have tried to encourage a diverse set of voices that speak both to the reader and to each other.

But this diversity also reveals some commonalities. Perhaps most obvious amongst them is a recognition of the social construction of gender and sexual identities and practices. For many commentators, the appreciation of the cultural and historical situatedness of both gender and sexuality is so commonplace as to be banal. Nevertheless, it is submitted here that it is an insight that deserves and benefits from repetition. For many engaged in social struggle, after all, recognition of the 'performativity' of gender and sexuality remains fertile with potential (Butler, 2004).

Another shared concern amongst the contributors to this book is a cautious approach to legal engagement. While law may be a pragmatically useful site for the advancement of change, we should remember that the considerable 'power of law' does not make it an 'all-powerful' discourse (Smart, 1989). Relatedly, many of the chapters in this collection are indebted to the work of Michel Foucault. Despite the fact that Foucault expressed little direct interest in either law or feminism, his many insights into the complexity of power have proven to be a useful theoretical 'toolkit' of value for both feminists and scholars of sexuality (see, for example, Munro, 2001; 2003). To appropriate Foucault is, of course, also necessarily to recognise that he never claimed to provide a 'grand theory' of social change or the conditions of oppression. That said, his analysis does usefully assist us in understanding the power of law, not only to prohibit and censure, but also to regulate, normalise, and produce identities and practices in different historical periods and cultural contexts (Foucault, 1979; 1980a; 1980b).

In this volume, then, we seek, not a 'grand reconciliation', but to carry on a conversation across identities and politics. The book begins with issues of long-standing importance to feminist theory and practice: Vanessa Munro analyses harm and privacy in the context of the Sexual Offences Act 2003 in England and Wales. In this chapter, Munro provides a new 'twist' to concepts that have long been central, not only to feminism, but to liberalism itself. She provides a critical reading of the discourse that surrounds the Act, providing insights into debates over the relationship between law and morality. Those same debates are also of importance to Matthew Weait, in his consideration of recent case law surrounding the sexual transmission of HIV. Weait's specific interest is in the way in which the concept of 'responsibility' gets translated into criminal regulation and on the impact which this may have on individuals and communities 'at risk'. This critical reappraisal of the criminal law's intervention in sexual negotiation also animates Sharon Cowan's contribution. Focussing specifically on the provisions on rape under the Sexual Offences Act 2003, Cowan examines the law's use of consent as the threshold for permissible sex. Unlike many others who have criticised the model of consent that dominates the legal imagination, however, Cowan calls for its reformulation rather than outright rejection in the service of feminist goals.

A second theme reflected in this collection could be described as the ongoing problematics of gender and sexuality in theory and practice. The contributions of Carl Stychin, Rosemary Auchmuty, and Surya Monro exemplify this theme in particular. Stychin and Auchmuty provide differing, but complementary, perspectives on the UK's Civil Partnership Act 2004. While Stychin focuses on the way in which the discourse of contract law gets deployed in Parliamentary debates (and in other legal contexts around sexuality), Auchmuty provides a critical and passionate analysis of the pitfalls of civil partnership from a lesbian feminist perspective. Meanwhile, Monro's chapter, with its focus on transgender politics and theory, provides a challenge to much feminist, as well as gay and lesbian, activism. Monro's emphasis on the fluidity of identity categories underscores the challenge that 'trans' presents for long established 'truths' in much feminist and sexuality theory and politics. In so doing, it also engages key debates that animate the terrain of sexuality scholarship regarding the relationship between 'feminist' and 'gender' approaches.

We move on from these chapters to consider three distinct theoretical perspectives on citizenship and legal institutions, provided by Margaret Davies, Davina Cooper and Daniel Monk. Taken together these chapters illustrate the breadth of scholarship in the field on sexuality theory today. More specifically, Davies' chapter articulates an important intervention into critical legal pluralism, with a specific focus on subjectivity and sexuality. Her work challenges traditional jurisprudential notions of the subject of law, bringing feminism and sexuality into a world dominated too often by legal positivism. Cooper provides a complementary analysis, which interrogates the concept of 'unthinkability' in local government sexuality politics. Her contribution also demonstrates historical shifts which have occurred since the 1980s in the political realm, illustrating the complex interaction between the theoretical, the political and the experiential. Meanwhile, Monk's contribution provides a third perspective on the construction of sexual citizenship that focuses on the treatment of teenage pregnancy. The body of the pregnant girl is depicted in Monk's analysis as a site in which narratives of adolescent sexuality and childhood innocence clash, intersect, and occasionally merge. The role which sex education plays as a controlling mechanism in this context is also interrogated.

Finally, building on concerns about sexual agency, our focus turns in the final part of this collection to the global, and more specifically to the dilemmas of sex and survival under conditions of globalisation. Ratna Kapur's chapter provides a rich account, grounded in postcolonial analysis, of the ways in which issues of sex and sexuality have been deployed in contemporary legal discourses of prostitution and sex trafficking. She problematises the tendency to provide a one-dimensional perspective, which preserves the imperialist perception of the vulnerable third world 'other' and downplays the narratives of sexual agency that some women provide. It is a similar concern which animates Otto's analysis of sex between UN peacekeepers and the populations that they protect. In the wake of the UN's zero tolerance stance, Otto examines the impact of this policy on practices of 'survival sex', on the welfare of the local people involved and on the public image of the UN as a global institution. Our last chapter, by Kotiswaran, interrogates the regulation of sex workers through an analysis grounded in the political economy of the developing world. Her analysis, with its consideration of markets and work, provides an important corrective by highlighting the economic impact of sex as paid and unpaid labour.

Taken together, we hope that readers will agree that this volume provides a rich assortment of perspectives on law, feminism, and sexuality. As editors, we are indebted to all of our authors for their generous intellectual contributions. We also thank Beverley Brown and Colin Perrin for their unstinting support of the project at Routledge-Cavendish since its inception. Finally, we thank Tricia Allen for her superb assistance in the production of the manuscript.

Bibliography

Butler, J (2004) *Undoing Gender*, New York: Routledge.

Crenshaw, K (1994) 'Mapping the Margins: Intersectionality, Identity Politics and Violence Against Women of Color' in M Fineman and R Mykitiuk (eds) *The Public Nature of Private Violence*, New York: Routledge, pp 93–118.

Finley, L (1989) 'Breaking Women's Silence in Law: The Dilemma of the Gendered Nature of Legal Reasoning' *Notre Dame Law Review* 64, pp 886–910.

Foucault, M (1979) *Discipline and Punish – The Birth of The Prison* (trans. A. Sheridan), London: Vintage.

Foucault, M (1980a) *The History of Sexuality, Volume I* (trans. R Hurley), London: Vintage.

Foucault, M (1980b) *Power/Knowledge – Selected Interviews and Other Writings 1972–77* (ed. C Gordon), New York: Pantheon.

Harris, A (1990) 'Race and Essentialism in Feminist Legal Theory' *Stanford Law Review* 42, pp 581–616.

Herman, D (1994) *Rights of Passage: Struggles for Lesbian and Gay Legal Equality*, Toronto: University of Toronto Press.

Kapur, R (2005) *Erotic Justice: Law and the New Politics of Postcolonialism*, London: Glasshouse Press.

MacKinnon, C (1982) 'Feminism, Marxism, Method and the State' *Signs* 7(2), pp 515–44.

MacKinnon, C (1987) *Feminism Unmodified: Discourses on Life and Law*, Cambridge, Mass: Harvard University Press.

Monro, S (2005) *Gender Politics: Citizenship, Activism and Sexual Diversity*, London: Pluto Press.

Munro, V (2001) 'Legal Feminism and Foucault: A Critique of the Expulsion of Law' *Journal of Law and Society* 28(4), pp 546–67.

Munro, V (2003) 'On Power and Domination: Feminism and the Final Foucault' *European Journal of Political Theory* 2 (1), pp 79–99.

Rubin, G (1984) 'Thinking Sex: Notes for a Radical Theory of the Politics of Sexuality' in C Vance (ed.) *Pleasure and Danger: Exploring Female Sexuality*, New York: Routledge, pp 267–319.

Sharpe, A (2002) *Transgender Jurisprudence: Dysphoric Bodies of Law*, London: Cavendish.

Smart, C (1989) *Feminism and the Power of Law*, London: Routledge.

Stychin, C F (1995) *Law's Desire: Sexuality and the Limits of Justice*, London: Routledge.

Wishik, H (1985) 'To Question Everything: The Inquiries of Feminist Jurisprudence' *Berkeley Women's Law Journal* 1, pp 64–77.

Chapter 1

Dev'l-in disguise?

Harm, privacy and the Sexual Offences Act 2003

*Vanessa E Munro, King's College, University of London**

According to the then Home Secretary, the Review of Sexual Offences in England and Wales, which produced the 2000 *Setting the Boundaries* Report, signalled the beginning of a process that would lead to 'a new code of sex offences to take us into the new century' (Home Office, 2000: 2). While many of the recommendations set out in this report, and in the subsequent Government White Paper entitled *Protecting the Public*, were subject to protracted debate and substantial modification, by commissioning this Review, the Home Office did indeed put in motion a legislative process that would ultimately lead to the passing, in 2003, of the Sexual Offences Act.

In a context in which all criminal law interventions offer insight into the operative concerns and normative standards of a given community, this chapter will subject the ideology underpinning the Sexual Offences Act to critical scrutiny. More specifically, it will question whether this legislation, in creating space for state intervention in areas of socio-sexual life that were hitherto of little interest to the criminal law, fails to live up to its liberal rhetoric of respect for privacy. In so doing, it will examine the legacy that has been left by the Sexual Offences Act and will evaluate the extent to which it fulfils its promise to leave in its wake a forward-thinking code, supportive of the demands for autonomy and diversity that have come to dominate modern society.

The first section of this chapter, then, will examine the liberal tenets that explicitly animate the Sexual Offences Act, namely respect for personal freedom, on the one hand, and protection against (other-imposed) harm, on the other. Having done so, however, discussion will also draw attention to the existence of another, less candidly acknowledged, ideology, which was also influential upon the reform process. According to this latter approach,

* With the usual caveats, my thanks are due to John Tasioulas and Carl Stychin for their comments on an earlier draft of this chapter. I am also indebted to the contributors who attended the Work In Progress Seminar at King's College in September 2005 for their helpful comments on the version of the chapter presented there, and to Matthew Weait for suggesting the title.

sexual offences should be developed in such a way as to affirm and preserve moral consensus and righteousness within the community.

With the parameters of this potential ideological conflict highlighted, discussion in the second section will move on to look more directly at some of the criticisms that have been lodged at the Sexual Offences Act to date. More specifically, this section will examine the emerging claim that the Act's treatment of child sexual activity and prostitution-related activity ultimately undermines its liberal pretensions by supporting an agenda, according to which deviance from the sexual norm, and the offence which such deviance may cause others, in itself justifies criminal intervention.

To the extent that these criticisms highlight the existence of a tension between a focus on 'harm' and 'privacy', on the one hand, and on 'deviance' and 'offence', on the other, they can be seen to offer a concrete manifestation of, and testing ground for, the long-standing debate in analytical theory over the legitimacy of the law's role as an enforcer of conventional morals. Having situated the Sexual Offences Act and its critique in the context of this debate throughout the first and second sections of this chapter, discussion will move on in the final part to subject the notions of 'harm' and 'privacy' reflected in the work of key protagonists (i.e. Mill and Devlin) to scrutiny.

Deploying insights derived from feminist theoretical analysis and epistemological method, the precariousness of these notions, both in their own terms and in relation to one another, will be highlighted. Having done so, the final section will reflect on the implications of this for debate over the legal enforcement of morals in general, and for the Sexual Offences Act in particular. More specifically, it will argue that the shortcomings of the Act's treatment of child sexual and prostitution-related activity may lie less in having extended the reach of the criminal law *per se*, or in having criminalised conduct solely on the basis of 'offence', and more in having determined what is to count as relevant offensive conduct on an insufficiently critical basis.

Liberalism in tension: the philosophy behind the Sexual Offences Act 2003

In a context in which the pre-existing law on sexual offences contained a number of provisions that dated back several decades, there was clearly a need for the kind of sustained reflection and modernisation initiated by the Home Office in its *Setting the Boundaries* Review. But it was not only the drive to modernise 'archaic' laws that provided the impetus for legislative action. The social climate within which the Review emerged was also one in which there had been a broadening 'acknowledgement of the widespread existence of sexual abuse, particularly directed against children and other vulnerable people' (Lacey, 2001: 4). Exercised both by the public sensitivity to, and concern (or, some would argue, panic) about, paedophilia and by the gathering momentum of the 'New Labour' commitment to stamp out antisocial behaviour that undermines the fabric of the community, the Home Secretary's foreword to *Setting the Boundaries* identified the need to strengthen, as well as modernise, the law on sexual offences (Temkin and Ashworth, 2004: 328).

Placing their liberal credentials at the forefront, both the *Setting the Boundaries* Review and the *Protecting the Public* White Paper asserted as their guiding principles a belief firstly that 'the criminal law should not intrude unnecessarily into the private lives of adults' and secondly, therefore, that 'most consensual activity between adults in private should be their own affair' (Home Office, 2000: 5). While the exact boundaries of what can and cannot be consented to in private remains the subject of ongoing debate, this notion that there is and should remain a private sphere of life that is, 'in brief and crude terms, not the law's business' clearly resonates with the sexual offences rhetoric that has dominated in the UK since the time of the Wolfenden Report into Homosexual Offences and Prostitution (Home Office, 1957).

In addition, though, and here the contemporary approach continued to mirror its Wolfenden predecessor, the Review also acknowledged that this affirmation of the right to sexual freedom must be counterbalanced by an acceptance that there are certain circumstances in which constraints need to be imposed in order to protect others from harm. Central amongst those circumstances are those 'where sexual activity is not consensual or where society decides that children and other very vulnerable people require protection and should not be able to consent' (Home Office, 2000: 5). Thus, the Review adopts a framework of respect for personal freedom, subject only to the requirement to avoid harming others, which replicates Mill's famous position that 'the only purpose for which power can be rightfully exercised over any member of a civilised community, against his will, is to prevent harm to others' (Mill, 1996: 13).

While *Setting the Boundaries* and its reforms thereby pay considerable lip-service to Mill, there are, however, aspects of the underpinning philosophy that appear to undermine the strength of these liberal ideals. Indeed, as Lacey has argued, the dual commitment in *Setting the Boundaries* to the protection of privacy and to the infliction of harm to others as the sole basis for state intervention rest uncomfortably alongside a blend of other rationales for the criminalisation of sexual conduct, including in particular a 'quasi-moral' rationale which reflects 'the idea that sexual offences embody social standards of right and wrong' (Lacey, 2001: 5).[1]

This kind of rationale for criminalisation is in itself problematic to the extent that it assumes the existence of a shared popular consensus as to what

---

1   Of course, referring to this alternative rationale as 'quasi-moral' is not intended to imply that the harm principle is not itself also grounded in moral consideration, namely in the moral consideration that coercive state intervention is justified when harm is inflicted upon others.

constitutes 'right' and 'wrong' behaviour in the sexual arena. As a number of commentators have pointed out, in the context of an increasingly diverse and heterogeneous community, the faith which is thereby placed in the existence of this kind of sexual 'conscience collective' is highly questionable. Despite this, however, the Home Secretary's foreword to *Protecting the Public* talks repeatedly about 'our common values', which, he warns, could be 'undermined by the behaviour of a minority' (Home Office, 2002: 5). In so doing, he alludes to the existence of a communitarian dimension to the sexual offences reforms that is barely acknowledged in the individualistic rhetoric of the liberal philosophy.

In addition, this alternative rationale for criminalisation is controversial, since it fails to give clear guidance on the criteria by which standards of right and wrong are to be determined. To the extent that they focus on the *harmfulness* of the conduct to others, there exists the possibility of a happy coincidence between this 'quasi-moral' rationale and its liberal counterpart. But there is no apparent need for the criteria to be determined in this way. Thus, this approach has the potential to subvert the Review's explicit commitment to the harm principle by legitimating the criminalisation of behaviour that deviates from the norm of 'appropriate' sexuality, even where that behaviour harms no-one, or at least harms no-one other than the individual.

Where the wrongfulness of sexual conduct is to be determined by the moral majority, be they real or imagined, and where such determinations of wrongfulness in themselves constitute legitimate grounds for legal intervention, this alternative rationale for criminalisation limits personal freedom to deviate from the norm. In so doing, it grafts on to the underside of the *Setting the Boundaries* Review an ideology that appears to be more in keeping with Devlin than Mill – an approach within which a shared moral fabric not only exists, but needs to be protected, through the criminal law, from the deleterious effects of deviance, the existence of which could undermine and disintegrate the bonds that hold our community together (Devlin, 1965). Even when non-conformance with the norm appears as ostensibly harmless, therefore, under this approach, rejection of the standards that unite the community, and the offence which this causes to others, may justify legal intervention; as indeed may the desire, stemming from that offence, to protect an individual from the degradation that s/he self-imposes through his or her intentional non-conformance with moral norms.

Thus, the 'quasi-moral' rationale that Lacey identifies as implicated within the *Setting the Boundaries* approach, when pressed, appears to risk undermining the official story of the Review, which reflects the Millian tenet that a person's own well-being, physical or moral, does not provide sufficient warrant for paternalistic coercion. Developing this insight, a number of the emerging critiques of the resultant Sexual Offences Act have illustrated the ways in which, despite an explicit philosophy of respect for privacy, personal freedom and an exclusive concern with conduct causing harm to others, the legislation has also introduced a series of provisions that reflect a more paternalistic, moralistic, and it has been argued, repressive, rationale for criminalisation. To the extent that this is true, Lacey has concluded that the concern with harm put forward in the Review is 'a guiding rather than a limiting principle', since 'though the shade of John Stuart Mill stands behind the Review's references to harm and its appeal to the value of autonomy, an equally important concern is that of protection' (Lacey, 2001: 5). Importantly, however, as will become apparent as we turn our attention more directly to the Sexual Offences Act in the following section, the concern for protection operating in this context extends not only to vulnerable individuals, but also to society at large and in particular to its fragile moral fabric.

The Sexual Offences Act 2003: setting or skewing the boundaries?

After a lengthy period of consultation and negotiation, following on from the publication of the *Setting the Boundaries* Review, the Sexual Offences Act 2003 emerged. This legislation not only consolidated the law in this area, but also created a range of new offences and substantially modified a number of pre-existing ones. The reach and complexity of the Sexual Offences Act is such that it is not possible to offer a comprehensive discussion of all of its provisions within this chapter. Thus, discussion here will concentrate on highlighting those parts of the Act, criticism of which indicates that, despite its apparent support for boundaries of state intervention born of necessity and grounded in the avoidance of harm to others, there are certain reforms brought about under the Sexual Offences Act that reflect a different position both on the rationale for criminalisation and on the parameters of personal privacy.

Sexual activity between minors

Notwithstanding the assertion in *Setting the Boundaries* 'that many forms of potentially harmful or dangerous sexual conduct are not most appropriately or effectively regulated by criminal law', commentators have been quick to point out (and often to lament) the 'striking' reach of the provisions under the Sexual Offences Act relating to child sexual activity (Lacey, 2001: 9). With the backdrop to the legislation being one dominated by popular concern about paedophilia and with both *Setting the Boundaries* and *Protecting the Public* flagging protection of children from abuse as a key priority, a series of offences were designed to capture adult predators who cause harm to children by engaging them in a sexual encounter. Under ss 5 to 8 of the Act, it is an offence for anyone to rape, penetrate, or sexually assault a child who is under the age of 13, or to cause that child to engage in sexual activity. In addition, under ss 9 to 12, it is an offence for anyone, who does not reasonably believe that a child is over the age of 16, to engage in sexual activity with a child under that age, to cause that child to engage in sexual activity, to engage in sexual activity in the presence of that child or to cause that child to watch a sexual act.

Some child liberationists may, of course, object to these provisions on the basis that they are too heavy-handed – this kind of blanket prohibition on a child's consent to sexual activity, it is argued, unduly restricts his or her autonomy, particularly where the more mature child may have the requisite capacity to consent to sexual intimacy. In response to this, it should, however, be noted that just because a child may have the capacity to make an informed choice regarding participation in sexual activity, this does not in itself mean that their participation may not also prove to be harmful. Survey data from the US indicate that over 25 per cent of girls have a first sexual experience that, although consensual, was also felt by them, either at the time or subsequently, to be 'unwanted' (Raphael, 2000: 49). In a context in which premature sexual experiences, even when consented to, can result in physical and psychological harm, there may therefore be good reason for caution in accrediting too much weight to expressions of sexual consent even from otherwise competent minors.[2] Thus, there would appear to be some justification for the blanket approach taken by the Act, grounded in a concern to protect children from harm in situations where their sexual partner is older, more experienced, and more likely to wield persuasive power or influence over them.

Certainly, for the purposes of current discussion, the criticisms of the Sexual Offences Act with which we are concerned in this chapter do not, for the most part, object to the criminalisation of this kind of scenario: perhaps precisely because, when restricted to adult offenders, these offences appear more compatible with the liberal rhetoric of non-intervention except where necessary to prevent harm to others. By contrast, however, the extension of these offences beyond the conduct of adult predators, to cover all forms of sexual behaviour *between* children, has been the subject of more animated criticism. Section 13 of the Act expressly stipulates that any person under the age of 18 can also be held liable for one of these child sexual offences, even where both parties have given their consent. In thus leaving a 15-year-old child who engages in consensual sexual activity with an age mate potentially liable to up to five years' imprisonment, the Sexual Offences Act has attracted criticism for criminalising conduct that is argued to be both harmless and

---

2   For further discussion of this survey, see Abma *et al.*, 1998. Of course, adults too may consent to sexual encounters that prove harmful, and the question of whether, and how, the law should deal with this is a complex one (see Munro, 2005).

potentially positive for young people, and for thereby betraying its liberal premises regarding justifiable intervention.

As these critics point out, consensual sexual experimentation with age mates is a 'universal part of everyone's growing up' (Bennion, 2003: 13), particularly for pubescent children aged between 13 and 16. Certainly, empirical studies have consistently found that pubescents tend to have their first non-penetrative sexual experience much earlier than the Sexual Offences Act would allow, with the average age being 14 for girls and 13 for boys (Wellings *et al.*, 1994: 40; Erens *et al.*, 2003: 5). Although, as noted above, such experiences may sometimes prove harmful, they are by no means necessarily so, and, according to Bennion, much of the harm that is generated may be the result of embarrassment or shame produced as a consequence of others' disapproval. In addition, these critics point out that, without going to the extreme of condoning adult–child sexual relations in the name of child liberation, it is clear that considerable harm may be generated by restricting children's ability to sexually experiment with age mates and by labelling children who do so either criminal or potentially criminal.

Together, these considerations have led a number of commentators to conclude that, even if there is a legitimate ground, based in consideration of harm, for the Act's blanket prohibition of sexual activity between adults and minors, there is no such justification in regard to its prohibition of all such activity between minors. As Spencer puts it, 'the new law is exceptionally heavy-handed', since it renders 'theoretically punishable' a range of behaviour for which it would be 'scandalous' if anyone were prosecuted (Spencer, 2004: 347). Supporting this position, Bainham and Brooks-Gordon also point out that these provisions create 'an unwarranted proliferation of criminal liability where no identifiable harm has yet occurred' (Bainham and Brooks-Gordon, 2004: 261) and extend the criminal law in ways that are clearly disproportionate to the aim of protecting children from abuse.

Thus, it has been argued that the child sexual offences represent a clear example of the Act's unprecedented extension of the criminal law into intimate areas of socio-sexual life, and of the justification of that intervention in something other than harm prevention alone. While the alternative rationale for criminalisation in this context is not always articulated by those who lodge this critique, it is generally assumed to be a 'quasi-moral' one, reflecting what Bennion would refer to as 'sex negativism' (2003: 6) and what others might refer to as a concern to preserve the sexual purity of youth. To the extent that this undermines the official policy of non-intervention in the absence of identifiable harm, it is argued by these critics that these offences support a counter-narrative grounded in 'right' and 'wrong' ways of expressing sexuality, which sits at odds with the standard liberal commitment to freedom and diversity.

Given the difficulties which our society has traditionally experienced in dealing with the idea of child sexual desire, it is perhaps unsurprising that such a narrative interjects into our notions of protection and vulnerability in this context. Likewise, it is perhaps unsurprising to find a similar 'quasi-moral' rationale for criminalisation overriding non-interventionism and harm criteria in the Act's response to one of the other areas of sexuality with which society has frequently struggled, namely prostitution.

Prostitution-related activity

In purporting to undertake a wholesale review of sexual offences in England and Wales, it might have been anticipated that the *Setting the Boundaries* Report would have taken the opportunity to conduct a thorough examination of prevailing prostitution policy. This, however, did not in fact occur. Indeed, despite a context in which several other jurisdictions had recently taken steps towards a more tolerant approach to sex industry regulation, the Review largely side-stepped the ideological and regulatory questions at the root of any such alternative legislative response.[3] Modernising the form, but not the tone or substance, of pre-existing offences relating to causing or inciting (s 52), or controlling (s 53), prostitution for gain and brothel-keeping (s 55), the Sexual Offences Act took its lead from the Government's *Protecting the Public* White Paper. This Paper, according to the then Home Secretary, adopted the view that the sex industry is a 'sub-world of degradation and exploitation' to be purged, and a 'terrible trade' that 'bedevils' communities with its off-spins of 'antisocial behaviour' and 'mafia-style criminality' (Hansard, 2002).

Throughout the entire process leading up to the Sexual Offences Act, it was assumed, therefore, that the selling of sex is inherently exploitative, such that activities which encourage, facilitate or benefit from prostitution necessarily involve the infliction of harm on others. But, as has often been pointed out, this assessment is far from uncontroversial. Indeed, while many campaigners have dedicated considerable energy to justifying this view (Jeffreys, 1997), a number of others have argued that there is nothing inherently exploitative in a commercial sexual transaction. Such campaigners have argued that the harm in prostitution comes, not from the commodification of sex *per se*, but from the conditions in which prostitutes are forced (by virtue of their industry's current illegality) to operate, and from the social stigma and official surveillance that is imposed upon them under the current regime (for discussion of these 'prostitution debates', see O'Connell-Davidson, 1998; O'Neill, 2001).

---

3 While the subsequent Home Office Review, *Paying the Price: A Consultation Paper on Prostitution* (2004), might have been hoped to yield more satisfactory results, its response, *A Coordinated Prostitution Strategy* (2006) does not in fact indicate any significant change in approach.

While these debates over the conceptualisation of prostitution are heated, they are central to what justifies the criminalisation of the sex industry under a classical liberal approach, namely its harmfulness. For a number of commentators, therefore, the failure of the Review and the Sexual Offences Act to engage with these debates represents a telling ambivalence as to the legitimacy of this liberal rationale as the operative basis for criminalisation. Indeed it has been argued that, in a context in which the legislators could not *but* have been aware of the controversy over the harmfulness of prostitution, this uncritical affirmation of the need to punish prostitution-related activity paradoxically reflects the way in which prostitution has been conceived of as an exception to, rather than as an exemplar of, the liberal mantra of non-intervention in the absence of identifiable harm (Lacey, 2001; Bainham and Brooks-Gordon, 2004).

By adopting the approach reflected in the White Paper, the Sexual Offences Act extends special protective measures to adult sex workers whose vulnerability, although real in many cases, is arguably not of the sort which the classical liberal view would normally recognise as precluding the possibility of consent (Lacey, 2001: 5–6). Critics argue that this over-extends the reach of the criminal law into this area of socio-sexual life and infantilises sex workers by rendering them prima facie victims of abuse. What's more, it does so, according to these critics, not primarily, or at least not exclusively, out of a concern with the protection of the women themselves, but rather out of a concern with the preservation of our shared moral fabric. As Lacey puts it, the case for criminalising prostitution-related activity under the Sexual Offences Act emerges as grounded less in a concern about abuse of vulnerability or harm, as the official rhetoric implies, and more in a conviction that 'the commodification of sex is unacceptable and should be prohibited' (Lacey, 2001: 10).

To the extent that this is so, this sets up these prostitution-related offences as another example of the way in which the Sexual Offences Act, while purporting to adopt a non-interventionist stance concerned exclusively with the prevention of harm, simultaneously supports criminalisation in instances where there is no unequivocal harm caused to another. In the context of prostitution, critics have argued that the harm accruing to the sex worker is debatable and undefended, and the rhetoric which emerges throughout the reform process is one focussing on the 'wrongfulness' of prostitution, on the moral degradation it inflicts on those who sell sex, and on the need to protect society from the decline in moral standards and the threat to public order which a more tolerant approach to the sex industry might encourage. Once again, therefore, while the guiding principles asserted as forming the foundation of the sexual offences reform prioritise Millian ideas of privacy, personal freedom and sexual diversity, it is argued that the Act reflects a competing rationale for criminalisation that appears more concerned with affirming sexual norms and protecting the moral fabric of the community from the negative effects of deviance.

A boundary askew?

While there have been a number of promising developments brought about by the Sexual Offences Act, what the discussion in this section has illustrated is the existence of considerable disquiet among some critics over the way in which certain offences intrude into hitherto untouched areas of socio-sexual life and find their justification for so doing in a claim to protect the moral fabric of the community. As Bainham and Brooks-Gordon argue, this generates some 'strikingly illiberal' provisions that ignore the fact that harm to the individual must be established before criminalisation can be justified and that extend into areas of private life and sexual morality that should have remained 'none of the law's business' (Bainham and Brooks-Gordon, 2004: 290).

Re-setting the boundaries?

Although sympathetic to the concerns expressed by these critics over the treatment of child sexual and prostitution-related activity, it will be argued in this section that the shortcomings of the Sexual Offences Act lie less in having abandoned an exclusive focus on harm as such, and more in failing to reflect critically upon the ways in which what is deemed to be 'right' or 'wrong' may be relevant in justifying criminalisation.

Borrowing insights developed from feminist analysis, it will be suggested here that many of the criticisms lodged at the Sexual Offences Act, and in particular those discussed in the previous section, have inappropriately reified the concepts of harm and privacy that have formed the bedrock of traditional liberal rhetoric. Indeed, by automatically treating with suspicion reforms that do not fit this liberal model, these criticisms have failed to deconstruct the boundaries of what constitutes the private and what counts as harm under the dominant approach. In so doing, they have reaffirmed the purported neutrality and inevitability of these concepts in a context in which feminist analysis has long-since highlighted their partiality and malleability.

Building on feminist insights to initiate a more complex analysis of these liberal tenets, this section will revisit the failings of the Sexual Offences Act with a view to offering an explanation that differs somewhat from that reflected in the criticisms examined above. In addition, by interrogating the central concepts of privacy and harm directly, this analysis will permit scope for a reappraisal of the parameters of the debate between Mill and Devlin over the law's enforcement of morals. In particular, it will question the extent to which the sanctity of the private sphere, supported in liberal rhetoric, in fact facilitates the pursuit of personal freedom in the way that is often claimed. And in a context in which we take our place in a complex network of relationships with others, it will illustrate the artificiality of the distinction between harm and offence that has dominated positions on each side of this debate.

Privacy and harm: the Sexual Offences Act and beyond

As was discussed in the first section of this chapter, at the forefront of the official approach to the Sexual Offences Act was a commitment to respecting the right to privacy. In the context of sexuality, this respect for privacy has traditionally manifested itself through the imposition of a general embargo on state intrusion into the bedroom, except under very limited circumstances. While preserving a realm of private life which is none of the law's business is not in itself necessarily controversial from a feminist perspective, considerable concern has been expressed regarding the ways in which the boundaries dividing the public and private spheres have been drawn. As Pateman has argued, the division between public and private has operated to insulate the injustices that arise in the latter sphere from scrutiny or reform (Pateman, 1989). And in a context in which those injustices are predominantly visited upon women, this laissez-faire approach emerges as deeply problematic. Indeed, the question arises: for *whom* is this non-interventionist policy securing freedom?

The boundaries of public and private drawn and maintained in liberal theory emerge, under a feminist analysis, as deeply political and inherently constructed. Indeed, determinations of what counts as public and what counts as private are the result of a conscious process of decision making. The downside of this has been that those with power in society, typically men, have been able to relegate sexual and familial situations in which women are most vulnerable to the unregulated private sphere. But the upside of the constructed nature of the private sphere lies in the potential thereby offered for subversion and for shifting the public/private boundary in ways that are more productive for women. Indeed, the feminist slogan that 'the personal is political' is intended both to highlight the extent to which non-intervention by the state into the private sphere is itself a political choice and to campaign for greater state intrusion into hitherto unregulated areas where this is necessary to secure women's freedom.

The criticisms of the Sexual Offences Act discussed in the previous sections have highlighted its apparent duplicity in expressing a commitment to the right to privacy, on the one hand, whilst simultaneously jettisoning this commitment in specific contexts in order to adopt a heavily interventionist response. While it is no doubt prudent to approach reforms that intervene in hitherto unregulated areas of private life with some caution, as these critics do, it is submitted that there is a danger here of assuming that the mere fact of extension of the criminal law into these areas *in itself* gives rise to legitimate condemnation. While this affirms the 'symbolic and normative power of "the private" as a category that frames our perceptions of the world' (Weait,

2005: 99), it does so in a way that threatens to stagnate the inherently con-structed, and thus contingent, boundary delineating the content of public and private life. In so doing, the approach thus informing many of the criti-cisms lodged at the Act's interventionism appears to ignore feminist insights regarding the politicised nature of this boundary. What's more, it threatens to pose obstacles of principle to re-imagining that boundary in ways that may secure women's freedom through further intervention.

The problems which this presents from a feminist perspective are amplified, furthermore, as suspicious critics of the Act move forward from this reifica-tion of current forms of the public/private binary to seek out justification for new interventions from a pre-selected set of considerations grounded in the liberal concept of harm. As noted in the previous section, most criticisms of the Act's treatment of child sexual activity and prostitution 'down tools' relatively quickly upon discovering no evidence of clear and unequivocal harm in the absence of intervention. This focus on harm as the pertinent threshold criteria has, of course, been the hallmark of the traditional liberal rationale for criminalisation. But it is far from unproblematic. Indeed, much feminist analysis has sought to deconstruct this conception of harm and to highlight the extent to which it demands an unduly formulaic and partial understanding of injury. As will be argued in the following discussion, to the extent that this analysis has merit, many of the criticisms of the Sexual Offences Act examined above ignore its relevance in the context of sexual offences reform. In so doing, they disguise both the particularity of this liberal conception of harm and the partiality of its claim that it alone can provide the basis for legitimate criminalisation.

In a context in which feminist analysis has highlighted the tendency, in a patriarchal society, for laws to reflect the concerns of male authors rather than female others (or at least to reflect the concerns of women only as refracted through men's cognition), it is perhaps unsurprising to find disquiet over the partiality of the dominant conception of harm. Feminism has long-since been alert to the ways in which 'the harms, minimisation of which is largely assumed to be in some way the "point" of law, have for most of our history not included the harms suffered distinctively or disproportionately by women' (West, 1997: 9). Thus, the refusal of the law to grant a right to abortion, for example, represents the failure of its male authors to acknow-ledge the harm suffered by women forced to endure an unwanted pregnancy. Similarly, the law's reluctance to recognise marital rape reflects male incredu-lity at the suggestion that intercourse with one's husband, even when not consented to, may be harmful. But beyond the gender-specific experiences that have led to the marginalisation of certain characteristically female harms from the purportedly neutral benchmark, there is a further source of concern. Indeed, it has often been argued that the way in which the law, particularly the criminal law, conceives of the concept of harm is itself highly specific. Within the liberal tradition, the concept of harm is treated as denoting an injury, typically inflicted upon the body, which can be identified independently of both the context in which it takes place and the understanding of the experience from the point of view of the people involved. While this represents one of the ways in which what we experience as harmful can be identified, it is by no means the only way. In this light, then, this notion of harm, largely unquestioned in liberal thinking, and in the criticisms of the Sexual Offences Act above, emerges as itself a construction, which is created as coherent and self-evident only through a process that deliberately renders other experiences of harm incomprehensible or irrelevant.

When coupled with the overarching analysis of the impact of patriarchy on law's cognition of gender-specific injuries, this recognition of the constructed nature of the liberal concept of harm has proven useful in facilitating feminist campaigns in areas, such as pornography, in which it is argued that women's experiences of harm have been excluded or ignored. Indeed, in a context in which the women depicted in pornographic images may have consented to their production and distribution, and in which no direct link between pornography and sexual violence has been established, liberal frameworks for conceptualising harm have struggled to see any basis for legitimate concern. Despite this, however, a number of commentators, most famously MacKinnon, have worked tirelessly to highlight the negative impact which pornographic images can and do have on women (MacKinnon, 1989). In particular, she has argued that the experience of having one's sexuality as a women objectified through such depictions constitutes a real harm, of the sort which, despite failing to conform to the conventional liberal understanding, ought to be recognised by the law.

While these claims regarding the harm inherent in pornography are undoubtedly controversial, their value in the present context lies in their ability to highlight the limitations of the standard liberal conception of harm and to illustrate the potential which exists for redeploying that notion in new ways through the process of sexual offences reform. In addition, this work on pornography is useful since it provides a concrete illustration of the way in which the concept of harm has traditionally been constructed in opposition to the concept of 'mere offence'. Indeed, it has often been argued by liberals keen to defend pornography that what feminist analysis denotes as harm reflects nothing more than the offence which sexualised imagery may generate; an offence which cannot in itself justify prohibition (Dworkin, 1981). Inherent in the liberal construction of harm, then, is the idea of its involving something other than, or more than, 'mere offence'. This understanding is apparent, moreover, not only in the context of specific engagements with sexual offences reform, but also in the very parameters which define the debate between Mill and Devlin, through which the legitimacy of criminalising 'merely' offensive, cf. harmful, conduct is considered.

It is precisely this distinction between harm and 'mere offence' that also dominates the criticisms of the Sexual Offences Act discussed above. Indeed, the force of most of these criticisms has lain in the apparent illegitimacy of criminalising conduct that is merely offensive, since such conduct is, by definition, not harmful in any sense that should justify criminalisation. While, as we have seen, this replicates the approach adopted by various other theorists, the uncritical perpetuation of this distinction is lamentable. Duff and Marshall, for example, have recently suggested that this distinction ultimately provides an unhelpful distraction from the substantive concerns that ought to dominate considerations of the legitimacy of state intervention (Duff and Marshall, 2006). In addition, as Tasioulas points out, assuming the legitimacy of this distinction is not only distracting but also distorting, since it obscures the ways in which causing offence can itself constitute harm (Tasioulas, 2006).

Building on the feminist mandate to reflect upon and draw attention to forms of harm that do not meet the technical notion of injury supported in the liberal conception encourages a more flexible approach within which a relevant harm may be understood simply as involving a wrongful set-back to another's interests. Where this is the case, moreover, it is perfectly plausible that conduct which another finds offensive could cause harm in a way that may be relevant for the purposes of justifying criminalisation. Thus, the distinction between 'mere offence' and harm emerges as an artificial one which, when interrogated, provides no clear rationale for limiting law's ability to respond to offence *per se*.

On the face of it, however, this claim that it may be legitimate to criminalise conduct solely on the basis of the offence it causes to others appears to offer little more than a return to Devlin. Such a move would, of course, give rise to legitimate concern, not only amongst feminists, but also amongst anyone concerned to ward off repressive regulation of sexuality. Indeed, it has been widely noted that the Devlin approach has the potential to justify severely regressive outcomes, including, for example, the criminalisation of homosexuality or premarital sex, so long as the sense of revulsion from 'the man on the Clapham omnibus' is sufficiently strong. But it is precisely in adopting an approach that thereby concentrates on the extent of the offence caused, rather than also on its reasonableness, that Devlin's thesis becomes problematic and that the approach to criminalising offence discussed here represents a departure.

Although Devlin argued that social cohesion required a shared set of moral beliefs, it is telling that he did not demand that these beliefs needed to be 'fair', 'well-informed' or 'rational'. Indeed, as Dworkin notes in his discussion of Devlin's work, 'what is shocking and wrong is not the idea that the community's morality counts, but his idea of what counts as the community's morality' (Dworkin, 1966: 1001). To the extent that this is true, there is in fact no need for us to determine the legitimacy of criminalising offensive conduct on the basis of such 'conventional' rather than 'critical' morality. On the contrary, we can subject an experience of a wrongful set-back to one's interests as a result of offence to scrutiny to ensure that the mere existence of this response, even when shared by a majority of the population, does not justify criminalisation unless that response itself has a rational and well-informed basis.

Granted, evaluating the rationality and competence of strong and widely held reactions to specific forms of sexual conduct is by no means an easy task and there is a perpetual risk to be warded against of merely cloaking irrational prejudices with a rational explanatory form. But this alone is no reason to resort to Devlin's conventional 'mob' morality or to reject, with liberalism, the reality that some experiences of offence constitute a harm of the sort that the law ought to protect us against. There is, after all, a value in holding up critical morality as the standard which the law should reflect, even where fulfilling this standard is demanding.

Moreover, to the extent that striving to meet this standard requires us to empathise with, if not temporarily adopt, the standpoint of others, and to communicate with suspended judgement and mutual respect, the insights of feminist method may be of considerable assistance. Along with Habermas, a number of feminists have highlighted that respectful communication between two (differently positioned) interlocutors can yield more enlightened ethical positions (Habermas, 1992). Developing a distinctively feminist perspective on this communication, however, such theorists have demanded not only respect for, but also empathy with, the standpoint of 'concrete' others (Benhabib, 1992). In addition, they have combined this with a sensitivity (often lacking in Habermas' own account) to the power disparities that affect each person's ability to enter into the dialogue and to articulate their perspective in terms that are both true to themselves and intelligible to others (Meehan, 1995).

In the specific context of the Sexual Offences Act, this revised approach to what constitutes harm and offence, and to how these concepts are related, permits scope for reappraising the criticisms discussed in the previous section, which have assumed that the criminalisation of conduct on the basis of 'mere offence' is itself problematic. If we follow the arguments presented here, however, the problem with the Act now emerges as quite different. Indeed, it is not so much that it betrays its liberal pretensions by criminalising offensive conduct or by intervening into previously unregulated areas of life, but rather that it does so without any examination of the grounds on which underlying determinations of 'right' and 'wrong' have been made.

This tendency is clearly apparent, for example, in the provisions relating to child sexual activity and prostitution discussed above. A prominent rationale for criminalisation in these areas has been the moral disapproval which active child sexuality or the commodification of sex have traditionally invoked. While this disapproval was no doubt operative in determining the reach and form of the resultant offences under the Act, its presence was rarely explicitly mentioned in the reform process, and thus no scope was provided in which its legitimacy could be scrutinised.

More prominent examples of this dangerously uncritical approach emerge, moreover, if we turn our attention to some of the offences created towards the end of Part I of the Sexual Offences Act where, as Lacey notes, 'the idea of "indecency" . . . . survives to haunt its less critical approach to matters of public order and offence' (Lacey, 2001: 9). In relation to the offences of sexual penetration of a corpse (s 70) and sexual intercourse with an animal (s 69), for example, it is striking that the only justification given for their creation in either the Bill, the White Paper or the *Setting the Boundaries* Review was that such conduct is 'deviant' and 'profoundly disturbed'. Significantly, no assessment was undertaken to ensure that the offence thereby generated sprung from an objective and rational basis (disrespect of the dead, of animals, or of human sexuality perhaps), rather than simply from abstract disapproval.

Both Spencer and Bennion, in their critiques of the Sexual Offences Act, lament the lack of any discernible system of morals and values (Bennion, 2003: 9) or any 'intelligible philosophy as to what sort of behaviour the criminal law should and should not prohibit' (Spencer, 2004: 360). Building on that criticism, it is submitted in this chapter that what is most troubling about the Act is not so much the fact that some of its provisions target conduct that is deemed, in the words of Devlin, to be 'vile and vicious', but rather that the determination of what counts as 'vile and vicious' is dependent on what legislators imagine would offend the 'moral majority'. By adopting such an approach, the Sexual Offences Act not only fails to pay adequate respect to its symbolic role in defining and underpinning social assumptions of sexual normality (Lacey, 2001: 13), it also produces a depressingly detached and potentially conservative framework for regulating sexuality into the twenty-first century.

Conclusion

Many of the criticisms of the Sexual Offences Act developed to date have challenged the legislation on the grounds that it justifies its reforms through an inconsistent set of rationales, some of which prioritise non-intervention and classic notions of harm, while others prioritise community morals and protection against offence. It has been argued here, however, that, in itself, there may be nothing contradictory, incoherent or illiberal about such an approach. That said, it has been suggested that the Act does nonetheless continue to risk generating an illiberal regime through its adoption of a wholly uncritical and populist conception of what should constitute the morals of a community, and of what should justify a reaction of offence. Ultimately, therefore, the problem with this Act is not that it criminalises on the basis that conduct is 'wrong', 'unacceptable' or 'deviant' but rather that it does so without adequate scrutiny, in a context in which such scrutiny is central to ensuring that forms of sexual behaviour are not criminalised merely as a result of prejudice, misinformation or ignorance.

Bibliography

Abma, J, Driscoll, A and Moore, K (1998) 'Young Women's Degree of Control over their First Intercourse: An Exploratory Analysis' *Family Planning Perspectives* 30(1), pp 14–17.

Bainham, A and Brooks-Gordon, B (2004) 'Reforming the Law on Sexual Offences' in Brooks-Gordon *et al.* (eds) *Sexuality Repositioned: Diversity and the Law*, Oxford: Hart Publishing, pp 261–96.

Benhabib, S (1992) *Situating the Self: Gender, Community and Postmodernism in Contemporary Ethics*, London: Polity Press.

Bennion, F (2003) *Sexual Ethics and Criminal Law: A Critique of the Sexual Offences Bill 2003*, Oxford: Lester Publishing.

Devlin, P (1965) *The Enforcement of Morals*, Oxford: Oxford University Press.

Duff, A and Marshall, S (2006) 'How Offensive Can You Get?' in Simester and von Hirsch (eds) *Incivilities: Regulating Offensive Behaviour*, Oxford: Hart Publishing, pp 57–90.

Dworkin, R (1966) 'Lord Devlin and the Enforcement of Morals' *Yale Law Journal* 75, pp 986–1006.

Dworkin, R (1981) 'Is There a Right to Pornography?' *Oxford Journal of Legal Studies* 1(2), pp 177–212.

Erens *et al.* (2003) *National Survey of Sexual Attitudes and Lifestyles II*, London: National Centre for Social Research.

Habermas, J (1992) *Moral Consciousness and Communicative Action*, Cambridge: MIT Press.

Hansard (2002) 19 November 2002, at Column 507.

Home Office (1957), *Report of the Committee on Homosexual Offences and Prostitution*, Cmnd 247, London: HMSO.

Home Office (2000), *Setting the Boundaries – Reforming the Law on Sexual Offences*, London: Home Office Communication Directorate.

Home Office (2002), *Protecting the Public – Strengthening Protection against Sex Offenders and Reforming the Law on Sexual Offences*, Cmnd 5668, London: HMSO.

Home Office (2004), *Paying the Price – A Consultation Paper on Prostitution*, London: Home Office.

Home Office (2006), *A Coordinated Prostitution Strategy and A Summary of Responses to Paying the Price*, London: Home Office.

Jeffreys, S (1997) *The Idea of Prostitution*, Melbourne: Spinifex Press.

Lacey, N (2001) 'Beset by Boundaries: The Home Office Review of Sex Offences' *Criminal Law Review*, pp 3–14.

MacKinnon, C (1989) 'Pornography: On Morality and Politics', in *Towards a Feminist Theory of State*, Cambridge: Harvard University Press, pp 95–215.

Meehan, J (ed.) (1995) *Feminists Read Habermas: Gendering the Subject of Discourse*, New York and London: Routledge.

Mill, J S (1996) *On Liberty*, Ware: Wordsworth Classics.

Munro, V (2005) 'Concerning Consent: Standards of Permissibility in Sexual Relations' *Oxford Journal of Legal Studies* 25(2), pp 335–52.

O'Connell-Davidson, J (1998) *Prostitution, Power and Freedom,* Cambridge: Polity.

O'Neill, M (2001) *Prostitution and Feminism: Towards a Politics of Feeling*, Cambridge: Polity.

Raphael, J (2000) *Saving Bernice: Battered Women, Welfare and Poverty*, Boston: Northeastern University Press.

Spencer, J (2004) 'The Sexual Offences Act 2003: Child and Family Offences' *Criminal Law Review*, pp 347–60.

Tasioulas, J (2006), 'Crimes of Offence' in Simester and von Hirsch (eds) *Incivilities: Regulating Offensive Behaviour,* Oxford: Hart Publishing, pp 149–72.

Temkin, J and Ashworth, A (2004) 'The Sexual Offences Act 2003: Rape, Sexual Assaults and the Problems of Consent' *Criminal Law Review*, pp 328–346.

Weait, M (2005) 'Harm, Consent and the Limits of Privacy' *Feminist Legal Studies* 13, pp 97–122.

Wellings, K *et al.* (1994) *Sexual Behaviour in Britain: the National Survey of Sexual Attitudes and Lifestyles*, London: Penguin.

West, R (1997) *Caring for Justice*, New York: New York University Press.

Chapter 2

On being responsible

Matthew Weait, Birkbeck, University of London*

> Far from apologizing for their promiscuity as a failure to maintain a loving relationship, far from welcoming the return to monogamy as a beneficent consequence of the horror of AIDS, gay men should ceaselessly lament the practical necessity, now, of such relationships, should resist being drawn into mimicking the unrelenting warfare between men and women, which nothing has ever changed.
>
> (Bersani, 1987: 218)

> Finding and using the implicit and explicit theories that inform the personal, political, and educational approaches to preserve the lives of sexual dissidents is not just an immediate project: *it is our lives.*
>
> (Patton, 1996: 139)

> To infect an unsuspecting person with a grave disease you know you have, or may have, by behaviour that you know involves a risk of transmission, and that you know you could easily modify to reduce or eliminate the risk, is to harm another in a way that is both needless and callous. For that reason, criminal liability is justified unless there are strong countervailing reasons. In my view there are not.
>
> (Spencer, 2004b: 448)

Introduction

These three quotations reflect, in different ways, for different reasons, and from within different intellectual and political traditions, some of the central problems with responsibility. It may, as is implied by Leo Bersani, be something to be resisted insofar as it impels sexual dissidents to adopt a 'responsible' monogamous heteronormative sexuality. Or it may, as Cindy Patton suggests, be a concept whose mortal significance demands that it be understood and deployed practically and politically. Or it may, as John Spencer forcefully

* I should like to thank the editors for their patience and comments, and Nicky Priaulx for being an indefatigable source of inspiration and the most excellent of critics.

argues, be an immanent, desirable and necessary quality of human beings – and one which, if denied or abused, justifies the imposition of public censure and punishment. Each of these perspectives on responsibility, and each of the positions they reflect, is sustainable. Each is a perspective that captures something about what 'being responsible' means. Being responsible is being true to oneself and to the values that inform the way in which one lives one's life and treats others. Being responsible is to engage with ideas and concepts, and to argue for a particular way of understanding them, in a way that is ethically and politically defensible. Being responsible is to accept and internalise the judg(e)ment of others, and to acknowledge that responsibility is both self-directed and other-directed, private and public, personal and political.

In this chapter I want to explore these various dimensions of responsibility, and their implications both for legal critique generally and for feminist legal critique in particular. To do this I will be using the vexed subject of criminal liability for the sexual transmission of HIV. This is something about which I (and others) have written extensively (Weait, 2001; 2005a; 2005b; 2005c; 2005d; see also Smith, 1991; Laurie, 1991 (Scotland); Alldridge, 1993; Ormerod and Gunn, 1996; Dine and Watt, 1998; Chalmers, 2001; Spencer, 2004a; 2004b; Warburton, 2004) and it is not my purpose to explore the specifically doctrinal contours of the debate. Instead, I want to think critically about the ways in which the essence of that debate might provide us with an insight into what I consider to be the fundamental problem in criminal law theorising about responsibility. That problem, simply put, is this: the vast majority of those criminal law theorists who have engaged with the idea of responsibility have adopted (more or less uncritically) a moral-philosophical framework which takes the responsible agent as the foundational unit of analysis (see for example Moore, 1997; Tadros, 2005). This means that when engaging in discussions of what it is to be responsible their focus and emphasis – whether or not they are engaging in critique or criticism – are centred on the capacities and/or characters that human beings *qua* individuated agents possess, or on the choices they make. According to these analytical approaches, being (held) responsible requires either (a) a set of capacities – including (but not limited to) cognitive skills, self- and other-awareness, foresight of consequences resulting from willed action, and an understanding of right and wrong; (b) that the person chose (consciously) to act in a particular way, and that the choice was freely made; or (c) that the person's conduct was in some way expressive of his or her character. Irrespective of one's preferred mode of analysis, a person's capacities, choices or character are thus both constitutive of agency and a basis on which their exercise or expression – or non-exercise and non-expression – can be (morally) evaluated. Put another way, the individual agent, that person's actions, and the consequences that they (are seen to) produce, provide the conceptual framework within which theories of responsibility are built; and responsibility provides the conceptual framework within which the actions of individual agents are, and may legitimately be, judged. Legal theorists for whom capacity, choice and character provide an adequate, if ever refinable, basis for thinking about responsibility and those for whom such analytical categories provide a point of critical departure, are therefore caught in an ultimately self-referential mode of reasoning about what being, and being held, responsible means.

More importantly, and this is the nub of my argument, this kind of theorising, whatever its particular concern and focus, takes the criminal law as a given, and – whether explicitly or implicitly – asserts that the conduct, consequences and people with which it is concerned can be and are appropriately analysed and critiqued in terms both of the criminal law's own institutionalised logic and the moral and political traditions within which it is embedded. Because of this, such theorising – while important in enabling us better to understand that logic and the principles which inform criminal law – is necessarily constrained in its understanding of what 'being responsible' means. My argument is that while we may learn much about the criminal law's construction of responsibility from such theorising, because the criminal law is itself a conservative institution the function of which is not to liberate but to repress, censure and condemn, it precludes us from thinking differently, laterally and imaginatively about the very conduct, consequences and people that are the objects of its repression, censure and condemnation. The fact that criminal law cannot, as I hope to show, respond adequately to people's lived experience of responsibility, or be responsive to difference and specificity, does not mean that radical critics – feminist and otherwise – who think that this is problematic are ham-strung. Far from it. It is my contention that we can use the very constraints and limitations of criminal law as the justification for arguing, should there be the desire and the political will to do so, that criminalising certain conduct, consequences and people may be unhelpful, counter-productive and unjustifiable. Put more strongly, it is my contention that with respect to some conduct, some consequences and some people, 'being responsible' as lawyers, whether theorists or practitioners, entails recognising the importance and value of developing sound and defensible arguments for de-criminalisation. The fact that we inhabit a society governed by the constraints of *realpolitik* and deafened by the clamour of populist retributivism, in which an ever more extensive and punitive system of criminal law is understood as *the* mechanism that can provide *the* solution, does not mean that we should allow our imaginations to rot.

The structure of this chapter is as follows. In the first section, 'The responsible subject', I explore the meaning of law's (responsible) subject. In the second section, 'Responsibility, risk and the criminal law', I address the criminal law's response to responsibility and risk taking, with particular emphasis on problems associated with its approach to recklessness, consent and disclosure. I conclude by advancing some arguments for the decriminalisation of reckless HIV transmission.

The responsible subject (of criminal law)

It is not possible to talk about being *responsible* without first being clear about *being* responsible. In the context of law and legal theory this necessarily entails addressing the question of legal subjectivity. Only subjects of law are legally accountable at law. Therefore, being held to account depends on first satisfying the conditions necessary to be treated as a legal subject. In the context of criminal law – these conditions are framed in terms of identity and capacity (understood in terms of cognitive functioning and willed action), and organised around certain rebuttable presumptions. Thus, an adult human being is presumed to operate with a set of mental capacities that link conduct (and any consequences of that conduct) to volition, and unless – by virtue of immaturity or mental impairment – it is not possible to make that link, prima facie liability is established. A second condition of (criminal) liability is, in keeping with the principles of 'orthodox subjectivism', a requirement that the legal subject exhibit fault of a kind necessary for the offence (which will typically set out the fault requirements) to be made out. Such fault, expressed usually in terms of intention, recklessness or knowledge (whether with respect to conduct, consequences or circumstances), expresses – for want of a better term – the *moral dimension* of legal subjectivity. A legal subject that meets the primary capacity condition will only be treated as responsible (that is, criminally liable) if they also exhibit, through voluntary action, certain morally significant states of mind with respect to that action. Those states of mind (intention, recklessness, etc.) provide, where present, justification for the moral condemnation that criminal liability represents. They, along with the capacity condition, also reflect the particular moral philosophical and liberal political heritage that underpins contemporary Anglo-American criminal law. From a philosophical perspective they represent a Kantian commitment to treating people as ends, not means. To be treated as a responsible subject is to have one's humanity acknowledged and respected. To be held responsible for those actions which define subjectivity in these terms is to have that subjectivity affirmed (see for example Gardner, 2003). From a liberal political perspective, these states of mind and the presumption of capacity are constitutive of personhood. Personhood depends on freedom of action and on individual self-realisation. To be held personally responsible is to have one's autonomy – the central liberal value – respected.

One of the most important aspects of *legal* subjectivity in the criminal context is that its meaning is established through the process of adjudication. Adjudication is based on reconstruction. The legal settlement of conflict, where this concerns the determination of liability for the conduct or consequences that have brought about such conflict, provides the occasion for identifying the rights and responsibilities of the legal subject. While the nature of such subjectivity may be a necessary and prior inquiry when determining legal claims relating to status and entitlement, in a world without dispute there would be no need to determine (via a retrospective analysis of the capacities and character manifested in *this* person's behaviour on *that* occasion) the conditions or criteria that should and must be met before responsibility for acting in a particular way, or for bringing about particular effects, can be established. A consequence of this is that the legal subject that is constructed through adjudication (at trial and on appeal) is one that is necessarily embedded within the social, economic, and political processes and values that have contributed over time to the development, and informed the values, of adjudicative procedure and reasoning. This means that the legal subject of adjudication is one that can only be framed – in our legal system – within the logic of due process under the rule of law. As such, *legal* subject-ivity, and the responsibilities it entails, are (and must be) of a kind that only make sense for the law if they are premised on assumptions of equality, generality, and neutrality. And, it follows, the construction of subjectivity and responsibility through law can only provide an account of subjectivity and responsibility for law, and this account is one that will inevitably occlude the reality, and deny the relevance of, inequality, specificity and partiality.

Taken together, our moral-philosophical, liberal-political and due process inheritance have combined to produce an idealised model of the rational, prudent person whose self-fulfilment and self-realisation depend on respect for autonomy, on choices that are freely made, and on relationships – whether of an economic, political, social or intimate nature – that are entered into voluntarily, as an expression of individual will. This dominant model of personhood, which finds expression in the discourse of legal reasoning about subjectivity, necessarily produces an account of responsibility that further distances it from the diversity and uniqueness of people's individual, relational and social experience. The responsible subject is responsible *for* (and only for) that behaviour and those effects that can be identified with the necessary criteria of personhood (rational choices freely made within a coherent and internalised moral universe as the result of deliberative cognitive processing) (see, further, Hart, 1968); and the responsible subject may thus only legitimately be held responsible (and, in the context of criminal law, punished), where his actions and their effects manifest – or may be interpreted as – a failure to exercise the responsibility that defines him as a subject of, and for, law. Understood in this way, it is not merely the adjudicative process that has the (inevitable and necessary) effect of denying the legal subject's humanity (it has none to deny); such denial is a consequence of that process being informed by the very values that provide its content. Law is necessarily reductivist. People are, and must be, reduced to persons. Responsibility is, and must be, reduced to the quality that defines persons. To be held responsible is to have one's personhood respected and one's legal subjectivity acknowledged; and to have one's personhood respected and one's legal sub-jectivity acknowledged implies an acceptance of the account of responsibility on which these depend.

For critical criminal law theorists this descriptively thin but normatively potent account of subjectivity and responsibility is one that poses interrelated significant theoretical, methodological and – critically – political challenges. These challenges stem from the fact that endogenous critiques which focus on doctrinal inconsistency in the treatment of subjectivity and responsibility may, while exposing incoherence, end up simply highlighting that incoherence; and exogenous critiques which seek to evaluate their legal meaning in light of social 'facts', cultural traditions, psychological insights, ethical values or political ideologies run the risk of reducing law to, or criticising it for being, something it is not (nor can ever be). This is not to suggest that it is theoretically futile to argue that the inherent (and inescapable) contradictions in the criminal law's treatment of responsibility are the result of a positivising project that seeks, but necessarily fails, to exclude questions of communal morality and human sociality from questions of liability (see for example Norrie, 1993; 2000); nor that it is unimportant to emphasise the way in which a pervasive legal rhetoric of rationality serves to provide a legitimating gloss on interpretations and decisions that serve dominant socio-economic interests (see for example Kelman, 1980–81); nor that it is fruitless to point to the fact that for the criminal law to acknowledge the 'real world', and to renounce its conceptual formalism, would (because such formalism is necessary for the individualised blaming function that is criminal law's essence) be both undesirable and logically impossible (Seidman, 1996). Such critical insights, along with those which emphasise the historically contingent and socially constructed nature of legal subjectivity (see for example Norrie, 1993; Lacey, 2001a; 2001b) and the extent to which it is determined by procedural and evidential rules (see for example Farmer, 1996) have provided an important and necessary foil to those whose work affirms, whether implicitly or explicitly, the dominant liberal and/or moral-philosophical conceptual heritage in criminal law theorising (see for example Hart, 1968; Moore, 1997; Horder, 2004; Tadros, 2005).

The same is true of specifically feminist theorising about the criminal law. Feminist legal theory has ensured that sex and gender are acknowledged as a (and for some such theorists *the*) critical issue for any legal scholarship that seeks to contribute to the broader political goal of eliminating unjustified discrimination against people on identity grounds. But, like critical legal scholarship more generally, it too has had to confront subjectivity and responsibility as these are understood within law and for law. As far as subjectivity is concerned, the brightest illumination that feminist scholars have shone into the dark recesses of conventional legal scholarship is the fact that law's subjects (or objects, depending on one's point of view) have bodies – bodies which (depending on their sex) bleed, gestate, give birth, nurture, have the capacity for pleasure and pain, connect with other bodies in conflict, love and sex, bodies which work, live and die (see, generally, Naffine and Owens, 1997). This insight (and it seems remarkable to us now that it could ever be characterised as such), has done much to alert other than the most unreconstructed in the legal academy to the differential impact that law – neutral, impartial and therefore 'fair' – has in fact had, and continues to have, on differently sexed/gendered human beings. And it is an insight that has resulted in some significant successes (in establishing the rights of women to non-discriminatory treatment in the workplace, for example), even if these successes are ones that are moderated by continuing disparities in socio-economic opportunities between the sexes. But the assertion and (partial) recognition of sexed/gendered human embodiment, while it has been critical to, and (in certain contexts) effective as part of, the feminist political project of asserting equality on grounds of status, has – I believe – been a far more complex and vexed project within the sphere of legal reasoning and adjudication.

As I have attempted to explain above, the subject of legal reasoning is necessarily without substantive content. It is important to be clear here. I do not mean that liberal legal reasoning is incapable of articulating and accommodating difference (whether that be in matters of gender, race, sexuality etc.). Indeed, it is one of the reasons for liberalism's continued domination in the industrialised West as a political philosophy and/or mode of governance (Dean, 1999) that it has managed to recognise and give at least partial effect through legislation to the claims of marginalised groups. Rather, what I mean to suggest is that this recognition and the effecting of these claims is successful (where it is) at the level, and as the result of, political struggle within liberal democratic polities. They do not (and cannot, I believe) succeed within the confines of liberal legal reasoning itself. And it is this which I think creates a fundamental problem for feminist theorising about law. Legal reasoning does of course have discriminatory effects; and it may, as some have argued, be explained at least partly in empirical terms (the fact that the common law has been developed by a patriarchal legal profession that has been overwhelmingly male and insensitive to the position and experience of women). But while such analysis may possess descriptive truth, it cannot – I would suggest – provide an adequate theoretical basis for understanding the treatment of women (or, for that matter, men) within *adjudicative* processes that both construct subjectivity via determinations of responsibility and determine responsibility via the construction of subjectivity.

For feminist legal theorists with an intellectual and political commitment to the values of liberalism (see for example Baer, 1990; for critiques see West, 1988; Tong, 1989; Naffine, 1990; Lacey, 1998),[1] the fact that men and women

---

1   It is notable that in their critiques of liberal legal feminism, neither Mackinnon (1987) nor West (1988), nor many critics for that matter, actually refer to any particular authors whose work could be characterised as such. It is possible that the 'liberal legal feminist', whose identity remains a mystery, has simply become the lurking liberal bogeywoman against whose windmills it is useful (and all too easy) to tilt.

are – and should so be treated as – equal, the wrong of the law has been its failure to deliver on its promise of equality. Because the job of law is to acknowledge, respect and advance the 'truth' of women's equality with men, an equality that is strongly associated with the other liberal values of autonomy and freedom of choice, it is difficult for such theorists to avoid the conclusion that women's subjectivity before the (criminal) law is, and should be treated as, identical to that of men and that – similarly – their responsibilities in law are (and should be) no different.[2] Thus, a woman who murders is as much a murderer as a man who murders – inasmuch as she, like him, possesses, and should be treated as possessing, the same capacity to form an intention to kill or cause grievous bodily harm (or, within character-based theories, that her conduct is capable of manifesting as vicious a character as a man's). The impact on her may be different (e.g. with respect to the loss into care of any child she may have), and the causes of her conduct may be significantly affected by a life of male oppression and violence, but these are peripheral to the fundamental principle, and one to be addressed with regard to local and particular effects rather than in such a way as to deny the truth of equal legal subjectivity and equal responsibility. (It should be emphasised that I am concerned here with the construction of responsibility in law as I have defined this, not with culpability.) The question of whether a woman who murders is as morally culpable as a man will (as it is when determining the relative culpability of different men, and different women, who kill or commit other crimes) depend on their particular motives and circumstances. The law (if we include sentencing) may be able to, and generally does, reflect these differences, but this is an analytically separate question. Similarly, claims that certain defences, such as provocation and self-defence, are less easy to deploy for women than for men – claims grounded both in physiological difference and in more fundamental arguments about the structure and legal development of the defences themselves – are not ones that can easily be made (within a liberal theoretical framework) at the same time as asserting the 'truth' of equality before the law, or denying the importance of difference.

Liberal legal feminists are, thus, caught in a bind when it comes to questions of responsibility. On the one hand, their position is largely consonant with the law's own view of the responsible subject of law – one that is framed in terms of agency, equal treatment, choice and autonomy; and, to that extent, the law's failure to treat responsible-woman no differently from responsible-man (where it does so) may be counted a 'success' (at least in terms of formal equality). The difficulty is, of course, that the different and

---

2   I emphasise criminal law here because there are those who as 'welfare liberal feminists' would argue that, in the context of employment (for example), preferential treatment or positive discrimination is justified in order to redress systemic socio-economic imbalances in opportunity (Tong, 1989: 29).

often discriminatory effects of formal legal equality for women – where these exist – produce a gendered (in)justice because of those effects. Remedying these, without renouncing formal equality claims, is – I would suggest – impossible within law's adjudicative rationality, because law is not, in matters of establishing responsibility, concerned with those effects (or, for that matter, causes). Nor, and this is the other part of the bind, can any liberal feminist project that seeks to remedy law's failure to articulate the 'truth' of equality, by emphasising the embodied nature of the legal subject, fare any better. For while this can serve to highlight the aforementioned effects, and may provide persuasive arguments for law reform aimed at minimising or eliminating discrimination based on status (and bear real fruit in this respect, as equal opportunities legislation has demonstrated), it will and can have – if I am correct in my analysis – no impact on the law's construction of its subject (which is, and must be, disinterested in gendered and sexed corporeality). And it follows that if law is disinterested in – and structurally resistant to – the corporeality of its subject, then it must inevitably follow that such corporeality (and the affective dimensions of human life) will, and must, be treated as irrelevant in the construction of the subject-as-responsible.

For feminists coming from different political and theoretical traditions responsibility is – I would suggest – no less problematic, though for different reasons. For radical feminist legal theorists, who start from the position that men and women are unequal, and that women are structurally oppressed by patriarchy the (overtly political and strategic) task is to effect legal change so as to bring about the equality that the rule of (patriarchal) law denies. In the work of Mackinnon, Dworkin and others who share their fundamental assumptions, the central mission is socio-economic and cultural transformation through law. Within such a theoretical and ideological framework, any woman who believes subjectively that she is not disempowered (especially in the context of sexual relationships and intimacy with men), is – according to extreme radicals – labouring under a false consciousness produced precisely because of her structural disempowerment (see for example Mackinnon, 1982; 1983). The political-personal response to such disempowerment might entail participation in a revolutionary project grounded in a rejection of theist religion, heterosexuality and 'femininity' (e.g. Daly, 1973; 1978; 1984); or it might demand attempts to construct a sexuality not defined with respect to that of men, or appropriated by them for their own ends (e.g. Mackinnon, 1982; 1983; 1987); or it might involve attempts to introduce legislation, or support test cases, whose purpose is to outlaw particular modes of subjugation (such as pornography, prostitution or the marital rape exemption). The point is that whatever strategies are deployed in pursuit of these laudable ends, they are – ultimately – powerless when it comes to influencing, and, I would suggest, irrelevant to questions concerning the construction of subjectivity and responsibility through adjudication. This, let me make it quite clear, is essentially a descriptive claim. I am not arguing that it is good, or just, or fair that women's felt (or denied) experience of disempowerment, oppression and subjugation is ignored in determinations of responsibility; just as I would argue similarly with respect to the experience of minority ethnic communities or those who are otherwise culturally, socially or economically marginalised. The point I want to make is that the legal adjudicative process when concerned with determining responsibility will, and must, ignore such truths because that is what law will, and must, do.

This can be succinctly explained using two scenarios appropriate to the subject matter of this chapter.

Scenario 1

John is a married man who sometimes visits Sarah, a sex worker. As a result of unprotected sexual intercourse with her, John is infected with HIV. He discovers this during medical tests for a life insurance policy, but he does not tell his wife and continues to have unprotected sex with her. As a result she too is infected with HIV.

Scenario 2

Sarah is a sex worker who has a client called John. He likes having unprotected sex, for which she charges him more. During routine ante-natal testing she discovered that she was HIV positive. When John next visits her she does not volunteer information about her HIV status. As a result of sex with Sarah, John is infected with HIV.

These scenarios can self-evidently be unpacked in a variety of ways. Here, I simply want to make the following preliminary observations before going on to explore in more detail some problems with the criminal law's construction of responsibility in cases such as these. First, at a purely biological/ physiological level of analysis, none of the characters would be HIV positive but for the fact that (a) someone earlier in the chain of transmission was also HIV positive and because (b) each engaged in conduct that carried with it the risk of transmission. HIV is something that exists in people who are, or have been, connected with others in some way. It is more aptly understood as a disease of communities, not of individuals. Second, from an abstract moral-philosophical perspective, it is arguable that if both Sarah and John are understood as being responsible for onward transmission of the virus through their failure to disclose known HIV status and for failing to practise safer sex, then they are responsible in precisely the same way. Each may be viewed as a cognitively aware agent with the capacity to make choices, and who has made a choice. And both may be judged and found wanting for their failure to regard and take into account the interests of those whom they knowingly expose to the risk of transmission. Third, and here is where it gets more complicated, I would suggest that this moral-philosophical approach (the one that, as we shall see, underpins criminal law's response) is one that feminists would find deeply problematic. The liberal would, if she is true to the essence of liberalism, have to accept that both John and Sarah are knowledgeable, autonomous and responsible agents who are equally accountable for their actions. From a liberal perspective, based on the premise of equality, there is no way of legitimately distinguishing between the two. If John is responsible and someone who may justifiably be censured and punished, so then is Sarah.

For radical feminists, who would start from the premise of inequality, there would – I suggest – be an even more profound difficulty. As compared with John, Sarah would be viewed (as a result of participation in sex work, or – more basically – through institutionalised heterosexual relations with men) in a position of such structural and relative powerlessness that she is more properly understood as a victim than as a responsible and accountable agent. Both she, and John's wife, are in a space so different from that of him, that to view Sarah and John as both equally responsible in any meaningful sense would be anathema. Any criminal law that held both Sarah and John responsible for transmission in the same way, and for the same reasons, would thus be unjust (in its failure to recognise power differentials and substantive inequality between the sexes). This is not to suggest that women in such contexts are necessarily to be treated or constructed as 'victims' for all purposes – it is not my intention here to deny women's agency. Rather, it is to suggest that a radical feminist perspective on her responsibility confronts profound problems when attempting to think about how her responsibility within the confines of legal adjudication can and should be conceptualised. Whatever the political and socio-economic truth of the radical analysis (and it is one to which I am sympathetic), it is one whose logical conclusion – the criminalisation of men like John who infect women with HIV but not of women like Sarah who infect men – is one that would necessarily undermine one of the most basic premises of the rule of law, and which could not be achieved without dismantling the most fundamental principle informing the process of legal adjudication on questions concerning responsibility: that one's sex, gender, race, ethnicity, sexuality, relationships with others – in short one's lived identity – are irrelevant, and must be so.

Neither liberal nor radical theoretical positions provide, or can provide, an adequate or authentic theory of responsibility that will deliver justice for people through law. Simply put, this is because law (as I have suggested above) is not – nor can be – concerned with what it is to be a human being (whether male or female, black or white, old or young, healthy or diseased, rich or poor, gay or straight, confused or secure), and is not – nor can be – concerned with what a *human-being-responsible* actually means. Because the legal construction of subjectivity and responsibility is – and can only ever be – a self-referential, self-interested and self-legitimating process, it will and must exclude any dimensions of human experience that would, if acknow-ledged, undermine the methodology upon which criminal law depends to justify the account of subjectivity and responsibility necessary for its continued functioning.

The choice is therefore stark, both for feminists and others committed to a critical analysis of the function and impact of criminal law. Either there must be a political project that seeks to explore and defend justifications for differential approaches to responsibility in law (a project that would of necessity be a radical one, and which would have to engage beyond sex and gender with other multiple and intersecting modes of oppression and domination); or, if it is thought that such a project is so radical that it is destined to failure at the level of practical politics, there must be a political project that engages with the pros and cons of selective decriminalisation. For if it is accepted, as I argue, that law must deny the relevance of different contexts and identities in determining the responsibility of the legal subject, but that this has undesirable effects, then the only way of addressing those effectively is outside law. It is this latter position that I seek to defend here. To do so, I will first set out in brief the criminal law's approach to respon-sibility in the context of HIV transmission, with particular emphasis on the relevance of, and problems with, disclosure of known HIV status to existing or prospective sexual partners.

Responsibility, risk and the criminal law: the case of HIV transmission

Recklessness and risk taking

English criminal law only imposes criminal liability on those who (a) satisfy the conditions of legal subjectivity (see above); (b) whose conduct and state of mind accord with the definitional requirements of the offence in question; and (c) those who, where (a) and (b) are satisfied, lack a recognised defence. In the context of liability for the transmission of HIV these conditions are met in the following way. The Offences Against the Person Act 1861 (OAPA 1861) (the statute under which they may be criminalised) makes it an offence to cause serious bodily harm to another person either intentionally or recklessly.[3] What constitutes serious bodily harm for the purpose of charg-ing the defendant with the offence is a matter for the police and Crown Prosecution Service,[4] and is a question of fact for the jury at trial. It is a requirement of the OAPA 1861, as well as general principle of criminal law,

---

3   This is, of course, a paraphrase. Liability for causing serious bodily harm with intention to do such harm is set out in s 18; liability for recklessly causing such harm is set out in s 20.

4   See the CPS Charging Standards: http://www.cps.gov.uk/legal/section5/chapter_c.html.

that the causing of the harm must be unlawful, so a person who has a valid defence may not be held criminally liable, despite causing the harm and having the requisite mental state. Thus, a person who intentionally or recklessly transmits HIV to another is criminally liable unless that other person consents to the risk of transmission (a defence that has been developed by the appellate judiciary as a matter of common law).

Analysed from a liberal juridical perspective this summary is unremarkable. If, as is socially and culturally accepted by most if not all people, being infected with HIV amounts to a serious harm,[5] and a person causes that harm, then unless that person is in some sense morally innocent and not properly at fault, then, in the absence of any consent to the risk of such harm occurring (a defence that affirms the liberal principles of autonomy and choice), she may be legitimately held to account and punished. And there are some who would defend this analysis as the only legitimate 'way of seeing' responsibility in this context (see for example Spencer, 2004a; 2004b). However, it is important – I believe – to unpack these elements to fully understand what the consequences of analysing responsibility in this way can be.

Ignoring for present purposes the important question of the ways in which harm is constructed in cases involving HIV transmission (Weait, 2001; 2005b), the key issues here relate to the meanings of recklessness[6] and consent, and the implications of those meanings for people living with HIV and those to whom such people may transmit the virus. Let us take first the meaning of recklessness. This entails consciously taking an unjustifiable risk (Herring, 2004: 150–3; Norrie, 1993: 58–82). What does conscious risk taking mean here? Let us assume for the moment that, when a person who is HIV positive has sex with a partner which carries with it the risk of transmission, this involves unjustifiable risk taking (though we will revisit certain problems with this below). If that is assumed, we need to be clear about what is meant by 'conscious' in this context. There are two ways in which this could be understood. One would demand merely that the defendant was aware of the possibility that she might be HIV positive, and the other would require certain knowledge of HIV positive status. If the former were the relevant test it would clearly set the parameters of potentially liable people extremely wide.

---

5 For a feminist critique of the meaning of harm see Conaghan (1996; 2002). For more general discussion see Feinberg (1984), Dan-Cohen (2002).

6 I do not deal with intentional transmission here for a number of reasons. First, it is extremely difficult in the sexual context to establish intentionality (a) because even if a person wanted to transmit the virus during intercourse this is not something over which they can exercise agency (in the same way that a person can exercise agency over a broken bottle); (b) because even if it is not someone's purpose to transmit, the risk of transmission on any one occasion does not approach anything like the 'virtual certainty' necessary for a jury finding of intention using the indirect approach. Second (and for the reasons given) there have been no cases – at the time of writing – where a person who has transmitted HIV has been convicted for doing so under s 18.

All those who are in fact HIV positive and who do not know this, but know (for example) that they have engaged in sex, or shared injection drug equipment, with people about whose HIV status they are unaware and by whom they could have been infected, would be reckless. Such a test would also, arguably, render responsible – for the purposes of the criminal law – those who belong to identifiable social, ethnic or national communities with higher HIV prevalence than the general population. Whereas it might be considered unreasonable (by any jury required to address the issue) for an HIV positive white woman in rural Wales to assume that she might be infected, the same might not be true with respect to a black man from sub-Saharan Africa, a sexually active gay man from central London, or a female sex worker.[7] Although it is not articulated explicitly, it is possible that these reasons informed the Court of Appeal in *R v Konzani* when it held that an HIV positive person who transmitted the virus would only be reckless for the purposes of liability under s 20 of the OAPA 1861 if, at the relevant time, she knew that she was HIV positive (for instance via a test result that had been communicated to her).[8] It is to be welcomed that the Court of Appeal has limited the scope of those potentially liable by its imposition of a knowledge requirement.

However, there are at least two consequences that demand particular comment in the context of a chapter on the meaning of what it is to be responsible. First, although there is (as yet) no empirical research to confirm or refute the possibility, the fact that a person can only be held criminally liable for the transmission of HIV if he or she knows their status, may provide people (especially, perhaps, those who think they may be positive, or who are members of high prevalence populations) with a disincentive to establish their status. If 'being responsible' as a sexually active person entails – as some may argue – the acquisition of knowledge that enables one, and one's partners, to make fully informed decisions about the risks one is taking, and (which is equally important) to access Highly Active Anti-Retroviral Treatment (HAART) that can have the effect both of prolonging life and rendering one less infectious through reducing viral load, then a principle of criminal law that may disincentivise testing may legitimately be questioned. Second, it is clear from the law's approach that knowledge of status (as opposed to merely risk-taking behaviour, which may also, as a matter of fact, be engaged in by

---

7 It is estimated that of the approximately 70,000 people living with HIV in the UK, one-third remain undiagnosed. Approximately 1:500 of the adult population is HIV positive. Nearly 50% of all new diagnoses in the UK in 2004 were among black African men. An estimated 45% of people living with HIV in the UK are gay men (see, for further statistical information, AIDSMAP www.aidsmap.com, and the UK Health Protection Agency (http://www.hpa.org.uk).

8 *R v Konzani* (2005) 2 Crim App R, para 41. For an alternative interpretation see Spencer (2004a, 2004b).

HIV positive people ignorant of their status) is understood as a significant determinant of responsibility for adverse consequences. Within a liberal analysis of criminal law this makes perfect sense, since knowledge is central both to the identity of the cognitively aware, rational, choice-making, agent and to the legitimacy of punishing those who, armed with such knowledge, make the (morally) wrong choice or act irrationally and contrary to the interests of others.

The difficulty with this, though, is that those with such knowledge are not, as we shall see below, necessarily in a position to behave as rational, dehumanised, agents would in an ideal world. If, as I suspect some readers would agree, the liberal focus on legal judgment being grounded in a person's autonomous choices is one that is problematic because of its gendered assumptions and effects (see for example West, 1988) then determinations of responsibility based on knowledge are similarly problematic. If we think that the HIV positive woman who knows her diagnosis, but finds it difficult or impossible to resist unprotected sex with a male partner should be punished and sent to prison for up to five years when she infects him, then all well and good. But if we think that this is at least *potentially* undesirable and unjust then we need to question what the relevance of knowledge of status in determinations of responsibility should be. We can either, as I have suggested above, develop a political project which argues that there should be gender sensitive approaches to the meaning and effects of knowledge (which would be problematic given that knowledge is so intimately bound up with choice, agency and thus with the way in which law constructs responsibility); or we can question the very legitimacy of criminalising reckless transmission on the basis that its effects are ones that may contribute further to the oppression of women (and those from high prevalence populations who are, typically, socially, culturally and economically marginalised).

Just as the function of knowledge is problematic when determining the meaning of conscious risk taking, so is risk taking itself. A person who knows that he is HIV positive may seek to eliminate or minimise the risk of transmission to a partner by abstaining from, or only practising, safer sex. The most common way of practising safer sex, where the sex involved carries with it a risk of transmission, is to use a condom. But condoms are not 100% effective, and – even when used properly – can fail. Is the HIV positive man who knows his status but uses a condom reckless when, as a result of condom failure, he transmits HIV to his partner? And is the HIV positive woman who knows her status, but asks her partner to use a condom reckless when, as a result of condom failure, she transmits HIV to hers? From a common-sense perspective the man who uses a condom, and the woman who requests that one be used, are being responsible. They are doing what safer sex campaigns have encouraged for the past 20 years. But is this way of being responsible, or seeking to act responsibly, one that the law recognises? Arguably not. Applying the strange logic of law, the HIV positive person with knowledge of status who uses a condom to prevent or minimise the risk of transmission is the very person who is aware of the risk of transmission – just as Lord Templeman commented in *R v Brown* (a case involving sado-masochistic sex) that the fact the appellants sterilised the needles they used was evidence of their awareness of the risk of infection.[9] Condom use is thus, perversely, prima facie evidence of an awareness of risk. Of course, this is not an issue if HIV is not transmitted; but a case will only arise for decision if it has been. And if HIV has been transmitted despite the use of condoms, the 'responsible' behaviour has failed to deliver the intended and anticipated protection. It remains to be seen whether the Crown Prosecution Service will prosecute where condoms have been consistently used,[10] and the courts have not yet directly addressed the question of whether a defendant who uses condoms is to be treated as reckless (or, more specifically, whether such conduct amounts to unjustifiable risk taking). The point is that if the person living with a known HIV diagnosis attempts to be responsible in a sense, and in a way, meaningful to him or to her, there is no guarantee that this will be acknowledged as such by the law.[11]

Disclosure and consent

Let us assume that there exists a defendant who knows that he is HIV positive and has in fact transmitted the virus to a sexual partner. Questions about the relevance of condom use aside, on what basis may he avoid liability? The answer lies in the defence of consent; and it is here, I would suggest, that some of the most fundamental problems about the law's construction of responsibility are exposed (see, generally, Wertheimer, 2003). In *R v Dica*[12] the Court of Appeal held that it is open to a defendant to raise the defence that the person to whom he transmitted the virus consented to the risk of transmission. The Court distinguished between consent to the deliberate infliction of actual or serious bodily harm (which cannot provide a defence: *R v Brown*) and consent to the risk of such harm (which can). It did this on classic liberal grounds. Mulling, *inter alia*, on the problems that would arise

---

9 [1994] AC 212 at 220 (HL).

10 There is, at the time of writing, a CPS review of prosecution policy in cases involving the transmission of sexually transmitted infections.

11 The question of whether the use of condoms should preclude liability has long been a topic of debate in common law jurisdictions. In 1991 in Australia, the Intergovernmental Committee on AIDS Legal Working Party recommended the availability of a 'protective measures' defence (Canberra: Department of Community Services & Health, 1991), and the prosecutor in the Canadian case of *R v Ssenyonga* (1993) 81 CCC (3d) 257 (Ont Ct (Gen Div) was of the opinion that the use of condoms should provide a defence (see, Elliott, 1997: Appendix A: 11). The Report makes the same recommendation.

12 [2004] QB 1257.

for the sero-discordant[13] Roman Catholic couple who know each other's status and who are conscientiously prevented from using contraception, and on the possibility of criminalising the man who knows that conception may present significant health risks to his partner, the Court stated that:

> These, and similar risks, have always been taken by adults consenting to sexual intercourse. Different situations, no less potentially fraught, have to be addressed by them. Modern society has not thought to criminalise those who have willingly accepted the risks, and we know of no cases where one or other of the consenting adults has been prosecuted, *et al.* one convicted, for the consequences of doing so.
>
> The problems of *criminalising* the consensual taking of risks like these include the sheer impracticability of enforcement and the haphazard nature of its impact. The process would undermine the general understanding of the community that sexual relationships are pre-eminently private and essentially personal to the individuals involved in them. And if adults were to be liable to prosecution for the consequences of taking known risks with their health, it would seem odd that this should be confined to risks taken in the context of sexual intercourse, while they are nevertheless permitted to take the risks inherent in so many other aspects of everyday life . . .[14]

In short, to deny someone a legally recognised right to consent to the risks inherent in sexual intercourse (and to deny the correlative defence that recognition of that right entails) would, in the Court's view, amount to such a significant infringement of autonomy that only Parliament should be able to sanction it.[15]

The problem with this is, of course, what is meant by consent (or an honest belief in it) for these purposes. This is not an idle academic question. For the person who knows her HIV positive status and who in fact transmits the virus to her partner, the answer that is given will make the difference between liberty and imprisonment.[16] And the answer to the question, according to English law, is this. Whether or not there was consent, or an honest belief in

---

13 Ie one partner HIV positive, the other HIV negative.

14 *R v Dica*, paras 50–51 (emphasis in original).

15 Ibid., para 52.

16 A conviction under s 20 of the OAPA for the reckless transmission of HIV has, in all cases, been treated as a serious offence justifying long terms of immediate custody (from two to four and a half years on each count in the eight cases on reckless transmission decided in England and Wales at the time of writing). This is particularly noteworthy since (a) only 55% of those over 18 sentenced for a s 20 offence in 2003 (N: 3,811) received an immediate custodial sentence; (b) of that 55% (N: 2,078) only 4% received sentences of more than three years (Sentencing Advisory Council, 2005: Annexes B and C).

consent, is a question of fact for the jury. If the prosecution fails to prove to the criminal standard that there was no such consent, or belief in consent, the defendant will be entitled to a not guilty verdict and will be acquitted. That much is straightforward. The real issue is the way in which the Court of Appeal has given guidance on what will count as consent for the purposes of enabling a defendant to rely on it, as matter either of fact or honest belief. Just as we saw that there are two ways in which conscious risk taking may be understood (see above, 'The responsible subject'), so there are two ways in which it is possible to argue that consent to risk exists. First, it is possible to argue that a person who agrees to have unprotected sex with a partner whom they know to have had risky sex in the past, or multiple partners, or a history of injection drug use, or who is from a high prevalence population, has consented to the risk of HIV transmission (just as they could be said to have consented to the risk of any other sexually transmitted infection). Such an argument is one that, taken to its logical conclusion, would treat a person as having consented to the risk of transmission if he is infected by someone about whose status he is ignorant or unsure (on the basis that unless one knows for certain that a partner is HIV negative there is always the possibility that he or she may be HIV positive).

This way of understanding consent is one based, therefore, on a person's general knowledge of the risks associated with unprotected sex; and it is one that would enable a defendant to argue that a partner's willingness to engage in unprotected sex in the absence of particular knowledge (about the defendant's HIV positive status) was the basis for his honest belief in the existence of such consent. This, it should be obvious, would – in the real world of criminal trials – result in the differential treatment of defendants who, at a purely formal level of analysis, have behaved identically. For example, it is not far-fetched to suggest that a jury hearing a case against John (from scenario 1 above) would be unwilling to accept that he honestly believed his wife was consenting to the risk of transmission; but they might be willing to accept that Sarah (the sex worker) honestly believed that John was so consenting. For whereas a jury is likely, I suggest, to deny the husband the right to assert an honest belief in the consent of a wife who has no reason to assume infidelity and its attendant risks, it may well be willing to accept that a sex worker might honestly believe that a punter who engages in unprotected intercourse with her has consented to the risk of infection (on the basis that he would be aware that she is a woman who is willing to have unprotected sex with men). The same would be true, I believe, where transmission occurs between gay men having unprotected sex in a sauna. The very fact that a man is willing to have such sex with another in such an environment might well be treated as either demonstrating *de facto* consent or, alternatively, that the defendant in a case arising from transmission in such a context is entitled to the defence of honest belief (though the response might be different if there was a significant age gap between the parties and the jury considered there to be a disparity in the parties' understanding of risk).

These hypotheticals are intended to illustrate the ways in which a defence of consent based on general knowledge could result in some defendants being found guilty and others not, for reasons which are not to do with their conduct or state of mind (which are identical in each case) but on a normative evaluation by the jury of the relationship between, and identities of, the parties and of the context in which sexual transmission occurs. Although it is possible to construct an argument in favour of such an approach (it is one that can, for example, provide the basis for a theory of shared responsibility since it precludes the criminalisation of those who infect partners who are aware of the risks they are taking) it is one that the Court of Appeal has, in *R v Konzani*, firmly rejected. Instead, it has chosen to limit the availability of the defence of consent by holding that a defendant may not rely on it unless the consent is a 'conscious' or 'willing' one. And consent will only have these qualities, which amount to a requirement of *informed* consent, where the person to whom HIV is transmitted has particular knowledge of the risk to which she or he is exposing himself with this particular defendant. Put simply, unless the HIV positive person discloses known HIV status to the partner whom he subsequently infects, it will not (bar exceptional circumstances)[17] be possible to argue either that the partner consented to the risk, or that he honestly believed that there was such consent. In the words of the Court of Appeal:

> Silence in these circumstances is incongruous with honesty, or with a genuine belief that there is an informed consent. Accordingly, in such circumstances the issue either of informed consent, or honest belief in it will only rarely arise: in reality, in most cases, the contention would be wholly artificial.[18]

This approach, which in effect imposes a test of reasonable belief, and which is at odds with the approach taken elsewhere in the criminal law relating to offences against the person, is one that may have certain immediate attractions both to liberals and radicals. For the liberal, it is an approach that allows the defence of consent, but only if that consent is based on the knowledge that permits the exercise of autonomous choice (see, generally, Law Commission, 1995: Appendix C). It thus has the potential to protect the defendant, but only if other important conditions relating to the experience of the complainant are met. For the radical (in this context one who believes

---

17 The Court gives the example of a complainant who has met the defendant in a hospital where he is receiving treatment for an AIDS-related illness: *R v Konzani*, para 44.

18 *R v Konzani*, para 42.

that the subjectivism of liberal legal reasoning prioritises the interests of men) it is an approach that prevents a man from avoiding liability for harming a woman on the basis of asserting an honest, but unreasonable, belief (something for which many have fought in the context of rape law reform, and which finds expression in the Sexual Offences Act 2003) (Temkin and Asworth, 2004). Although this way of establishing the scope and availability of the defence of consent may address the concerns of those who have been critical of its operation in common law jurisdictions – especially those in favour of an approach based on positive assent (see for example Bronitt, 1994; Hall and Longstaff, 1997; Lacey, 1998) – I think we should be wary of interpreting this as the Court undergoing a Damascean moment of feminist enlightenment. The test it has established may have affirmed a mode of 'being responsible' that answers the concerns of some critics; but its focus on disclosure of known HIV status – which is now the litmus test of the defence's availability – fails to acknowledge the very real difficulties that disclosure poses, for both women and for men living with HIV. It is these difficulties that I want to explore, before concluding the chapter with some more general observations about how we might think about what 'being responsible' means.

Responsibility and disclosure

Common sense suggests that a person who is HIV positive should disclose this fact to those people with whom he has, or intends to have, a sexual relationship in the course of which HIV transmission may occur. It is the *responsible* thing to do (see for example Novick, 1994; Bruner, 2004). In this context therefore 'common sense' has a strong normative component, closely associated with 'being responsible'. Disclosure provides those to whom HIV may be transmitted with a fact that enables them, in theory at least, to make an informed decision about whether to enter into, or continue, a sexual relationship with an HIV positive person and – if they choose to do so – to decide the nature and limits of any sexual interaction. Disclosure ought to be made because not doing so undermines any 'consent' which existing or potential partners may give to such interaction. Failure to disclose, according to this analysis, precludes those partners from exercising their autonomy and has the potential, at least, to violate their bodily integrity. Put bluntly, failure to disclose may result in sexual interaction which in turn may result in onward transmission of the virus to someone who, had they known the risk, might have been able to avoid infection.

Such 'common sense' is perfectly reflected, as we have seen, in English criminal law's approach to disclosure. There is no legal obligation to disclose; but an HIV positive person who fails to do so prior to infecting a sexual partner will find it all but impossible to argue successfully that there was consent to the risk of transmission, or that he honestly believed that there was such consent. Assuming that he is aware of the risk of transmission at the relevant time (on the basis of having received an HIV diagnosis), and is thus legally reckless, he will be guilty under s 20 of the OAPA 1861. He may legitimately be punished not because he has caused the victim serious injury, but because that injury is an unlawful one – unlawful because of the absence of consent to the risk of its occurrence. It is the absence of consent which enables us to describe such injury as a legally relevant harm. In contrast, where there has been prior disclosure, and as a consequence of this the 'victim' has consented to the risk of transmission, the self-same injury is not unlawful, and therefore not a legal harm. The decision to accept the risk of transmission is an expression, or realisation of, personal autonomy and the person who is the source of infection cannot, from a liberal legal theoretical perspective at least, be said to have violated it.

The criminal law's approach to disclosure – one of common sense imbued both with a readily comprehensible morality and a faultless liberal logic – is, I suspect, immediately appealing to many. It is one that we may intuitively understand, whether as members of the general public who may be called upon as jurors in a case involving the sexual transmission of HIV, or as legal academics and lawyers educated and trained within a common law tradition in which that morality and logic is entrenched. But it is also, I would argue, an approach whose limitations and potential for injustice are substantial, and which should therefore be subjected to close and careful scrutiny. More specifically, in the context of this chapter, it is important to recognise that it is an approach whose intuitive appeal reflects certain assumptions about knowledge, reason, choice, and action – categories of thought which are themselves the product, and constitutive, of a particular liberal-political and moral-philosophical model of what it is to be human, and a human-being-responsible. It is an approach that assumes the 'truth' of the neutered rational agent, guided (and therefore legitimately judged) according to both deontological and consequentialist principles: deontological because it is an approach that assumes that there is an essential, categoric, 'right' (disclosure) and 'wrong' (non-disclosure) in this context; consequentialist because it is an approach that assumes that the non-discloser may legitimately be judged on the basis that he has treated his partner as means towards his own ends. As I have argued earlier in this chapter, it is inevitable that the law deploys this model; but it is precisely because such a model is inevitable if we comprehend what 'being responsible' means through a logic of adjudication that we need, I think, to reflect on whether that logic is one that can deliver real justice for real people.

Disclosure in law and in life

The function of disclosure in cases involving the reckless transmission of HIV is to enable the court to determine whether the person to whom HIV was transmitted may be treated as someone who has given consent to the risk of transmission (and is therefore not properly characterised as the victim of a crime who has been harmed), or whether the defendant honestly believed that there was such consent (and is therefore not properly characterised as the perpetrator of a crime). As such, in cases where HIV positive people who are aware of their diagnosis infect others, disclosure operates as a critical marker of (legal) responsibility. But whereas the mere fact of disclosure operates (and can only operate as) a decontextualised, atemporal, signifier for law,[19] it operates as a far more complex indicator of responsibility for those living with HIV and AIDS and who must determine whether, and if so how, to disclose to people with whom they have, or anticipate, an intimate physical relationship. This means that it is important to understand and interrogate the dynamics of disclosure itself. This is the case because if the decision not to disclose is understood simply as a rational, selfish and self-serving choice made by people who want to 'use' others as means to their own ends, and which denies them the right to make informed choices of their own, the justification for punishing such people is, at least in a criminal justice system informed by Kantian retributivism, a strong one. If, however, the decision not to disclose is not properly characterised in this way then the justification is significantly weaker. Put more strongly, it may be possible to argue that not disclosing may – under certain conditions, for some people – be appropriately understood as either a responsible or reasonable course of action, and that to punish such people who transmit HIV without first disclosing their status to those whom they infect *using non-disclosure as a reason to do so* is unjustifiable.

So why do people not disclose their known HIV positive status to those with whom they have had, have or intend to have, sexual relationships?[20] There is substantial evidence to suggest that perceived stigma associated

19 It is important to recognise that whereas law treats disclosure as something that either has, or has not, happened, it is better understood as a process that – where it occurs – may take place over time. It may also involve the use of non-verbal cues, and be either oblique ('we need to use condoms') or direct ('I am HIV positive'). As a result, some people living with HIV may subjectively believe that they have disclosed, but be treated as if they have not. Similarly, a person to whom disclosure has been made may not recognise it as such, or understand the implications. Given that liability for reckless transmission may only be avoided if there is consent to risk, disclosure per se may not provide an HIV positive person with a defence.

20 In a recent US probability sample 42% of the gay or bisexual men, 19% of the heterosexual men, and 17% of all the women reported any sex without disclosure, predominantly within non-exclusive partnerships. Across all groups, 13% of serodiscordant partnerships involved unprotected anal or vaginal sex without disclosure, with no significant difference between groups (Ciccarone *et al.*, 2003). For a recent overview of the extensive research literature on disclosure by HIV positive people to their past and current partners, see Simoni and Pantalone (2004).

with HIV[21] is an important factor for many[22] in decisions about disclosing to non-intimate others (for example family, friends and work colleagues) (Derlega *et al.*, 2002; see also Klitzman and Bayer, 2003). Especially for those who are HIV positive but asymptomatic (and therefore 'discreditable' rather than 'discredited' – Goffmann, 1963), there may be a very real interest in maintaining privacy, or – put another way – keeping an HIV positive diagnosis secret. As far as non-disclosure to existing or prospective sexual partners is concerned, there is some evidence that this is not associated with concerns about stigma as such (Derlega *et al.*, 2002), but by more immediate, situated and interpersonal considerations. Unlike disclosure in other contexts, disclosure to sexual partners is complicated by its assumed correlation with the risk of HIV transmission (assumed, because there is no clear evidence to support the claim that disclosure is necessarily and positively correlated with the practice of safer sex – for an excellent critical review see Simoni and Pantalone, 2004). Whatever that correlation may in fact be, there is substantial empirical evidence that a significant proportion of people who are HIV positive do not disclose this fact to sexual partners. Reported reasons for this include fear of rejection (Perry *et al.*, 1994; Simoni *et al.*, 1995; Moneyham *et al.*, 1996; Gielen *et al.*, 1997; Kilmarx *et al.*, 1998; Levy *et al.*, 1999); concerns about discrimination (Moneyham *et al.*, 1996; Gielen *et al.*, 1997; Petrak *et al.*, 2004); concerns about privacy and confidentiality (Perry *et al.*, 1994; Simoni *et al.*, 1995; Moneyham *et al.*, 1996); fear of abuse and violence (Gielen *et al.*, 1997; Gielen *et al.*, 2000); and the desire to protect the feelings of others (Levy *et al.*, 1999; Petrak *et al.*, 2001).

One response to these explanations for non-disclosure would be that they are simply irrelevant to the question of responsibility (i.e. liability) because they equate to motive. The person who kills for profit is as much a murderer as the person who kills to gratify sadistic desire; and so the person who fails to disclose because of privacy concerns, or because of a fear of rejection by a partner is as culpable as the person who fails to disclose his HIV status because, for selfish reasons, he wants unprotected sex with a partner who he believes will refuse this if his status is known. Viewed in a purely ethical light, it is difficult to deny the strength of this argument. Just as non-maleficence is a central principle informing the physician's duty to a patient, so it may be

21 Stigma here is understood not simply as a deeply discrediting attribute of individuals, but in relational terms (Goffmann, 1963). Numerous studies have articulated the negative associations (with homosexuality, promiscuity, injecting drug-use, etc.) that HIV and AIDS have in the minds of the non-HIV positive general public (see for example Derlega *et al.*, 1998; Lemieux *et al.*, 1998; Herek and Capitanio, 1999).

22 It is important to recognise that the experience of, and response to, stigma varies depending on, *inter alia*, the sexuality, gender and ethnicity of the person concerned (see for example Petrak, 2001). Furthermore, the more substantial a person perceives the risk of stigma to be, the less likely they are to disclose (see for example Alonzo and Reynolds, 1995; Siegel, 1998).

argued that an HIV positive person's duty to a sexual partner is to do them
no harm. Similarly, a Kantian commitment to the categorical imperative
would demand that the truth be told. Others should not be treated as means
to one's own ends. The law, however, is not (and can never, nor should not,
be) an institution that effects such principles or imperatives *tout court*. If it
were otherwise then many conscious and deliberate acts that in fact have
adverse consequences on others would, by virtue of that fact alone, justify
their criminalisation – and this would spread the net of criminal liability far
too widely. It is arguable therefore, that a failure to disclose known HIV
status, while ethically problematic, does not – in itself – justify the imposition
of liability. However, as things currently stand, 'being responsible' in the
English criminal law relating to the reckless transmission of HIV entails a
de facto, if not *de jure*, obligation to disclose known HIV status. Although it
is the practising of safer sex that minimises the risk of transmission and not
the fact of disclosure, it is the latter that has been established as a key
determinant of liability in cases where transmission has occurred. Coupled
with a failure on the part of the Court of Appeal to clarify whether the use of
condoms will preclude a finding of recklessness, and a refusal to accept that
general knowledge of the risks associated with unprotected sex is relevant to
the question of whether consent exists, this emphasis on disclosure is one that
affirms a model of responsibility based on the principles of liberalism at the
expense of the lived experience of people with an HIV positive diagnosis.
Never mind that the HIV positive woman who fails to disclose because she
fears violence or the loss of economic support will be sent to jail if she infects
a male partner who would not agree to using a condom even if asked to do
so. Her failure to respect his interests, irrespective of her attempts to be
responsible in a way that is manageable for her, means that she may legitimately be subject to public censure and punishment. To the extent that the
defence is available in principle, but not in practice, its concession to human
fallibility – and the protection it is intended to provide – is all but illusory.

And this is, of course, only to be expected. The criminal law denies – or, put
more strongly and accurately, must deny – the relevance of people's lived
experience of what it is to be responsible and of their ability to behave
responsibly in particular contexts, at particular times, with particular people
and with regard to particular behaviours. It must deny the relevance of
such experience and such ability because to do otherwise would result in an
infinitely individuated mode of criminal adjudication that would undermine
the very function of a legal system within a liberal democratic polity – which
is to establish and sustain a set of behavioural standards that apply equally to
all, and against which all may legitimately be judged. In the context of
criminal law's response to the sexual transmission of HIV, this means that a
person's actual ability to discuss HIV positive status with partner(s), the
nature of the relationship between that person and the partner (for example
husband and wife, casual sex partners, client and sex worker), the respective

gender and sexual orientation of the partners, and the context in which viral transmission occurs (for example matrimonial bed, sauna, or brothel) are all irrelevant to the question of liability for such transmission. They may not be irrelevant for the purposes of deciding whether to prosecute a particular incident of transmission (it may not be thought to be in the public interest, or there may be evidential difficulties), or for determining questions of culpability at the sentencing stage in the event of a guilty verdict; but for the purposes of establishing whether the HIV positive defendant *was* responsible for transmitting the virus to someone else, and whether that defendant should be held responsible *for* doing so (which are the issues that inform questions of criminal liability in this context), these factors can, and must, be ignored.

Of course, for some people this is not a problem. It is the solution. Within the paradigmatic mode of legal reasoning it is essential to essentialise, that is to translate (and by doing so abstract and reduce) facts in the world to elements that can be 'read' by law. If we accept, without question, that HIV transmission is a harm with which the criminal law should be concerned, that the cause of such harm can be located in the actions of a particular agent, that the requisite fault element is established if there exists proof of a specified mental state with respect to transmission on the agent's part, and that the only way of avoiding liability (if all these elements are present) is the existence of a legally recognised defence, then it is inevitable that people aware of their HIV positive status who transmit HIV to their partners will be treated as responsible for doing so. But, and this is critical, such a conclusion is only inevitable *if* one frames one's thinking about responsibility by applying the internal and inexorable logic of the criminal law, and by accepting the philosophical principles and established analytical categories upon which it is based.

Concluding remarks: 'being responsible' and the decriminalisation of reckless transmission

I began this chapter by arguing that the criminal law's approach to the question of responsibility is one based on a model of subjectivity that will, and must, deny the specificity of individual human experience. For those, like me, who have been brought up within a democratic polity, who take the rule of law as both a given and as fundamental, who are the product of a legal education whose source material manifests values informed by a tradition of liberalism, and whose conduct is judged according to a set of particular philosophical assumptions about what it is to be a person, it requires a significant leap of imagination (or, possibly, a complete suspension of disbelief) to be able to question the premises that underpin what it is to be, and be held, responsible in such a society at such a time. Those premises deny – or at the very least marginalise – the relevance of my gender (male), my class (middle), my sexuality (gay), my colour (white), my ethnicity (Caucasian), and my political status (British citizen). They ignore – or at the very least marginalise – the relevance of time in which I am living, my biography, my relationships, my character, and my political and spiritual beliefs. They are premises which assume that the individual human being is the locus – or at the very least the starting point – of any inquiry, but demand a prior distillation of homeopathic intensity. For the theoretician of responsibility wedded to the articulation and/or elaboration of the conventional account, the richness, variety and complexity of what it is to live as a human being is abstracted to a set of cognitive processes, volitions and choices. The object (and subject) of the inquiry – who becomes, through this process of abstraction, simply an agent – is assumed to have a moral compass; but it is a moral compass whose origin, range, and content is treated as a given and which functions simply as a means of evaluating the agent's conduct against the (same) moral compass that all other agents, whether individually or collectively, are assumed to possess.

If I am correct in my assertion that a criminal law informed by these moral, philosophical and political principles will, and must, have these effects; and if it is accepted that those effects may have adverse consequences both for individuals attempting to live responsible lives, and for public health more generally (to the extent that the criminalisation of HIV transmission may have adverse effects on the management and control of the epidemic)[23] then it seems to me that there are – as I suggested earlier – two choices. The first is to reflect the reality of individual experience in adjudicative processes concerned with determinations of responsible subjectivity. For reasons I have set out, I believe this to be politically unrealistic since it would mean dismantling the most fundamental premises and values that inform the rule of law. This is not to argue – let me be clear – that political projects which seek to address the adverse *effects* of adjudication, feminist and otherwise, should not be pursued. Such projects are important and can lead to beneficial outcomes for people whose interests the law fails to recognise and protect. Rather, it is simply to suggest that attempts to seek substantive justice for individual human beings by particularising the legal subject are doomed to failure.

The second choice, and one that I believe could serve to promote a more authentic and socially beneficial approach to the meaning, practice and expression of responsibility than that which the law constructs and reinforces, is to decriminalise the reckless transmission of HIV. This, to be sure, is a radical suggestion which will be rejected by those who believe that the

---

23 It is not only the potential disincentive to establishing one's HIV status that may result from limiting liability to those who know for certain that they may infect others: the *de facto* requirement to disclose one's HIV positive status to partners may lead those to whom no disclosure is made to assume (wrongly) that a non-discloser is HIV negative. See, more generally, Elliott (1997), UNAIDS (2002), AIDSFONDS (2004).

function of the criminal law is to articulate the moral sentiment of a society that (a) treats HIV infection as a harm, (b) views unjustifiable risk taking and non-disclosure as reprehensible, and (c) constructs the person to whom HIV is transmitted as a victim. For those who subscribe to such a view – and I am under no illusions as to their prevalence – decriminalisation is unthinkable; and such people are unlikely to be converted by any argument, least of all that which I advance here.

Nevertheless, I do think it is important to question the premises upon which this view is based. First, those who accept the legitimacy of criminalisation need to recognise that it is based on an individualised model of fault and conduct that ignores the fact that HIV exists in populations and that its transmission occurs between people. Each person who transmits HIV to another is someone who was him- or herself infected. If HIV is understood as a social fact rather than merely as a quality or characteristic of individuals, it becomes legitimate to develop responses to transmission that centre on the social consequences and benefits of any intervention rather than on the censure of particular people. Such consequentialist thinking is, no doubt, anathema to those committed to a Kantian analysis of responsibility; but I would argue, if our principal concern is (as I think it must be) the eradication of this dreadful virus through the prevention of onward transmission, that such an analysis has the potential to do us more harm than good. Second, the approach that the criminal law has adopted towards responsibility for transmission is one that denies the relevance of particular individuals' attempts to behave responsibly (by practising safer sex rather than disclosing status for example). To the extent that it does so, it undermines those attempts and ignores the very real impediments and barriers to behaving as the law demands. Third, criminal law (unlike tort law) is not concerned with fault allocation. If a defendant meets the conditions for liability he will be held responsible; if not, he will be absolved. And yet there are strong, public health centred, arguments that emphasise the importance of joint and shared responsibility for sexual health (see for example Gostin, 1989). To the extent that the criminalisation of reckless transmission establishes a perpetrator/victim dyad – even in cases where the 'victim' was aware of the risks she was taking when she engaged in unprotected sex *despite* the lack of disclosure – the law is serving to undermine this important public health message. Finally, an argument for the decriminalisation of reckless HIV transmission is emphatically *not* an argument for the decriminalisation of all reckless conduct that harms the interests of others. Legal reasoning in the common law tradition is grounded in analogy. As such, it is tempting to deploy a general account or analysis in other contexts. While it may be that the pragmatic approach I have advocated here may have application elsewhere – that is for others to judge; and some may argue that the wider implications of the position I take here is one that would, if applied in other contexts, have morally and politically unsupportable effects. I am not, however, arguing for a principle of general application. What I am arguing is that where the negative social impact of criminalisation in a particular context has the potential to outweigh any social benefits it might achieve (as I believe is the case here) it is legitimate to question whether criminalisation is justifiable.[24]

I want to end this chapter by reminding ourselves of what we must not forget. HIV transmission occurs between human beings. Those human beings may be male or female, hetero-, homo- or bisexual. They may be infants, adolescents, or adults. They may be mothers, fathers or carers. They may be orphans. They may belong to any ethnic, religious, or national group. They may be in marital, casual, committed or commercial sexual relationships with others. They may be HIV negative or HIV positive. They may know their HIV status, have unconfirmed beliefs or be ignorant about it, or not have given it a moment's thought. They may consider themselves to be 'at risk', or immune. They may know or believe, rightly or wrongly, their sexual partner(s) to be HIV positive, or HIV negative. They may understand the way in which HIV is transmitted, be unsure, or ignorant. Those who have contracted HIV may have been infected more than decades ago and be asymptomatic, or they may have been infected last year and have been diagnosed as suffering from an AIDS-related illness. They may have contracted HIV through maternal-fetal or perinatal transmission, a blood transfusion, needle sharing in the course of injecting drug use, consensual sexual intercourse or rape. They may have taken no precautions against transmission, or attempted unsuccessfully to protect themselves. They may have a high or negligible viral load. They may have access to care, treatment, advice and support, fail to take advantage of these where they are available, or be denied such services. They may know the identity of the person who infected them, or neither know nor care. They may feel ashamed, empowered, stupid or unlucky (or all of these things). They may voluntarily disclose their HIV positive status to those with whom they have sex of a kind that poses a risk of transmission, or stay silent. They may tell the truth if asked, or they may lie. They may not care about infecting others, or they may take every precaution against doing so. They may feel responsible for their infection, or that someone else is responsible for infecting them.

The point to be made is this: HIV affects everyone, whether they are positive or negative, and whether they know this or not. It affects them in different ways, in different contexts and for different reasons. Those who are HIV negative may, unless they take precautions against transmission in situations where that is a risk, become infected; those who are HIV positive may, unless they take precautions, infect others. There is, therefore, for those in each category a responsibility, both to themselves and to others, to minimise the risk of onward transmission. This simple truth of prevention, central to safer sex and health promotion initiatives in the field of HIV and

24 For an interesting discussion of this point in the US context see Lazzarini *et al.* (2002).

AIDS, nevertheless fails to capture – as the variety of experience, attitudes, emotions and statuses described above demonstrate – what being responsible means and entails, both for people living with HIV/AIDS and those at risk of infection. Nor does it give any indication of how people, individually or in their relations with others, are able to put, or are prevented from putting, their understanding of what being responsible means into practice. Put more simply, being responsible in the time of AIDS is both critically important and deeply problematic; and it is something that the criminalisation of reckless transmission fails abjectly to address.

Bibliography

AIDS FONDS (2004) *'Detention or Prevention?' A Report on the Impact and Use of Criminal Law on Public Health and the Position of People Living with HIV*, Amsterdam: AIDS FONDS.

Alldridge, P (1993) 'Sex, Lies and the Criminal Law', *Northern Ireland Legal Quarterly* 44, pp 250–68.

Alonzo, A A and Reynolds, N R (1995) 'Stigma, HIV and AIDS: An exploration and elaboration of a stigma trajectory', *Social Science and Medicine* 41, pp 303–15.

Baer, J (1999) *Our Lives Before the Law: Constructing a Feminist Jurisprduence*, Princeton: Princeton University Press.

Bersani, L (1988) 'Is the Rectum a Grave?' in D Crimp (ed.) *Cultural Analysis, Cultural Activism*, Cambridge, Mass: MIT Press.

Bronnit, S H (1994a) 'The Direction of Rape Law in Australia: Toward a Positive Consent Standard', *Criminal Law Journal*, pp 249–53.

Bruner, D 'High-Risk Sexual Behavior and Failure to Disclose HIV Infection to Sex Partners: How Do We Respond?', *AIDS & Public Policy Journal*, 19 (1/2), pp 11–36.

Cane, P (2002) *Responsibility in Law and Morality*, Oxford: Hart Publishing.

Chalmers, J (2001) 'Sexually Transmitted Diseases and the Criminal Law', *The Juridical Review* 5, pp 259–78.

Chalmers, J (2002) 'Criminalisation of HIV Transmission', *Journal of Medical Ethics* 28, pp 160–3.

Ciccarone, D *et al.* (2003) 'Sex Without Disclosure of Positive HIV Serostatus in a US Probability Sample of Persons Receiving Medical Care for HIV Infection', *American Journal of Public Health* 93 (6), pp 949–54.

Conaghan, J (1996) 'Gendered Harm and the Law of Tort', *Oxford Journal of Legal Studies* 16, pp 407–31.

Conaghan, J (2002) 'Law, Harm and Redress: A Feminist Perspective, *Legal Studies* 22 (3), pp 319–39.

Daly, M (1973) *Beyond God the Father: Toward a Philosophy of Women's Liberation*, Boston: Beacon Press.

Daly, M (1978) *Gyn/Ecology: the Metaethics of Radical Feminism*, Boston: Beacon Press.

Daly, M *Pure Lust: Elemental Feminist Philosophy*, Boston: Beacon Press.

Dan-Cohen, M (2002) *Harmful Thoughts: Essays on Law, Self and Morality*, Princeton: Princeton University Press.

Dean, M (1999) *Governmentality: Power and Rule in Modern Society*, London: Sage.

Derlega, V J *et al.* (1998) 'Reactions to an HIV-positive man: Impact of his sexual orientation, cause of infection, and research participants' gender', *AIDS and Behavior* 2, pp 239–348.

Derlega, V J *et al.* (2002) 'Perceived HIV-related stigma and HIV disclosure to relationship partners after finding out about the seropositive diagnosis', *Journal of Health Psychology*, 7, pp 415–32.

Dine, J and Watt B (1998) 'The Transmission of Disease During Consensual Sexual Activity and the Concept of Associative Autonomy' *Web Journal of Current Legal Issues* 4.

Elliott, R (1997) *Criminal Law and HIV/AIDS: Final Report*, Montreal: Canadian Legal Network and Canadian AIDS Society.

Farmer, L (1996) *Criminal Law, Tradition and Legal Order: Crime and the Genius of Scots Law 1747 to the Present*, Cambridge: Cambridge University Press.

Feinberg, J (1984) *Harm to Others*, Oxford: Oxford University Press.

Gardner, J (2003) 'The Mark of Responsibility', *Oxford Journal of Legal Studies* 23, pp 157–71.

Gielen, A *et al.* (1997) 'Women's Disclosure of HIV Status: Experiences of Mistreatment and Violence in an Urban Setting', *Women's Health* 25, p 19 *et seq.*

Gielen, A *et al.* (2000) 'Women's Lives After an HIV-Positive Diagnosis: Disclosure and Violence', *Maternal and Child Health Journal* 4, pp 111–20.

Goffmann, E (1963) Stigma: *Notes on the Management of Spoiled Identity*, Prentice Hall, New York.

Gostin, L (1989) 'The Politics of AIDS: Compulsory State Powers, Public Health and Civil Liberties', *Ohio State Law Journal*, pp 1017–58.

Greene, K, Derlega, V J, Yep, G A, and Petronio, S, (2003) *Privacy and Disclosure of HIV in Interpersonal Relationships: A Sourcebook for Researchers and Practitioners*, Mahwah, New Jersey: Lawrence Erlbaum Associates.

Hall, R and Longstaff, L (1997) 'Defining Consent', *New Law Journal*, p 840 *et seq.*

Hart, H L A (1968) *Punishment and Responsibility*, Oxford: Oxford University Press.

Herek, G M and Capitanio, J P (1999) 'AIDS and Stigma and Sexual Prejudice', *American Behavioural Scientist* 42, pp 1130–47.

Herring, J *Criminal Law: Text, Cases and Materials*, Oxford: Oxford University Press.

Horder, J (2004) *Excusing Crime*, Oxford: Oxford University Press.

Intergovernmental Committee on AIDS, Legal Working Party *Legislative Approaches to Public Health Control of HIV-Infection*, Canberra: Department of Community Services and Health (February, 1991).

Kelman, M (1980/81) 'Interpretive Construction in the Substantive Criminal Law' *Stanford Law Review* 33, pp 591–673.

Kilmarx, P *et al.* (1998) 'Experiences and Perspectives of HIV-Infected Sexually Transmitted Disease Clinic Patients After Post-Test Counselling', *Sexually Transmitted Diseases* 25, pp 28–37.

Klitzman, R and Bayer, R (2003) *Mortal Secrets: Truth and Lies in the Age of AIDS*, Baltimore: Johns Hopkins University Press.

Lacey, N (1998) *Unspeakable Subjects*, Oxford: Hart Publishing.

Lacey, N (2001a) 'Responsibility and Modernity in Criminal Law' *Journal of Political Philosophy* 9, pp 249–76.

Lacey, N (2001b) 'In Search of the Responsible Subject: History, Philosophy and Criminal Law', *Modern Law Review* 64, pp 350–71.

Laurie, G T (1991) 'AIDS and Criminal Liability Under Scots Law', *Journal of the Law Society of Scotland* 36, pp 312–17.

Law Commission, *Consent in the Criminal Law: A Consultation Paper* (No. 139) London: HMSO.

Lazzarini Z et al. (2002) 'Evaluating the Impact of Criminal Laws on HIV Risk Behavior', *Journal of Law, Medicine and Ethics* 30, pp 239–55.

Lemieux, R et al. (1998) 'The persuasive effect of the AIDS NAMES quilt on behavioural intentions', *Communication Research Reports* 15, pp 113–20.

Levy A et al. (1999) 'Disclosure of HIV Seropositivity', *Journal of Clinical Psychology* 55, pp 1041–9.

MacKinnon, C (1982) 'Feminism, Marxism, Method, and the State: An Agenda for Theory', *Signs: Journal of Women in Culture and Society* 7(3).

MacKinnon, C (1983) 'Feminism, Marxism, Method, and the State: Toward Feminist Jurisprudence', *Signs: Journal of Women in Culture and Society* 8(4), pp 635–58.

MacKinnon, C (1987) *Feminism Unmodified*, Cambridge, Mass: Harvard University Press.

Moneyham, L et al. (1996) 'Experiences of Disclosure in Women Infected With HIV', *Health Care Women International* 19, pp 209–21.

Moore, M (1997) *Placing Blame*, Oxford: Oxford University Press.

Naffine, N (1990) *Law and the Sexes: Explorations in Feminist Jurisprudence*, London: Alan & Unwin.

Naffine, N and Owens, R (eds) *Sexing the Subject of Law*, London: Sweet and Maxwell.

Niccolai, L et al. (1999) 'Disclosure of HIV Status to Sexual Partners: Predictors and Temporal Patterns', *Sexually Transmitted Diseases* 26, pp 281–5.

Norrie, A (1993) *Crime, Reason and History: A Critical Introduction to Criminal Law*, London: Weidenfeld & Nicolson.

Norrie, A (2000) *Punishment, Responsibility, and Justice: A Relational Critique*, Oxford: Oxford University Press.

Novick, A 'What Are the Responsibilities of HIV-Infected Persons? What Are the Reciprocal Responsibilities of Society?', *AIDS and Public Policy Journal* 9(2), p 55 et seq.

Ormerod D C and Gunn M J (1996) 'Criminal Liability for the Transmission of HIV', *Web Journal of Current Legal Issues* 1.

Patton, C (1996) *Fatal Advice: How Safe-Sex Advice Went Wrong*, Durham: Duke University Press.

Perry, S W et al. (1994) 'Self-disclosure of HIV infection to sexual partners after repeated counselling', *AIDS Education and Prevention* 6, pp 403–11.

Petrak, J A et al. (2001) 'Factors associated with self-disclosure of HIV serostatus to significant others', *British Journal of Health Psychology* 6, pp 69–79.

Seidman, S (1996) 'Points of Intersection: Discontinuities at the Junction of Criminal Law and the Regulatory State', *Journal of Contemporary Legal Issues* 7, p 97 et seq.

Sentencing Advisory Council, *Assaults and Other Offences Against the Person*, (Consultation) (2005).

Siegel, K et al. (1998) 'Stigma management among gay/bisexual men with HIV/AIDS', *Qualitative Sociology* 21, pp 3–24.

Simoni, J and Pantalone, D (2004) 'Secrets and safety in the age of AIDS: does HIV disclosure lead to safer sex?', *Topics in HIV Medicine* 12 (4), p 109 *et seq.*

Simoni, J M *et al.* (1995) 'Women's self-disclosure of HIV infection: Rates, reasons and reactions', *Journal of Consulting and Clinical Psychology* 63, pp 474–8.

Smith, K J M (1991) 'Sexual Etiquette, Public Interest and the Criminal Law', *Northern Ireland Legal Quarterly* 42, pp 309–31.

Spencer, J R (2004a) 'Liability for Reckless Infection: Part 1', *New Law Journal*, pp 384–5.

Spencer, J R (2004b) 'Liability for Reckless Infection: Part 2', *New Law Journal*, 448.

Sullivan, K M and Field M A (1988) 'AIDS and the Coercive Power of the State', *Harvard Civil Rights-Civil Liberties Law Review* 23, pp 139–97.

Temkin, J and Ashworth A (2004) 'The Sexual Offences Act 2003: (1) Rape, Sexual Assault and the Problems of Consent', *Criminal Law Review*, pp 328–46.

Tong, R (1989) *Feminist Thought: A Comprehensive Introduction*, London: Routledge.

UNAIDS (2002) *Criminal Law, Public Health and HIV Transmission: A Policy Options Paper*, Geneva: UNAIDS.

Warburton, D (2004) 'A Critical Review of English Law in Respect of Criminalising Blameworthy Behaviour by HIV+ Individuals', *Journal of Criminal Law* 68(1), pp 55–77.

Weait, M J (2001) 'Taking the Blame: Criminal Law, Social Responsibility and the Sexual Transmission of HIV', *Journal of Social Welfare and Family Law* 23, pp 441–57.

Weait, M J (2004) '*Dica*: Knowledge, Consent and the Transmission of HIV', *New Law Journal*, pp 826–7.

Weait, M J (2005a) 'Criminal Law and the Sexual Transmission of HIV: *R v Dica*', *Modern Law Review* 68(1), pp 120–34.

Weait, M J (2005b) 'Harm, Consent and the Limits of Privacy', *Feminist Legal Studies* 13, pp 97–122.

Weait, M J (2005c) 'Knowledge, Autonomy and Consent: R v Konzani', *Criminal Law Review* October, pp 763–72.

Weait, M and Azad, Y (2005) 'The Criminalization of HIV Transmission in England and Wales: Questions of Law and Policy', *HIV/AIDS Policy and Law Review* 10 (2), pp 1–12.

Wertheimer, A (2003) *Consent to Sexual Relations* Cambridge: Cambridge University Press.

West, R (1988) 'Jurisprudence and Gender', *University of Chicago Law Review* 55, pp 1–42.

Chapter 3

'Freedom and capacity to make a choice'

A feminist analysis of consent in the criminal law of rape

*Sharon Cowan, University of Edinburgh**

Introduction

This chapter explores the role of consent in the context of rape, in (re)constructing certain kinds of sexual choices. Consent has been described as a 'remarkable power(s) of personhood', and has historically been associated with notions of autonomy and choice (Hurd, 1996: 121). To focus on consent as the distinguishing feature between wanted and unwanted physical contact is to say that it is an appropriate measure of respect for our autonomy: 'Consent derives its normative power from the fact that it alters the obligations and permissions that collectively determine the rightness of others' actions' (Hurd, 1996: 124). This view of consent as the focal point of self-rule has historically relied upon a liberal perspective, involving the protection of one's autonomy to make choices as to one's sexual intimate relationships and contacts. According to Gardner and Shute (2000), in the context of rape, the concept of consent is valuable and necessary because it allows people to act as moral agents. The ability to genuinely consent is *constitutive* of sexual autonomy (2000: 207). Consent and autonomy are, it seems, inseparable.

In the context of sexual assaults, autonomy is most commonly defined along the lines of the recent formulation by the Scottish Law Commission:

> Autonomy is a complex idea but in the context of legal regulation of sexual conduct it involves placing emphasis on a person freely choosing to engage in sexual activity . . . Where a person participates in a sexual act in respect of which she has not freely chosen to be involved, that person's autonomy has been infringed, and a wrong has been done to her.
>
> (2006: paragraph 2.3)

* Countless thanks are due to both Gillian Calder and Victor Tadros for conversations and suggestions that helped to clarify my thinking on many issues. Thanks also to Vanessa Munro and Carl Stychin for invaluable editorial assistance.

Many feminists have critiqued this notion of consent, particularly in the context of rape. For example, as Nicola Lacey points out in relation to the UK government's Home Office Review of Sexual Offences, *Setting the Boundaries*, which was enacted in amended form in England and Wales by the Sexual Offences Act 2003: '[t]he shade of John Stuart Mill stands behind the Review's references to harm and its appeal to the value of autonomy' (2001: 5). Lacey problematises the standard liberal view of autonomy and consent as individualistic and removed from a social context: 'In focusing on an individualised notion of consent, rather than the conditions under which choices can be meaningful, the prevailing idea of sexual autonomy assumes the mind to be dominant and controlling, irrespective of material circumstances' (1998: 117). A more nuanced understanding of how human interactions take place, particularly in relation to sexual intimacy, is required if consent is to prove a valuable and workable concept in rape. For any formal right to consent or refuse to have effect, the substantive elements of the right – an appropriate range of options and a real opportunity to choose between them – must also be present (Weait, 2005). Further, consent does not operate in a vacuum and is relational, and dependent on social interaction rather than individualistic decision making.[1] A formal contract model of consent does not capture the underlying power imbalances that may exist before 'negotiation' takes place, and may portray each choice as an isolated snapshot, rather than reflect the interconnected nature of choice: 'The law [of rape] presents consent as free exercise of sexual choice under conditions of equality of power without exposing the underlying structure of constraint and disparity' (MacKinnon, 1989: 175). Therefore, the structural constraints upon the process of choice also merit scrutiny. The central issue then is whether the notion of consent is equipped to address questions of power and agency inherent within the notion of sexual choice, and take on the broad task of substantively distinguishing between wanted and unwanted (that is, legal and illegal) interpersonal contact.

This chapter will consider these questions in relation to rape, and particularly with regard to recent reforms on the law of rape introduced by the Sexual Offences Act 2003. Legal rules on consent in rape have long been of concern to feminists and other critical scholars, especially with respect to the issue of protecting (or failing to protect) sexual autonomy. This chapter provides an analysis of the places where law disregards a seemingly valid refusal of sexual intimacy, and the cogency of the bases on which decisions to accept/disregard refusals are made, thereby demonstrating law's role in (re)constructing sexual choices. This discussion raises serious concerns about the protection of sexual integrity, and the power of law in constructing

---

1   Cf. Archard (1998). For a defence of feminist liberalism, and a conception of positive autonomy in the form of 'capabilities', see Nussbaum (1999).

sexual agency. Legal processes of validating or rejecting consent also tell us something about the kinds of sexual agents law helps to construct (Lacey, 1998: 103).

Examining law's (re)construction of consents and refusals raises a further question – namely, is there something special about the way consent should work in rape, which would necessitate a distinct body of theorising about consent, or is consent something we can conceptualise generally across criminal law? An argument for a general ethical concept of consent has been made by Monica Cowart. She claims that we should have one view of consent for the purposes of all human activity, and define consent in an 'unbiased, systematic manner that can be theoretically applied' (2004: 496). A rich and precise understanding of the concept of consent can be gained through the teasing out of some underlying principles, or minimum conditions of consent. These principles would both do justice to the idea of what consent is for, and make it a practically useful concept. Cowart's main planks of genuine consent are: that the act of consent must match the consenter's intention; there must be a mutual understanding of the thing being consented to (including minimum standards of communication); and that subjectively speaking, the consenter must feel that they have a genuine range of choices from which to choose.

While there is no opportunity here to engage with each of these minimum conditions, in this chapter I argue that general principles of genuine consent, perhaps along the lines of Cowart's schema, are possible and necessary to make consent practically and conceptually useful. Consent is a concept which we can fill with either narrow liberal values, based on the idea of the subject as an individual atomistic rational choice maker, or with feminist values encompassing attention to mutuality, embodiment, relational choice and communication. In the following sections I will argue that we can formulate general principles for genuine consent – for example whether the interaction between parties involves mutuality, agency, respect for bodily integrity, and communication – and further, that a substantive legal analysis of how consent operates in particular sexual contexts can guide us as to whether sexual contact is genuinely wanted or not, and whether such behaviour should be criminalised. The project then is to address both the principles and the process of genuine consent. By analysing current formulations of rape law in light of feminist understandings of how consent should work, I will argue that while there is room to broaden out the notion of consent in order to protect sexual integrity and autonomy, contemporary provisions on rape are caught within traditional liberal notions of consent which reflect a concern with the actions and bodies of women, whilst failing to recognise substantive questions of freedom and capacity to make genuine choices. This argument is made with particular attention to rape law reforming provisions introduced in England and Wales by the Sexual Offences Act 2003.

In both Scottish and English/Welsh jurisdictions amongst many others, rape is defined as sexual intercourse without consent. Feminists have long documented the problems of operationalising consent in this context, particularly concerning the subject of whether force (and correspondingly physical resistance) is necessary to show lack of consent.[2] The issue of consent is further complicated by the fact that the legitimacy of sexual intercourse is a both a question of the *actus reus* of rape – whether the complainant in a rape trial actually consented to the sexual intercourse, and of the *mens rea* – whether the defendant understood the complainant to be consenting. Here the contentious issue often takes the form of the question, should a mistaken belief in consent have to be reasonable, or just merely honest?

The Sexual Offences Act 2003 rejects an entirely subjective test of the defendant's state of mind – s 1(2) requires that the defendant's belief should be 'reasonable in all the circumstances'. The Act represents an important (though for some disappointing) effort to update and reform the law on sexual offences. This chapter focuses in detail on the relevant provisions of the 2003 Act regarding the *actus reus* and *mens rea* of rape, namely, the creation of a statutory definition of consent, and the test for assessing the defendant's belief in consent. The argument here is that despite the recent reforms, law continues problematically to construct consent where proper attention to context would suggest none exists. This legal reconstruction of events occurs in cases where it should not, that is, where non consent should be obvious, and it occurs because of the difficulties inherent within the concept of consent itself, and because of the unsatisfactory way in which the test of belief in consent has been articulated. In the discussion below it will be argued that a feminist reading of consent which protects women's sexual embodied autonomy continues to be displaced by the legal application of consent. The chapter concludes by drawing together some thoughts about the role of consent as it operates in rape law, asking whether consent is a 'meaningful concept' (MacKinnon, 1989: 178), and noting that the question of whether consent can protect sexual autonomy and bodily integrity through the criminal law, requires both general principles of consent, and an offence specific contextual analysis.

What counts as consent? The *actus reus*, and s 74 of the 2003 Act

On advice from the Law Commission, the Home Office (2000) Review *Setting the Boundaries* (on which the Sexual Offences Act 2003 was based) recommended a statutory definition of consent that could be put to juries, along-

---

2   'Reasonable' physical resistance to force is still required to show non-consent in many US states (Schulhofer, 1998).

side a non-exhaustive list (which by the time of the Act's implementation had become an exhaustive list) of circumstances where the validity of consent would be questionable. The Sexual Offences Act 2003 provides the following definition of consent:

s 74 'Consent'

For the purposes of this Part, a person consents if he agrees by choice, and has the freedom and capacity to make that choice.

Section 74 tries to give flesh to the bones of the concept of consent by referring to the surrounding circumstances of a choice rather than simply the moment of assent. The definition acknowledges that consent is not a simple matter – that issues of, for example, capacity, coercion, manipulation and fraud are intimately connected to establishing consent. However, the definition does not really help us to answer the most difficult questions, primarily those related to freedom and capacity.

Freedom

Freedom is a difficult concept to define, and since one might argue that no choice is truly free in the sense of being completely unconstrained, the question is, just how free does a choice have to be before it is valid? What is the meaning of genuine consent as opposed to acquiescence or submission? And what counts as free agreement in the face of non-violent coercion? For example, if a woman submits to having sex with her partner because she knows that otherwise he will not give her housekeeping money and she will not be able to feed her children, is that rape under this definition? If a prostitute agrees to have sex with a client because she knows that otherwise her pimp will beat her later, does she have freedom and capacity to make that choice?[3] The instinctive response here may be that these are not free choices, but it seems unlikely that those kinds of cases, even though they arguably meet the definition, will be considered rape in court (suspending disbelief and assuming cases such as these ever reached a court). Even though these choices do not in theory fit the definition of 'free', juries and courts in practice often interpret broad terms such as freedom and capacity narrowly (Finch and Munro, 2005).

And what sorts of information must such a person have before she is said to have the freedom to make the choice? The possibility of using the concept of informed consent as part of the law of rape was rejected by the Law

---

3   Ormerod (2005: 600) suggests that in developing the s 74 definition courts may draw on the rules governing analogous areas of coercion and consent such as freedom to resist in duress cases. See also Tadros (2006).

Commission in their report *Consent in Sexual Offences* on the grounds that it might focus inappropriate jury attention on the complainant in a rape trial, 'by diverting minds to the irrelevant issue of the lack of wisdom of the consent given' (footnote 10). But, as is shown in relation to fraudulent rapes, the information a complainant has about her partner does impact upon her ability to genuinely consent.[4] The centrality of a particular piece of knowledge or information to the desirability of sexual intimacy will vary but it is arguable that where one's sexual and bodily integrity is violated by way of a lack of relevant information or knowledge, this would mean that the relevant freedom, required to make a genuine choice, is not present.

Capacity

At the time of writing, since 2004 (the Act came into force in May of that year) there have been 119 reported cases citing the 2003 Act.[5] It is clear that none of the 119 cases refer to s 74 or the terms of the statutory definition of consent. However, in one recent case, judicial interpretation of consent in light of the new legislation is to be noted. The 2005 case *R v Gardner* addresses the notion of consent as it applies to an intoxicated 14-year-old girl's ability to consent to digital penetration by a 19-year-old boy.[6] The defendant actually pleaded guilty to sexual activity with a child under s 9 of the 2003 Act, to which consent is not a defence, but appealed on sentence. While no issue of liability turns on the issue of consent in this case, consent was the subject of judicial interpretation. The appellant entered the bathroom while the victim was being sick, kissed her and propositioned her. She was unable to answer because she was vomiting. He then penetrated her. At the trial the defendant claimed to have thought that the complainant was being sick from a stomach bug rather than through alcohol consumption, even though she had been carried into the house very drunk, placed in a bedroom, and the defendant had agreed to check on her every ten minutes (he changed his story at the time of sentencing and acknowledged that he had known she was drunk). In sentencing, the trial judge accepted that 'what the defendant had done was consensual', even if it was drunken consent and despite the fact that the young woman had been 'taken advantage of' (paragraph 11). Further, the appellate court also accepted that the defendant had reasonably believed there to be consent, even though he knew she was drunk, and although, as they themselves said, the defendant knew she was only 14 and that 'consent could not possibly justify what he was doing' (paragraph 15).

---

4   Such as *R v Flattery* (1877) 2 QBD 410; *R v Williams* (1923) 1 KB 240.
5   As at 26 January 2006. Some of these do not involve offences brought under the Act but refer to other 2003 Act provisions, such as sex offender orders, and many of them are sentencing appeals. Appeal cases obviously do not tell us what happens at a discursive level in jury trials for rape.
6   (2005) EWCA Crim 1399.

Given the paucity of judicial or other guidance on the meaning of consent, particularly as it is defined under s 74 of the 2003 Act, this judgment demonstrates the very real concerns of having a vague definition of consent which is left open to case-by-case interpretation by individual judges and juries. The finding that not only was there reasonable belief in consent, but that consent existed, albeit drunken and under-age, is open to fundamental challenge. A 14-year-old girl who is extremely drunk and vomiting at a party, unable to communicate with a defendant about what he wants to do (to her), nevertheless, according to the Court, does appear to have the capacity to make the choice to consent. But what was her range of realistic options whilst in this state? For autonomy and choice to have any positive meaningful content, they have to be accompanied by a range of options to choose from if the power to consent/refuse is to carry any weight. It is accepted by the court in *R v Gardner* that the consent is both under-age and drunken, but it is still held to be consent.[7] The judicial reluctance to accept that a person who has voluntarily intoxicated themselves could be raped has a long history – Kim Stevenson (1999) for example notes 'the comment of Mr. Justice Willes in 1856, doubting that the offence of rape could be committed "upon the person of a woman who had rendered herself perfectly insensible by drink" (*The Times*, 6 December 1856)'.

Surely here the issue is one of the level of intoxication, rather than whether or not intoxication was self-induced. Where a person is drunk to the point of vomiting, or to the point of memory black-out, the reason for being in such a condition, including the notion of fault in bringing it about, is irrelevant to a meaningful understanding of consent. Consent cannot be valid, and further there can be no reasonable belief in consent, if one party is in a condition, self-induced or otherwise, where communication is compromised to this degree. The Home Office have recently recognised that intoxication presents a serious problem in establishing whether or not there was consent, and have produced a consultation paper (2006) to prompt discussion on how to deal with incapacity through intoxication. They have recommended a statutory definition of capacity, but this does not address the issue, highlighted in *R v Gardner*, of the defendant's claim to reasonable belief *despite* incapacity.

While the language of reasonable belief in consent was used in the case, the 2003 Act's s 74 definition of consent is not discussed or even mentioned by the appeal court.[8] It remains to be seen then how the statutory definition will

---

7   A similar conclusion was reached recently in a case in 2005 where the court said that a drunken consent is still consent; see 'Call for inquiry after rape case collapses over "drunken consent" ' Clare Dyer, *Guardian* 24 November 2005.

8   The original case at trial is not reported and therefore it is not clear whether the definition provided by s 74 was discussed in the first instance.

be operationalised. Some, for example MacKinnon, would argue that attempts to reformulate consent are merely manipulations of a fundamentally flawed concept, and that the problems evident here are merely symptoms of the real malaise of using a model of consent in the first place, a model which ignores the argument that 'consent is a communication under conditions of inequality' (MacKinnon, 1989: 182). While it seems incredibly important that a law which protects sexual autonomy should criminalise serious infringements of that autonomy, including non-consensual sexual assaults such as rape, at the same time it appears that consent is not doing the necessary work in this respect. Despite the 2003 Act's focus on consent in the *actus reus* as being pivotal in protecting sexual autonomy, the lack of proper engagement with or guidance on questions of substantive context under which consent is given means that s 74 may not in fact make any difference, other than its symbolic message, to jury findings of guilt and responsibility.

The question of context is, however, tricky – contextual analysis can provide an excuse for a focus on the behaviour of the victim, and what can be inferred from that, as opposed to the blameworthy failure of the defendant to participate in communication about the mutuality of desire. Legal discussion which informed the development of the 2003 Act demonstrates just such a focus on the victim which fails to properly respect sexual integrity. For example, it was envisaged by the Law Commission in their *Consent in Sexual Offences*, which formed part of the Home Office report *Setting the Boundaries*, that any statutory definition of consent, while termed as free agreement, should make it clear that consent could be express or implied, and could be 'evidenced by words or conduct, whether present or past' (2000, paragraph 2.12).[9] While this formulation does not form part of s 74, it indicates that in the contemporary conceptualisations of consent that underlie the 2003 Act, there is evidence of a lingering failure to separate a truly meaningful definition of what consent is, from whether or not a defendant has reasonable reasons to suppose that there is consent.[10] Past or present behaviour of a complainant, while relevant, is *only* relevant to the defendant's belief in consent, not to whether consent itself exists on this particular instance.[11] Therefore such considerations should not form part of a statutory definition of consent, the point of which is to help juries decide whether genuine

---

9 Available as an appendix to *Setting the Boundaries*.

10 This conflation is also enshrined within the 2003 Act itself in that the list of rebuttable and non-rebuttable presumptions in ss 75 and 76 apply to both the question of whether there was consent, and as to whether the defendant had a reasonable belief that there was consent. For critique see Ormerod (2005: 602–11); Ashworth and Temkin (2004); Tadros (2006).

11 Barring extremely unlikely exceptional instances (for example where V asks D in advance to have sex with her, whenever she is asleep or drunk). Thanks to Victor Tadros for raising this point.

consent was present, and to signal to juries that consent is ideally based on mutual agreement.

Feminist critiques of legal discourse on rape have included the way in which past or present sexual (or indeed non-sexual) conduct has been taken by defendants to imply consent to sexual contact. These critiques, combined with the wealth of research that suggests that men often misinterpret women's behaviour as sexual interest (Archard, 1998: 34; Anderson, 2005: 117–20), make the Law Commission's recommended inclusion of these potentially problematic inferences within a definition of consent even more surprising. That these changes to the definition of consent were meant to form the centre-piece of supposedly modernising and reforming legislation is problematic indeed.[12]

At any rate, since there is no statutory guidance as to how to interpret s 74, the way in which the 2003 Act's statutory definition of consent will be inter-preted in the courts offers another avenue for reflection and anticipation. In Victoria, Australia, the positive consent standard in rape, where consent is defined as free agreement, is supported by judicial guidelines on directing the jury as to consent (Bronitt, 1994). Under the 2003 Act, however, there is as yet no guidance or model direction from the Judicial Studies Board that might assist judges in addressing juries on the meaning of consent in s 74, and '[s]ince juries will have their own basic understanding of "freedom" and "choice", the value of a direction along these lines would be to challenge stereotypical thinking' (Temkin and Ashworth, 2004: 336). Without such guidance, a phrase such as free agreement might be interpreted overly narrowly by judges and juries, as Munro and Finch have found (2005). On the other hand, it has been suggested that leaving it to the Judicial Studies Board to set guidelines, rather than Parliament, is both undemocratic, and unpromising (Tadros, 2006; Temkin and Ashworth, 2004). What is clear is that judges and juries need to have a broader contextual view of consent that does not focus solely on the victim's behaviour and what the defendant has inferred from that, but rather whether the victim did in fact have freedom and capacity in relation to her contact with the defendant.

So much for the recent reforms regarding the *actus reus*. What of the role of consent in *mens rea* of rape? How does consent operate in relation to the defendant's mental state?

Consent, the *mens rea* and reasonable belief

The historical lack of a reasonableness requirement in belief about consent, which has historically marked the rape laws of many jurisdictions, has been subject to strong criticism for many years. Feminists claimed that the honest

---

12 Archard (1998: 35–7) critiques the Husak and Thomas (1992) model of consent, which is based on 'social conventions' around consent to sex, for exactly the same reasons.

belief rule panders to those who believe, as it was argued by the defendants in *DPP v Morgan*,[13] that even when a woman says no, she really means yes (Wells, 1982). In practice there may be few real 'Morgan' cases where a defendant is acquitted on the basis of a genuinely mistaken though unreasonable belief in consent, since the more unreasonable the mistake the less genuine the jury might think the belief is. Bronitt (1992: 306–7) claims that research has shown that the risk of a defendant being acquitted under this standard has been overestimated. However, it is possible that if the *actus reus* of rape were redefined to include, for example, clients who have sex with prostitutes who are coerced into prostitution, there may be some clients who unreasonably but genuinely do not question the validity of the consent, and these cases would be 'Morgan'-type cases. In my view however, if the client cannot provide a reasonable, ethical explanation for his lack of thought or knowledge of the coercion (such as lack of capacity) the encounter should be seen as non-consensual.

Feminists also emphasised the symbolic importance of criminalising unreasonable mistakes as to consent in sexual intercourse. Men's unreasonable beliefs about women's sexual (and non-sexual) behaviour should not be reflected in standards that assess criminal liability. Legal rules must reflect the aspiration that men ought to ground their belief in consent in the practice of proper and mutual communication with their sexual partners. This is especially true, it is often said, since a law which requires defendants to have taken reasonable steps to discover whether or not complainants are consenting would not put too high a burden on defendants, and would clarify any ambiguity that might exist, thereby protecting defendants from criminal responsibility for mere misunderstandings, while protecting the sexual autonomy of complainants (Archard, 1998: 144–5; Temkin and Ashworth, 2004: 340). However, Catharine MacKinnon articulates what is troubling about a dichotomised approach of subjective versus objective standards:

> Interpreted this way, the legal problem has been to determine whose view of that meaning constitutes what really happened, as if what happened objectively exists to be objectively determined . . . As a result, although rape law oscillates between subjective tests and objective standards invoking social reasonableness, it uniformly presumes a single underlying reality, rather than a reality split by the divergent meanings inequality produces.
>
> (1989: 180)

MacKinnon's argument is that an apparently objective interpretation of what counts as consent in the first instance is not so, because under

13 [1976] AC 182.

conditions of male supremacy, which are embodied in the law, consent is never freely given. Objective and subjective legal standards are not polar opposites but in fact reflect the same view point – that of the defendant.[14] A simple move towards a reasonable belief standard does not address the question that MacKinnon raises – reasonable according to whom? She says: '[t]o attempt to solve [the problem of rape] by adopting reasonable belief as a standard without asking, on a substantive social basis, to whom the belief is reasonable and why – meaning, what conditions make it reasonable – is one sided: male-sided' (1989: 183). However, the switch to a reasonable belief standard is arguably still necessary and important. MacKinnon's argument is not an argument against moving from honest to reasonable belief *per se*, but against doing so without concurrent engagement with questions of substantive equality – that is, the context and conditions under which consent are achieved and understood. With regard to substantive law, what this might mean in practice is both moving to a reasonable belief standard, but alongside some rigorous reassessment of what counts as consent in the first place in rape law, as discussed above. In any case it seems that there is a strong case for adopting a standard of reasonable belief in consent; as Nicola Lacey has suggested: 'Symbolically . . . it is crucially important that rape law be reformed so as to express an unambiguous commitment to the positive integrity as well as the full humanity of both rape victims and men accused of rape' (1998: 122).

The 2003 Act in England and Wales purports to move towards a standard where the defendant must have a reasonable belief in the complainant's consent. However, the actual provision states:

Section 1(2). Whether a belief is reasonable is to be determined having regard to all the circumstances, *including any steps A has taken to ascertain whether B consents.* (My emphasis.)

On one level this definition is an improvement on the pure subjective test – it introduces an element of reasonableness, and goes as far as requiring that the jury, in determining whether or not A's belief is reasonable, take into account whether or not A has made an attempt to find out if B is in fact consenting. The approach is modelled on similar provisions in other jurisdictions such as s 273.2(b) of the Canadian Criminal Code[15] which states that mistake is not available as a defence to a charge of rape if D 'did not take reasonable steps in the circumstances known to the accused at the time, to ascertain that the complainant was consenting'. Arguably, the explicit inclusion of this criterion encourages *positive action* by the defendant to establish consent in order for his defence of reasonable belief to be persuasive (Bronitt,

14 Cf. Archard (1998: 87–9).　　15 *Criminal Code*, RSC 1985, as amended.

1994). If we accept that the law of rape should have consent as its central plank, and we will return to this question, s 1(2) embodies a positive communicative standard of consent (Bronitt, 1994) rather than allowing the defendant to rely on his own assessment without trying to communicatively establish whether his assessment is correct. This is definitely a step in the right direction. Anderson claims that rape laws built upon the requirement for communication or negotiation would 'protect the values that rape law should be designed to protect. It would maximize autonomy and equality and minimize coercion and subordination. It would require people to treat their sexual partners with respect and humanity' (2005: 107). Section 1(2) of the 2003 Act could be seen as a move towards a more 'communicative model of sexuality' (Bronitt, 1994), assuming that steps taken are based on some express communication between parties. It is at least possible that inclusion of reasonable steps within the 2003 Act statutory framework signals recognition that belief in consent should involve some level of positive action to establish whether or not there is mutual desire.

On another level however the provision is still deeply troubling. For one thing, reference is made to what is reasonable *in all the circumstances*, and the question remains as to what this means in practice in the courtroom. What circumstances will be relevant to the assessment of reasonableness? It is not unforeseeable that circumstances will include personal characteristics of the accused. Will reasonable in all the circumstances therefore mean in effect a return to what is reasonable for the defendant given his wider belief system?[16] What if the accused has led an especially sheltered life, in a rural place, within a sexist family, has not been schooled in the shifting gender power relations of the twenty-first century, and believes a sexual partner to be consenting despite her protestations; will it be reasonable for him to think she is consenting? Without further guidance, 'reasonable in all the circumstances' does not address MacKinnon's point as to the question of *reasonable to whom*, and indeed may mean what is reasonable for the defendant.

According to the Government's Sexual Offences White Paper *Protecting the Public*, (which formed the basis of the 2003 Act), it was envisaged that *reasonable* would be assessed according to a purely objective standard, and that this was crucial not only symbolically but also because the existing subjective honest belief standard might be partially responsible for the low conviction rate in rape, in that victims of rape may perceive that the legal system is biased against them and therefore will 'not report incidents or press for them to be brought to trial' (Sexual Offences White Paper 'Protecting the Public', paragraph 32). The White Paper states:

16 On the 'Ethics of Belief' see Tadros (2005: chapter 9).

'Reasonable' will be judged by reference to what an objective third party would think in the circumstances. The jury would however have to take into account the actions of both parties, *the circumstances in which they have placed themselves* and the level of responsibility exercised by both.

(Paragraph 34, my emphasis)

'*The circumstances in which they have placed themselves*' is a potentially problematic phrase, raising questions of allocation of responsibility, which themselves in turn evoke the most misogynist judicial statements made in 1980s rape trials, when certain judges deemed women to be responsible for precipitating rape because of the clothes they were wearing, or the behaviour they had 'indulged' in, such as hitch hiking.[17] It is based on a notion of prior fault. The phrase also assumes autonomous choice and agency when 'placing' oneself in a situation, rather than acknowledging the complex relational and always constrained nature of choices. Part of the problem with interpreting 'reasonable' in this way is that it is open to jury (as well as judicial) prejudice, especially in the law of rape. In Munro and Finch's work on mock juries' assessments of responsibility in intoxicated rape cases, jurors were given a rape case, and asked to decide whether there had been consent according to s 74 of the 2003 Act. One of the jurors expressed the view that the victim, by getting drunk, had *put herself* into a position where she no longer had the freedom and capacity to make a choice and that this somehow diminished the degree to which s 74 could protect her (Finch and Munro, 2006). The outcome for the victim here, and consequently the defendant's liability, is again seen in terms of the victim's own responsibility, and not the inherent structural power relations that form the framework for her capacity to consent. It is, as Steven Box once said, just as ridiculous to address questions of men's liability for rape by focusing on the lack of precautions – including not drinking – taken by women, as it is to assess the liability of bank robbers by focusing on the precautions (alarms etc.) taken by the banks (1989: 134). This approach of allocating blame to victim or defendant tends towards seeing responsibility as a 'zero sum game' where any responsibility borne by the complainant, as contributing to the rape, is deducted from the responsibility borne by the defendant (Archard, 1998: 139).

There was much debate on the reasonableness test during the passage of the Sexual Offences Bill through Parliament. By the end of that process, the test had been downgraded from a purely objective one (as espoused by the White Paper, quoted above) to its present format of 'reasonable in all the circumstances'. During the debates in the House of Lords this shift away from a purely objective standard of belief in consent was seen as a workable compromise, and a necessary one in order to ensure that those with mental

17 See for example Patullo (1984).

incapacities, who may be unable to appreciate that a partner was not consenting, would not be found guilty of rape. In the intervening period between the government's Sex Offences Review *Setting the Boundaries*, the Home Office White Paper *Protecting the Public*, and the 2003 Act itself, many competing views were expressed on the propriety of an objective test. Proposed amendments to the Bill explicitly suggested that, when assessing whether a belief in consent was reasonable, the jury should be required to take into account personal characteristics of the defendant. This was rejected in the House of Lords, as it would excuse a defendant on grounds that 'should not absolve him of guilt' such as sexist attitudes.[18] However, in rejecting this requirement, it was suggested that it would be for the jury as a matter of fact to decide which of the defendant's characteristics would be relevant in assessing the reasonableness of his belief.[19] When asked by Baroness Kennedy to reassure the House that 'relevant characteristics' would be limited to those characteristics such as age and mental impairment, Lord Falconer replied that:

> [i]t would be unwise for me to restrict the precise characteristics to which a judge could direct a jury. It will depend upon the circumstances of a case. The noble Baroness is obviously right to refer to the enduring characteristics of age and mental impairment but I should not like to rule out other circumstances. One will have to leave it to the good sense of judges and juries.[20]

Lord Falconer's answer is reminiscent of the way in which the reasonableness test had evolved in the context of the defence of provocation, most notably in the case of *R v Smith (Morgan James)*,[21] and indeed Lord Cooke in the House of Lords debates on the Sexual Offences Bill approvingly drew a direct comparison between their formulation of reasonableness, and the provocation test of reasonableness.[22] The developing legal rules on what is reasonable in the law of provocation have been the subject of much debate and criticism, particularly where these rules have tended towards an 'overly subjectivised' standard which allows for a defendant's unreasonable (unethical) background beliefs to excuse his provoked response (Tadros, 2005: 352).[23] Indeed, recently the decision in *Smith (Morgan)* was rejected 6:3 by the Privy Council in *Attorney General of Jersey v Holley*,[24] and the court explicitly stated that the standard of self-control expected of the reasonable

---

18 Lord Falconer, HL Debates, 2 Jun 2003, Column 1073.
19 Lord Falconer, HL Debates, 2 Jun 2003, Column 1074.
20 HL, 2 Jun 2003, Column 1075.   21 [1999] QB 1079; affd [2001] AC 146.
22 HL, 17 Jun 2003, Column 675.
23 See also generally Tadros (2005: chapters 9 and 13); Cowan and Tadros (2006).
24 [2005] UKPC 23.

man was objective, and should not be judged as being the self-control of the defendant himself, as interpreted by the jury.[25]

In the context of rape, as in provocation, leaving to the jury the decision as to what is reasonable in the circumstances is dangerous and unnecessary. It is dangerous because, as feminists and other critical scholars have long argued, what is 'reasonable' in the deeply gendered area of rape, should be matters for legal principle informed and judicial guidance rather than subject to jury prejudice and manipulation by the defence; unnecessary because if the concern of the government (as it seemed to be) was to protect those who do not have full mental capacity (including the young) to appreciate a lack of consent, they could have explicitly and legislatively excluded them, or provided them with a defence without jettisoning 'reasonableness' (Temkin and Ashworth, 2004: 341). Building in a defence for such defendants is only one way of proceeding; the point here is that if we retain a consent-based system we could require consideration of some subjective characteristics of the defendant, such as age, when assessing belief in consent. But the kinds of questions we should ask about the defendant's belief formation should not simply be left to the jury as a matter of fact without any guiding legal principles. Thus the fact that the subjective test of reasonableness may be coherently and consistently developed across the offence of rape and the defence of provocation is something to be regretted rather than celebrated. And as Temkin and Ashworth suggest: 'It therefore seems possible that the new element of absence of reasonable belief in consent, which forms part of the four major offences in the Act, may not impose greater duties on defendants than does the present law' (2004: 342).

What is deemed reasonable then, in the circumstances of establishing consent, depends very much on societal views of responsibility. And responsibility, as feminists have argued, is a deeply gendered notion. It is a notion that is especially problematic within the field of sexual relations, as is also evidenced by the debates over what it is *reasonable* to tell a prospective partner about one's HIV status, raised by the English cases *R v Dica* and *R v Konzani*, and the Scottish case *HMA v Kelly*.[26] The crucial issue again is by whose standards are we measuring reasonableness. In rape trials, the answer will undoubtedly be the jury's. The question remains then as to whether the present formulation of 'reasonable' can do the kind of work the Government White paper envisaged it could do to combat the problems of an over-subjectivised belief in consent. Posturing that a return to an objective and reasonable standard is both symbolically necessary (which seems broadly right) and will have a positive impact on poor rape conviction rates (which is

---

25 Followed by *R v Mohammed* [2005] EWCA Crim 1880.

26 *R v Dica* [2004] Crim LR 944; *R v Konzani* [2005] EWCA Crim 706; *HMA v Kelly* (Glasgow High Court, unreported, February 2001).

far from obvious), but then allowing that standard to retain an inherent unknown amount of subjectivity by way of the imprecise phrase 'reasonable in all the circumstances', seems, at best, contradictory.

Further, leaving this to the discretion and moral standards of the fact-finders might well perpetuate an unacceptable degree of uncertainty in the law (Bronitt, 1992: 299). It is important that the term 'reasonable' should be interpreted in light of feminist critiques of reasonableness so as to meet demands that the legal system does not reflect male norms (MacKinnon, 1989). The problems of using a reasonable standard are not addressed by leaving the vague phrase 'reasonable in all the circumstances' to the jury and hoping for the best. Clearer direction on what is reasonable, or even what is *un*reasonable, perhaps by enacting a list of examples, might be preferable (Cowan and Tadros, 2006). The content of the list and whether the list takes the form of evidential or conclusive presumptions are crucial questions which are not dealt with here. However, it is important in principle to have legislative guidance, based on principles of respect and mutual communication, and that will protect sexual autonomy and bodily integrity. This is preferable to an unguided case by case analysis by fact-finders, of the types of situations where a defendant's simple reliance on: 'I thought she was consenting', will not be adequate to provide a defence. Arguably the 2003 Act does not provide clear enough guidance here, and leaves much of the work of interpretation of key phrases, such as freedom, capacity and reasonable, to the jury. Where there is any room for doubt about what counts as consent, or as to the meaning of an act such as kissing, consent to sexual intercourse should not be presumed; rather reasonable steps should be taken by the person wishing to claim consent, to establish mutual agreement to sexual activities. While the 2003 Act requires the jury to take into account whether or not the defendant has taken reasonable steps to establish consent, what counts as reasonable, and the question of reasonable to whom, are left unaddressed. Perhaps most importantly, any modification of the *mens rea* of rape, in terms of belief in consent, arguably cannot take place without concomitant changes to the *actus reus* of the offence as discussed above. The vague quasi-objective test adopted by the 2003 Act is, for many reasons then, unsatisfactory.

Consent or no consent?

While not all apparently consensual behaviours, such as SM, are legitimate in the eyes of the law, consent carries with it a kind of 'moral magic'[27] reflecting the idea that certain behaviours are legitimate only if they are consensual. The absence of valid consent renders physical intimacy an assault of one kind or another. Notably, law can and often does interpret circumstances and

---

27 The term is borrowed from Hurd (1996).

behaviours to read consent into a seemingly non-consensual encounter. The above discussion of the current law regarding rape and reasonable belief in consent demonstrates this phenomenon. In terms of the legal treatment of consent, a yes is not always a yes and a no is not always a no. When we consent to or refuse physical intimacy then, criminal law always has the trump card in finally establishing whether or not our consents or refusals are legally valid. This means that any expression of sexual autonomy is always subject to a final reading and pronouncement by law. In many places, then, the concept of consent continues to fail to meet the aim of protecting bodily and sexual autonomy. So what should we do about consent?

The answer here takes on a different significance depending on the context of the question. For example in SM, it appears that consent is a very import-ant aspect of both interpersonal rules of engagement that individuals who take part in SM construct for themselves, and also of the legal rules govern-ing the legitimacy or otherwise of physical and sexual contact. Without clear and precise boundaries of consent it becomes difficult to distinguish SM from violent unwanted sexual contact. In SM, consent allows people to construct the grounds and boundaries of their own choices, and their own sexual agency. Consent here therefore plays a crucial role. But whether or not lack of consent by itself fully captures the wrong done in rape is another question. Tadros (2006) argues that in some cases of rape, lack of consent is not the most important aspect of the denial of sexual autonomy – in violent rape, for example, the wrong perpetrated is centred on the force used, rather than the lack of consent by itself.

Many have concluded that rape laws are too dependent on the notion of consent as a central element of the definition of the offence, and that this dependence leads to an inappropriate focus on the behaviour and conduct of the victim.[28] Consent should therefore be displaced. One alternative would be to provide a list of situations or conditions under which non-consensual intercourse is conclusively presumed. Some jurisdictions have adopted this alternative (the Sexual Offences Act 2003 is a diluted version of this model) and rejected consent as the basis of part of or all of their law on rape, maintaining that robust laws governing sexual assault can be enacted without resort to such an unhelpful (both practically and theoretically) concept as consent. For example, New South Wales, Australia, has formulated rules on violent assault that do not refer to consent, and South Africa is in the process of reforming its laws, with recommended new provisions that do not include the notion of consent.[29] In both jurisdictions, consent is retained as a defence, but does not form part of the definition of the offence that the prosecution has to prove beyond reasonable doubt.

Alternatively, Tadros (2006) has proposed a system of differentiated rapes,

28 See Tadros (2006).   29 See Artz and Combrinck (2003).

not ordered hierarchically, but each with a substantive definitional content that describes the harm caused (rape by coercion, drug-assisted rape, rape by force for example), which have these circumstances rather than consent as their central element. Other options have been suggested – the 'fair opportunity to exercise your will' and the 'negotiation' model to name but two.[30] A more radical reform has been proposed by Simon Bronitt (1994), who suggests that in circumstances such as where violence is present, or where there are certain blameworthy mistakes, consent would be neither part of the offence definition nor provide a defence, providing the accused had knowledge or recklessness as to these circumstances (rather than the victim's consent).

Given the practical problems of operationalising consent in rape, as discussed earlier, it is not surprising that there has been such a range of proposals to reject the concept as a definitional element. It appears that the Sexual Offences Act 2003, despite its attempt to grapple with some of the problems historically associated with consent, may in the end reproduce some of the worst consequences of relying on the concept. Giving consent a less central role – that is, as a defence rather than part of the offence definition, will ameliorate the position of the victim, and her lawyer, in trying to prove beyond reasonable doubt that she did not consent. However, in cases where consent is raised as a defence, if the defendant can initially show enough evidence of consent, it will then be a matter for the defendant to prove on a balance of probabilities that the complainant did consent, and many of the same issues of behaviour, dress, previous sexual history and so on, which have caused problems in rape trials for many years will return to haunt us, albeit at a procedurally different stage. Further, Graycar and Morgan (2002) argue that reforms in Michigan, where consent is now a defence rather than part of the definitional element of the offence, have not prevented heated arguments in the courtroom about consent, and that these continue to focus on familiar negative stereotypes of femininity, and on women's behaviour and responsibility for their own safety.

The short answer, as feminists have long known, is that tinkering with the law on sexual offences does nothing to undermine entrenched social views about the apportionment of responsibility between men and women in sexual assault cases. For example, a recent Amnesty International Poll in the UK found that one in three people believe that women are at least partially responsible if they are raped.[31] Focusing on law, substantive or procedural, does not address fundamental underlying social inequalities, particularly those related to gender roles and stereotypes, and these must be addressed if we are to see a decrease in sexual assault and an increase in conviction rates.

---

30 Tadros (1999) and Anderson (2005) respectively. For others see Power (2003); Bronitt (1994).
31 See 'One in three blames women for being raped' David Fickling, *Guardian*, 21 November 2005.

There are very clear limits to what the substantive law can achieve in this area. Even a reforming focus on the many procedural stages of criminal justice where rape and sexual assault cases 'fall out' of the system, as recently described by Liz Kelly *et al.* (2005), must be accompanied by changes in advocacy practice, professional training and codes of conduct for criminal justice agents, and judicial guidelines (Lacey, 2001: 12). Given that we cannot refuse to engage with law completely,[32] there is a strong case for giving consent a much less central role in the law regarding rape and other sexual offences. Rejecting consent as a definitional aspect of rape by providing a non-exhaustive list of situations under which sex is deemed to be rape, is one step towards a more context driven approach to assessing whether or not a particular sexual encounter was wanted. Temkin and Ashworth highlight that in Canada and those Australian jurisdictions which list non-consensual situations in their legislation (such as Victoria), the list is non-exhaustive (2004: 338).[33]

Having some sort of reasonable standard for belief in consent is also an important part of this move. In this sense the 2003 Sexual Offences Act appears superficially to have met the aims of reform, but in substance there remains much work to be done regarding proper guidance on what is reasonable, to whom, and when.[34] Despite attempts to statutorily define consent in rape, the very fact that questions of what is reasonable for the defendant to believe is left to juries, without proper guidance, alongside a system of gendered laws that retains rape as a distinctive offence perpetrated penetratively, only by men, together mean that it is almost impossible to escape the more detrimental effects of using consent in the courtroom. In this respect the 2003 Act has hung on to a concept that is unavoidably tainted with gendered and heteronormative notions of victim precipitation or responsibility, and of the passivity of the complainant. Whilst we still have jury trials for rape, in an adversarial system, with a separate gendered offence of rape, the way forward must be to concentrate on substantively assessing the surrounding context and conditions of the sexual encounter. Rather than focusing on the (non)sexual behaviour of the victim this would entail that juries, guided by clear principles on what counts as consent, engage in proper analysis of the respect for bodily integrity, and quality of communication, negotiation and mutuality between the parties.

Bibliography

Anderson, M (2005) 'Negotiating Sex' *Southern California Law Review* 78, pp 101–138.

---

32 Cf. Smart (1989).   33 See also Bronitt (1994).
34 For critiques of other aspects of the 2003 Act, see Temkin and Ashworth (2004), Ormerod (2005), Spencer (2004), Lacey (2001), and Bainham and Brooks-Gordon (2004).

Archard, D (1998) *Sexual Consent*, London: Westview Press.

Ashworth, A and Temkin, J (2004) 'Rape, Sexual Assaults and the Problems of Consent' *Criminal Law Review*, pp 328–46.

Artz L and Combrinck H (2003) ' "A Wall of Words": Redefining the offence of rape in South African Law' *Acta Juridica*, pp 72–91.

Bainham, A and Brooks-Gordon, B (2004) 'Reforming the Law on Sexual Offences' in Brooks-Gordon, B, Gelsthorpe, L, Johnson, M and Bainham, A (eds), *Sexuality Repositioned*, Oxford: Hart, pp 261–96.

Box, S (1983) *Power, Crime and Mystification*, London: Routledge.

Bronitt, S (1992) 'Rape and Lack of Consent' 16 *Criminal Law Journal*, pp 289–309.

Bronitt, S (1994) 'The Direction of Rape Law in Australia: Toward a Positive Consent Standard' *Criminal Law Journal*, pp 249–53.

Cowan, S and Tadros, V (2006) 'Some reflections on *mens rea*', paper presented to Rape Reform Workshop, Edinburgh University School of Law, 30 April 2006 (on file with author).

Cowart, M (2004) 'Consent, speech act theory, and legal disputes' *Law and Philosophy* 23 (5), pp 495–525.

Finch, E and Munro, V (2005) 'Juror Stereotypes and Blame Attribution in Rape Cases Involving Intoxicants: the Findings of a Pilot Study' *British Journal of Criminology* 45, pp 25–38.

Finch, E and Munro, V (2006) 'Breaking Boundaries?: Sexual Consent in the Jury Room' *Legal Studies* 26 (3), pp 303–20.

Gardner, J and Shute, S (2000) 'The Wrongness of Rape' in Jeremy Horder (ed.) *Oxford Essays on Jurisprudence* (Fourth Series), Oxford: Oxford University Press.

Graycar, R and Morgan, J (2002) *The Hidden Gender of Law* (2nd edn), Sydney: Federation Press.

Home Office (2000) *Setting the Boundaries: Reforming the Law on Sexual Offences*, London: HMSO.

Home Office (2006) *Convicting Rapists and Protecting Victims – Justice for Victims of Rape*, London: Home Office.

Hurd, H (1996) 'The Moral Magic of Consent' *Legal Theory* 2, pp 121–46.

Husak, D and Thomas G (2001) 'Rapes Without Rapists: Consent and Reasonable Mistake' *Philosophical Issues* 11, pp 86–117.

Kelly, L *et al.* (2005) *A gap or a chasm? Attrition in reported rape cases* (Home Office Research Study 293), London: HMSO.

Lacey, N (1998) *Unspeakable subjects: feminist essays in legal and social theory*, Oxford: Hart.

Lacey, N (2001) 'Best by Boundaries' *Criminal Law Review*, pp 3–14.

Law Commission (2000) *Consent in Sexual Offences: A Report to the Home Office Sex Offences Review*, London: HMSO.

MacKinnon, C (1989) *Towards a Feminist Theory of the State*, Cambridge, Mass.: Harvard University Press.

Nussbaum, M (1999) *Sex and Social Justice*, New York: Oxford University Press.

Ormerod, D (2005) *Smith and Hogan Criminal Law* (11th edn), London: Butterworths.

Patullo, P (1984) *Judging Women: A Study of Attitudes that Rule our Legal System*, London: Civil Liberties Trust.

Power, H (2003) 'Towards a Redefinition of the *Mens Rea* of Rape' *Oxford Journal of Legal Studies* 23, pp 379–404.

Schulhofer, S (1998) *Unwanted Sex: The Culture of Intimidation and the Failure of Law*, Cambridge, Massachusetts: Harvard University Press.

Scottish Law Commission (2006) *Rape and Other Sexual Offences* (Discussion Paper 131), Edinburgh: The Stationery Office.

Smart, C (1989) *Feminism and the Power of Law*, London: Routledge.

Spencer, J (2004) 'The Sexual Offences 2003: Children and Family Offences' *Criminal Law Review*, pp 347–60.

Stevenson, K (1999) 'Observations on the Law Relating to Sexual Offences: the Historic Scandal of Women's Silence' *Web Journal of Current Legal Issues*.

Tadros, V (2005) *Criminal Responsibility*, Oxford: Oxford University Press, pp 218–22.

Tadros, V (2006) 'Rape without Consent' *Oxford Journal of Legal Studies* 26, pp 515–43.

Weait, M (2005) 'Criminal Law and the Sexual Transmission of HIV: *R v Dica*' *Modern Law Review* 68(1), pp 120–33.

Wells, C (1982) 'Swatting the Subjectivist Bug' *Criminal Law Review*, pp 209–20.

Chapter 4

De-meaning of contract

Carl F Stychin, University of Reading

Introduction

This chapter is provoked by two legal episodes which speak to the connections between personal relationships, and the language and law of contract as the basis for their regulation. I interrogate these two episodes in order to consider whether and how contract as a discourse and ideology might be appropriate (or not) as a way to think about, for example, the legal regulation of same-sex (and other) relationships. In so doing, the analysis will consider wider issues concerning the institution of marriage itself, and how lesbian and gay and feminist theory understands both personal relationships and contract. Thus, this chapter might be seen to provide (yet) another interpretation of the 'sexual contract' in light of what may be new political dynamics at work around the family today in Britain. My reading can be located within a substantial body of scholarship which seeks to engage with contract from a feminist perspective, and the two examples concern same-sex relationships explicitly.

Episode one: civil partnerships

The lost language of contracts

My first example is taken from the parliamentary debates (and reactions to them) around the UK's Civil Partnership Act 2004. This legislation creates a new legal status of 'civil partner' in the law, which is available to those same-sex couples who choose to register their relationships. The status straddles the boundaries of marriage and 'not-marriage', which has led critics of the Act to describe civil partnership as marriage in all but name. It carries both the rights and responsibilities of marriage, and the state benefits that are accorded to married couples (such as exemption from inheritance tax) on the basis of the assumed public good that comes from living as a committed couple. Yet, it also preserves the formal status of marriage for opposite-sex couples. In this way, the Government sought to satisfy the demands of parts of the lesbian and gay communities, while also avoiding the 'backlash' that often accompanies the opening of the institution of marriage to same-sex couples.[1]

Some (but not all) conservative critics of the legislation responded to the proposed bill in a fairly sophisticated fashion, resorting not to overtly homophobic language, but rather in terms of the number of people who are in need of the protection and benefits offered by law. That is, the argument runs, civil partnership should be available to all those in committed relationships who choose to register them, and opponents of the legislation further suggested that its basis should be explicitly contractual. Specific examples that were cited included carers, friends, spinsters, and spinster sisters, who may all live intertwined lives, but for whom the benefits of the Act will be unavailable (because they are not lesbian and gay couples). Thus, the legislation, it was argued, should be expanded to cover anyone who wishes to take advantage of a new state sanctioned *contractual* basis to govern their relationship (a contract which would have many of its terms dictated by statute). On this point, an amendment was made in the House of Lords to replace the term 'relationship' with 'contract', as part of a wider strategy of amendment to include carers, siblings and other dependent relationships. Opponents argued that if civil partnership is *not* marriage (the Government's officially stated position), then what can it be except a domestic contract? And, if contract, then surely anyone can contract, if contract is a universal.

Conservative Baroness Wilcox made this precise point, when she argued for the extension of civil partnerships, and she did so through repeated references to contract:

> These civil contracts will, I hope, be extended or adapted to bring mutual security and comfort to spinsters, bachelors, carers and other partnerships who are also disadvantaged by not being able to marry. To these groups, such contracts would bring financial security and peace of mind, particularly in old age. Too many of us live alone . . . society will benefit greatly if more long-term partnerships are encouraged.
>
> (*Hansard*, Lords, 22 April 2004, 395)

Thus, the Government should encourage more of us to live intertwined lives. Of course, nothing stops the making of agreements to structure personal relationships. Rather, the issue in the debates was the state benefits that flow (or not) to those relationships. However, the question that remains, and which is one of the foci of this chapter, is the way in which the language of contract itself became a term of political significance in the debates. The Government

---

1   I examine the way in which civil partnership straddles this boundary in more detail in Stychin, 2005: 548–53.

opposed (and ultimately defeated in the House of Commons) the amendment and extension of the Act, and there are many explanations (pragmatic and principled) as to why it was so opposed to that extension. Also interesting is the way in which the *language* of contract was opposed by the Government, which claimed that, to understand relationships through that lens, is somehow demeaning to same-sex civil partners and (presumably) to married couples. As Labour Baroness Scotland explained in the House of Lords debate:

> We still believe that 'relationship' is of real importance and signifies a difference from a mere 'contract'. We are dealing with intimate connections between people and we do not think that 'contract' accurately expresses what we are seeking to uphold. . . . We are talking about the tender relationships that can happen within families, relationships of support. They are relationships. They are not contracts and we think that it would be inappropriate to describe them as such. It demeans the quality of the relationships that we hope that people in these partnerships will be able to enjoy.
>
> (*Hansard*, Lords, 1 July 2004, 395)

The pressure group Stonewall (2004: 3) made a similar point in response to the proposed amendment:

> Referring to the loving and committed long-term relationships of homosexual couples as 'contracts' is demeaning, and downgrades the nature of their commitment. . . . A civil partnership is more than just a contract, the very concept of which does not fit within family law which has traditionally been based on relationships. . . . A civil partnership, like any family structure, is not a negotiable contract with optional components. This is why the contractual analogy is unsuitable.

One could argue that these interventions should be read in terms of the *realpolitik* of the debates. They are attempts to counter quite a clever political move by opponents of the Civil Partnership Act. But the argument can be taken more seriously than that, and I want to argue that it captures something about how contract is viewed in the realm of personal relationships. More specifically, it speaks to popular understandings of contract itself. In this regard, the perception of contract held by Baroness Scotland, the pressure group Stonewall, and many others, accords with some feminist and lesbian feminist commentators who, as Elizabeth Kingdom (2000: 6) has argued, 'have tended to be politically hostile to contract as an ideology for reading social relations'. This understanding of contract is grounded in a 'contract as commerce' model, involving the self-interested, rational, hard bargaining social actor who is engaged in endless discrete exchanges. As Linda Mulcahy (2005: 4) summarises this view, 'contractual relationships have been understood as being motivated and fuelled by separation, possessive individualism, certainty, security of transaction and standardisation . . . a callous cash nexus divorced from intimacy, in which exchanges are the only way in which individuals come to recognise the needs of others'.[2] This is the bargain/exchange model at its most masculinist.

It is this model of contract that, I would argue, is in the collective minds of Baroness Scotland, Stonewall, and other critics when they reject the amendments to the Civil Partnership Act. It is a conception of contract based on the self-interested actor who negotiates over the terms to secure an agreement most to his or her personal advantage (financial or otherwise), and who presumably breaks the contract when it is in his or her self-interest (economic or otherwise) to do so. In this interpretation, prenuptial agreements might be viewed with suspicion by critics of the classical contract model; not simply on the basis that they may be a product of unequal bargaining power (a frequent and well-founded criticism) but more fundamentally because they are demeaning to the relationship itself. As well, it is worth noting the extent to which the language of care infuses the parliamentary debate and supporters often answer claims regarding contract and exchange as the basis for relationships, with arguments centred on care (see Stychin, 2005: 562–66). To some extent, this may signify the emergence of an 'ethic of care' within parliamentary discourse (see Gilligan, 1982).

If one does understand contract through this lens of the self-interested rational actor, then there are quite understandable reasons why the Government must reject this discourse to explain personal relationships. The granting of the status of civil partner – and the Civil Partnership Act does not merely recognise private rights, it confers public benefits and imposes legal responsibilities – must be limited to the 'deserving'. The status must be containable and restricted to those who have 'legitimately' become partners. As with the status of marriage, the justification for the conferral of public benefits is dependent upon the myth that only 'true believers' (the 'in love') have entered into the relationship (and will contribute to the public good). If partnership[3] (or marriage) becomes deconstructed as a commercial relationship founded on mutual self-interest (especially on tax and immigration matters), then we are forced into interrogating the dichotomy of the legitimate and the illegitimate marriage. When is a marriage or partnership a fraud because it is made solely for self-interested reasons? When is a partnership 'real' from the perspective of the state? What are its necessary components? Alternatively, when is a marriage (or partnership) *not* entered into for reasons

---

2   I am indebted here to John Wightman's (2000: 99) description of what he calls the second phase of feminist engagement with contract from the mid-1980s: a critique of contract doctrine as a whole. See also Brown (1996), Goodrich (1996) and Wheeler (2005).

3   One might note here a double meaning to the word 'partnership' – business or personal?

of self-interest? Is there ever a purely altruistic relationship? This is the genie that must be kept in the bottle.

To repeat, the Civil Partnership Act does not only enforce contracts, it sets many of the terms of the relationship and provides a framework of regulation as between state and couple, including the provision of public benefits. The justification put forward for this Act is the fact that civil partnerships (like marriage) are special – they are not exchange based nor are they entered into by self-interested actors. Rather, they are in some way transcendental, care based, 'packages' of rights and responsibilities which leave no room for nego-tiation around many of the terms (those set by the legislation). Otherwise, there can be no reason to prioritise and single out the same-sex couple (and the married couple) from any other agreement between people to share lives jointly. In particular, the unmarried heterosexual couple with a domestic contract looms large in the background. This limits the scope of the status in numerical terms (and its financial implications for the state). For this series of reasons, the exchange based model must be rejected and, as a consequence, the Government also has a justification as to why the couple cannot opt out of (or 'pick and mix') the terms of the Civil Partnership Act to form their own personalised contract.

This analysis raises a more fundamental question, namely, why would we think that understanding our personal relationships in terms of an exchange based model is demeaning? In fact, the institution of marriage has been understood as contractually grounded by some political theorists since the time of John Locke (1698: 78), who described marriage as a 'voluntary Compact between Man and Woman'. Moreover, the twentieth century has been characterised in terms of 'the gradual rise to legal prominence of an Enlightenment contractarian model of marriage' (Witte, 1997: 196). My inquiry in this chapter, however, is not historical in focus. Rather, my question is whether there is political utility in the language of contract as a way of imagining personal relationships. Should critical, feminist, lesbian and gay scholars and activists consider reclaiming the discourse of contract as having political possibilities that might otherwise be lost?[4]

Bargain relationships?

Perhaps the most famous critique of contract was provided by Carole Pateman (1988) in her book *The Sexual Contract*. Her argument has been so often

---

4 An interesting parallel can be drawn between the progressive political possibilities of *con-tract*, which I develop in this chapter, and arguments that *property* discourse also contains within it the kernels of a feminist politics, characterised by connectivity and altruism (as opposed to alienation and commodification). Some years ago, I examined the potential and limitations of property for feminism, which is particularly relevant in the medical law context: see Stychin (1998).

repeated that it is now almost legendary – that 'contract is far from being opposed to patriarchy; contract is the means through which modern patriarchy is constituted' (1988: 2). Pateman's story is that the 'social contract' is a fraternal contract centred in the public sphere which 'establishes men's political right over women – and also sexual in the sense of establishing orderly access by men to women's bodies' (1988: 2). Civil freedom, in Pateman's account, is dependent upon the patriarchal right generated by the social contract to which women have no part. They are not endowed with the capacity to contract. The fact that, constitutively, being an individual within civil society is dependent upon a set of masculinist capacities that women do not possess, means that the marriage contract cannot be understood as a contract proper. It can never be an exchange between free individuals entered into within the public sphere. Rather, 'with the establishment of marriage and the pretence of a contract, men's domination is hidden by the claim that marriage allows equal, consensual sexual enjoyment by both spouses' (1988: 159).

Thus, Pateman concludes that marriage is not a contract, but a status, which explains why the 'contract' is not concluded at the moment of the marriage ceremony – the time of the meeting of minds – but rather, at the moment of conjugality – the exercise of the patriarchal right (1988: 164). The individual in contract is a patriarchal category *per se*, and to understand marriage in contractual terms is a diversion from the fact that it represents a consolidation of patriarchal right (for example, it demands obedience). For feminists to turn to contract as a way of comprehending their relationships with men – certainly in understanding marriage – becomes something akin to a form of false consciousness. As Pateman argues, 'in the victory of contract, the patriarchal construction of sexual difference as mastery and subjection remains intact but repressed' (1988: 187).[5]

Pateman's account of the sexual contract has been subject to considerable discussion and critique, but it does provide important insight into the relationship between status and contract, and public and private spheres. In particular, Pateman observes that the attraction of contract discourse for feminists is its promise of a universal category that can include women within the public sphere. As she points out, 'there can be no predetermined limits on contract, so none can be imposed by specifying the sex of the parties' (1988: 167). However, Pateman rightly notes that the potential for contract as a universal category is dependent upon the ability to enter the public sphere of civil society; which, she argues, is constitutively closed to women.

This is a crucial point in thinking through the political utility of contract

5   For example, the common law rule that the crime of rape did not exist as between a husband and wife was originally justified by Sir Matthew Hale (1736: 629) on the basis of 'matrimonial consent and contract'. For the judicial abolition of the rule, see *R v R* [1991] 4 All ER 481.

and exchange. One of the key criticisms of Pateman has been that her story of contract is a highly essentialist and absolutist one, in which a particular historical legacy is assumed to continue uncomplicated and uncontested (Okin, 1990). Nancy Fraser (1993: 175) has argued, in relation to Pateman's resort to a master/slave dyadic, that we require a more nuanced analysis focusing on the conditions in which many women enter contracts; contracts of employment, for example, in 'sex-segmented labor markets' in which there remains a 'gender division of unpaid labor'. The apparent move from status to contract in understanding male–female relationships, Fraser argues, cannot be understood simply as 'old master/subject wine in new contractual bottles' (1993: 180). The meanings of masculinity and femininity are subject to cultural contestation and, so too, contract and exchange are not static constructs impervious to change. Moreover, it has been argued that Pateman's fraternal patriarchy needs some qualification through a recognition of the way in which the social contract was also historically constituted through racial and class based exclusions (Boucher, 2003: 35–6). Relatedly, Pateman pays little heed to the possibility that some women resisted the sexual contract throughout history, and did manage to engage in forms of exchange in civil society (see Wheeler, 2005).

Furthermore, there are a number of commentators who have defended contract as a way of understanding personal relationships that may not be inimical to a feminist, progressive, and lesbian and gay politics. John Wightman (2000: 100) has described this as a 'third phase' of feminist engagements with contract: a recognition that 'contract law contains within it resources which could render it more appropriate to handling intimate relationships'. Here the work of Elizabeth Kingdom (2000) on cohabitation contracts provides a good example. She emphasises that, although contract may conceal relations of unequal bargaining power, it may also be capable of fostering more progressive norms. Kingdom's work is instructive in alluding to the status/contract binary. She refers to the potential for contract in terms of the move away from status. Kingdom describes the latter as 'the imposition of a sovereign standard of uniform social relations'; whereas contract is based on 'the dignity of the parties' (2000: 23). As a consequence, *contra* the Civil Partnership Act debates, the notion of contract becomes centred on dignity rather than being demeaning to relationships. Status becomes equated with the tyranny of uniformity; contract with empowerment.[6]

Much of the scholarship which defends the potential for contract relies heavily on the insights of Ian Macneil and the relational contract theory;

---

6   It could be argued that contract has a particular feminist appeal in the domain of opposite-sex relationships because of foundational inequalities grounded in gender difference, which are reproduced through the status of marriage. However, I want to argue in this chapter that the political possibilities of contract are of relevance to relationships more generally, for reasons which I hope become clear.

a theory which has been popularised in recent years by David Campbell.[7] Ironically, Macneil has not been particularly interested in personal relationships, and quite rightly because his theory is an attempt to correct the classical understanding of commercial relations. Briefly, Macneil has sought to provide an alternative to a model of discrete contracts based on unbridled immediate self-interest and, indeed, based upon an entire series of neoclassical assumptions about economic behaviour involving commercial parties. In its place, he has shown that, within commercial relations, we find a 'relational constitution of all contracts', involving a set of norms that includes co-operation, relationality, and commonality, in which the value of maintaining a long-term good relationship supersedes the model of the individual immediate wealth maximiser (Campbell, 2001a: 5). As he states, 'the participants . . . view the relation as an ongoing integration of behaviour which will grow and vary with events in a largely unforeseeable future' and the examples he gives include a marriage and a family business (2001a: 22). Key to relational contract theory is the fact that the 'preservation of the relationship itself is one of the objectives of the parties', and the norms and rules of that relationship may shift and evolve over time, in such a way that may well not have been imagined when the contract was formed (Leckey, 2002: 10).

What I think Macneil offers to many feminist and lesbian and gay commentators on personal relationships is what I call an anti-essentialist understanding of contract.[8] That is, in terms of the values which underpin contract, Macneil is clear that there are both discrete and relational elements to all contracts and this, in turn, is rephrased as an ongoing tension between the values of individualism and communalism; or even self-interest and altruism (Campbell, 2001a: 51).[9] This tension resides within contract doctrine and ideology. Kingdom (2000: 23), in particular, is attracted to this rethinking of the values of contract: 'these new readings of contract loosen the ideological hold of the official doctrine whereby parties to contract are abstracted from their communities, and because they demand consideration of the social matrix'. Kellye Testy (1995: 220) makes this claim even more strongly, highlighting the ambiguity of contract, 'while contract's commitments to the ideologies of individual autonomy and consent has undeniably had oppressive effects, contract has a deep commitment to other ideologies as well, particularly those of fairness and connectivity'.

Even some of those theorists who are critical of the uses of contract in understanding personal relationships would not disagree with the political

---

7   For a very comprehensive introduction to Macneil's work, see Campbell (2001b). For an illuminating interpretation of Macneil, see Campbell (2001a).

8   By way of contrast, for an alternative 'law and economics' approach, see Bush (2001).

9   It is a tension that equally can be found in the related concept of autonomy, which, I have argued, contains within it both the possibilities of connection, as well as alienation, see Stychin (1998: 219–23).

sentiments of commentators such as Kingdom and Testye. For example, Ruthann Robson and S E Valentine (1990: 526) are critical of contract ideology in understanding lesbian relationships because 'the dominant ideology of contract theory "colonizes" lesbian aspirations; contract "makes sense" and disallows other ways of thinking'. Yet, they are themselves imagining, I would argue, a neoclassical understanding of contract that Macneil rejects. At the same time, it may be significant that Robson and Valentine conclude their critique of contract with the more ambiguous point that 'the goal of lesbian legal theory must always be for lesbians to use contract rather than be used by it' (1990: 528), suggesting that there may be elements of contract that can be reclaimed.

These observations underscore the limitations of Pateman's analysis of contract. The critique of marriage and gender relations, I would argue, may lie in the contradiction which commentators such as Macneil have pointed to as embedded within contract doctrine between the discrete and relational; between individualism and communalism; between self-interest and altruism. The gender critique of contract should focus, not as Pateman argues, on an originary story of the social contract, but on the way in which the contradictions have themselves been embedded within gender relations, such that they are central to the distinction between public and private spheres; civil society and the household; the political and the familial. In this way, the critique of contract mirrors much feminist critique of liberal citizenship and of liberalism itself. This has been usefully highlighted by Wendy Brown (1995) in her commentary on Pateman. Brown argues that 'the constitutive terms of liberal political discourse depend upon their implicit opposition to a subject and set of activities marked "feminine" ' (1995: 152), a sexual division of labour, and a 'gendered antinomy between individual and family as well as in the terms expressing the respective ethos of civil society and the family: "self-interest" on the one hand and "selflessness" on the other' (1995: 161). Liberalism thus demands that the 'self-interested subject of liberalism both requires and disavows its relationship to the selfless subject of the household' (1995: 162).

Thus, the very contradiction that relational contract theorists identify as embedded within contract ideology has been profoundly socially constructed as gendered within the terms of liberalism. If that is the case, though, it may suggest that pro-contract feminists are unrealistically optimistic about the potential for contract to rectify the limitations of status in our understanding of relationships. As Janice Richardson (2004: 113) asks, where exactly are these egalitarian, non-hierarchical contracts in the world today? So too, if lesbians and gays are embedded within liberalism, then they are unlikely to be able to transcend the constitutive limitations of liberalism in organising their relationships. Consequently, perhaps Robson and Valentine are correct in claiming that contract is irredeemable as a way of organising relationships in an egalitarian fashion. That argument, however, may be too powerful because it suggests that liberalism is itself beyond hope, and unless we can transcend it, we are 'stuck'.

But feminists and others also have recognised the potential and power of liberal discourse for the reform of gender relations, and a similar argument can be made about contract in the realm of relationships. Both liberalism and contract are full of contradictions that can be exploited. On this point, I want to argue that same-sex relationships may provide useful insights into thinking about the potential of contract as a way of tackling the limitations of liberalism that Brown (1995) and others have underscored. Once again, relational contract theory is helpful. Macneil's theory highlights the importance of shared norms within relationships and within the wider contracting community as a basis for the preservation of ongoing contractual relationships. This is one of the points that Wightman suggests highlights the difference between personal relationships and commercial relationships – marriage and marital like relations cannot be embedded within a set of communal norms. Wightman (2000: 107) argues that 'this is partly because the parties are not participating in practices which shape a set of norms which commonly apply to a category of situations . . . [there is] no equivalent to "sector wide" understandings'. Each relationship, he argues, has its own particular trajectory and dynamic. At the outset of a relationship there may be no shared understandings at all on many major issues. This is hard to imagine in the context of a commercial relationship.

I wonder, though, whether this is necessarily the case. After all, the status of marriage historically was dependent upon a whole ideology of norms which constituted appropriate behaviour and roles within marriage. There was a common set of understandings which were created and transmitted. These norms reflected and helped constitute the liberal public/private distinction, and the gendered notions of ownership of the self and indeed the gendered construction of the liberal self. As a political matter, then, contract may provide a useful way in which lesbians and gays (and others) might construct counter-narratives – new communal norms – going to the question of 'how to' construct relationships in ways which resist Brown's 'gendered antinomy between individual and family'. Perhaps this is one of the potential benefits of new family forms, and might well be a more progressive *political* response to the Civil Partnership Act; rather than the dominant response of claiming a sameness of relationship forms and a desire for status rather than contract. These narratives might problematise the liberal notions of public and private; serve to delink the private familial realm from the sexual realm; provide greater recognition of changing dynamics and roles within relationships; shift away from the dyadic model of 'coupledom'; and allow us to rethink the role of friendship in relationship. They would challenge the hegemony of the narrative of traditional, sexualised marriage.

The second limitation, it is sometimes argued, in Macneil's relational contract model applied to personal relationships lies in the role of altruism.

One of Macneil's most significant insights is his claim that, in relational contracts, individual utility maximisation may be foregone in order to preserve the long-term relationship, resulting in ongoing co-operative adjustment of mutual obligations (Campbell, 2001a: 22). From this, it might be extrapolated that, at certain points, contracting parties in commercial, relational settings may appear to be acting altruistically towards each other. This clearly flies in the face of classical contract doctrine, in which there is little room for the notion of ongoing contractual adjustment. This, again, is very appealing for those pro-contract feminists, such as Kingdom, who see relational contracting as opening up a potentially wider set of values to draw upon in understanding a relationship as contractual. Wightman (2000: 113) claims, however, that despite Macneil's offhand references to familial relationships as exemplifying relational contract theory, it is in the notion of altruism that the analogy between the commercial and the familial breaks down. He argues that the idea(l) of co-operation in contracting has 'radically different implications in intimate relationships compared with commercial contracts'. At the end of the day, even in the most relational commercial contract, the exchange principle still holds true. The temporality of the exchange is different from the classical, discrete model of contracting, but it remains a bargain rather than an act of 'pure' altruism. Wightman (2000: 116) argues that, by contrast, intimate relations cannot be categorised in this way. These relationships are better defined in terms of 'genuine altruism', which undercuts their definition as contracts at all. Such relationships are non-instrumental. In Wightman's (2000: 125) words, 'there is reciprocity without bargain'. A model of exchange (commerce) is distinguished from a model of altruism (familial).

These concerns may help us to understand the negative reaction to the invocation of the language of contract in the Civil Partnership Act debates. I would argue that the hostility to contract, displayed by government members and Stonewall, amongst others, in part reflects a concern about the construction of civil partnerships as anything other than altruistic. To the extent that contract is informed, ultimately, by exchange, then it seems inevitably to slide into a model of self-interest (as opposed to altruism) which leads, in turn, to the conservative reaction to civil partnership as entered into by self-interested individuals who seek to secure benefits and 'special privileges'. Entering a civil partnership then becomes a purely rational self-interested decision by the utility maximising individual (or couple); a point which also could be made about entering the institution of marriage, to the extent that it too is interpreted in contractual, rather than status-based, terms. Furthermore, this argument provides an explanation for why the Government was keen to highlight that this was a status package of rights and responsibilities – it was not a 'pick and mix' contract in which the parties were free to choose the terms that best advantaged them. Moreover, any public benefit was balanced, it was argued, with individual responsibilities (benefits were offset by costs). A discourse of care and mutual support must not be replaced by the language of exchange and contract.[10]

However, the reproduction of this binary between exchange and altruism in understanding personal (as opposed to commercial) relationships is problematic. Clearly, the proponents of the Civil Partnership Act are ideologically committed to the construction of relationships in terms of altruism rather than exchange. In large measure, I think that this is because they are reproducing, in substance, the status of marriage for another group on the basis of being similarly situated. The Labour Government has demonstrated its ideological commitment to a traditional understanding of the status of marriage, as being the locus of care in society (see Stychin, 2005: 548). But there is a difference between recognising that our personal relationships involve care, on the one hand, and the rejection of a bargain/exchange model, on the other. That is, the characterisation of relationships in terms of altruism reproduces the liberal binary construction of self-interestedness and familial selflessness; the public sphere, and the household; male and female. Bargain is the realm of the public sphere, civil society, and work (male); altruism is the realm of the home, the private sphere, and the family (women).[11] Of course, you could argue that all liberal subjects are founded on this tension between exchange and altruism – a tension which Macneil claims rests within contract doctrine itself (Campbell, 2001a: 51–5). But to the extent that liberalism remains grounded in a gendered division of spheres of life, then there is a danger that this splitting will occur on a gendered basis within relationships. Women become associated with altruism, men with commerce, and this can be reproduced within same-sex relationships rather than challenged. I would argue that the debates did nothing to undermine that gendered model.[12] One danger may be that, in the absence of the discourse of contract, there is little space for articulating the idea of a bad bargain for women, or the usefulness of other contract doctrines in the realm of personal relationships: frustration; mistake; misrepresentation. These concepts may only make sense through a model of exchange, but seem to me to be no less relevant to the world of relationships.

Mulcahy (2005: 8) has argued that Macneil's theory of relational contract allows us to think about contracts as relationships, rather than relationships

---

10 I recognise that there are two separate issues at play here: whether people take on a legal status for practical, self-interested reasons; and whether we should understand those relationships through a model of exchange and bargain, during their lifetime.

11 Relatedly, children are largely *assumed* to exist outside of the realm of productivity, contract, and economic exchange within western society. However, as Zelizer (1985) has shown, this 'sentimentalisation' of children is only a twentieth-century social construction. Thanks to Libby Schweber for drawing this point to my attention.

12 There are obvious similarities here with the debates around the value and limitations of Carol Gilligan's (1982) ethic of care and ethic of justice model for women.

as contracts. My argument, however, is that it is through thinking about contracts in more value-open terms that we may be liberated to think about relationships in richer, contractual terms, which may be politically useful and challenging. It allows us to consider whether exchange and bargain are themselves appropriate (or problematic) as a way of understanding our actions, in a context in which we also recognise a complex set of values (co-operation, trust, connection) underpinning agreements. In other words, we can come to accept that, in our personal relationships, 'we are all inconsistently selfish and socially committed at the same time' (Mulcahy, 2005: 12).

I now want to move on to another reason why I claim that contract has a political utility, and here I return to the binary of status and contract. For groups such as Stonewall, the 'prize' has been the granting of a status from 'on high': the status of 'civil partner' accorded by the state. For the Labour Government, it is clear throughout the debates that this is a status which is constructed as containable, naturalised, and limited. The status of civil partner is available to a particular group of people who meet an imagined set of cultural criteria. They are 'like' 'married couples' (another essentialised category) and are worthy of a status because they are similarly placed. By being so essentialised, they can rightfully claim the status. Legal and cultural status thus connect.

The language of contract, however, is potentially troubling in the context of a status (Diduck and Kaganas, 1999: 57–8). Contrary to the historical claim that we have experienced an inevitable movement from status to contract (including with respect to our understanding of the institution of marriage), Jon Goldberg-Hiller (2002: 84) has made the important argument that we should understand status and contract as existing in a dialectical relationship between the abstract identity and the socially integrated self. One can see this in the civil partnership debates. The status of civil partnership is defended (and defended against a reimagining and broadening of the category in terms of contract) through a communitarian ideology, namely, the demonstrated public good of the relationship form. This category has *earned* its status by replicating marriage in substance if not form. Contract, by contrast, has a 'limitless, democratic character' (Goldberg-Hiller, 2002: 85). It is lacking in 'natural social boundaries' and, in the context of relationship recognition, it becomes a more difficult site for the articulation of governmentality (2002: 95). This is absolutely clear in the debates, in which civil partnerships appear highly disciplined and normalised.[13] The status of civil partner is a controlled and limited one, which is potentially made more

---

13 Goldberg-Hiller (2002: 86) points to the prevalence, in an employment context, of a 'post-Fordist discourse' of the corporate family/team, rather than the language of exchange/bargain. The example underscores the dangers of the language of altruism replacing that of exchange and bargain.

unruly by the claims to universality of contract. This presents a challenge to the way in which we understand relationships, because of the potential to democratise them. Rather than being demeaning, contract may be able to strip relationships of any essential meaning.

Episode two: the desire for law

I turn now to my second contract episode, which graphically exemplifies the relationship between contract and personal relationships. This is a Chancery Division judgment about professional negligence: *Sutton v Mishcon de Reya and Gawor & Co.*[14] In this case, the claimant, Sutton, sued two firms of solicitors for professional negligence. The case concerned the drafting of a 'deed of cohabitation' and a 'deed of separation', on which Sutton had been advised by each of two firms. The cohabitation agreement expressly made reference to a document, described as a 'statement of trust', which had been drawn up by Sutton and another man, Staal, that set out the details of their proposed 'master and slave' relationship (at p 838). This included Staal turning over his income of £6,000 a month to the claimant, and making him, Sutton, heir to his considerable estate. In return, Sutton was to treat Staal as a slave, to 'keep me in a firm grip, taking away all my personal belongings, and leaving me totally to your mercy' (at p 838). Complicated financial arrangements (including the transfer of the legal title to property) were negotiated with a detailed agreement which was clearly framed as an exchange – a *quid pro quo* – which, in the event, never came to fruition as the relationship ended. Staal required Sutton to leave the property. Although Sutton had moved into the property, cohabitation had never taken place.

The court held that, on the facts, there was no professional negligence involved in this case, and that such a contract could not be enforceable. The distinction drawn by Hart J was between a contract between persons who are cohabiting in a relationship which may involve sexual relations; and a contract for sexual relations outside marriage. The latter is not enforceable on the grounds of public policy; it 'was an attempt to reify an unlawful ideal' (at p 847). In the context of a master and slave contract, Hart J points to a particular difficulty – distinguishing the 'fantasy' elements of the contract from the 'real' terms. If Staal wants to be a 'real' slave, then it would be difficult for any court to ever hold that there was not undue influence in the transfer of property. If, on the other hand, the financial provisions of the cohabitation agreement were part of the fantasy, then there is no intention to create legal relations (at p 848). Interestingly, Sutton argued that the master and slave roleplay was only a small part of the cohabitation relationship and, in fact, was not a part that he found particularly fulfilling (at p 848). Sutton

14 [2004] 1 FLR 837.

claimed that this was a straightforward agreement to govern a planned long-term spousal-type relationship, like any other. He thus sought to reimagine his contractually based arrangement as a status relationship, so as to 'normalise' it for the court.[15]

What does *Sutton v Mishcon de Reya* suggest about the contract relationship? Politically, it is clear what Pateman would conclude. Towards the end of *The Sexual Contract*, she alludes to the use of contract to frame the sadomasochistic relationship, describing it as 'a dramatic exhibition of the logic of contract and of the full implications of the sexuality of the patriarchal masculine "individual" ' (Pateman, 1988: 186). *Sutton* could be read as evidence of the way in which contract is, as Pateman argues, central to the patriarchal construction of sexuality. It might be said to underscore the incongruous character of an alliance between feminism and contract, through a reproduction of the original sexual contract.

On the other hand, *Sutton* demonstrates the universality and ungovernability of contract; its potential to structure relationships through the notion of exchange but in ways which defy respectable liberal citizenship. It could even challenge the classic liberal conception of autonomy and individuality while, at the same time, exemplifying the universality of liberal autonomy demonstrated through one's ability to contract. The case, I would argue, underscores the ambiguity and ultimately the potential for ungovernability and excess of contract in the structuring of personal relationships.

The idea of excess is related to Peter Goodrich's (1996: 23) claim that the historically constructed masculinity of contract is linked to the notion of the impersonal exchange 'at arm's length', 'beyond the terrain of the body and so outside of the confines of sex, gender or even of desire'. *Sutton* crosses that line between contract (and, more generally, law) and desire, leaving the Court to reproduce the boundary that separates subjectivity, femininity, and desire, from objectivity, masculinity and commerce. The contracting parties in *Sutton* force the law to confront desire, not only for a particular relationship form, but also a desire for law itself (not unlike, perhaps, Stonewall's desire for the legal regulation of civil partnerships).

Concluding thoughts

> If there are as many types of contract as there are societies, our focus should be on the type of society we want rather than on contract itself.
>
> (McLellan, 1996: 238)

---

15 A reading of the case also demonstrates the frequently articulated concern of commentators about unequal bargaining power in relationships, although it appears that Staal (the slave) possessed most of the bargaining power.

In this chapter, I have sought to explore the possibilities that 'contract thinking' might provide in understanding relationship forms. Ultimately, I share David McLellan's belief that we should aspire, in considering these issues, to think utopian possibilities concerning the kind of relationship and the kind of society in which we want to live. Nevertheless, I disagree with McLellan's argument that contract is a limiting, depoliticising, and 'dead end' approach to that venture. I maintain, by contrast, that contract can potentially 'open up' questions that otherwise are stifled by the dominance of a status approach. For those who find the current hegemony of marriage, marriage-like same-sex relationships, and 'family values' to be constraining, contract may provide an alternative language that is productive and enabling, in its recognition of the tensions inevitable within relationships. Although I do not claim, in this chapter, to provide a prescription for a new legal framework to govern relationships, it may be that contract discourse can give us an enriched way of understanding the *process* of living in relationships and their evolution over time.

In making this argument, I do not want to unduly valorise contract, nor do I underestimate the problem of inequality of bargaining power.[16] But it also should be remembered that the very language of inequality of bargaining power, and the legal consequences that follow, emerged through contract doctrine, underscoring the tension identified within contract. Even McLellan (1996: 244), who seeks to build upon marriage as 'an institution whose resonances are deeply informed by timeless memory and myth' concedes that 'it is open to question whether a relationship of status is more egalitarian than one which is based on exchange'. Rather, at its finest, contract can signal, not a depoliticisation nor privatisation of relationships, but an alternative, and perhaps more radical politics. It provides a flexible and empowering discourse through which we can articulate our entry into relationships and the evolution of relationships over time. Such a politics can loosen the disciplinary stranglehold that the current statuses on offer seem to possess (and may even challenge the limitations of liberalism). To that extent at least, contract deserves not to be demeaned.

Bibliography

Boucher, J (2003) 'Male Power and Contract Theory: Hobbes and Locke in Carole Pateman's *The Sexual Contract*', *Canadian Journal of Political Science* 36, pp 23–8.

Brown, B (1996) 'Contracting Out/Contracting In: Some Feminist Considerations', in Bottomley, A (ed.), *Feminist Perspectives on the Foundational Subjects of Law*, London: Cavendish Publishing, pp 5–15.

Brown, W (1995) *States of Injury*, Princeton: Princeton University Press.

Bush, D (2001) 'Moving to the Left by Moving to the Right: A Law & Economics Defense of Same-Sex Marriage', *Women's Rights Law Reporter* 22, pp 115–38.

---

16 Nor do I claim to have an answer to difficult legal questions, such as the extent to which prenuptial agreements should be respected by courts.

Campbell, D (2001a) 'Ian Macneil and the Relational Theory of Contract', in Campbell, D (ed.), *The Relational Theory of Contract: Selected Works of Ian Macneil*, London: Sweet & Maxwell, pp 3–58.

Campbell, D (ed.) (2001b) *The Relational Theory of Contract: Selected Works of Ian Macneil*, London: Sweet & Maxwell.

Diduck, A and Kaganas, F (1999) *Family Law, Gender and the State: Text, Cases and Materials*, Oxford: Hart Publishing.

Fraser, N (1993) 'Beyond the Master/Subject Model: Reflections on Carole Pateman's *Sexual Contract*', *Social Text* 37, pp 173–81.

Gilligan, C (1982) *In a Different Voice*, Cambridge, MA: Harvard University Press.

Goldberg-Hiller, J (2002) *The Limits to Union*, Ann Arbor: University of Michigan Press.

Goodrich, P (1996) 'Gender and Contract', in Bottomley, A (ed.), *Feminist Perspectives on the Foundational Subjects of Law*, London: Cavendish Publishing, pp 17–46.

Hale, M (1736) *History of the Pleas of the Crown*, London: E and R Nutt, and R Gosling.

Kingdom, E (2000) 'Cohabitation Contracts and the Democratization of Personal Relations', *Feminist Legal Studies* 8, pp 5–27.

Leckey, R (2002) 'Relational Contract and Other Models of Marriage', *Osgoode Hall Law Journal* 40, pp 1–47.

Locke, J (1698) *Two Treatises of Government*, Laslett, P (ed.) (1960), Cambridge: Cambridge University Press.

McLellan, D (1996) 'Contract Marriage – The Way Forward or Dead End?', *Journal of Law and Society* 23, pp 234–46.

Mulcahy, L (2005) 'The Limitations of Love and Altruism – Feminist Perspectives on Contract Law', in Mulcahy, L and Wheeler, S (eds), *Feminist Perspectives on Contract Law*, London: Glasshouse Press, pp 1–19.

Okin, SM (1990) 'Feminism, the Individual, and Contract Theory', *Ethics* 100, pp 658–69.

Pateman, C (1988) *The Sexual Contract*, Cambridge: Polity.

Richardson, J (2004) *Selves, Persons, Individuals*, Aldershot: Ashgate.

Robson, R and Valentine, SE (1990) 'Lov(h)ers: Lesbians as Intimate Partners and Lesbian Legal Theory', *Temple Law Review* 63, pp 511–41.

Stonewall (2004) 'Parliamentary Briefing', www.stonewall.org.uk.

Stychin, CF (1998) 'Body Talk: Rethinking Autonomy, Commodification and the Embodied Legal Self', in Sheldon, S and Thomson, M (eds), *Feminist Perspectives on Health Care Law*, London: Cavendish Publishing, pp 211–36.

Stychin, CF (2005) 'Couplings: Civil Partnerships in the United Kingdom', *New York City Law Review* 8, pp 543–72.

Testye, KY (1995) 'An Unlikely Resurrection', *Northwestern University Law Review* 90, pp 219–35.

Wheeler, S (2005) 'Going Shopping', in Mulcahy, L and Wheeler, S (eds), *Feminist Perspectives on Contract Law*, London: Glasshouse Press, pp 21–49.

Wightman, J (2000) 'Intimate Relationships, Relational Contract Theory, and the Reach of Contract', *Feminist Legal Studies* 8, pp 93–131.

Witte, J (1997) *From Sacrament to Contract*, Louisville: Westminster John Knox Press.

Zelizer, VA (1985) *Pricing the Priceless Child*, New York: Basic Books.

Chapter 5

Out of the shadows

Feminist silence and liberal law [1]

Rosemary Auchmuty, University of Westminster

On 5 December 2005 the Civil Partnership Act came into force in England and Wales and the first 'gay weddings' were celebrated on 21 December.[2] The Act gives same-sex couples who register their partnerships virtually the same rights and responsibilities as married spouses. It has been hailed not only as a victory for legal equality and human rights for gays and lesbians, but as a huge step forward in the public recognition of the existence and validity of same-sex relationships. 'It will also', declared Ben Summerskill, Chief Executive of the gay legal lobby and advice group Stonewall, 'send a powerful signal to young people who are growing up gay that when they grow up their relationships will be treated in the same way as their straight friends' (Summerskill, 2005).

Well, maybe. We shall see. It is too early yet to assess the long-term impact of the Act. But, if so, I for one will be disappointed. One of the reasons I am proud to be a lesbian is because of the *differences* between the ways many lesbians organise their lives and the mainstream forms of heterosexual relating, including marriage (Dunne, 1997; Dunne, 1998; Auchmuty, 2003). I write as a middle-aged lesbian feminist, for whom the personal remains political, and as someone who believes, in the words of the late Andrea Dworkin, that:

> The real core of the feminist vision, its revolutionary kernel if you will, has to do with the abolition of all sex roles – that is, an absolute transformation of human sexuality and the institutions derived from it.
>
> (Dworkin, 1982: 12)

---

1 The title of this chapter is adapted from a famous lesbian 'pulp' novel by Ann Bannon, *Women in the Shadows* (1959), which dates from the period when a lesbian sub-culture was developing in a climate of repression. Sheila Jeffreys describes this as 'the most pessimistic of her novels' (Jeffreys, 1994: 17), which bears out my thesis that ultimately silence is not good for us. I see such novels as symbols of the paradox of silencing for lesbians.

2 The first registrations in Northern Ireland took place on 19 December and in Scotland on 20 December. In fact 13 gay partnerships were recognised by special dispensation throughout the UK before these dates, generally because one of the partners was dying (Chrisafis, 2005).

What struck me about the advent of civil partnerships was that, although there was considerable right-wing opposition to the Bill, both from those who wished to preserve the heterosexual character of marriage and from those who were simply anti-gay, little criticism was heard from what is known as 'the lesbian and gay community'. Stonewall appeared to speak for us all in its promotion of civil partnerships as an equality measure, and its enthusiasm drowned out any radical critique from the left.

In reality, beyond the liberal face of the 'lesbian and gay community' there exists what Mark Vernon, writing in the *Guardian* on 28 October 2005, called 'a profound hesitancy' (Vernon, 2005). Civil partnerships had not been high on the wish-list of many lesbians and gay men so, when presented with the actuality, we were not sure how to react. The Civil Partnership Act 'seemed to catch many of us out', Catherine Donovan and Marianne Hester remarked at a Gay Divorce Symposium in May 2006.³ Our earlier indifference meant that few of us had had any input into the terms of the debate, and such debate as did take place was conspicuous for the paucity of either queer or feminist contribution. That is not to say that *no one* expressed any caution or disagreement, but the dominant tone was overwhelmingly celebratory and uncritical.⁴ In spite of two centuries of feminist suspicion of the institution of marriage, and at least 30 years of gay pride in our difference from heterosexuals, in the end any of the reservations we might have felt about embracing a marriage-like institution went unpublicised and ignored.

Aims of the chapter

My aim in this chapter is *not* to provide a feminist critique of the Civil Partnership Act,⁵ but to analyse the reasons why a feminist critique of civil partnerships has been largely absent from the discussions both before and after the passing of the Act; to explore the consequences of this silence; and to consider whether there remains any point in speaking out, now it is a *fait accompli*. I am sure there are many in the UK who believe that civil partnerships are an unqualified benefit and who would regard any criticism from within the 'lesbian and gay community' with some astonishment, wondering how *anyone*, and especially a lesbian or gay man, could make anything but approving noises about the reform. And no one would deny that there are many good things about the Civil Partnership Act. Summerskill is right to say it demonstrates greater social acceptance of homosexuality and

---

3   In a presentation entitled 'Same-Sex Relationships: When Things Go Wrong'. King's College, London, 20 May 2006.

4   One exception was the critical stance of Peter Tatchell, whose articles appeared repeatedly in the quality press at this time, promoting the idea of a legally supported civil partnership open to any committed relationship, including family and friends. See for example Tatchell (2005).

5   For a critique of some of its principles, see Auchmuty (2004).

will serve to enhance that level of acceptance. We are already seeing this in the press coverage. In the weeks between the coming into force of the Act on 5 December 2005 and the first registrations, lesbian and gay couples were featured on television and in newspapers in unusually positive representations, in marked contrast to the articles about the Pope's ban on gay priests and the evangelical homophobia in the Church of England which had been news in preceding weeks. In emphasising the things these couples had in common with heterosexuals – love and commitment, shared homes, wedding plans – gays and lesbians were for once presented as *normal*, not exotic; not a problem, not evil or Other. That felt simultaneously very comfortable and very momentous, because it was so new.

So feminists along with everyone else could happily celebrate the 'equality' achieved by this legislation in one area of gay and lesbian life. But that does not mean that the development is beyond criticism. For this was not a reform we all asked for; it is an opportunity many of us will choose not to embrace; and some of us suspect that, far from marking the achievement of substantive equality for gays and lesbians, civil partnerships will prove a disappointment to many, a disaster for some, and a step *backward* in the pursuit of justice and fairness for all, since they leave many people unfairly outside the beneficial regimes and do little to challenge the structural inequalities of the marriage model.

There is a long tradition of feminist critique to the effect that the marriage model cannot be the route to real equality. 'We should all be familiar with, and keep in mind, the ways in which marriage has operated to reproduce women's dependency and inequality', Susan Boyd and Claire Young remind us (Boyd and Young, 2003: 758). We ignore this at our peril. Marriage was a focus of feminist concern during both the first and second waves of feminism[6] and, while many of the first wave presented their arguments in terms of what was wrong with the *current* marriage form (for example Smith, 1854; but see also Hamilton, 1909), campaigning vigorously to change the most egregiously awful aspects of the institution (Perkin,1989), the second wave came to see marriage as almost beyond redemption, something to be avoided by all liberated women (for instance, Barrett and McIntosh, 1982; Smart, 1984; Ettelbrick, 1997). These generalisations mask considerable variations in

6 'First-wave feminism' is an expression used to describe the women's movement of the Victorian and Edwardian periods, which won substantial rights for women in the fields of education, work and family law, and which culminated in the achievement of the vote (Strachey, 1928; Levine, 1987). 'Second-wave feminism' describes the women's movement that began in the late 1960s and for which there is no agreed finishing point. Some would like to think that it is still going on; others conclude that we presently live in a 'post-feminist' world, either because gender equality has been achieved (which is patently not true) or because of the advent of a powerful anti-feminist backlash. See for example Spender (1983a); Mitchell and Oakley (1986); Coppock, Haydon and Richter (1995).

lived experience, of course, and it is as true to say that a good proportion of first-wave feminists avoided marriage even though they could not publicly condemn it, as that many second-wave feminists chose to marry for a range of personal or practical reasons, whilst maintaining a critical overview. The important thing to bear in mind is that feminists have never seen marriage as a neutral choice, let alone a benefit to be unreservedly embraced. It has *always* had to be justified. But civil partnerships do not seem to be problematised in this way, and one has to ask why not.

Does anyone really understand this law?

The most obvious reason why civil partnerships have not been subjected to the same critique as marriage is undoubtedly uncertainty concerning the law. That most people are not quite clear on the legal implications is hardly surprising given that 'civil partnership' means something quite different in other jurisdictions and that the two Private Members' Bills that preceded the UK Government's Civil Partnership Bill differed in quite significant ways from the final Act.[7] Initially the civil partnership was perceived as an *alternative* to marriage, open to heterosexuals as well as gays and lesbians, on the French, Dutch or Belgian model. People familiar with this kind of civil partnership will have seen it advocated for those who rejected 'the traditions, history and the connotations associated with marriage', as one New Zealand couple explained in an *Observer* article (Scott, 2005a). The British civil partnership, on the other hand, is directed at those who wish to *embrace* these very qualities.

If you do not understand what is going on, you hardly feel qualified to comment; and there is ample evidence that many people do not realise that civil partnership in England is effectively *marriage* for gays and lesbians, as far as the law is concerned. As Baroness O'Cathain, a critic of civil partnerships, declared in the House of Lords debates on the Bill:

> The Government insist that a civil partnership is not gay marriage. The name is clearly different, but anyone with any nous can see that the legal rights are the same.
>
> (Quoted in Barker, 2004: 315)

The sole legal differences between marriage and civil partnerships are (1) the name (2) the definition (marriage is 'the union . . . of one man and one

---

7   Both Bills would have opened the civil partnership to unmarried heterosexual couples as well as same-sex couples, and the rights were not the same as those enjoyed by married people. Lord Lester's Bill was particularly interesting in proposing community of property for civil partners (see n. 21 below).

woman')[8] and (3) the requirement that the marriage relationship be a sexual one, but not the civil partnership. Thus adultery is a ground for divorce[9] but not for dissolution of a civil partnership, and non-consummation is a ground for annulment of a marriage[10] but not of a civil partnership.

I do not wish to minimise these differences. For many radical feminists, the very act of sexual intercourse operates to institutionalise male domination and female subordination (see, for instance, Dworkin, 1982; Friedman and Sarah, 1982; MacKinnon, 1987; Jeffreys, 1994). Carole Pateman (1988) argued that consummation established the male conjugal right, shifting the marriage 'contract' to a relationship of *status*. More recently, Nicola Barker has suggested that the absence of sex in the Civil Partnership Act opens up the possibility of including non-monogamous and non-sexual relationships within its legal protection, which may in turn affect legal and social ideas of the marriage norm (Barker, 2006).

Nevertheless, I would argue that the omission of sex from the civil partnership legislation was largely a pragmatic decision: the Government was anxious to avoid the thorny and, for many, distasteful problem of defining what exactly constitutes same-sex sexual practice. Moreover, there is evidence that some gay men had lobbied against an adultery ground for dissolution of a same-sex relationship. 'Many gay couples with perfectly solid bonds between them may not want such a tight definition of fidelity to govern their relationship', wrote one spokesman in the *Stonewall Newsletter* (Davies, 1999).

Nevertheless, in terms of legal rights and responsibilities, marriage and civil partnership are virtually the same. Yet both the Government (White, 2004) and a number of commentators have insisted that an institution which is not called marriage, while *effectively* the same thing, *is* not and *cannot* be the same thing as long as it bears a different name. The Government's message seems to have been intended to placate traditionalists and religious groups who believed the sacred institution to be under threat, and those for whom same-sex marriage might be seen as carrying tolerance too far. Indeed, it has been argued that the relatively easy acceptance of civil partnerships by the UK legislature was due to the way that Government proponents carefully distinguished them from marriage. I have even heard it said that the physical form of the Act – with every provision laid out in full instead of a simple, short instruction to add 'or civil partner' whenever the word 'spouse' appeared in any Act – was meant to deter opponents from reading the whole 400-plus pages and thereby recognising its real implications.[11] If so, it was a successful ploy, but in the long run a self-defeating one. Mark Harper, family law solicitor and long-term supporter of Stonewall and same-sex marriage, has

---

8 *Hyde v Hyde* (1866) LR1 P & D 10 at 133.
9 Matrimonial Causes Act 1973, s 1(2)(a).   10 Ibid., s 12.
11 Said at an ESRC seminar on 'The new family', London, 25 February 2005.

publicly warned that couples are likely to register their partnerships without realising the consequences, 'partly because we were told repeatedly it isn't the same thing as marriage' (Dyer, 2005). The Government's obfuscation about the naming of the reform may end up fooling more than its opponents.

For many lesbians and gays, however, the name is the goal, the pursuit of which has been strengthened by the availability of same-sex marriage in an increasing number of other jurisdictions in the world.[12] On the day the Act came into force, Celia Kitzinger[13] was quoted in the *Guardian* as saying scornfully, 'this is hardly cutting edge' (*Guardian,* 5 December 2005, p 9). Two days later her partner, Sue Wilkinson,[14] observed, 'Separate is still not equal' (*Guardian,* 7 December 2005, Letters to the Editor). These two women, a lesbian couple married in Canada in 2003, went on to seek recognition in the English courts of their marriage *as* marriage under s 55 of the Family Law Act 1986 and arts 8, 12 and 14 of Sched 1 to the Human Rights Act 1998. 'Civil partnerships are an important step forward for same-sex couples, but they are not enough', they told Liberty, which sponsored their case. '*We want full equality in marriage*' (Liberty, 2005, my emphasis).[15]

Inevitably, they lost their challenge. The judge (Sir Mark Potter, President of the Family Division) held, first, that capacity to marry was governed by the law of the parties' domicile (here, England) and, second, that the courts when seeking to determine whether legislation is compatible with Convention rights must:

> distinguish between permissible judicial interpretation by way of . . . modification of the meaning of words in a statute and impermissible adoption of a meaning inconsistent with a fundamental feature of the legislation.[16]

Since case law had so far ruled that the need for two sexes in a marriage *was* a fundamental feature of the English law, such a momentous change as the petitioners sought would require Parliamentary intervention.

While widely reported, I would guess that the case has done little to clarify the legal status of civil partnerships in the eyes of the general public. What they are likely to take from the media reports is an idea of *difference* – because if marriage and civil partnership were the same, then, surely, as in Canada or the Netherlands, it would have the same name?

---

12 At the time, the Netherlands, Belgium and two Canadian provinces, followed soon afterwards by Massachusetts, Spain, Canada as a whole and South Africa.

13 Psychology professor and pioneer of lesbian studies in the UK (for example Kitzinger, 1987).

14 Another distinguished psychology professor, co-founder of the journal *Feminism & Psychology*.

15 For details of this action, see http://equalmarriagerights.org, accessed 7 September 2006.

16 *Wilkinson v Kitzinger and Others* [2006] EWHC 2022 (Fam) (31 July 2006), para 37.

The triumph of romance – aided by commerce

Marriage delivers a mixed-bag of positives and negatives, some of which depend on the personalities of the parties to the marriage (and their associates), some on the level of preparedness and expectations they bring to the union, and some about which they have no choice whatsoever. Among the last-named are the legal and financial 'rights and responsibilities' that each jurisdiction attaches to the institution at a particular moment in history. Marriage, in other words, is a different thing in different countries.

In England and Wales, civil partners have been offered the same mixed-bag of positives and negatives as married couples 'enjoy' today, which the publicity around the legislation (in particular, that put forward by an exultant Stonewall) has managed to present as a gift-wrapped bundle of generalised *benefits* that 'level up' lesbian and gay couples to equality with married heterosexuals. That the process involves a good deal of levelling *down*, especially in financial matters, has been skilfully concealed beneath the tinsel and glitter.

So much for preparedness and expectations, then. In its treatment of civil partnerships, the gay advice organisation Stonewall has followed the time-hallowed English tradition of ensuring that couples contemplating a legal union should know as little as possible about its legal and financial implications. This has always been the preferred way for English couples to enter marriage – in general ignorance of the law, secure only in the love and trust the parties have for each other – and has led, perhaps in consequence, to this country's having the highest divorce rate in Europe (Bunting, 2004: 6). Two in every five marriages now end in divorce (Rowan, 2004: 10).[17] Surveys reveal profound disillusionment and surprise among those whose relationships have broken down, not just because of what they discovered about the personal dynamics of their particular marriage, but because they had simply not grasped what the institution of marriage *meant* in terms of law and access to money. 'People look at marriage through a romantic haze', observed a psychologist interviewed by the *Guardian*, 'but it's actually a business contract. . . . I have seen people for whom the wedding has been considerably more important than the marriage' (Taylor, 2005: 7).

Much of the publicity for civil partnerships has adopted an identical romantic focus, playing on susceptible emotions and causing the practical implications to recede into the background. Even the Lesbian and Gay Lawyers' Association expressed concern over this in the context of a survey of their own members, more than half of whom said they planned to register their own partnership. The Association's chairman, Andrea Woelke, commented:

---

17 Though the divorce rate actually fell slightly in 2005, particularly among younger couples; and one-fifth of people getting divorced had already been divorced once before (*Social Trends* 2005).

We expected to find a degree of lawyerly caution, because so many of our members are family lawyers and know all too well the drawbacks, as well as the advantages of marriage. Despite our work involving the breakdown of relationships, *romance seems to be triumphing over professional scepticism*. It is vital that people do take time to consider the full impact of the legislation before tying the knot – we don't want to see a rush of divorces.

(*Law Gazette*, 2005, my emphasis)

As if on cue, the day after the Civil Partnership Act came into force, Catherine Bennett declared in the *Guardian* that there had never been a better time to be a divorce lawyer:

Not only is the marital breakdown industry currently enjoying one of its best seasons since the figures peaked in 1996 (buoyed further by a series of prominent court battles between millionaires and their wives, including childless wives married for approximately five minutes), but now there's the prospect of hundreds of miserable gays coming on stream within a few years. Who could have anticipated this queue of victims, eager to fill the space left by heterosexual couples, who have seen what traditional marriage did to their friends and families?

(Bennett, 2005)

Bennett did not envisage that same-sex unions would be any more secure than heterosexual ones. Noting the popularity of the traditional white wedding with civil partners, she predicted that gay couples would:

observe all the other traditions associated with modern marriage, from the early snoring/map-reading disputes to less Thurberesque money resentments, wrangling over cleaning and cooking, and the never-to-be resolved question of whose work-life balance is causing the greater degree of martyrdom. After which it is but a short step – shorter if a child has arrived to complete the couple's happiness – to the traditional first visit to a Relate [ie marriage guidance] counsellor.

(Ibid.)

But can we be surprised if this happens? Turn to the pocket-sized handbook prepared and distributed by Stonewall, with financial support from Barclays bank, keenly alert to the value of the pink pound.[18] The cover shows two gold

---

18 '. . . big name companies such as Barclays bank . . . join the growing rush to cash in on a gay economy which is worth tens of billions of pounds. Barclays has just received research which showed that gays and lesbians enjoy a combined annual income of £60 billion . . . greater

rings with the legend 'You're gay, you're in love, You want to be together forever . . . GET HITCHED! A Guide to Civil Partnership'. As well as adopting all the symbols, metaphors and romantic myths of heterosexual marriage, this 'guide' perpetuates the cheerful disregard for legal accuracy and detail one finds in most English discussions of marriage outside the courtroom context. Copycat illustrations of confetti, wedding cakes and champagne waste valuable space that could be used to inform, with the consequence that the 'practical' advice is brief in the extreme and so general as to be misleading. One example will suffice, 'if you're receiving benefits, you will be dealt with the same as any other married couple'. It sounds very positive and 'equal'; but nowhere is it explained that this means you will be *worse off*, since means-tested benefits are lower for couples than for two individuals. One same-sex couple mentioned in an *Observer* article of 4 December 2005 were going to be £51.85 a week poorer as a result of the Civil Partnership Act (Scott, 2005c: 8).[19]

There are some who would argue that more precise practical advice would only be wasted on those who had already made up their minds to register a civil partnership – and certainly there is evidence that heterosexual couples planning to marry often evince no interest in legal detail (Hibbs *et al.*, 2001). But that is to assume that gays and lesbians, whose relationships have up to now been conducted outside the sanction of the law, would choose to take as little notice of the law as those who always have been able to invoke it. It is not in any case an excuse for not giving proper advice, especially given that Stonewall is an organisation with a specific concern for law.

Stonewall's 'guidance', such as it is, focuses on the mechanics of registration. 'So, how do we get started?' The dissolution process rates one line. Surely it would be useful to know the grounds for dissolution and the court's powers to redistribute assets on the ending of a relationship? But to contemplate *this* would be to spoil the romance of the occasion and to allow reason to taint decision making. The inheritance tax exemption for spouses is

---

disposable income than heterosexuals' (Campbell, 2005: 13). As Didi Herman notes in *The Antigay Agenda,* figures of this kind need to be treated with caution: they tend to exclude lesbians from the statistics (no surprise here) and respondents are often self-selecting rather than representative (Herman, 1997: 116–17). Indeed, the *Guardian* was forced to print a clarification the day after it published a similar article ('Gay men earn £10k more than national average'), acknowledging that the readers who responded to the survey conducted by the glossy magazines *Diva* and *Gay Times* might not 'reflect . . . the condition of gay people in general' (Curtis, 2006a, and *Guardian* Corrections and Clarifications, 24 January 2006). However accurate the findings, the bank was sufficiently persuaded to fund 300,000 copies of the Stonewall guide (Campbell, 2005: 13).

19 An illustration of this careless disregard for the financial realities can be seen in the statement by a Manchester lesbian couple interviewed in the *Guardian*, 13 October 2004, 'We do not have the figures of how much we will be better off but at least we will be entitled to the same treatment' (Carter and Glendinning, 2004).

highlighted, but no one points out that this is irrelevant to most readers: only six per cent of the population are currently liable for inheritance tax (Collinson, 2006). Of this number, the majority will inevitably be men or widows; yet I have heard lesbians who are clearly not wealthy enough to benefit from the exemption citing it as a reason for registering their partnership.[20] Children go unmentioned, except to note that civil partners might have to support their partners and children. *Might?* Whom, one wonders, is Stonewall addressing here? Older, childless gay men with substantial property? Certainly not young lesbians keen to have a family, or older lesbians who already have one.

On Stonewall's website, a set of 25 Frequently Asked Questions goes into slightly more detail, but suffers from the same faults. In answer to the question, 'Should we make a will?', Stonewall says: 'Even if you choose not to make a will, your civil partner will probably still inherit everything' (Stonewall, 2005a). *They will?* This is terrible advice, for registering a partnership, like marriage, invalidates all previous wills, while the intestacy rules give rights to children or parents on estates worth more than £125,000 (Scott, 2005b: 2). Once again, the possibility of dissolution is downplayed, being relegated to the very last question, still without details of grounds or consequences. When dissolutions start to happen, there are going to be some very surprised gay and lesbian 'divorcees' out there. Those who never realised that civil partnerships were so similar to marriage may not have grasped the fact that a fair share of their assets – particularly the real property and pension rights, if they have them – may have to be surrendered to an ex-partner. As lawyer Mark Harper warned:

> If you are keen to sign up, if things go wrong – and the average marriage lasts only 10 years – then you could be in for a shock. The rules on dissolution of a civil partnership are precisely the same as those on divorce.
>
> (Jones and Collinson, 2005)

---

20 The problem with inheritance tax is that few people know how high the nil-rated band is (and it rises annually) or how it is calculated. They therefore imagine they will be liable when they will not. I venture to suggest that most of us will not be liable. A *Guardian* article (23 January 2006) suggested that 'Women have officially joined the pink pound' on the basis of a survey of lesbian earnings undertaken by the magazine *Diva*. This prompted the comment from the magazine's editor that, 'There's been a lesbian glass ceiling and this shows that women are breaking through'. Sally Munt, professor of cultural studies at Sussex University, was quoted as saying that there have always been 'extremely rich aristocratic lesbians, it's just that they've been less visible' (Curtis, 2006a). Both comments seem to me unscientific, and until we have proper statistics, I will continue to assume that childless lesbians are probably financially better off than heterosexual women with children, but that lesbians as a group will generally be poorer than gay men, because women earn less than men, and women with children least of all.

On the other hand, those who believed, as many English spouses do, that all their property is jointly owned,[21] may be equally startled to discover that neither marriage nor civil partnership gives a person on dissolution of their relationship an *automatic* right to a half-share.[22]

Even if there were no other reasons to speak out about civil partnerships, then, the shocking quality of Stonewall's 'advice' would be a compelling one. This is particularly so because Stonewall is such a prominent presence in discussions of the subject: to most people it *is* the voice of the 'lesbian and gay community'. In considering why Stonewall so spectacularly missed its opportunity to clarify the terms of the new law, I am driven to the conclusion that this was neither exactly deliberate nor simply wilful but the inevitable consequence of its propaganda strategy, which rolled three types of candidate for civil partnership registration – those who seek a public demonstration of their love and commitment,[23] those who want the symbols and trappings of heterosexual 'normality',[24] and those with financial motives[25] – into one rather muddled composite, and then had to present the final outcome as an unqualified benefit for all. This was particularly tricky given that the Act we got was so clearly a compromise, offering neither the very different form of

21 Community of property, where marital property is either owned in equal shares or (in the deferred form) divided into equal shares on divorce, is commonly found in American and continental jurisdictions. It has never been part of English law. Even the principle of equal division established in *White v White* [2001] 1 AC 596 gives rise to no *automatic* entitlement.

22 Though this very error was perpetuated in the article in which Mark Harper was quoted (Jones and Collinson, 2005), whose authors went on to say (and I am sure this is not what Harper told them!): 'Regardless of whether the couple have children, all assets built up during that time [ie of cohabitation before and after registration of the partnership] (irrespective of relative incomes) will have to be divided equally.' This is quite untrue, and an example of the media misinformation that dogged discussions before the coming into force of the Act.

23 'I imagined I'd never want a big do, but then I think about all the people I want there . . . So I think if we're going to do it, we should do it properly and make it the best day of our lives. . . . I don't think either of us needs to stand there and announce anything. It's more a confirmation of the commitment we've shown to each other over 15 years.' Gay male couple interviewed in McLean (2005: 35).

24 'Lots of my friends are getting married at the moment and settling down and having children. I want that too. . . . I want a beautiful day with my huge family and lovely clothes to wear and I want to be able to afford a nice holiday afterwards. Getting registered will be the best day of my life, just as it always has been for straight people.' Young Cardiff lesbian on civil partnership plans, Stonewall *Friends* (Winter 2003) p 9.

25 ' "Legal recognition" as next of kin would at least bring us some peace of mind. In addition, it would remove the current threat to a surviving partner that our home might be sacrificed to meet inheritance tax. . . . I really don't mind paying taxes but I don't see why I should pay twice what a heterosexual couple would, as is the current state.' Older South London gay man on civil partnership plans, ibid.

civil partnership that Stonewall had earlier supported,[26] nor same-sex marriage itself. In the end, Stonewall decided to pretend (or perhaps convinced itself) that the Civil Partnership Act satisfied both goals. It would have been more honest to tell the truth: this 'one-size-fits-all' model does not, in fact, suit everyone. The dumbing-down of Stonewall's advice insults its audience and was, in my view, a serious misjudgement.

Stonewall is not, of course, the sole source of information on civil partnerships, though it may well be the one most people turn to first. The Government's Women and Equality Unit web pages direct the seeker to the precise tax, pension and benefits implications as well as the grounds for dissolution and the rules concerning children – all the issues Stonewall's 'advice' ignores (Women and Equality Unit, 2005).[27] But practical detail, whilst essential for informed decision making, does not serve the same purpose as a critical assessment of the law, and that is what is so hard to find. *Someone* needs to offer this so that gays and lesbians know what to do.

On money matters this role has been assumed by the financial pages of the quality press. These, after some months of rather garbled reporting in the run-up to the Act,[28] made serious efforts to set the record straight ('Same-sex couples are learning a harsh lesson', *Guardian Money*, 26 November 2005; 'Equality at a price', *Observer Cash,* 4 December 2005; 'Civil partnership law to hurt some same-sex couples', *Guardian Money*, 3 December 2005). The trouble is that these pages are not widely read. Moreover, as with heterosexuals embarking on marriage, it was evident from the reporting that many gays and lesbians just did not want to know. Neither couple interviewed by Maria Scott in the *Guardian* (Scott, 2005b) was interested in having a prenuptial agreement to set down financial arrangements during and, if necessary, at the ending of a civil partnership. The gay men said, 'Clive's solicitor suggested it but we decided we wouldn't bother.' The lesbians declared, 'Everything can be easily split 50:50. But we are also quite sure that we will spend the rest of our lives together.' Their reluctance to make formal financial agreements might have been due to a well-founded faith in the security of their relationship, or could perhaps demonstrate the clear-sightedness of those who have long had to organise their money outside formal legal regimes. After all, courts are not bound by prenuptial agreements, though these have strong persuasive value. It might also represent a healthy resistance to the blandishments of a legal profession eager to seize this opportunity to enhance its client portfolio (Bennett, 2005). But it may just as easily reveal

---

26 When Angela Mason was Executive Director of Stonewall, she favoured a civil partnership open to 'everybody – gay, straight, friends, siblings – anybody who defines as a family' (Mason, 2001).

27 Their advice also carries useful links to counselling agencies such as Relate (for relationship breakdown) and Broken Rainbow (domestic violence).

28 For an example, see n. 22 above.

the naivety of the uninformed, who believe, as so many heterosexual couples also do, that legally regulated relationships are not so very different from relationships outside the law's control (Robins, 2005).

It is small wonder, then, that amidst this muddle of legal misinformation, misunderstanding and mixed messages we fall silent, not knowing where we stand, not knowing whom to believe, not knowing what to do.

Does anyone take marriage seriously?

On the day the Civil Partnership Act came into force, a *Guardian* editorial congratulated the British Government on doing 'something that is both progressive and well in advance of almost everywhere else' (*Guardian*, 5 December 2005). Leaving aside the observation that the trend in other parts of the world seems decidedly *more* progressive, in that Spain, Canada and South Africa have all conceded same-sex marriage since the Act was passed, what drew most praise from the *Guardian* was the fact that 'alone in the world Britain seems to have done it with a minimum of fuss'. I submit that this is hardly a matter of congratulation. The reality is that the measure passed with relative ease through Parliament because few people cared sufficiently strongly about it to join in the debates. It was consequently an easy concession for the Government to make.

It is clear that the general ignorance of the law can be partly ascribed to indifference. Prior to the brief upsurge in interest when the Act was coming into force, British lesbians and gays demonstrated little obvious enthusiasm for civil partnership rights.[29] The same was true of heterosexuals, reflecting a general *laissez-faire* attitude to marriage in a country where marital status is now socially irrelevant. With the exception of extreme traditionalists and those motivated by religious considerations, no one really cares whether people marry or not. Marriage has become almost a lifestyle choice. With the institution in serious decline over the past 30 years, English law – and not just family law – has made strenuous efforts to move with the times, extending to unmarried cohabitants (first heterosexual, then same-sex) benefits once

---

29 This statement has been called into question by the speed with which many same-sex couples appeared to take advantage of the new law once it came into force. All I can say is, their enthusiasm did not seem particularly evident *before* the Act was passed. Stonewall had been pushing for relationship recognition since about 2001, but it was only one among many concerns (which included, *inter alia*, equalising the age of consent for gay men, challenging the prohibition on gays in the armed forces, and outlawing discrimination against gays and lesbians in employment, education and the provision of services). Given developments abroad, *same-sex marriage* was a topic of theoretical debate, but I doubt if many British people had ever considered the possibility of a 'civil partnership', with all the rights of marriage, and *for same-sex couples alone*, until we were presented with the Government's proposals.

confined to spouses.[30] Conservatives may argue that confining benefits to the legally married helps to protect the institution of marriage, but that has not been the approach of the courts. In the House of Lords' judgment in *Ghaidan v Godin-Mendoza* [2004] UKHL 30, for example, Baroness Hale declared that 'The traditional family is not protected by granting a benefit which is denied to people who cannot or will not become a traditional family' (para 1483).[31] If restrictiveness serves no useful purpose, then, the sensible way forward is to make the law fit the reality – and this is what has been happening.

In one sense the Civil Partnership Act is an illustration of this process but, in another, it can be seen as a move against the tide. Family law long ago ditched the marital relationship as its central concern, along with its former title of 'matrimonial law', replacing it with a primary focus on the well-being of children in the complicated web of relationships that constitutes the twenty-first century British family. Journalist Anne Karpf captured this social change in an article in the *Guardian*'s 'Family' section on 17 December 2005 when she wrote:

> I was in a shop, picking up and putting down Christmas presents for my step-grandson ... when I looked down at my shopping list and was struck by the span of relationships it described. They included my sister's mother-in-law, my step-grandson's ex-wife, my nephew's girlfriend. Here was a web of kinship every bit as complex as that among the Iroquois Indians.
>
> (Karpf, 2005. See also Bunting, 2004)

Where there *has* been hype and media attention for the civil partnership – mainly in the period around the Act's coming into operation – much of this has been manufactured by commercial forces. The wedding industry (which includes the Local Authorities whose duty it is to perform the registrations) has been touting for business – *big* business, as it clearly perceived it, with rich gay men in mind. While Brighton and London's Westminster slugged it out for the title of Gay Wedding Capital of the UK, the founder of the 'Gay Wedding Show' declared that:

> We think it will be worth hundreds of millions of pounds here. A lot of guys are coming through who have been together fifteen or twenty years – they've got loads of money and they're not worried about the cost at all.
>
> (Spencer, 2005)

---

30 For example, protection against undue influence in mortgage contracts (*Barclays Bank v O'Brien* [1994] 1 AC 180) and the right to adopt children as a same-sex couple (Adoption and Children Act 2002) – see Auchmuty (2004: 114–16).

31 For comment on this point, see Probert (2005).

The Hilton hotel chain is 'offering tailor-made parties and even the chance to hold the ceremony at some hotels' (Campbell, 2005). Before long, couples who have hardly given a thought to registering will start to wonder if they should. This experience is not unlike the release of a new luxury item you do not need and never thought you wanted. Advertising makes it seem desirable, and when everyone around you is getting one, you feel you have to have one too. The timing of the first civil partnership ceremonies, just before Christmas, may have been fortuitous, but for the wedding industry it was also extremely fortunate.

If the British establishment had wanted to stir up renewed interest in marriage, however, extending its rights to gays and lesbians was certainly a good ploy. The publicity alerted heterosexuals as well as the target audience to some of the differences between the married and unmarried status and, given that the consensus was generally in favour of the rights marriage supposedly conferred, it seems not unlikely that a number of heterosexual couples were pushed in the direction of formalising their unions.[32] It was surely no coincidence that in the same week the Act came into force the recently retired President of the Family Court, Dame Elizabeth Butler-Sloss, complained about the lack of legal incentives to marry; the *Guardian* even placed the report of her speech alongside an article about gay couples tying the knot (*Guardian*, 6 December 2005).

This does not mean, of course, that the same-sex registered couple has become the new ideal couple for heterosexuals to emulate. Such would be a curious role for a coupling once seen as beyond the pale – the 'pretended family relationship' of s 28 Local Government Act 1988.[33] No, it merely represents the colonising by 'family values' of a new target group, with the subsuming of *all* deserving couples – gay or straight – into a homogeneous style of union based as far as possible on the heterosexual model. With marriage in long-term decline (despite small increases in the actual number of marriages for the last three years), this can be seen as an attempt to shore up what had fast been becoming a moribund institution.[34]

Is feminism in retreat?

While young people often reject both the tenets of and the need for feminism, older women may acknowledge continuing inequalities but sometimes

---

32 There has certainly been an enhancement of media interest in the topic of marriage since the Civil Partnership Act came into effect. See for example Russell (2005); Behr (2005); Hanman (2006); Odone (2006); Fyfield (2006); Burns (2006).

33 Local Government Act 1988 s 28 made the promotion of homosexuality illegal in schools and local government-funded venues. It was repealed in 2003.

34 In 2003 the marriage rate had declined by 36% from a peak in 1972 (*Social Trends 2005*). By 2011, it is predicted, unmarried adults will outnumber married ones (Behr, 2005).

question if feminist interventions have any force any more.[35] The lack of feminist engagement with the Civil Partnership Act would appear more comprehensible if we saw it simply as evidence of the death of feminism as a political movement. Certainly it is a salutary experience for those of us who lived through the period of feminist activism in the 1970s and 1980s to reflect on the huge differences between our lives now and then. Some of these differences are external – the social and political context is quite changed – but some are internal: *we* are quite changed too.

I do not believe that feminism is dead – there are plenty of young people out there who are hearteningly willing to embrace feminist principles (and even the name) – but certainly the fervour of the Women's Liberation Movement of the 1970s is long gone. Within the lesbian community, the radical feminist critique of the 1970s was quickly eclipsed by the 'sex wars' in the 1980s. 'Sexual radicals', as they called themselves, turning the notion of radicalism on its head, revolted against what they saw as the prescriptive (and proscriptive) lesbian feminist critique of heteropatriarchal sexual practices (Healey, 1996). Feminists found themselves forced into a defensive and, ultimately, silenced role (Jeffreys, 1994). What collectivist action remained regrouped around opposition to section 28 and support of AIDS victims. Other factors such as the Tory Government's destruction of the Greater London Council brought many lesbian services and formal networks to an end, killing off, in their turn, many of the *in*formal networks as lesbians moved into mainstream employment. We allowed ourselves to be seduced by the consumer culture of the 1990s: as Emma Healey asked, 'Why shouldn't lesbians own their own homes or drive their own cars?' (Healey, 1996: 165). Meanwhile a younger generation of lesbians was growing up who had known no political or economic climate but Thatcherism. Feminism no longer spoke to them: its very success meant that *they* did not feel oppressed. We cannot really be surprised, then, at the 'me-first' or at least 'me-too' approach that greeted the Civil Partnership Act. It was as much the product of its times as a reaction against the 'political correctness' of the lesbian feminists.

But what has happened to the Women's Libbers of yesteryear? Have we really all been bought off? Or is it simply a function of our increasing age that older feminists are more concerned for ourselves personally, and therefore less active politically? How much of our reluctance to speak out on questions of principle is due to our crowded working lives, which leave so little time for reflection or engagement with social issues; our efforts to cope with caring responsibilities (growing children, aging elderly relatives, sick or disabled partners); our own experience of ill-health and degenerating bodies; the

---

35 The title of the UK Political Studies Association's Women and Politics Annual Conference (February 2006) reflected this timely concern, 'Feminist Ethics, Feminist Politics and the States We're In: Critical Reflections in Uncertain Times'.

simple lack of time to think beyond our day-to-day activities? How much is due to our personal disappointment with the way the world has turned out? And how much to concern about our futures: our preparations for our ever-closer retirement, old age, and death?

I think all these factors are relevant, and the propaganda for the Civil Partnership Act plays into all our concerns. Are you scared of being ill in hospital and your partner being denied access? Then register your partnership, quick. Are you afraid your death will leave your partner unprovided for, without the benefit of your pension rights, obliged to sell the house? Then register! You can avoid all these worries if you just take this little step. (Of course, after all these years, you are never going to split up, so the possibility of having to sell the house and being economically strapped long before your death never crosses your mind.) The retreat from feminist activism may in the end be more accidental than intentional, more pragmatic than principled.

But there are many among us who will argue that our feminism – and feminism generally – is not actually in retreat. Many will point to the incorporation into our current working lives of feminist activities which in the 1970s and 1980s took place distinctly outside them. This is certainly true for the academic world, which embraced first Women's Studies and then feminist scholarship across the range of disciplines. While hardly mainstream today (this is particularly true of legal studies), feminism is now tolerated as one of many acceptable scholarly approaches, something that would have been unimaginable to first-wave feminists and academics right up to the 1970s.[36] So what has happened for some of us is that our feminist activism takes place largely in our work, not outside it.

But this mainstreaming has been neither easy nor total. I have tried to take the Civil Partnership Act into the classroom, where any attempt to engender reasoned discussion has proved uphill work. Where once I complained of students' liberalism (as opposed to radicalism), now I am often horrified by their *il*liberalism. With the rise of religious fundamentalism, we now have students who not only believe that homosexuality is incontestably wrong, but are not shy to say so in class – or to refuse to discuss the issue at all. In that kind of situation, one is almost obliged to reposition oneself as pro-civil partnership; we never get as far as the feminist critique. It is at moments like this that one feels grateful for the case law on the Human Rights Act 1998 which has made gay rights a given that students cannot contest, whether they want to or not.[37]

---

36 Evidence for this lies in the fact that in 2004 the Government generously funded the AHRC Centre for Law, Gender and Sexuality, where much of the research output is quite explicitly feminist.

37 An article in the *Guardian Education* which appeared just after the Act came into force offered useful advice on how to engage school students in discussion about the Civil Partnership Act (Turner, 2005).

What's wrong with rights?

Yet the rights culture has a lot to answer for. It has paradoxically made things more difficult for feminists. When the Human Rights Act was passed in 1998, the idea of 'rights' seized the public imagination in unprecedented fashion. It fitted well into the 'me-first' or 'me-too' ideology mentioned above, but it also seemed to offer a way forward for identity groups who had long been struggling for recognition and equality. It has proved quite successful for gays and lesbians in this respect.[38] In the process, however, the very word 'rights' has come to mean something very different from what it meant in the days of, for example, the movement for 'women's rights' in the nineteenth and early twentieth centuries. *Then*, rights were a philosophical idea, open to debate; now they are a legal institution, and, while the public may often misunderstand the scope of the Human Rights Act, for lawyers the only question is whether one falls within or outside the category enjoying them. 'Rights not only become reified,' wrote Didi Herman in 1990 of the Canadian situation, in an observation that has since become true of the UK, 'but people become dependent on the state (including the courts) to grant them rights that are essentially formal and unsubstantive' (Herman, 1990: 805).

Much has been written about the advantages and disadvantages of rights, many of the critiques coming from feminists (e.g. McColgan, 2000), but the overwhelming view is that they are a good thing. It would be hard to argue against this as a general proposition. No feminist could seriously oppose rights for gays and lesbians, and the pursuit of formal equality has always been one strong strand of feminist activity. But we must not lose sight of the shortcomings. First, the rights mentality assumes that people can be grouped into fixed and simple categories. The truth is that many people move between the categories: for example, heterosexuals may choose to 'become' gay or gays to 'become' heterosexual; more muddling still, there are plenty of self-identified heterosexuals who indulge in gay sex, and vice versa. Second, rights are hierarchical. Once people have been categorised into groups, it is inevitable that some will be eligible for a particular right and others not so. So, in deciding who is eligible to marry, the law lays down clear rules; and while it may be amended to allow some in, there will inevitably be others (perhaps equally deserving) who are excluded from its benefits. For example, on the subject of transsexuals, English law has already spoken. Those who adopt the opposite gender identity to their birth gender, and who undergo the required treatment, and whose partners are of the opposite gender to their chosen gender, may now marry. Other transsexual

---

38 For example, *Ghaidan v Godin-Mendoza* [2004] UKHL 30, which established the right of a man to succeed to the tenancy of his deceased same-sex partner as if he had been a spouse. The Human Rights Act has not, however, been so helpful to women as a group – for example, in rape trials.

couples may not.[39] It is likewise with civil partnerships. Only same-sex couples may register their partnerships and obtain the associated legal and financial benefits. Other couples (friends, relatives) who suffer similar legal and financial disadvantage may not. Not to speak of groups or individuals, who are altogether ignored by a measure that deliberately privileges couples (Auchmuty, 2004: 121–2). Some of the benefits of marriage can be contrived in alternative ways – through the making of contracts, trusts or wills, for instance – but the means are complex, expensive, and sometimes inaccessible.

These are disadvantages of the new law, but in terms of feminist silence an even more serious effect of the rights strategy has been to group lesbians with gay men. Not only does this separate us from other women in this context, leaving us divided and unsupported (for with women's campaigns numerical strength is vital), but it positions us alongside a class of men whose concerns are often very different from ours – for example, access to public sex is important to many more gay men than lesbians – and who are less likely to be concerned with issues more central to women's experience, like children and poverty.[40]

In the 1970s and 1980s, as Laura Cottingham explains, lesbian feminists tried hard to politicise gay men around gender issues, drawing their attention to, among other things:

> [t]he unequal division of labour and property between men and women, the relationship between violence and sexuality, the ethics of buying and selling people for sex, the hegemony of race in a racist society, the social configuration of male authority in political and personal life . . .
>
> (Cottingham, 1996: 9)

Then came the AIDS crisis and section 28 and, even as lesbians rallied to both causes, gay men found the perfect excuse to ignore feminism. Women's struggles seemed truly insignificant in the face of these more terrible threats. Whenever men and women are grouped together, it is men's voices – and men's interests – that prevail. 'Economically privileged gay men were especially

---

39 Gender Recognition Act 2004

40 I am not suggesting an essential gender divide here: Davina Cooper's research on the lesbian bath-houses of Toronto (forthcoming) gives the lie to any notion that *no* woman would be interested in public sex, while the idea that gay men never prioritise children is contradicted by the high-profile cases of gay male couples who have adopted. See, for instance, the delightful photograph the *Observer* chose to accompany its article 'Ban gay weddings, says Bush' (Harris, 2006), showing two gay men being married in San Francisco, each holding one of their twin daughters. I am torn between pleasure at this assumption-confounding vision and irritation that, once again, men are stealing the limelight (and getting the approbation) by presenting an entirely atypical example of gender roles, and in such a corny way: who would get married carrying a baby?

tired of hearing about issues that did not concern *them*' (Cottingham, 1996: 9) or that, as Terry Castle puts it, 'challenge[d] the moral, sexual and psychic authority of men so thoroughly' (Castle, 1993: 5).

The result was the disappearance of specifically female concerns from the 'lesbian and gay' agenda. Though for decades feminists have fought against the subsuming of women in 'man', against the masculine pronoun doing duty for the feminine,[41] and the consequent obscuring or actual elimination of women's experience, this is exactly what is happening when one speaks of 'gay' rights or 'pink' power. (You can be sure that the 'pink pound' is not a reference to *lesbian* wealth.) Even the expression 'lesbian and gay community', I would argue, with its explicit inclusion of lesbians, conjures up images of gay male culture: gay bars, drag, mardi gras.

As Terry Castle comments:

> The lesbian is never with us, it seems, but always somewhere else: in the shadows, in the margins, hidden from history, out of sight, out of mind . . . (She has seldom seemed as accessible, for instance, as her ingratiating twin brother, the male homosexual.)
>
> (Castle, 1993: 2)

Though routinely ignored, the lesbian may yet be trotted out when a particular image of the 'lesbian and gay community' is required, one that the gay man cannot easily represent, or that is needed to *counter* a less useful image associated with gay men. One of the arguments advanced in favour of civil partnerships and same-sex marriage was the beneficial *domesticating* effect that these would have on homosexual behaviour. The spectre of gay male promiscuity was clearly in people's minds here. As a result, one context in which one commonly saw representations of lesbians in the pro-reform propaganda was as a corrective to this notion, the lesbian serving as the domestic ideal, the faithful long-term partner, the good – these days! – mother (Patterson, 2000).[42] This new representation of 'lesbian', a contrast to all that had gone before – the sexual predator, the bull dyke, the nanny feminist, the sex radical – is the paradoxical beneficiary of the lesbian feminist custody battles and their insistence on the valuing of women's work and the virtues of lesbian motherhood. Tactically, she embodies the safe, boring sexual practice and the earnest, moral approach to relationships of the mythic lesbian feminist – *but where is the feminist critique?* (Boyd, 1989; Polikoff, 1992; Tasker and Golombok, 1997).

---

41 Though I was surprised and pleased to note that the Civil Partnership Act itself, unusually for British legislation, uses gender-neutral language.

42 See, for example, the photograph of a lesbian couple with their baby that accompanied Angela Mason's Director's message in the Stonewall *Newsletter* of Summer 2001 (Mason, 2001: 3).

This particular lesbian image was, I suggest, essential to the campaign, but that did not mean that Stonewall and other advocates of civil partnerships took seriously the financial concerns of lesbian mothers or lesbians generally as a poorer class, for the 'lesbian and gay community' had simultaneously to be presented as fun-loving party-goers with *lots of money* (Bowes, 2005). A rights strategy legitimises the simultaneous *inclusion* of lesbians – primarily in the domestic role – and their more general *exclusion*. The consequence for lesbians is that we cannot complain of being overlooked, yet in being confined to an image of domesticity feminists have long sought to transcend (and one typically unvalued in financial terms), while all other styles and facets of lesbian experience are suppressed, we are back where heterosexual women were 50 years ago.

Indeed, it is worse than this. The Civil Partnership Act, in meeting the demands of an articulate, wealthy group (mainly gay men with inheritance tax liabilities and pension rights to bestow on their partners), actually *penalises* the silent, poor group (those without such perks, those on benefits). The Act offers an off-the-peg union (in contrast to, for example, the French *pacte civil*) which explicitly shifts the burden from the state to the individual in a couple relationship.[43] UK law disaggregates the married couple for many legal purposes (income is separately taxed, for example), but one little-known consequence of the Civil Partnership Act is that not only will registered civil partners be treated as 'spouses' for the calculation of means-tested benefits (which include all those hidden tax credits calculated on the basis of the *couple's* income, not the individual's), but that so will *all* same-sex couples living together, whether registered or not. The reasoning behind this silent revolution is presumably that if civil partners are to be treated in the same way as married couples, then unregistered same-sex couples must accept being treated in the same way as unmarried heterosexual couples who live together – that is, that people should expect to be supported by their boyfriend or girlfriend and forgo their reliance on the state.

This saves the state money, of course. It also serves to 'domesticate' gay relationships, and it renders less affluent same-sex couples poorer still. Some may lose whole swathes of benefits and, since women as a group are generally less well-off than men, especially if they have children, lesbians will almost certainly suffer most.[44]

---

43 For a discussion of the same principle in operation in Canada, see Young and Boyd, 2006a.

44 That is not to say that the Civil Partnership Act contains no financial disadvantages for wealthier couples, though these tend to be left unspoken by the very sources that trumpet the inheritance exemption. To take one example, a couple who have two homes (as half a million Britons now do), if married or in a civil partnership, can get the capital gains tax exemption on only one of these. An unmarried or unregistered couple with two homes may get the capital gains tax exemption on both homes if each partner chooses a different home as their principal private residence.

Where are the heterosexual critics?

The feminist critique of marriage is venerable and voluminous.[45] Many feminists feel a deep-seated repugnance to an institution which has occupied a central role in feminist debate for 200 years. Even if we accept the argument that the legal reforms of the late nineteenth and early twentieth centuries succeeded in transforming the institution into an egalitarian form unrecognisable to the first-wave pioneers, we have the second-wave critiques (e.g. Comer, 1974; Bernard, 1976; Smart, 1984) and the evidence of sociologists and our own eyes to demonstrate that formal equality does not inevitably bring substantive equality with it, and that the supposedly egalitarian form of modern marriage masks a legally regulated power imbalance between the sexes. Many lesbians value their freedom from that particular form of legal tyranny, and increasing numbers of heterosexuals also choose to avoid the marriage bond. Heterosexual cohabitation has trebled over the past 30 years (Bunting, 2004) and is predicted to rise from about 2 million in 2003 to almost double that figure (3.8 million) in 2030 (Carter, 2005). While not all cohabitants do so on principle or forever, the fact that they do not marry *automatically* suggests an awareness that there might be reasons not to do so. This awareness may be unarticulated, but it is there.

What is so startling, then, is that so little of this heterosexual feminist insight into the pitfalls and perils of marriage has been translated into a critique of the virtually identical civil partnership. On 3 September 2004, for instance, Dea Birkett wrote a celebratory piece in the *Guardian* about the wedding she attended of some lesbian friends in Massachusetts (Birkett, 2004a). Just a month later, on 4 October, she signed her name to an article in the same paper representing the 'anti-'position in a debate on (heterosexual) marriage, headed 'To see this hollow institution as desirable is laughable'. 'Marriage isn't the gold standard for relationships,' declared Birkett, a long-standing feminist with a male partner and children. 'Singledom, in which someone is entirely free to leave if the relationship becomes intolerable, is surely a far more principled way to live' (Birkett, 2004b). But she had certainly not said this in her article on the lesbian wedding, which had been presented entirely from the equality angle as *a good thing* – apart from one unexpected and ironic aside that 'Equality can make you dull' (Birkett, 2004a: 7).

One obvious reason why heterosexual feminists might find it hard to criticise civil partnerships is that having to represent oneself as opposed to this particular equalising measure means appearing to align oneself with the homophobic right. In an era when easy messages and sound-bites are the

---

45 For a discussion, see Auchmuty (2004: 105; 2005: 57–8).

goal, anyone who tries to explain that she is pro-equality but opposed to same-sex marriage risks being branded as anti-gay. Silence in these circumstances is the obvious refuge.

A second reason for heterosexual reticence on civil partnerships may be because they view civil partnerships as an entirely different institution from marriage – one which avoids one of its central problems, its state-sanctioned control of women by men. But many of the feminist objections to marriage have been as much about state intervention and the consequent 'normalising' of couple relationships as about gendered power differentials. For example, 'It is the intervention of law into this arrangement that irritates most' (Fyfield, 2006). And it is clear that many heterosexuals do see marriage and civil partnership as more or less the same thing. I have heard heterosexual feminists express surprise that gays and lesbians should wish to embrace a civil partnership law which is identical with marriage but add that, if that was what the 'lesbian and gay community' wanted – and the government's extensive consultations on the bill indicated that it *was* what the 'lesbian and gay community' wanted – it was not for them to say otherwise.[46] This shows a commendable reluctance on the part of members of a dominant sexual group to speak on behalf of a subordinate group. We are all mindful of the feminist struggles of the 1970s and 1980s when black, working-class and lesbian feminists objected to the white, middle-class and heterosexual domination of the movement and their tendency to universalise women's experience on the basis of their own. In response to heterosexual feminists, however, I would ask wherein lies the difference between assuming everyone is heterosexual (which is what used to happen) and assuming all lesbians and gays share an identity of interests? Instead of being subsumed into heterosexuality, lesbians are now being subsumed into the 'lesbian and gay community', and differences *among* lesbians are erased. Either way, we are silenced; indeed, one could argue that we have *less* space to speak because the voices of gay men so often drown us out.

By abdicating judgment on civil partnerships, heterosexuals are adopting a cultural relativism that takes no account of inequalities of power within the subordinate group. One appreciates their sensitivity, but their silence on this matter – one on which many can speak from personal experience – consigns many of us to a community to whom our links are tangential, and leaves a yawning gap where the feminist view should be expressed.

In its tendency to overlook, if not deliberately suppress, female experience, the 'lesbian and gay community' is no different from other communities in a patriarchal society. We all need to be reminded that women often have more in common with each other than with the men in any shared social category, whether it be class, race, or sexuality. But the consequence for

---

46 At an ESRC seminar on 'The new family', London, 25 February 2005.

lesbian feminists is that, if the heterosexual feminists dare not speak out, for fear of treading on gay toes, then it is up to us.

But don't some lesbian feminists support civil partnerships?

The argument alluded to above – that heterosexual marriage can be distinguished from same-sex marriage or civil partnerships, on the ground that the latter does not involve the gendered power imbalance of heterosexuality – is a formidable one. It is certainly true that most of the second-wave critique of marriage was targeted at the opportunities it presents for men's exploitation of their wives: indeed, the institution of marriage was seen as *central* to women's oppression under patriarchy (Figes, 1970; Wandor, 1974). For later radical feminists, of course, it was not only marriage but heterosexuality itself that institutionalised women's oppression (Rich, 1980; Jackson, 1999; Jeffreys, 1994). For this reason, as Jeffreys later explained, 'Marriage is not on the agenda of lesbian feminists because it symbolizes and constructs women's subordination' (Jeffreys, 2003: 150). Yet this very understanding led a later group of lesbians to seek to *reclaim* marriage for lesbians and gay men, by pointing out that, since a same-sex version lacked the pernicious gendered dynamic of dominance and subordination, there could not be the same objection to it (Hunter, 1995; Calhoun, 2000). In this vision, the formal recognition of the egalitarian lesbian-feminist mode of relating offered an opportunity to reconfigure public notions of marriage as well as giving lesbian and gay couples genuine legal equality with heterosexuals. Same-sex marriage was therefore not only acceptable, but positively to be sought.

I would agree that same-sex unions offer alternative and potentially better models of relating than heterosexuality because of the absence of socially-enforced gender roles in the division of domestic tasks and the making of financial arrangements, and that this permits greater equality both within and outside the couple relationship (Auchmuty, 2003). But I doubt the transformative power of same-sex marriage (and still less civil partnerships) over heterosexual couples: as Boyd and Young remind us, 'queer families' have not necessarily 'challenged the ways in which families operate to perpetuate various hierarchies and inequalities, perhaps particularly economic hierarchies' (2003: 759). I suspect, rather, that legal recognition might actually disrupt the egalitarian ideal of many same-sex relationships.

The problem is that civil partnerships may push many same-sex couples towards a normative heterosexual mode of relating that will lead to the emergence (or re-emergence) of gendered power imbalances among gay and lesbian couples. I suggest that we shall see more and more role differentiation and enforced inequalities in same-sex couples as society imposes gender norms on us, either because that is the only way heterosexuals can conceive of a marriage-like relationship or because the couple's domestic, work and financial situation makes them impossible to avoid.

It seems clear, for instance, that more and more same-sex couples will have children in future. While this has been possible and achievable (for lesbians at least) for a good 30 years, it has never been common, and for gay men the idea is relatively new. But children are one of the *normal* attributes of marriage and so the desire to have them may become, in a sense, almost inevitable for many young gays and lesbians in a marriage-like union. Once you have children, there is an expectation (strongly encouraged by the absence of affordable alternatives) that one partner will provide the greater proportion of the childcare, and therefore spend more time in the home, with all the associated expectations about doing the housework and the concomitant loss of financial power that are the hallmarks of the heterosexual couple relationship. As one of Gillian Dunne's lesbian interviewees explained:

> Because by virtue of being home all day, it's very easy to slip into the old role models. 'You're at home all day, I am going out to work, where's my tea? Why isn't the house clean?'

> (Dunne, 1997: 190)

Evidence in the UK suggests that, up to now, lesbian couples with children have tried very hard to equalise childcare responsibilities, often in the face of serious social and workplace constraints (Dunne, 1998). But this kind of resistance may not long survive the ideological (and practical) pressures to behave more like 'normal' heterosexual couples.

Am I ascribing too much power to law to shape social relationships? I do not think so. The Civil Partnership Act was won on the basis that same-sex couples are 'just like' heterosexual couples, and therefore just as deserving of legal protection. These days some married women continue to give up paid work when they have children: this is a socially approved 'choice'. So why should civil partners not 'choose' to do the same thing? In come roles, out goes independence; there may be two women (or two men) in this relationship, but when one adopts the feminine role and the other the masculine, there may as well be a woman and a man (Jackson, 1999; Jeffreys, 2003).

I am not saying that all role differentiation is necessarily bad. Most couples share out the domestic tasks in one way or another, but one of the first and most fundamental struggles for feminists was against the kind of specialisation which was based on gender rather than aptitude or choice, and which consigned women to the least valued, least rewarded roles in society. It was not accidental that these roles were represented as those that women were best suited to (and would naturally 'choose'), nor that whatever men did was *always* more important than what women did. One could argue that there is potential for same-sex couples to confound the association of particular roles with one sex or the other, but what I fear we shall see in future will be, on the one hand, lesbian parents doubly disadvantaged with one unpaid full-time carer and one poorly-paid full-time worker and, on the other, gay male parents who are both in full-time, well-paid employment and have a nanny for their children, which their more substantial incomes will readily support. This will result in a situation where not only are undesirable inequalities introduced into the lesbian couple, but the values of the status quo are perpetuated in the wider society. Male power will continue to go unchallenged, and women will stay poor.

The long tradition of lesbian silence

Lesbian experience has been characterised by a long tradition of silence. It is strange how lives that were really lived, and lifestyles and cultures that formed domestic and social settings for thousands of women across the centuries, can have left so little mark on the world's collective history. Though more in evidence from time to time and place to place, in certain circles and in certain manifestations, lesbian life has gone largely unrecorded; and where it has been recorded, it has been quickly censored, erased, revised and re-interpreted to fit a normalising script. *It is as if it never happened.*[47]

Absent in life, the topic of lesbianism is also largely absent from law. That is not to say that lesbians have not suffered under English law, but lesbian sex was never specifically criminalised (except in the armed forces) as were sexual acts between men in the years 1885–1967. The old chestnut of Queen Victoria's refusal to accept the existence of such a vice is hardly an adequate explanation for the absence of a criminalising law.[48] But we know that some of those who opposed the attempt to include lesbians in the Criminal Law Amendment Bill 1921 argued that silence was a better policy than criminalisation. After suggesting in the House of Commons debates that lesbian perverts could be dealt with by the death penalty or the lunatic asylum, Lieutenant-Colonel Brabazon went on:

> The third way is to leave them entirely alone, not notice them, not advertise them. That is the method that has been adopted in England for many hundred years . . .[49]

In 1928, Radclyffe Hall's novel of lesbian love, *The Well of Loneliness*, was prosecuted and banned in England on grounds of obscenity. While the book is not, in the normal sense of the word, obscene, and its tendency 'to deprave

47 On silence in lesbian history, see Rich, (1980); Faderman, (1981); Duberman, Vicinus and Chauncey, (1989); Lesbian History Group, (1989); Castle, (1993); Donaghue, (1993); Oram and Turnbull, (2001).
48 By 1885 the sovereign had long since lost any genuine power of veto on legislation.
49 House of Commons Debates Vol 145 (8), Columns 1802–3.

and corrupt' (the legal definition) was grossly exaggerated, the impetus to ban it was fueled by a *Sunday Express* columnist's remark that he would 'rather give a healthy boy or a healthy girl a phial of prussic acid than this novel' (Baker, 1985: 223). In other words, he would rather kill young people than let them know lesbianism existed.

As Terry Castle explains:

> The law has traditionally ignored female homosexuality – not out of indifference, I would argue, but out of morbid paranoia. . . . [T]his seeming obliviousness should not deceive us. Behind the silence, we can often detect an anxiety too severe to allow for direct articulation.
>
> (Castle, 1993: 6)

The anxiety was about the contagious effect of a lifestyle that removed women from men's control. Radclyffe Hall's crime therefore was that she broke the silence, not simply in discussing the subject but in coming out by doing so. Hitherto a respected author, with a string of prizes and years of critical acclaim, she believed her reputation to be sufficiently established to sustain the critical attack such an action would engender and also to help to make her message palatable. She was wrong: if plenty of heterosexuals shunned her from then on, many famous lesbians of the time, too, while supportive in principle, were privately cross and probably threatened by the publication of the book (Baker, 1985: 235–6). For them the public silence surrounding lesbianism acted as a protective veil, enabling them to live a secret and, often, double life (think of respectable Vita Sackville-West, devoted wife of diplomat Harold Nicolson, lover of a dozen women or more), unsuspected and unsanctioned (Glendinning, 1983).

This is the paradox of silence. On the one hand, it cuts us off from recognition, a proud heritage, an independent culture. On the other, it allows that culture to exist, even to flourish, unmolested. Emma Healey has noted how the 'outsider' status of the lesbian brought with it 'a certain freedom':

> If we live outside society, then, very simply, we don't have to conform to society's mores to survive.
>
> (Healey, 1996: 53)

But once we become insiders, we not only lose some of the culture's special qualities and strengths, we also open ourselves up to surveillance and control, and we may be forced to 'conform to survive'.

So silence has often worked for us – since, as long as you stay in the shadows, you tend to be left alone – so it is natural for us to retreat into silence when we feel under threat. We hide away; we pretend we do not exist – or, rather, that we are just like everyone else; we draw as little attention to our relationships and personal life as possible. This was how British lesbians lived in the two decades following the second world war, more or less underground, partly by choice but partly as a result of official policy. An advice book for single women, for example, with the attractive title *Unmarried but Happy* (1947), touched briefly on same-sex attraction before the author drew back with the disclaimer:

> Books have been written about such sad cases, but I am not going to mention the titles of any, because I am convinced that such books should be read only by doctors, psychologists and moral welfare officers.
>
> (Eyles, 1947: 72)

Likewise, the Wolfenden Committee, set up to enquire into homosexual offences and prostitution, had almost nothing to say about lesbianism in its report, since lesbianism was not an offence (Great Britain, 1957).

British lesbians began to come out of their (self-)imposed silence in the late 1960s when the first lesbian social groups and newsletters were set up. Some became involved in the Campaign for Homosexual Equality and the Gay Liberation Front, but it was within the Women's Liberation Movement of the 1970s and 1980s that large numbers found a sympathetic home. These were the decades that saw so many volumes of coming-out stories we all began to tire of the genre. But they were also times of huge optimism, as we engaged in the lesbian-feminist project 'to make over our lives anew to fit into our vision of the feminist future', as Sheila Jeffreys put it (1994: xi). Lesbian fiction and film, the searching out of lesbian history, theorising around sexuality, and a great deal of political campaigning gave lesbians a public presence and a culture that was distinct from that of both heterosexual women and gay men. As we all know, however, a backlash followed the heady years of feminism. Though lesbians were never again as invisible as they had been, lesbian-feminist ideas were repudiated both from within the lesbian community and from outside it.

Section 28 of the Local Government Act 1988 was the outward and visible sign of a much broader attack on a separate women's culture. For lesbian feminists, section 28 was not solely or even primarily about sexual practice (Alderson and Wistrich, 1988). It was a response to lesbians' rejection of the patriarchal organisation of society, of a masculinity premised on the sub-ordination of women and a femininity that put men at the centre of women's lives. If, for the proponents of section 28, gay men must be silenced because they were not *real* men doing their foreordained work to sustain patriarchy, lesbians were even more dangerous, for by living without men they rejected male control in their private lives. Not only must this message not be allowed to be spread to young people, but lesbians, the very embodiment of the message, must be forced to retreat. *And we did.*

Not a single prosecution was ever brought under section 28, but its effects were far-reaching. Even if we thought ourselves to be beyond its jurisdiction, we were changed by it. We learned to live defensively. Benefiting from the gains won by the women's movement, we made our way up conventional career ladders. The better we behaved, the more we were rewarded. If our relationships were recognised, it was usually only unofficially and partially. It remained unsafe to proclaim oneself a lesbian in many workplaces, including universities (MacLeod, 2002). Notwithstanding legal changes to bring sexuality within discrimination and human rights law, the rise of religious fundamentalism did not make openness on these issues any easier.

This oppressive climate contributed to the limiting of radical knowledge that ensued. As long as they survived, feminist publishers like The Women's Press championed lesbian-feminist writing, but the anti-feminist backlash, the rise of competing political issues and the tenacity of the patriarchal version of the 'truth' all combined to restrict and suppress its production and dissemination, so much so that the next generation of young people grew up not only ignorant of lesbian and feminist history, but hostile to it.[50] Retreat into cautious silence, in such conditions, became almost an automatic reflex for feminists. In the 1990s many of us were content to let other people get on with campaigning: those with long memories knew only too well the perils of rocking the boat. Some of us concentrated on wider feminist campaigns, such as domestic violence, or on other causes, such as AIDS or peace; this had the effect of making our lesbianism seem a private, not a political, matter.

In retrospect, our silence seems more a gesture of hopelessness than of choice. If we spoke, we reasoned, no one would hear; or, if they did, our message would be co-opted and re-processed by the dominant group to suit their own agenda. Silence, in the end, is the language of the oppressed.

Conclusion

The advent of the Civil Partnership Act must make a difference. Sexualities and relationships which had once been 'private' are now 'public'. We have 'rights' that must be respected. Heterosexuals likely to come into professional contact with gays or lesbians – counselling and advice services, government and local government workers, lawyers and accountants, party organisers and shop assistants selling rings and wedding lists, hotel and restaurant staff – will have to be briefed and trained on how to deal with this new client group. It will soon be impossible for anyone to say they have never met a lesbian or gay man, a comment routinely made a decade ago.

This new public exposure is our chance to speak out. And we should. First, we need to *inform*. I would like lesbians to *know*, at least, what civil partnership really entails before they fall into the same traps that generation

---

50 This always happens, of course. My generation certainly failed to appreciate the achievements of our mothers' era. See Spender, (1983b).

after generation of married women have fallen into, and generation after generation of feminists have warned against. Knowledge does not necessarily prevent foolish decisions but it is certainly a better protection than ignorance and error. And I would like heterosexuals to have more sense of how lesbians live and of the differences between and among heterosexual and same-sex relationships. (Enough has been said about the *similarities* in the campaigns for recognition.)

The second reason we must speak out is to provide a critique. At the moment it seems as if only one voice is speaking for the 'lesbian and gay community' in the UK, and that voice has embraced civil partnerships uncritically. We must represent the views of those who, by choice or fate, 'live their lives in different and non-conformist ways [and who are not or] do not want to be the "conventional" couple that the law tries to make them be,' as Boyd and Young put it (2003:786). By naming what we perceive to be the drawbacks of the civil partnership model we have been given, and pointing out the possibility of better alternatives both in existence and for which we could campaign, we may help people to make an informed choice.

The Civil Partnership Act offers us an opportunity we would be foolish to ignore. Stripped of the protective veil of anonymity, and presented with a choice we never had to make before (well, are *you* going to register??), we can no longer stay silent. Otherwise, decisions will continue to be made according to preconceived ideas about what 'lesbians and gays' are like, or based on a heterosexual model which may not be appropriate, or in response to the loudest – generally male – voice. Once made, these decisions may well be self-perpetuating: marriage will be shored up rather than re-modelled on more egalitarian lines; same-sex couples will become increasingly indistinguishable from heterosexual couples; and those radical alternatives envisaged by lesbian and heterosexual feminists alike will be lost to sight.

Postscript

I began writing this chapter before the Civil Partnership Act came into force. As the months passed and the invitations to friends' partnership ceremonies rolled in, I felt more and more depressed at the evident lack of feminist caution. But early take-up figures have proved reassuring – first, because the numbers are not so great as to offer much of a boost to the marriage model, and second, because a clear gender difference is emerging, with twice as many gay men as lesbians registering their partnerships (McKie, 2005; Curtis, 2006b). This result surprised many people, and was ignored by others. But I think it is very telling. While recognising that such a statistic can be interpreted in a variety of ways, I suggest that one possibility is that lesbians recognise that a marriage-like institution has little to offer women, and that their relationships would not be enhanced by legal regulation. Perhaps the feminist message was not, after all, lost in those silent decades.

Bibliography

Alderson, L and Wistrich, H (1988) 'Clause 29 [*sic*]: Radical Feminist Perspectives', *Trouble & Strife* 13, pp 3–8.

Auchmuty, R (2003) 'When Equality is not Equity: Homosexual Inclusion in Undue Influence Law', *Feminist Legal Studies* 11, pp 163–90.

Auchmuty, R (2004) 'Same-sex Marriage Revived: Feminist Critique and Legal Strategy,' *Feminism & Psychology* 14, pp 101–26.

Auchmuty, R (2005) 'The Rhetoric of Equality and the Problem of Heterosexuality', in Mulcahy, L and Wheeler, S (eds) *Feminist Perspectives on Contract Law*, London: Cavendish Publishing, pp 51–74.

Baker, M (1985) *Our Three Selves: A Life of Radclyffe Hall*, London: GMP Publishers.

Barker, N (2004) 'For Better or For Worse? The Civil Partnership Bill [HL] 2004', *Journal of Social Welfare and Family Law* 26, pp 313–24.

Barker, N (2006) 'Sex and the Civil Partnership Act: the Future of (Non) Conjugality', *Feminist Legal Studies* 14, pp 241–59.

Barrett, M and McIntosh, M (1982) *The Anti-Social Family*, London: Verso.

Behr, R (2005) 'Why will I wed? It's love, actually', *Observer*, 13 March 2005.

Bennett, C (2005) 'Counsellors and divorce lawyers, rejoice – a long queue of new and wealthy victims is heading your way', *Guardian G2*, 22 December 2005, p 7.

Bernard, J (1976) *The Future of Marriage*, Harmondsworth: Penguin.

Birkett, D (2004a) 'My best friend's gay wedding', *Guardian Women*, 3 September 2004, pp 6–7.

Birkett, D (2004b) 'To see this hollow institution as desirable is laughable', *Guardian Women*, 4 October 2004, p 11.

Bowes, G (2005) 'The pink honeymoon', *Observer Escape*, 4 December 2005, p 5.

Boyd, S B (1989) 'What is a "Normal" Family? *C v C (A Minor)*', *Modern Law Review* 55, pp 269–78.

Boyd, S B and Young, C F L (2003) ' "From Same-sex to No Sex"?: Trends towards recognition of (same-sex) relationships in Canada', *Seattle Journal for Social Justice* 1, pp 757–93.

Bunting, M (2004) 'Family Fortunes', *Guardian Supplement: Life in 2020*, 25 September 2004, pp 4–7.

Burns, T (2006) 'It takes more than two people to make a marriage', *Guardian*, 31 August 2006.

Calhoun, C (2000) *Feminism, the Family, and the Politics of the Closet: Lesbian and Gay Displacement*, Oxford: Oxford University Press.

Campbell, D (2005) '3.6m people in Britain are gay – official', *Observer*, 11 December 2005.

Carter, H (2005) 'Marriage rate to decline', *Guardian*, 11 March 2005.

Carter, H and Glendinning (2004) 'Verdict: It is about being accepted in society', *Guardian*, 13 October 2004.

Castle, T (1993) *The Apparitional Lesbian: Female Homosexuality and Modern Culture*, New York: Columbia University Press.

Chrisafis, A (2005) 'Champagne, pedicures, and a place in history for the Belfast brides', *Guardian*, 19 December 2005.

Collinson, P (2006) 'Inheritance tax should be raised not scrapped', *Guardian Money*, 26 August 2006, p 4.

Comer, I (1974) *Wedlocked Women*, Leeds: Feminist books.

Coppock, V, Haydon, D, and Richter, I (1995) *The Illusions of 'Post-Feminism': New Women, Old Myths*, London: Taylor & Francis.

Cottingham, L (1996) *lesbians are so chic*, London: Cassell.

Curtis, P (2006a) 'Gay men earn £10k more than national average', *Guardian*, 23 January 2006.

Curtis, P (2006b) 'Twice as many men as women start civil partnerships', *Guardian*, 23 February 2006.

Davies, E (1999) 'The marriage debate', *Stonewall Newsletter*, July 1999, p 12.

Donoghue, E (1993) *Passions between Women: British lesbian culture 1668–1801*, London: Scarlet Press.

Duberman, M B, Vicinus, M, and Chauncey, G (1989) *Hidden from History: Reclaiming the Gay and Lesbian Past*, London: Penguin.

Dunne, G (1997) *Lesbian Lifestyles: Women's Work and the Politics of Sexuality*, Basingstoke: Macmillan.

Dunne, G (1998) *Living Difference: Lesbian Perspectives on Work and Family Life*, Binghamton, New York: Haworth Press.

Dworkin, A (1982) 'Renouncing Sexual "Equality" ', in *Our Blood*, London: The Women's Press, pp 10–14.

Dyer, C (2005) 'Thousands prepare to tie the knot', *Guardian*, 5 December 2005.

Ettelbrick, P (1997) 'Since when is marriage a path to liberation?' in Baird, R and Rosenbaum, S (eds) *Same-sex Marriage: the Moral and Legal Debate*, Amherst, New York: Prometheus books, pp 164–8.

Eyles, L (1947) *Unmarried but Happy*, London: Gollancz.

Faderman, L (1981) *Surpassing the Love of Men: Romantic friendship and love between women from the Renaissance to the present*, London: Junction books.

Figes, E (1970) *Patriarchal Attitudes: Women in Society*, London: Faber.

Friedman, S and Sarah, E (eds) (1982) *On the Problem of Men*, London: The Women's Press.

Fyfield, F (2006) 'It's all about respect', *Guardian*, 28 August 2006.

Glendinning, V (1983) *Vita: The life of Vita Sackville-West*, Harmondsworth: Penguin.

Great Britain, Committee on Homosexual Offences and Prostitution (1957) *Report*, London: HMSO.

Hall, R (1928) *The Well of Loneliness*, London: Cape.

Hamilton, C (1909) *Marriage as a Trade*, London: Chapman and Hall.

Hanman, N (2006) 'Partnership of equals', *Guardian*, 1 June 2006.

Harris, P (2006) 'Ban gay weddings, says Bush', *Observer*, 4 June 2006.

Healey, E (1996) *Lesbian Sex Wars*, London: Virago.

Herman, D (1990) 'Are We Family? Lesbian rights and women's liberation', *Osgoode Hall Law Journal* 28, pp 789–815.

Herman, D (1997) *The Antigay Agenda: Orthodox Vision and the Christian Right*, Chicago: University of Chicago Press.

Hibbs, M, Barton, C and Beswick, J (2001) 'Why Marry? – Perceptions of the Affianced', *Family Law*, March, pp 197–207.

Hunter, N D (1995) 'Marriage, Law and Gender: a Feminist Inquiry', in Duggan, L and Hunter, N D (eds) *Sex Wars Sexual Dissent and Political Culture*, New York and London: Routledge, pp 107–22.

Jackson, S (1999) *Heterosexuality in Question*, London: Sage.

Jeffreys, S (1994) *The Lesbian Heresy: a feminist perspective on the lesbian sexual revolution*, London: The Women's Press.

Jeffreys, S (2003) *Unpacking Queer Politics*, London: Polity.

Jones, R (2005) 'Civil partnership law to hurt some same-sex couples', *Guardian Money*, 3 December 2005, p 8.

Jones, R and Collinson, P (2005) 'Another step forward for same-sex couples', *Guardian Money*, 2 July 2005, p 2.

Karpf, A (2005) 'What do you call your step-grandson's ex?', *Guardian Family*, 17 December 2005, p 2.

Kitzinger, C (1987) *The Social Construction of Lesbianism*, London: Sage.

Law Gazette (2005) 'Gay lawyers wooed by civil partnerships', press release, 1 December 2005, www.lawgazette.co.uk/news/breaking/.

Lesbian History Group (1989) *Not a Passing Phase: Reclaiming Lesbians in History 1840–1985*, London: The Women's Press.

Levine, P (1987) *Victorian Feminism 1850–1900*, London: Hutchinson.

Liberty (2005) 'Couple Challenge UK Stance on Gay Marriage', press release, London, 11 August 2005.

McColgan, A (2000) *Women Under the Law: The false promise of human rights*, Harlow: Pearson.

McKie, D (2005) 'Don't forget the flat-nosed', *Guardian*, 22 December 2005, p 28.

MacKinnon, C (1987) *Feminism Unmodified: Discourses on Life and Law*, Cambridge, Mass: Harvard University Press.

McLean, G (2005) 'And So to Wed', *Guardian Weekend*, 19 December 2005, pp 32–41.

MacLeod, D (2002) 'I live a lie every day', *Guardian Education*, 26 March 2002, pp 10–11.

Mason, A (2001) 'All "Out" for partnership rights – we are family', *Stonewall Newsletter*, summer 2001, p 3.

Mitchell, J and Oakley, A (eds) (1986) *What is feminism?* Oxford: Basil Blackwell.

Odone, C (2006) 'Reader, I married him. And here's why', *Observer*, 4 June 2006.

Oram, A and Turnbull, A (2001) *The Lesbian History Sourcebook: love and sex between women in Britain from 1980 to 1970*, London: Routledge.

Papworth, J (2005) 'Same-sex couples who are learning a harsh lesson', *Guardian Money*, 26 November 2005, p 4.

Pateman, C (1988) *The Sexual Contract*, London: Polity.

Patterson, C J (2000) 'Family Relationships of Lesbians and Gay Men', *Journal of Marriage and the Family* 62, pp 1052–69.

Perkin, J (1989) *Women and Marriage in 19th-Century England*, London: Routledge.

Polikoff, N (1992) 'Lesbian Mothers, Lesbian Families: Legal Obstacles, Legal Challenges', in Maggiore, D (ed.) *Lesbians and Child Custody: A Casebook*, New York: Garland.

Probert, R (2005) 'Same-sex Couples and the Marriage Model', *Feminist Legal Studies* 13, pp 135–43.

Rich, A (1980) *Compulsory Heterosexuality and Lesbian Existence*, London: Onlywomen.

Robins, J (2005) 'Partners, but not for pensions', *Observer Cash*, 11 December 2005, p 13.

Rowan, A (2004) 'To have and to hold?' *Guardian*, 4 October 2004, p 10.

Russell, J (2005) 'The love business', *Guardian G2*, 25 January 2005, pp 6–8.

Scott, M (2005a) 'Marriage rights without the rites', *Observer Cash*, 3 July 2005, p 1.

Scott, M (2005b) 'Same-sex relationships: the law falls in line at last', *Observer Cash*, 25 September 2005, pp 2–3.

Scott, M (2005c) 'Gay wedding bells a wake-up call for all partners', *Observer Cash*, 4 December 2005, pp 8–9.

Smart, C (1984) *The Ties That Bind: Law, marriage and the reproduction of patriarchal relations*, London: Routledge and Kegan Paul.

Smith, B L (1854) 'A Brief Summary, in Plain Language, of the Most Important Laws Concerning Women', in Lacey, C A (ed.) *Barbara Leigh Smith Bodichon and the Langham Place Group*, London: Routledge and Kegan Paul, 1987, pp 23–35.

Social Trends 2005, www.statistics.gov.uk/cci/nugget.asp?id+1044, accessed 20 September 2006.

Spencer, M (2005) 'Race is on for pink wedding pound', *Guardian*, 5 December 2005.

Spender, D (ed.) (1983a) *Feminist Theorists: three centuries of women's intellectual tradition*, London: The Women's Press.

Spender, D (1983b) *There's Always Been a Women's Movement This Century*, London: Pandora Press.

Stonewall (2003) *Friends* [magazine], Winter.

Stonewall (2005a) 'Frequently asked questions'. www.stonewall.org.uk/information-_bank/partnership/civil_partnershipact/152, accessed 14 September 2005.

Stonewall (2005b) *Get Hitched! A Guide to Civil Partnerships*.

Strachey, R (1928) *The Cause: A short history of the women's movement in Great Britain*, London: Virago reprint, 1978.

Summerskill, B (2005) 'Remember! Remember! The 5th of December', *Stonewall Friends*, Winter, p 4.

Tasker, F L and Golombok, S (1997) *Growing Up in a Lesbian Family: Effects on Child Development*, New York: The Guildford Press.

Tatchell, P (2005) 'Let's get sex out of the equation', *Observer Cash*, 6 January 2005 p 11.

Taylor, D (2005) 'It Often Pays to Wait', *Guardian*, 9 September 2005.

Turner, L (2005) 'Sing if you're glad to be recognised by the law', *Guardian Education*, 13 December 2005, p 7.

Vernon, M (2005) 'Coming Out as Friends: civil partnership is about more than erotic love, and gays could help to change society', *Guardian*, 28 October 2005.

Wandor, M (1974) 'The Conditions of Illusion', in Allen, S, Sanders, L and Wallis, J (eds) *Conditions of Illusion*, Leeds: Feminist Books, pp 186–207.

Women and Equality Unit (2005) 'Civil Partnership Act 2004 – Frequently Asked Questions', www.womenandequalityunit.gov.uk/lgbt/faq.htm, accessed 13 September 2005.

Young, C F L and Boyd, S B (2006a) 'Challenging Heteronormativity? Reaction and resistance to the legal recognition of same sex partnerships', in Chunn, D, Boyd, S and Lessard, H (eds) *Feminism, Law, and Social Change: (re)action and resistance*, forthcoming.

Young, C F L and Boyd, S B (2006b) 'Losing the Feminist Voice? Debates on the Legal Recognition of Same Sex Relationships in Canada', *Feminist Legal Studies* 14, pp 213–40.

Chapter 6

Transgender

Destabilising feminisms?

Surya Monro, Leeds Metropolitan University

> Feminist legal theorists, despite differences in schools of thought, are uni-
> fied in their basic belief that society is patriarchal – shaped and dominated
> by men. Feminist jurisprudence, then, provides an analysis and critique
> of women's position in patriarchal society and examines the nature and
> extent of women's subordination.
>
> (Kelly Weisberg, 1996: xviii)

There has been a persistent tendency amongst feminist legal theorists to
assume a discrete female/male system of categorisation (see Olsen, 1995;
Weisberg, 1996; and Barnett, 1998). In the 1990s, complex, pluralist
approaches to legal feminism were developed, alongside a movement to reject
grand theory (Richardson and Sandland, 2000: 2). Postmodernist approaches
to feminist jurisprudence provide a sophisticated account of gender, decon-
structing the notion of 'woman', and exploring the political difficulties that
this entails (Barnett, 1998: 196–7). However, whilst there has been considerable debate about the definitions of 'woman' and 'gender', discussions have
generally overlooked those subjects who identify as gender fluid or diverse,
thus reinforcing notions of gender binaries.[1] Intersex and transgender (trans)
subjects remain marginalised, and the implications that they raise for feminist
legal theory continue to be overlooked. This may perhaps relate to the broader
tendency within feminisms to police transgender and thus reinscribe gender
binaries, an issue that is addressed in this chapter.

This chapter aims to explore the challenges that trans and intersex pose to
feminisms by developing and critiquing gender pluralist theories. Gender
pluralism involves conceptualising gender as more than a male/female binaried system – as well as including women and men, it encompasses people who
identify as an intersex, third, fourth, or other genders, people who experience

---

1   One exception in the jurisdicial literature is Sharpe's (2002) incisive account of the ways in
    which trans destabilises heterosexist legal discourse.

multiple genders, people who move between genders, people who are not sure what their gender is, and people who choose to identify as 'other than male or female', or as non-gendered. Gender pluralist theories draw on post-structuralist feminisms, addressing gender change and multiplicity whilst allowing for aims concerning equality to be pursued. However, there is a difficulty with gender pluralist stances, in that they could support a universalist, 'one size fits all', approach to gender politics, where, because everyone is seen as equal, the specificity of different people's experiences and their positions in society are masked. This approach would, because inequalities remain unseen and unchallenged, reinforce structural inequalities (the forces that shape social hierarchies, often in hidden and assumed ways). Tensions between the universalism of 'rainbow alliance'[2] approaches to lesbian, gay, bisexual and transgender (LGBT) politics, and more particularist or separatist positions (which focus on the specificities of the experiences of different groups), mirror this dynamic. Overall, this chapter addresses two related debates regarding gender diversity and theory: (a) the relationship between 'difference' or particularist approaches to gender, and 'equality' or universalist positions, and (b) the tension between 'feminist', as opposed to 'gender' approaches.[3]

The chapter will begin with a brief methodological note. It will then describe the ways in which trans blows apart gender binaried – and the related sexual orientation binaried – identity categorisations which have formed the (albeit disputed) lynchpin of much feminist thinking. The chapter then outlines and examines gender pluralist alternatives, which draw on, but perhaps supersede, feminisms. The chapter explores gender pluralist theories in relation to universalist/particularist debates, before looking at how these debates play out via the prism of LGBT community politics. The chapter concludes with some brief comments regarding the 'feminist' versus 'gender' debate.

It is important to point out that some authors conceptualise gender as being determined by processes concerning sexual orientation, others see sexuality as resulting from gender, whilst still others see gender and sexuality as being interwoven, so that gender identities are shaped by our sexual orientation and vice versa (see Richardson, 2000). I adopt the latter stance. Also, whilst I provide a critique of radical feminist approaches to transgender, it is important to note that other feminist interpretations[4] have been developed, including the work of Califia (1997) and Hird (2002). Furthermore, whilst my focus is on gender, I would like to emphasise the importance of other structuring factors such as 'race' (see for example McClinton, 1995; Harper et al., 1997).

---

2   Rainbow alliances involve alliances across different identities, and a recognition of equality, but also of difference.
3   My focus is primarily on debates regarding universalism and particularism.
4   Or interpretations that draw on feminisms.

Lastly I would like to point out that this chapter focuses not specifically on feminist jurisprudence, but rather on feminist theory as a whole.[5]

My data has been drawn from four main studies. Firstly, I utilise an in depth exploration of trans politics, which I conducted during the 1990s. This included transsexuals, intersex people, cross-dressers, drag kings and queens and others. Secondly, I have used material from a large ESRC-funded study of lesbian and gay equalities work in local government (this included bisexuals and trans people to an extent) which took place in 2000–03.[6] Thirdly, I have included data from a small study of gender and sexual diversity in India, which I conducted in 2003. Lastly, I interviewed a number of bisexual, lesbian and gay, and trans people during 2003, as a way of updating the earlier study on transgender. In keeping with the usual norms (see Kirsch, 2000), I shall identify myself at this stage as a female-bodied bisexual, who does not identify as trans in any substantial way at present, but who has explored some trans identities in the past. I have identified the people who took part in the research projects as research contributors, and their contributions can be distinguished from the literature by the absence of dates in the text. They are quoted by name unless a preference for anonymity was expressed. The projects that contributors took part in are identified in some cases by the following: Transgender Politics (a); Lesbian and Gay Equality in Local Government (b); Gender and Sexual Diversity in India (c), and LGBT research (d).

The troubling of gender categorisation

Trans and intersex provide a fundamental ontological challenge to the gender binaried system to which feminists refer. The majority of trans people and cross-dressers exist within a gender binary system, identifying as either male or female, and some of these reinforce gender stereotypes and gender binaries via their identities and forms of presentation.[7] However, there is a range of other people who identify in gender diverse ways. I shall describe these forms of gender diversity here. Intersex is perhaps the most profoundly disruptive identity. It provokes a questioning of the gender binary system on two levels – physical, as the various conditions subsumed under the umbrella term of intersex involve physiological characteristics (for example,

---

5 I would also like to note that dealing with intersectionality and with the cross-cultural variations in gender and sexual categorisation is outside of the scope of this chapter. Interested readers can refer to Bullough and Bullough (1993), Herdt (1994), Feinberg (1996), Ramet (1997), and Prieur (1998).

6 Reference number R29005538. I would like to acknowledge the contributions of Davina Cooper and Jean Carabine to the project.

7 Via, for example, cosmetic surgery, choice of dress and make-up – of course, non-trans people also reinforce gender binaries via such means.

chromosomal, hormonal and gonadal) which are other than (or a mixture of) those conventionally associated with males and females; and identity, as research contributions showed that in some cases intersex people wish to have an identity that is other, or in addition to, male or female (projects (a) and (d)). Non-gendered, 'third space' (see Nataf, 1996), multiply gendered (sometimes called 'gender plural'), androgynous and multi-gendered people may also destabilise the discrete gender binaried system.

Some of the research contributors (projects (a) and (d)) identified as other than male or female. For example, Simon Dessloch, an FTM trans person,[8] said that he felt himself to be in-between, or neither, or both, or third sex. Similarly, Christie Elan Cane, who started life as female, said in 1998:

> I don't feel male or female, and I say that I'm basically third gender because I can't identify as male or female . . . I mean I'm still trying to unravel how I wanted to be, I wondered whether maybe I could be part of both, which is not how I feel any longer but I sort of went through several stages along, trying to express and figure out how I felt, but now I feel I'm neither. I can't relate to male and female.

Gender fluidity may also destabilise gender binaries. For example, contributor Zach Nataf described the way that, during the early stages of his transition from female to male, he felt more like a man on some days and more transgendered on others, and that this depended to an extent on who he was with (see also Bornstein, 1994). Butch dyke Hamish described gender fluidity as a state in itself, whilst gender transient Phaedra Kelly said:

> It's about a discipline of duality with an open mind, without changing sex with hormones, with pills, with injections or surgery, living one's dualism as much as possible. If I am Phaedra, I allow elements of Bruce through, and there is no self hating or loathing going on. If I am Bruce, I allow elements of Phaedra – it's horses for courses, but like the transvestite, and to some degree the trans person living full time, I live with a separate identity. I have accepted my separate identity as well.

Transsexuality can in some cases be seen as a space beyond gender binarisms. Cameron (1996) frames transsexuality as an in-between place outside of gender duality, while Stone argues that 'a trans person currently occupies a position which is nowhere, which is outside of the binaried oppositions of gendered discourse' (1991: 295). This was mirrored by some contributors, for example, Christie Elan Cane discussed moving beyond the gender

---

8   Someone who started life as biologically female but who identifies as male; often FTM transsexuals have surgery and hormone treatment to support their male identity.

system and being non-gendered. 'Gender fuck' also disrupts gender binaries. 'Gender fuck' refers to conflicting sex/gender signals; in some cases these are consciously taken on as part of identity (see Halberstam, 2002). Kate N' Ha Ysabet explained that:

> . . . if I have a penis and big tits that's gender fuck, if I wore makeup and butch clothing that's gender fuck. And what's quite interesting is that androgyny is acceptable because there's a reason for that, but gender fuck isn't, because people go 'oh, OK' but with gender fuck its this thing of 'shit, I'm getting two sets of signals' and it feels like you're having a drum and bass mix on one side and classical music on the other and you're going 'Oh my God which am I going to listen to?'

The troubling of sexual orientation categorisation

The multiplicity and fluidity demonstrated by some forms of intersex and trans destabilises gender binaries in a way which is profoundly relevant to sexual orientation categories. The sexual orientation categories that are used in the West – lesbian and gay, heterosexual, and bisexual – are based on the gender binary system. In other words, being heterosexual means being attracted to people of the opposite sex, whereas being lesbian or gay entails same sex attraction, and bisexuality involves attraction to both males and females. Gay, lesbian, and heterosexual sexualities rely on the notion that people are only attracted to people of one sex (this can also be termed 'mono-sexual'), that there are only two sexes and genders, and that people can be identified as clearly falling within one of them. The term 'bisexuality' also implies two sexes and genders, although it may provide more space for fluidity:

> . . . it depends partly on which strand of bisexuality you're talking about. Some bi people are coming simply from the 'I like men, and I like women'. On the other hand, some people who consider themselves part of the bi community have gone a lot further to rejecting the significance of gender. Some bi people don't think the gender of the person they're with is important at all, and are therefore equally happy with people of other genders than men and women.
>
> (Jennifer Moore)

Our system of sexual orientation categorisation is problematised by gender diversity (see Rothblatt, 1995) physically, in terms of sexual expression, and socially, in terms of identity. Whilst the majority of people can relate to notions of same-sex or opposite-sex attraction, the categories of LGB (lesbian, gay, and bisexual) and heterosexual are insufficient in describing, for example, attraction between an androgyne and someone who identifies as gender transient. Sexual orientation categories based on the gender binary system are disrupted by physical gender diversity. The genitals of some gender diverse people are physiologically 'other' than those usually associated with women and men (although, of course, they may identify as male or female). For example, at the 1998 Transgender Film Festival, Del LaGrace Volcano (an initially female bodied person who took testosterone) displayed photographs of his and other people's phalloclits, which resemble small penises enwreathed in labial lips. Sex between people with non-standard genitals is unlikely to fit heterosexual, gay, or lesbian sexual norms. As FTM trans person James Green told me: 'First of all I never had sex as a woman, and I will never have sex as a man. You know, I will always in that sense be other. And I cannot pretend that I'm not a transgender male.'

What alternatives are there to sexual orientation binaries? Sexual orientation can be constructed in non-binary forms. For example, Queen and Schimel (1997) discuss the notion of 'omnisexual' (attracted to multiple genders), and the term 'pansexual' was coined by Firestone (1970) to mean diverse, unbounded desire. Other alternatives include for instance 'trannie lover'. These terms are not widely used, even in the sexual fringes where people are conversant with sexual orientation fluidity. Individuals and groups continue on the whole to use existing definitions, even when they do not fit very well. For example, Annie Cox, a MTF trans person defined herself as a 'woman who loved woman' although she has a penis, whilst Rosario (1996) describes a study of the partners of gay FTM trans people who were happy with their partners having vaginas, despite identifying as gay. These issues also apply to the category of bisexual:

> John: some bisexuals are aware of the way in which gender diversity problematises the category of bisexual . . . I am careful to say I am attracted to more than one gender. We need strategically to use 'bisexual' as it's known – I am uncomfortable with pansexual and omnisexual. Bisexual is sufficient to freak people out, if we go further, it is even more alienating than with bisexuality.

> Interviewer: You don't see 'bisexual' as binaried?

> John: No – I am uncomfortable about the 'bi' aspect and the 'sexuality' aspect – I want an equivalent to 'lesbian or 'gay [in which lifestyle and political aspects are acknowledged].

> Inteviewer: What are the implications of this for third or intersex people?

> John: There's an option of being monosexual – you could only be attracted to one type . . . I think sexual identity comes from gender identity, and if you identify as male or female you can slot into gay and lesbian categories, it's much easier.

Overlap of categories can occur when people move through a number of different spaces or identities. For example contributor Kate More said 'The only space I don't occupy, I think, is bisexual. And yet, in every way taking gay, lesbian, straight, whatever into consideration, taking all three roles, that would make me bisexual I suppose.' This kind of statement problematises assumptions underpinning mainstream forms of sexual orientation category, where a single sexual identity that is taken over a period of months or years, is assumed.

Overall, gender and sexual orientation binaries can be disrupted by transgender and intersex in a number of ways.[9] The binary based categories of female and male, lesbian, gay, heterosexual and bisexual cannot therefore be seen as discrete or as the only forms of categorisation that are possible.

Feminisms and gender diversity

How have feminists dealt with the troubling of gender and sexual orientation categories that trans and intersex provoke? Transgender has been a divisive and volatile issue for the feminist movement (see Whittle, 1998), with disputes concerning the presence of transsexual women in women only space taking place since the 1970s. Feminist debates about transgender have centred around the work of (mostly radical) feminists, especially Raymond (1980; 1994), Daly (1984), and Jeffreys (1996),[10] although, as noted above, other feminist analysis has also been developed (see for example Feinberg, 1996; Califia, 1997; Hird, 2002). Jeffreys, Daly and also Greer (1999) broadly follow the work of Raymond, who argued that transsexuals who identify as women are really men, and that transsexuality is a patriarchal means of reinforcing gender stereotypes (1980). Raymond saw MTF transsexuals as deceptively invading women's space, minds and emotions. She stated that 'All transsexuals rape women's bodies by reducing the real female form to an artefact, and appropriating this body for themselves' (1980: 104), and that 'The transsexually constructed lesbian-feminist feeds off woman's true energy source, ie her woman-identified self. It is he [*sic*] who recognises that if female spirit, mind, creativity and sexuality exist anywhere in a powerful way it is here, among lesbian-feminists' (1980: 108). Raymond argues that lesbian feminists who accept transsexual women are 'guilty of mutilating their own reality' (1980: 119). Overall, her position can best be summarised by this quote: 'I contend that the problem with transsexualism would best be served by morally mandating it out of existence' (via legal limitations on changing sex) (1980: 178). Raymond has continued to argue that transgender people reinforce, rather than challenge gender norms, although she does provide

9 Although trans and intersex people do not always disrupt gender binaries and sometimes their identities can reinforce the gender binary system, as noted elsewhere.
10 See also Heilbrun (1998).

some suggestion of recognition that trans may not simply be an evil patriarchal tool, in her statement that 'A real sexual politics says yes to a view and a reality of transgender that instead of conforming to gender, really transforms it' (1994: 632).

The radical feminist stance on trans has had a profound and damaging impact on relations between trans people and the feminist movement. Since the feminist debates of the 1970s, typified by Raymond's position on transsexuality, transsexual women have experienced a very considerable amount of exclusion from the lesbian and feminist communities. This has included, for instance, female transsexual employees in women's organisations being forced to resign, transsexual women who have been raped being refused support by Rape Crisis Centres, and Women's Centres excluding them (Monro, 2000). The trans people who took part in the study on transgender politics were unanimous in their rejection of the radical feminist position, which was seen as victim blaming, abusive, erasing of trans people's agency, and limited, given the many gender positions that trans people occupy. The only caveat was provided by one transsexual commentator, who suggested that Raymond's (1980) critique of the gender stereotyping that took place in the medical establishment was an important catalyst for change.

Raymond's work (1980; 1994) is flawed in a number of ways. Methodologically, her research can be seen as unethical because she deceived her subjects when gaining access by failing to let them know she had an antitranssexual agenda (Califia, 1997) and misrepresented them, for example by denying their experience of being female by referring to them as male. This goes against feminist methodological guidelines such as honesty and empowerment of participants (Reinharz, 1992). Raymond's notions of transsexuals invading and taking over women's space are largely unfounded. As one contributor said, her thinking is irrational – transsexuals have not been known to rape women, and the use of rape as a metaphor is insulting to rape victims and denies the extent to which transsexuals are at risk of sexual abuse. Raymond's account is problematic in other ways; theoretically and in terms of political strategy. She shifts between biologist and constructionist accounts of gender,[11] arguing that transsexual women are unequal to genetic women because they are born male, and, together with other feminists such as Greer

---

11 Biological, or nature, approaches to gender frame sex and gender as being determined by physiology, chromosomes and hormones – and there is a tendency for men and women to be seen as inevitably different and as being suited to different occupations and social roles because of these differences. Such approaches are termed 'biologically essentialist' because they conceptualise the essence of sex and gender as being determined by biology. Constructionist, or nurture, accounts envisage biological sex as playing a small part (or no role at all, in strong constructionist accounts) in the way that people are gendered – most of the differences between women and men are seen as being due to the way that people are brought up, and the social and cultural forces that influence people to take certain roles.

(1999), uses biological factors in her pronouncements on transgender people (for example, transsexual women can never be 'real' women because they were born as boys). A biological stance is, in itself, untenable because there are wide chromosomal and hormonal variations in sex in the general population (Rothblatt, 1994). Raymond's constructionist account is also problematic: she sees transsexual women avoiding experience of patriarchy because they are brought up as male. Whilst this rings true to a degree, many transsexual women experienced themselves to be female early in their lives, and have acted accordingly, only to be sanctioned by the gender normative system. In addition, transsexual women experience sexism in the same ways that other women do. The idea that transsexual women cannot construct themselves as female supports gender determinism – the idea that people cannot change their gender identity – and is politically regressive because it could also imply that it is impossible for men and women to change traditional, sexist roles and beliefs.

It appears that the issue at the root of the radical feminist attack on trans is the perceived threat that transgender poses to radical feminism. As I demonstrated above, trans scrambles gender binaries, because trans people cross genders, or exist between or outside of female/male categories. The difficulties that this raises has led to gender inconsistency being suppressed (More, 1996). Several of the trans contributors suggested that the reasons for Raymond and other feminist's attacks on transsexuality were due to their own self-interest. For example:

> I think for me it was about the power of a small group of, you know, privileged white feminists who wanted to make the definitions about who was in and who was out and who was right and who was wrong, and, you know, build a power base of their own and the book [*The Transsexual Empire*] was part of that.
>
> (Zach Nataf)

> It's about other people creating their own empires especially the Janice Raymonds of this world . . . over and over again, whether it's the level of very local politics. Like who should be allowed into Women's night at Paradise [club], who should sit on the Police, you know the gay and lesbian police committee . . .
>
> (Stephen Whittle)

Why has the radical, separatist stance on transgender had such purchase on the feminist, lesbian and trans communities? It is partly because of the historical context in which it was developed; a women's community that was formed in reaction to women's experiences of male domination and oppression and that perceived itself to be embattled. Non-trans women's fears, grounded in the realities of women's inequality, became manifest via

the scapegoating of gender minorities. This was possible because the fundamental aspects of radical and separatist feminisms meant that people who
transgressed gender binaries were ontologically incomprehensible: they did
not fit within a gender binaried world view. Perhaps the impact that these
types of stance had is also linked to the way in which they diametrically
opposed the dominant medical construction of transsexuality. There was a
lack of a middle ground, where the progressive part of Raymond's work (the
critique of a homophobic, sexist, gender binaried medical establishment)
could be utilised, but the transphobic part rejected. This has been com-
pounded by the lack of feminist discourse that is supportive of trans people
(including transsexuals), with the exception of trans authors, for example
Feinberg (1996) and Califia (1997),[12] as well as others such as Hird (2002).

Trans identities and politics highlight the way in which feminist aims
concerning the dismantling of the gender system remain unmet by the
radical feminist stance on gender.[13] Ironically, a focus on distinctions between
women and men may act to reinforce the gender binary system, if this is
adhered to long term rather than being used as a temporary, limited, strategy.
Questions concerning strategies in which the interests of one group (in this
case women) are foregrounded, risking the erasure of others, are central to
the universalist/particularist debate. I shall explore this debate below, after
outlining alternatives to the radical feminist approach to trans and intersex.

Gender pluralisms

The problematisation of gender and sexual orientation binaries provokes an
evaluation of gender theories, including feminisms, masculinity studies, and
poststructuralist and queer approaches. These approaches seem to be limited
when dealing with trans and intersex (see Monro, 2005), leading into an
exploration of conceptual alternatives to the gender binary system that draw
on, but perhaps move beyond, them. These alternatives are primarily constructionist, but are inclusive of an element of biological or other essentialism
where this forms a basis for people's lived experience (see Monro, 2000;
2005). They can be divided into three ideal types:

The expansion of male and female categories

Expanding gender binary categories involves theorising femininities and
masculinities as diverse, and as including people who have bodies or social

---

12 Califia was not self-identified as trans at the time of writing the text to which I refer.
13 Even though some early radical feminists aimed for androgyny. For example, Millet (1970)
    discussed an androgynous future in which individuals evaluate and integrate masculine and
    feminine traits, whilst Firestone (1970) envisaged the development of technology enabling the
    end of male-female gender differences based on biology.

roles that are different to those traditionally associated with women and men, for example, intersex people living as male or female (see Dreger, 2000). As Halberstam (2002) suggests, the elasticity of gender binary categories allows gender diversity to be subsumed into 'male' and 'female' – at least to an extent. The expansion of binary categories is conceptually related to notions drawn from masculinity studies. The notion of masculinities as plural involves moving away from an understanding of masculinity as white, middle class, heterosexual and able-bodied, towards thinking about masculinities as multiple, and the notion of some masculinities as hegemonic, whilst others are subordinated (see Hearn and Morgan, 1990: 11). Hearn and Collinson discuss 'distinctions between gay, non-hierarchic heterosexual, and hierarchic heterosexual; between white and black, between non-fathers and fathers; unpaid carers, paid carers, and non-carers; and non-violent, violent, and militant masculinities' (1994: 107). This understanding of femininities and masculinities as plural is helpful in theorising gender and sexual diversity, because it includes people such as camp gay men, butch women, and trans people who have undergone full sex reassignment. In other words, if there are lots of different masculine identities, then adding in a few more types of masculinity which involve people who do not have conventionally male bodies and/or traditional male identities is not such a big deal – and, it becomes easier to look at the structural differences between people with these masculinities and others.[14]

There are limitations to the 'expanded gender binaries' model, which can be illustrated by looking at the notion of female masculinities. Halberstam (2002) describes a range of female masculinities, for example tomboys, butch dykes, and masculine heterosexual women. This interpretation of gender risks co-option of what can be seen as transgressive and positive identities that are arguably female, not male (for example butch). In other words, if these people become seen as male rather than female it makes it harder to support variation amongst women, and reinforces female stereotypes. In addition, if masculinity is de-essentialised and delinked from male bodies, it becomes slippery and hard to characterise, relying on ideas that reinvoke social inequalities, such as rationality and aggression. In other words, if biology is not seen as contributing to male identities, social factors such as gender roles become the distinguishing features of such identities, and traditional roles mark out gender binaries, for example, Halberstam suggests that 'Masculinity in this [USA] society inevitably conjures up notions of power and legitimacy' (2002: 356). Such a movement is politically retrogressive, foregrounding rather than dismantling gender stereotypes. Another key problem with the expanded binaries model is that it fails to include those people who fall more fully outside of the gender binary system, and because of this defuses the potential for gender pluralism because some alternative identities

14 The same is of course true of femininities.

are subsumed into 'male' and 'female'. However, it is a pragmatic strategy, broadening out options concerning gender to a degree generally. It enables some people with diverse sexualities and genders to gain social rights and acceptance. An obvious example would be the improved legal and social position that many transsexuals are currently experiencing in the UK, following the Gender Recognition Act 2004.[15]

Moving beyond gender

Feminist authors such as Lorber (1993) argue for the 'degendering' of society. The notion of degendering, which is used here to mean moving beyond gender categorisation altogether, can be linked to an extent with gender liminality, which means 'an "in-between" place' (Feinberg, 1996: 143) (although liminality is in fact a non-male/female gendered space). As shown above, authors such as Stone (1991), Bornstein (1994) and Cameron (1996) describe transsexuality as a place outside of duality. Notions of degendering and gender liminality are useful for conceptualising gender diversity. A number of contributors discussed the need for a less heavily gendered society – for example, the use of 'male' and 'female' on forms when sex/gender is irrelevant to the matter at hand. In a society where there is less concern with gender, androgynous and gender ambiguous people would face less barriers to social inclusion, and gender norms overall would be less heavily enforced. A certain amount of degendering is clearly helpful in achieving a more equal, inclusive society. However, there are some difficulties with the 'degendering' approaches.[16] Identity categories seem to be necessary as a basis for cultural and political organisation. If a strategy focused on erasing gender is pursued, the minority gender groups, and those who have less power (including non-trans women), are likely to be disadvantaged because the default dominance of men and non-transgender people will remain unchallenged. In addition, it is questionable as to whether it is ever possible to fully degender – an individual might try to do so, but others will assign a gender to that person. In itself degendering is an inadequate approach, because of the power of existing systems of categorisation and the related structural inequalities. Faced with a universalist

---

15 Of course, the expansion of gender categories does not necessarily lead to increased social rights for gender and sexual minorities. The practice of intersex genital mutilation, where intersex infants and children have surgery that is unnecessary for physical functioning with the aim of making them fit better into the binary gender system, is a particular case in point. The Intersex Society of North America recommends not doing surgery unless physically necessary, and waiting until the child can make an informed choice about surgery – in the meantime a gender will be assigned to enable social functioning – which is a less draconian version of the 'expansion of male and female categories' model (www.isna.org/faq/patient-centered enabling).

16 One issue is that once fluidity is named, it becomes a space which people can inhabit (see Prosser, 1998), and is therefore arguably no longer a non-category.

gender vacuum, existing hegemonic norms (ways of seeing the world that reinforce inequalities) are likely to be reasserted, and marginalisation of people with different genders and sexualities will be perpetuated.

Gender pluralism

A further theoretical strategy concerns conceptualising gender as plural, and as a spectrum, a field, or intersecting spectra or continua. Gender is seen as being more finely grained than is the case with the binary system, and as being formed via the interplay of different characteristics associated with gender and sexuality. Gender pluralism involves 'calls for new and self-conscious affirmations of different gender taxonomies' (Halberstam, 2002: 360). It involves conceptualising gender as 'fields' or 'groupings' of – in some cases overlapping – masculinities, femininities, and gender diverse identities. It could entail the more widespread use of pronouns such as 'ze' and 'hir' (see Feinberg, 1996) for people who chose them as alternatives to male/female pronouns. More gender possibilities also means acknowledging that the categories of 'lesbian', 'gay', 'bisexual' and 'heterosexual' cannot encompass all sexual orientations, and complementary terms are likely to become more widespread.

There was support for gender pluralism amongst some of the research contributors to projects (a) and (d), some of whom discussed the way that they would prefer to identify as something other than female or male if this was socially possible. For instance, sex and gender as a continuum or as a spectrum was discussed by contributor Ann Goodley, who said:

> I see the main problems being that society and indeed children, in other words all of us, are programmed to only see in black and white, in monochrome. A concept I actually see as a rainbow, or many shades of grey, I prefer to see it as a rainbow, that's more positive, the grey areas are actually the technicolor colours between black and white. I believe that there are elements of all the colours in everybody, but that people knee-jerk into one column or the other quite often in Western patriarchal society. And I think that's damaging.

Some of the literature supports the spectrum model of sex and gender. Rothblatt (1995) discusses what she terms 'gender continuum theory', a shift away from bipolar sex/gender categories towards a multiplicity of genders. The notion of a gender and sex continuum may be expanded. For example, one (non-trans) bisexual contributor described genders as places in space rather than a continuum. Debates about the viability and advisability of a plural gender system will continue. One trans contributor (project d) said that the time was not right for a movement for third and other sexed/gendered people's rights, given existing social conservatism and bigotry and the need to fight other battles first, whilst another said: 'third gender – I resist that phrase, because all it does is rigidify, codify stuff' (James Green), and a further contributor argued that 'it's [third gender] got a sort of dustbin sense to it, even though I know people would use it for themselves' (Hamish). Gender pluralism could therefore be seen to perpetuate categorisation. Politically, the development/recognition of identities that are intersex, androgynous, third and other sex, or gender diverse in other ways is powerful and radical because it enables calls for justice and social change. It moves beyond the post-structuralist deconstruction of gender and sexuality binaries towards reconstruction, potentially towards a more diverse and tolerant society. Theoretically, gender pluralism allows for the inclusion of both essentialist and constructionist approaches to gender and sexuality, and it moves gender theory beyond the binary system.

Universalist panacea or particularist ghetto?

The 'politics of universalism' aims at the equalisation of rights, entitle-ments and immunities for everyone, or, at least, for every citizen. The polit-ics of difference, on the other hand, aims at recognizing the unique identity of concrete individuals and groups, their distinctness from everyone else.

(Axtman, 1996: 92)

This section aims to provide an analysis of universalism and particularism with reference to feminisms and trans politics. The tension between universa-lism and particularism is important for discussions concerning feminisms because questions concerning whether to foreground particular gendered groups, as opposed to appealing to universalist notions of equality, remains central. Feminisms, in foregrounding the concerns of women as a group, are a particularist form of politics.[17] Discussions concerning identity politics and particularism are found in the feminist legal literature, for example, Bridge-man and Millns (1998) bring together a number of debates about the tensions between equal rights oriented and diversity oriented political strategies. Related discussions are present elsewhere in the legal literature, for instance Ingram argues that 'Democratic fairness does not require that laws and policies advance the interests of everyone equally or identically – although it does require spreading risks and benefits fairly' (2004: 2). This section starts by evaluating universalism, before addressing particularism, and then arguing for a combination of these approaches.

According to Young, universalism entails citizens being defined by what they have in common, rather than differences, as well as universally binding rules and laws (see 1990: 114). 'It may signify the philosophical belief that

---

17 Although, the inclusion of all women is universalist and, as widely discussed in the feminist literature, may erase the differences between women (see Monro, 2005).

there is a fundamental human nature or human essence that defines who we are as humans' (Benhabib, 2002: 26). As Young (2001: 203) says, notions of universal humanity that override differences have been central to the struggle against social exclusion and status differentiation, making claims for equal rights possible. Universalism has a number of advantages as a political strategy. It acts as a 'level'; everyone is seen as equal and worthy of social inclusion, and, because it emphasises the equality of everyone, it can be used to challenge the prejudice that can become entrenched in subculture groupings, as well as the mainstream. Universalism is not strongly identity based, so that those occupying ambivalent, changing, or unconceptualised positions can be included, and it does not exclude people who do not have a particular identity. Because universalism is inclusive, it is resistant to being labelled as unfairly supportive of minorities.[18] On a conceptual level, universalist approaches provide a means of moving beyond a politics in which certain groups are potentially shut out or alienated.

Despite its advantages, there are difficulties with universalism. Insisting on a form of equality that ignores difference may perpetuate social exclusion. 'Blindness to difference disadvantages groups whose experience, culture, and socialized capacities differ from those of privileged groups' (Young, 2001: 207); bringing marginalised groups into the mainstream means that they have to play by the rules already established by more powerful groups. The notion of universalism also allows privileged groups to ignore their own specificity, so that their values and norms appear to be neutral and universal (Young, 2001: 208). In recent years, oppressed groups have rejected universalism and the assimilation that goes with it, and asserted separate group identities and interests that affirm difference as a positive thing (Young, 2001).

What of the alternatives to universalism, namely, particularist approaches? Current difference-based approaches enable the experiences of particular groups to be addressed in more detail than is possible with universalist approaches. Difference-based approaches enable groups to be treated as distinct classes, whilst at the same time recognising that particular groupings are cross-cut by (or formed in relation to) other socially ordering variables, such as class and ethnicity. The recognition of difference is important because the public adoption of identities that are visible, and that form a basis for organisation, is politically efficacious. As Carver says, 'working from the category of "women" has been and should continue to be successful' (1998: 27).

There are a number of problems with difference-based approaches to feminism and gender diversity. Particularist strategies demand that difference be conceptualised – people with fluid sexual orientations become known as 'bisexual'; people of diverse genders become classed as 'trans', and others,

---

18 A form of argument that is often used by right-wing critics of affirmative provision for groups facing discrimination.

who may have these tendencies but choose not to (or are not socially able to) express them, remain male or female, and gay, lesbian or heterosexual. Feminists who have fluid or changing gender identities are likely to be cramped by particularist strategies, and male feminists become something of an anathema.[19] Particularist strategies risk 'freezing' both established categories and established roles (for example, the social norm that dictates that women are primarily responsible for childrearing). The crucial irony, and an irony that has received considerable coverage in the literature, is that identity politics demands categorisation, but that that categorisation can then, in itself, become restrictive or hegemonic (see Dunphy, 2000: 75). Further subdivisions are one way of dealing with this problem. Alternative forms of identification, such as 'all genders', or 'polysexual', may solve the problem of categorisation becoming restrictive in some ways. These terms include those people who resist the current forms of identification usually used as a basis for particularist politics, potentially serving as a basis for the development of diverse rights claims.[20] The difficulty with very specific forms of identification (such as lesbian bisexual feminist) is that they are too narrow to form an effective basis for activism; the difficulty with broad categories is that they may lead back towards a universalising approach, risking obscuration of the specificity of experience and the effects of structural inequalities.

One way of addressing the limitations of both universalism and particularism is to fuse the two approaches. As Richardson and Sandland note, 'one cannot simply choose between "difference" and "equality" ', (2000: 2). The work of Mouffe (1993) and others can be adapted in developing gender pluralist feminism which includes both particularist and universalist strands. Mouffe (1993) argues for some level of universalism because democracy requires a certain amount of homogeneity – the acceptance of political principles by citizens. Mouffe (1993) and Nash (2002) both reject particularist notions of gender specific democratic citizenship. For Mouffe, this would mean essentialising identities and fixing notions of 'women'.[21] However, as Nash says, there is a certain amount of particularism and relational fixity involved in Mouffe's notion of radical politics, for example, she sees maternity rights as gender particular. Political positions that balance diversity and universalism are also found amongst writers in the field of sexuality, in particular Weeks (1995), who discusses radical humanism as involving a balancing of diversity against common values (such as equality and care). Some of the research findings from project (d) supported the fusion of universalist and particularist approaches, for instance:

19 See discussions about whether it is possible to be a male feminist (for instance Digby, 1998).
20 Relational forms of categorisation, such as 'lesbian-bisexual' may be useful in avoiding the privileging of specific (bisexual) identities (Hemmings, 1999: 198).
21 There is, however, a case for strategic essentialism, for example, arguing that transsexuality is an essential and immutable identity as a basis for rights claims (see King, 1993).

Interviewer: What are the advantages of 'one size fits all' versus diversity oriented approaches?

Contributor: My view would be that you need a bit of both. Just as we need the rights that heterosexuals have, but not all heterosexuals agree with marriage. It's about creating new approaches that might be relevant to heterosexuals and also to bisexual and trans people. But at the same time, it still needs to be about equality. Maybe there needs to be a minimal level of rights – something that is equivalent, not just the same. It is difficult, but, for example, me taking time off for childcare isn't relevant – but taking time off to care for older parents is.

(Co-ordinator, LGB consortium)

An approach that combines universalism and particularism appears to be the most appropriate means of supporting both women's equality and the equality of gender diverse people. The inclusive, equality oriented stance provided by universalism is crucial, whilst the attention to the interests of different groups, which is characteristic of particularism, is necessary in order to offset the assimilationalist tendencies of universalism. With gender plural-ist politics in general there would be a need to address gender differences when these were pertinent, for example, in the case of transitioning trans-sexuals, intersex newborn infants, and (following Mouffe, 1993) maternity issues. With respect to the different conceptual approaches outlined above, differences become apparent in relation to universalism and particularism. The 'gender pluralist' approach is universalist in including all genders, but particularist in recognising the differences between them, and potentially the structural inequalities underpinning gender relations. Gender pluralism involves the risks associated with both universalism and particularism, but may perhaps provide a means to integrate the two approaches. The other two strands of theory are more problematic. The 'expansion of male and female categories' approach to gender diversity can be particularist with respect to women and men, but subsumes all genders within a universalist binary sys-tem, which as noted above is flawed because it may erase some trans and intersex subjectivities, as well as differences between women. The 'moving beyond gender' approach is universalist in attempting to move beyond gender altogether, a position which leaves a void in which structures of inequality will continue to persist.

Regulating the communities

The relationship between universalist and particularist approaches to gender politics is evident in the dynamics that exist within, and between, the LGBT communities. The disruption to gender and sexual orientation categories that certain types of trans provoke has been regulated within both lesbian and gay, and trans, communities. Particularist, separatist approaches to LGBT politics appear now to have evolved into alliance-based politics in which universalist and particularist positions are combined. This section aims to outline some of the dynamics and tensions between the communities before discussing alliances with reference to universalism and particularism. Firstly, I briefly describe the historical background to some of the tensions between the communities, before examining rainbow alliances.

Trans people have historically been marginalized by the lesbian and gay communities (see for example Califia, 1997).[22] More (1996) discussed the way in which transgender implodes the established divide between gender and sexuality, in which femininity and masculinity, can, for example, be associated with heterosexuality, and cross-gender identities (butch and camp) associated with the lesbian and gay cultures. Trans people have been excluded from the lesbian and gay communities via various processes of regulation, for example, being shut out of venues and events, or inclusion on the basis that they are post operative only (see Monro, 2005). Transphobia in the lesbian and gay communities is linked with underlying identity conflicts, for example, Bergling (2001) relates the way in which effeminate or camp men are ostracised by the gay community due to the discomfort they provoke amongst other gay men.

As well as tensions between the trans and the lesbian and gay communities, there are also various conflicts within the trans communities. These seem to revolve around (a) hierarchical systems that mirror wider structural gender inequalities and (b) conflicts between particularist and more inclusive approaches. Until the 1990s, the goal for most transsexual people was on passing and assimilation into mainstream society as the gender to which they have been assigned, and the emphasis on conventional gender identities continues to be important for many transsexual people. External processes of regulation, in which gender clinics supported gender stereotypical trans people in making their transition and penalised others, were mirrored within the trans communities. A hierarchy developed within the transgender communities, with post-operative transsexuals placed at the top, followed by pre-operative transsexuals and then cross-dressers (see Bornstein, 1994). Clear presentation as the sex the person identifies as still seems to be valorised within large sections of the trans communities, for example, hyperfemininity tends to be seen as desirable within transvestite culture. This process acts to police gender, impacting the most heavily on people who cannot (or choose not to) fit into clear categories, for example, non-passing transsexuals and cross-dressers. For example:

22 I did not find any evidence for the marginalization of trans people within the bisexual communities.

I've been verbally abused, I've been threatened, and I've been warned that if I persist in going out in public without my wig, I'll get beaten up. Ironically, this behaviour has not come from the public, but from members of the [transvestite organisation] . . . some have even said that presenting as a mixture of male and female is unacceptable . . . freedom of choice is [an] anathema to some in the cross-dressing community.

(Holmes, 2003)

Since the early 1990s, when the radical transgender movement began, gender hierarchies have been challenged by trans people who wish to disrupt, or live outside of, the gender binaried system. For these people, passing as male or female may not be a goal (although it may be a survival strategy), and the older hierarchy is not subscribed to. A more particularist position, which affirms the existence of different gender identities, is being developed. Tensions between this stance and a more universalist and assimilationist one remain. For example, the gender pluralist problematisation of mainstream gender binaries that the non-male/non-female identities may involve can mean that gender binaried identities are not always assumed, and a transsexual may be more easily 'read' as transsexual; this makes passing harder. From a gender pluralist perspective, the conservative trans insistence on being closeted and on assimilating into mainstream society erodes a potential basis for organising, and perpetuates the social erasure of gender diversity. Tensions concerning inclusion are mirrored in debates within the movement, for example, concerning whether people with non-male/female identities should be included in a movement primarily run by transsexuals.

There appears to be a shift towards a politics of inclusion and diversity within the LGBT communities (see Monro, 2000; 2005). Notions of inclusivity across a range of areas have become more prominent, for instance a community member suggested that 'the (other) big issue that needs to be done with LGBT is enabling people to recognise that we are a totally inclusive community, so there are Black people, there are people with disabilities, we are all ages, we're mothers, fathers, we're colleagues'. These changes impact on the way that the communities are constructed. A representative of a national LGB organisation said:

Contributor: I'd say that LGBT is now the majority grouping used in discourse, and I think this will be future guidance. It came from the communities themselves, and a more assertive transgender community, some queer thinking.

Interviewer: Can you explain?

Contributor: A rethinking of traditional models. People are less grounded in a rigid politics of autonomy based on particular forms of oppression and so there are broader alliances, but also LGBT has been slow to link up with other alliances, such as race.

The changes in the sexual and gender minority community discourses are related to the formation of rainbow alliances. The term 'rainbow alliance' was developed as part of the queer movement towards embracing diversity and sexual and gender fluidity, and the recognition that the deconstruction of rigid gender and sexual categories necessitated forms of political organisation which were different from those associated with discrete or separatist identities. Instead of a politics bound up with being female, or lesbian, or gay, there is a movement towards a politics associated with the right to self-determination, with pluralisation, and with a celebration of diversity.[23] All parts of the gender and sexual spectrum are included in rainbow alliances, although in practice alliances are located around non-heterosexual and gender transgressive subjectivities. The rainbow symbolically covers both universalist, all-embracing politics (the whole rainbow) and an acknowledgement of diversity (the separate colours). Rainbow alliances provide a powerful means of unifying sexual and gender minorities and staking a claim for equality with heterosexual men and women, whilst also acknowledging differences between the various groupings. Rainbow alliances concerning gender and sexuality are indebted to anti-racist struggles, including those of Black feminists such as hooks (1984) and Hill Collins (1990). LGBT and queer politics intersect with some branches of the anti-racist movement, forming another set of alliances (see for example Conerley, 1996), but there are also ongoing tensions concerning ethnicity and alliances, for instance about the use (or not) of categories such as 'transgender' by non-Western gender diverse people (Roen, 2001).

Despite important reasons for the development of rainbow alliances, there are some difficulties with such alliances. The most important include (as noted above) conflicts over identity, and differences – including differences concerning ethnicity, ability, socio-economic class, nationality and other factors. Disputes over political aims and methods are also of central importance (separatism is quite clearly incompatible with rainbow alliances if it is seen as an ultimate political goal). Another problem concerns the extent of differences between the LGBTQI (lesbian, gay, bisexual, transgender, queer, intersex) communities. As contributor Jennifer Moore argued, 'it's important to distinguish between creating alliances to address political issues, and expecting to share social groups'. Even political alliances may be difficult

---

23 As noted above, some people utilise strategic essentialism to support sexual/gender equality rights claims. This can be advantageous in claiming the moral high ground, but can also perhaps feed into a victim-oriented way of framing identities, and support gender determinism to the detriment of others who experience gender and sexual identity to be malleable.

when there has been considerable hostility or ignorance, or where people cannot relate to those whom they might build alliances with. For instance intersex contributor Salmacis said:

> Well, the problem I've got with Pride is, I'm not male, I am not homo-sexual, I am not lesbian, I identify myself as female because I'm physic-ally predominantly female, and I'm comfortable with that, but I'm not a lesbian. I'm not heterosexual because I'm celibate. Apart from the fact that in most respects sex would be an impossibility anyway because it's been botched up . . .

Another difficulty with alliances concerns the impact of prejudice within the communities – for example, homophobia amongst transvestites and trans-sexuals, and transphobia amongst lesbians and gay men. These groups, in some cases, seek to distance themselves from what they perceive to be the stigmatised identities of other minorities; they hope to appeal to mainstream notions of normality and in so doing jettison other minority groups.[24] Clearly, experience of being a member of one minority does not automatically mean that people become sensitised to the needs and rights claims of other minor-ity groups, in fact, the research on trans (project (a)) indicated that stigmatisa-tion of other groups may be even more marked where identities are fragile or threatened, where identities are being consolidated in opposition to others (for example, butch lesbian identification of butch as a female rather than masculine identity), and/or where wider social stigmatisation is intense. Conflicts concerning the interests of different groups – a feature of particu-larist politics – are likely to continue, and appeals to universalist principles such as equality may go some way towards mitigating difficulties.

Conclusion

This chapter has suggested that feminist legal theorists have tended to overlook trans and intersex, and the ways in which these subject positions may challenge gender and sexual orientation binaries. It has critiqued traditional – in this case radical – feminist stances on trans, which act to regulate gender diversity and reinscribe gender binaries. The chapter outlines alternative theoretical approaches to trans and intersex: the 'expansion of male and female categories' approach, in which gender binaries are viewed as sufficiently elastic to include gender variation within them; 'degendering', in

---

24 This trend was also apparent in findings from research project (b), when contributors dis-cussed other areas of equalities initiatives. For example, some people working in the field of race equalities sometimes distanced themselves from LGBT equalities work, which was seen as more politically sensitive (as well as in some cases problematic on the grounds of faith).

which a movement away from any gender categorisation takes place, and 'gender pluralism', in which gender is viewed as a continuum, spectrum or universe, with a range of gendered positions, including female, male, trans and intersex. This latter approach is arguably the most politically radical, as it enables the establishment of currently socially erased identity categories as a basis for civil rights claims, whilst preserving the other categories, including women. The chapter then moves on to discuss issues concerning universalism and particularism, arguing that a combination of both approaches is necessary as a basis for praxis (political activism and theory). An examination of processes of regulation within the LGBT communities indicates, however, that conflicts between groups will continue. These tensions are mirrored at a more strategic level, in discussions regarding 'feminist' as opposed to 'gender' stances. It is to these that I now turn.

The universalism of gender pluralism and rainbow alliances could, if pursued without respect to the particularism of different groups and their interests, result in a universalist panacea in which the concerns of women are subsumed. This issue is one of concern to feminists such as myself, who might view the turn towards 'gender', as opposed to 'feminist', praxis with suspicion. However, a straightforward movement towards 'feminist' positions, as opposed to 'gender' positions, is also problematic, as it results in the erasure of gender diversity. Theoretically, feminist positions which continue to assume a male/female binary system are best matched with the 'expansion of male and female categories' approach to gender diversity, which enables feminist praxis to continue a reliance on gender and sexual orientation binarisms, but in a broader fashion. However, a more useful approach may perhaps be developed using gender pluralism. Gender pluralism allows for a particularist approach to gender equality which includes women as a very large contingent – trans and intersex people form much smaller groupings within the gender spectrum, and of these, many identify as female or male. Given the ubiquitous persistence of structural inequalities that disadvantage women, feminism would play a crucial role in gender pluralist praxis. Feminism, and the patriarchal forces it challenges, can be seen to cut across diverse genders, so that anyone who has inhabited, or partially inhabits, or is moving towards, a female subjectivity will find feminisms to be of direct relevance. For those who identify primarily as male but who are concerned with gender equality, feminism will also provide a key set of tools.[25] Moving back towards a universalist perspective for a moment, if the gender spectrum is envisaged as a whole, patriarchal forces form one of the central structuring forces, alongside gender binarism, hetrosexism/homophobia, ethnocentrism,

---

25 This type of approach draws on the work of standpoint epistemologists such as Harding (1986) in which women's social positions form the basis for research, although as noted in Monro (2000) these would be extended to include the standpoints of other groups.

racism, ageism and disablism. Therefore, overall, feminisms will continue to form a central plank of gender praxis. Perhaps what is indicated is the ability to move flexibly between 'feminist' and 'gender' positions; so that when the issue is one of women's rights (including trans and intersex women), feminism becomes central, and when the issue pertains to other gender groupings, other forms of praxis may become more relevant, although the feminist gaze would never become absent.

Bibliography

Axtman, R (1996) *Liberal Democracy into the Twenty-First Century: Globalisation, Integration and the Nation-State*, Manchester and New York: Manchester University Press.

Barnett, H (1998) *Introduction to Feminist Jurisprudence*, London, Sydney: Cavendish Publishing.

Benhabib, S (2002) *The Claims of Culture: Equality and Diversity in the Global Era*, Princeton, New Jersey: Princeton University Press.

Bergling, T (2001) *Sissyphobia: Gay Men and Effeminate Behaviour*, New York, London: Harrington Park Press.

Bornstein, K (1994) *Gender Outlaw: On Men, Women and the Rest of Us*, New York, London: Routledge Publications.

Bridgeman, J and Mullins, S (1998) *Feminist Perspectives on Law: Law's Engagement with the Female Body*, London: Sweet and Maxwell.

Bullough, V and Bullough, B (1993) *Cross-Dressing, Sex and Gender*, Philadelphia: University of Philadelphia Press.

Califia, P (1997) *Sex Changes: The Politics of Transgenderism*, San Francisco: Cleis Press.

Cameron, L (1996) *Body Alchemy: Transsexual Portrait*, San Francisco: Cleis Press.

Carver, T (1998) 'A Political Theory of Gender: Perspectives on the "Universal Subject" ', in: Randall V and Waylen G (eds) *Gender, Politics and the State*, London, New York: Routledge, pp 18–28.

Conerly, G (1996) 'The Politics of black lesbian, gay and bisexual Identity', in: Beemyn B and Eliason M (eds) *Queer Studies: A Lesbian, Gay, Bisexual and Transgender Anthology*, New York, London: New York University Press, pp 133–45.

Daly, M (1984) *Pure Lust: Elemental Feminist Philosophy*, London: Women's Press.

Digby, T, (1998) (ed.) *Men Doing Feminism*, London, New York: Routledge.

Dreger, A D (ed.) (2000) *Intersex in the Age of Ethics*, Maryland: University Publishing Group.

Dunphy, R (2000) *Sexual Politics: An Introduction*, Edinburgh: Edinburgh University Press.

Feinberg, L (1996) *Transgender Warriors: Making History from Joan of Arc to Dennis Rodman*, Boston: Beacon Press.

Firestone, S (1970) *The Dialectic of Sex*, New York: Bantam Books.

Greer, G (1999) *The Whole Woman*, New York: Alfred A Knopf.

Halberstam, J (2002) 'An Introduction to Female Masculinity: Masculinity without Men', in: Adams R and Savran D (eds) *The Masculinity Studies Reader*, Malden, Massachusetts and Oxford: Blackwell Publishers, pp 355–74.

Harding, S (1986) *The Science Question in Feminism*, Milton Keynes: Open University Press.

Harper, P B, McClinton, A, Munoz, J E and Rosen, T (1997) 'Queer Transexions of Race, Nation and Gender: An Introduction', *Social Text*, 15(3–4): 52–3.

Hearn, J and Collinson, D L (1994) 'Theorizing Unities and Differences between Men and between Masculinities', in Brod H and Kaufman M (eds) *Theorizing Masculinities*, London: Sage, pp 97–118.

Hearn, J and Morgan, D (1990) *Men, Masculinities and Social Theory*, London: Unwin Hyman.

Heilbrun C G (1998) 'Androgyny and the Psychology of Sex Differences', in: Eisenstein H and Jardin A (eds) *The Future of Difference*, New Brunswick, London: Rutgers University Press, pp 258–66.

Hemmings, C (2000) *Bisexual Spaces: A Geography of Sexuality and Gender*, New York: Routledge.

Herdt, G (ed) (1994) *Third Sex Third Gender: Beyond Sexual Dimorphism in Culture and History*, New York: Zone Books.

Hill Collins, P (1990) *Black Feminist Thought: Knowledge, Consciousness, and the Politics of Empowerment*, Cambridge, MA: Unwin Hyman.

Hird, M M (2002) 'Out/Performing Our Selves: Invitation for Dialogue' *Sexualities*, 5(3): 337–56.

Holmes, G (2003) 'Is that a Blank Sheet of Paper, or a List of Cross-dressers' Achievements?', unpublished, see www.totalclothingrights.org (last visited 11 October 2004).

hooks, B (1984) *Feminist Theory: From Margin to Center*, Boston: South End Press.

Ingram, D (2004) *Rights, Democracy, and Fulfillment in the Era of Identity Politics: Principled Compromises in a Compromised World*, Lanham, Boulder, New York, Toronto, Oxford: Rowman and Littlefield Publishers, Inc.

Jeffreys, S (1996) 'Heterosexuality and the Desire for Gender' in: Richardson D (ed) *Theorising Heterosexuality: Telling it Straight*, Buckingham, Philadelphia: Open University Press.

Kelly Weisberg, D (1993) (ed.) *Feminist Legal Theory: Foundations*, Philadelphia: Temple University Press.

King, D (1993) *The Transvestite and the Transsexual: A Case Study of Public Categories and Private Identities*, Aldershot: Avebury.

Kirsch, M H (2000) *Queer Theory and Social Change*, London and New York: Routledge.

Lorber, J (1994) *Paradoxes of Gender*, Newhaven, London: Yale University Press.

McClinton, A (1995) *Imperial Leather: Race, Gender and Sexuality in the Colonial Contest*, New York, London: Routledge.

Millet, K (1970) *Sexual Politics*, Garden City, New York: Doubleday.

Monro, S (2000) 'Transgender Politics', unpublished thesis: Sheffield, University of Sheffield.

Monro, S (2005) *Gender Politics: Citizenship. Activism, and Sexual Diversity*, London: Pluto Press.

More, K (1996) 'Let(TS)sbigay Together', *Radical Deviance: A Journal of Transgendered Politics* 2(2): 50–3.

Mouffe, C (1993) *Return of the Political*, London: Verso.

Nash, K (1998) 'Beyond Liberalism: Feminist Theories of Democracy', in: Randall V and Waylen G (eds) *Gender, Politics and the State*, London, New York: Routledge, pp 45–57.

Nataf, Z (1996) *Lesbians Talk Transgender*, London: Scarlett Press.

Olsen, F E (1995) (ed.) *Feminist Legal Theory 1: Foundations and Outlooks*, Aldershot, Singapore, Sydney: Dartmouth.

Prieur, A (1998) *Mema's House, Mexico City: On Transvestites, Queens and Machos*, Chicago: The University of Chicago Press.

Prosser, J (1998) *Second Skins: The Body Narratives of Transsexuality*, USA: Columbia University Press.

Queen, C and Schimel, L (1997) (eds) *Pomosexuals: Challenging Assumptions about Gender and Sexuality*, San Francisco: Cleis Press.

Ramet, S (1997) *Gender Reversals and Gender Cultures: Anthropological and Historical Perspectives*, London, New York: Routledge Publications.

Raymond, J (1980) *The Transsexual Empire: The Making of the She–Male*, London: The Women's Press.

Raymond, J (1994) 'The Politics of Transgender', *Feminism and Psychology* 4(4): 628–33.

Reinharz, S (1992) *Feminist Methods in Social Research*, New York, Oxford: Oxford University Press.

Richardson, J and Sandland, R (2000) (eds) *Femininist Perspectives on Law and Theory*, London, Sydney: Cavendish Publishing.

Roen, K (2001) 'Transgender Theory and Embodiment: The Risk of Racial Marginalisation', *Journal of Gender Studies*, 10(3): 253–63.

Rosario, V (1996) 'Trans (Homo) Sexuality? Double Inversion, Psychiatric Confusion, and Hetero-Hegemony', in: Beemyn B and Eliason M (eds) *Queer Studies: A Lesbian, Gay, Bisexual and Transgender Anthology*, New York, London: New York University Press, pp 36–51.

Rothblatt, M (1995) *The Apartheid of Sex: A Manifesto for the Freedom of Gender*, USA: Crown Publishers.

Sharpe, A N (2002) *Transgender Jurisprudence: Dysphoric Bodies of Law*, London, Sydney: Cavendish Publishing Limited.

Stone, S (1991) 'The Empire Strikes Back: A post-transsexual Manifesto', in: Epstein D and Straub K (eds) *Body Guards: The Cultural Politics of Gender Ambiguity*, London: Routledge, pp 280–304.

Weeks, J (1995) *Invented Moralities: Sexual Values in an Age of Uncertainty*, Cambridge: Polity Press.

Weisberg, K (1996) (ed.) *Applications of Feminist Legal Theory to Women's Lives: Sex, Violence, Work and Reproduction*, Philadelphia: Temple University Press.

Whittle, S (1998) 'Guest Editorial', *Journal of Gender Studies*, 7(3): 269–71.

www.isna.org/faq/patient–centered enabling (last visited 26 May 2006).

Young, I M (1990) 'Impartiality and the Civic Public: Some Implications of feminist Critiques of moral and political Theory' in Young, I M (ed.) *Throwing Like a Girl and other Essays in Feminist Philosophy and Social Theory*, Bloomington, Ind.: Indiana University Press, pp 92–113.

Young, I M (2001) 'Justice and the Politics of Difference', in: Seidman, S and Alexander, J C (eds) *The New Social Theory Reader*, London, New York: Routledge, pp 203–11.

Chapter 7

Beyond unity

Margaret Davies, Flinders University, Australia *

Introduction: legal separatism

Western law is traditionally understood as separate from the individual, in that Westerners do not regard our law as intrinsic to our identity. In contrast to ideas of law based in community, or culture, where the law might be regarded as part of one's identity, the liberal positivist model enshrines a myth of separation of legal system from legal subjects, both individually and collectively. At the same time, positivist legal theories imagine symmetrical conceptions of legal system and legal subject. Both system and subject are sovereign, self-determining, territorial, and autonomous. Thus, even though liberal positivist theory sees the individual as separate from its law, it nonetheless constructs subject and system as mirror images of each other.

The social field, by its nature less susceptible to an insistence on fixed boundaries, is foreclosed in many jurisprudential debates by this legal separatism. This is despite the role of the social in constructing and mediating legal subjects, legal systems, and the relations between them. Thus the many juristic dimensions of the social sphere – as the medium for contested representations of legality, as the site of political and moral struggles feeding into legal transformation, as a network of institutions and relationships in which the legal sphere is embedded, or as the field of emergent identities unrecognised by formal law – are erased by a legal theory based in a liberal dualism of law and its subjects. Positivist legal thought does understand law to be a social construction, but nonetheless maintains that – once law has been constructed – there is an institutional and conceptual separation of law from the social field. Critical legal theory has of course indicated how positivism 'maintains' such a position – the maintaining undertaken by positivist theory is both a theoretical position and the material practice of boundary

* This research was supported by an Australian Research Council Discovery Grant (project number DP0451107). I would like to thank the editors for their feedback at various stages of the drafting process, and Reeta Randhawa for research assistance.

maintenance for the formal law (Douzinas, Warrington and McVeigh, 1991: 25; Davies, 1996: 18–19).

Critical scholarship, including much feminist scholarship and sexuality scholarship, has also theorised a crisis or turning point for subjectivity, which is now seen as fragmented, hybrid, and plural. Not only is there plurality between subjects, but also within subjects (see for example Braidotti, 1994; Drakopolou, 2000; McCall, 2005: 1778). One aim of this chapter is to ask what the critique and pluralisation of subjectivity in feminist theory means for the conception of law. From one angle, it means that feminists and critical scholars are constantly discovering new forms of exclusion by law: insofar as law expects normative singularity, and society delivers diversity, there is an inevitable mismatch between the normative expectations of state law and the endless plurality of social life. This mismatch can hardly be corrected by instating new forms of subjectivity within law: the illimitable nature of social identities ensures that any new category will itself be exclusive and inadequate (Stychin, 2003: 20). From another angle though, the crisis in subjectivity has epistemological consequences for law, since diverse subjects read and interact with the law in a diversity of ways. If we genuinely believe that state law is socially embedded, and refuse the myths of legal separation and autonomy, then this diversity of readings and interactions has consequences for any theoretical characterisation of law. Therefore, I argue for a pluralised understanding of law, one which draws specifically upon the diversity of subjects in their multiple, overlapping and contested social spheres.

The plural in law is not simply a reflection of plural subjectivity (since the mirror imaging of system and subject mentioned above is probably contingent) but the consequence of law being intrinsically a social dialogue in process. My objective then is to refuse the legal myth of separation, and find ways of speaking about law which reclaim it as a democratic or participatory conversation. In the process, my aim is to add another voice to those who have been arguing for a much closer articulation between the sociology and the philosophy of law (Lacey, 1998; Norrie, 2000; Cotterrell, 2002).

The first half of the chapter (that is, the next two sections) is essentially an overview of developments in feminist and critical scholarship on both the subject and the concept of law. In these sections I describe how the idea of unity has become unsatisfactory for feminism, primarily in relation to our understanding of subjectivity, but also increasingly in relation to our understanding of law. The second half of the chapter is a tentative attempt to move beyond critique. It asks what resources feminist and critical theory offers for a reconceptualisation of law. I argue for a more pluralised and horizontal notion of law (see also Lacey, 1998: 157–64), and argue that such a view is already implicit in some feminist interventions in the practical legal sphere. Finally, rather than see a pluralised law simply as a theoretical alternative requiring the total abandonment of conventional legal theory and practice,

I argue that legal transformation is prefigured and tested by feminist and critical practices which refuse the traditional boundaries of law.

Beyond the unity of the subject

Critical legal theorists have become extremely attentive to matters of subjectivity in law, and in particular to the ways in which legal subjects are constructed through various modalities of inclusion and exclusion. This emphasis on the so-called 'subject of subjectivity' has developed in conjunction with the critique and displacement of the traditional white masculine norms of legal identity (a displacement which has at least been theoretical if not often practical). Such critiques are especially well developed in those approaches which take as their point of departure the several forms of social power or socialised force. Thus feminist critiques of law, sexuality critiques, race-based critiques, postcolonial critiques, as well as the more recent focus on refugees/asylum-seekers (Fitzpatrick and Tuitt, 2004), have been at the forefront of laying bare the mythologies of the legal subject. One characteristic strategy of such critiques, for instance, is to show how the allegedly universal or abstract subject is a pretext for a particular subject – often white, masculine, and heterosexual. When the abstract subject is marked by some otherness, such as femininity or Indigeneity, law has nonetheless shown a clear preference for reified ideals – the good (heterosexual) mother, for instance (Beresford, 1998) or the culturally static Indigenous community (Anker, 2004). The so-called 'universal' is revealed to be not universal at all, because in recognising persons before the law it normalises and excludes. The forms of such exclusion appear endless, and play out in many practical contexts.

Such exclusions are sometimes regarded as errors of representation, based on a failure to include resulting from ignorance or from the non-reflexiveness of lawmakers who have simply taken their own subjectivity as the model for all. Historically, the liberal solution has been to try to correct such errors, to ensure that the universal does truly include everyone meriting inclusion. The liberal approach includes by enlightenment and reform: namely, by rational argument illustrating a failure to include and by the consequential extension or reformulation of the category in question (Nussbaum, 2000). In the liberal world, our basic identities are singular: we are human units with clear boundaries, and independent agency. While liberalism recognises, indeed insists upon, the facts of human diversity and individuality, it nonetheless models subjects within a quite specific framework – as self-determining, ideally rational, consciously operating units.[1] The main issues for law are

---

1   There are many liberalisms, just as there are many positivisms, many feminisms, and many postmodernisms. I am interested here in two basic ideas in philosophical liberalism: first, the notion that human agents are individual units with a positive essence, however that is

whether we are adequately represented and how universal categories such as the subject and her/his rights, interests or capabilities can become truly inclusive. We have certainly seen a progressive liberal extension of legal subjectivity in formal terms, so that Indigenous people, women, sexual minorities, are more often than not *formally* regarded as legal persons and with few exceptions enjoy the full range of liberal rights.[2] The old status distinctions between types of legal person have been largely dismantled so that one basic form accounts for all manners of diversities. We all remain legally marked by our sex for some purposes – we cannot avoid a legal sex classification – but for most purposes formal legal subjectivity is unmarked by social classifications.

As critical scholars have argued of course, extension of an allegedly neutral category does not result in anything like full inclusion, since the more potent modalities of identity-construction in law are not formal legal principles but the socio-legal practices informing the interpretation and application of law. Standards of normality, reason or common sense give content to legal forms which in turn strengthen and legitimate such norms. Such perceptions lead to debate over whether it is possible to construct a truly inclusive legal person, or whether different types of subjectivity – such as specifically sexed subjects – ought to be formally recognised by law (Irigaray, 1993; 1996; cf. Cooper 2004: 86–8). The former approach preserves intact the liberal unity of both legal subject and legal system. The latter approach does nothing to challenge the boundaries of law, and while it appears to recognise diversity of persons, nonetheless retains an emphasis on essentialised identities and the associated imperative for subjects to belong to a normatively defined group (Cooper, 2004; Drakopolou, 2000: 213). In this way, legal recognition of multiple forms of subjectivity might also, ironically, reinstate (in a different form) the status categories which liberal activists, including feminists, fought so hard to eliminate.

In contrast to the liberal approach to subjectivity are others which emphasise inherent difference rather than merely the difference between subjects. These alternative approaches to subjectivity move away from essentialist descriptions, both of the human subject and of group-based identities. For instance, according to a structural understanding of meaning, any identity is constituted by the exclusion of an 'other'. Exclusion constitutes and also subverts identity (Laclau, 1996: 52–3). Legal subjects, for instance, have

---

construed; second, that these human entities are autonomous, in relation to each other and in relation to social, political and legal institutions. These ideas in a sense pre-exist core liberal values of freedom and equality.

2   There are of course still some notable exclusions, for instance the widespread, though diminishing, lack of equality for people in same-sex relationships.

typically been constituted by the exclusion of those who do not fall into the category, that is, those whose formal rights are curtailed in some way and are 'other' to the dominant norms. In recent years, much has been made of the otherness of the asylum-seeker, and how this threatening figure of exteriority is manipulated to constitute national identity and 'legal' as opposed to illegal subjectivity (Kyambi, 2004; Dauvergne, 2004). The so-called 'constitutive outside' is a necessary element of any identity although who or what is outside may vary, and as a result the inside/outside distinction is not given or rational but maintained by acts of discursive force: each term in the dichotomy is not self-contained but relies on its other in the process of any identity construction (Derrida, 1982: 13; Gasché, 1986: 128–31). Appreciation of this dynamic has led many to be extremely cautious of legal reforms aimed at achieving equality for same-sex relationships: legal recognition of one identity comes at the expense of the exclusion of non-recognised modes of existence. Moreover, the ubiquitous question 'equal to what/whom?' lurks behind all liberal equality measures (for example Loader, 2004: 121).

In addition to such formal-logical arguments, liberal faith in the universal subject has been questioned by psychoanalytical approaches which emphasise that psychic identity is intrinsically split between conscious and unconscious, and that there is an irrational underside of reason. More significantly, theorists of intersectionality (McCall, 2005), postcolonialism (Kapur, 2005), and multiple consciousness have emphasised the plural forms of power, the hybridity, and several social domains within which subjects find their identities. Identity is never simple pre-social atomistic unity, but is formed in plural socio-cultural spheres. The legal system is one arena through which subjects are interpellated, but its messages are not always clear, and it is but one among many normative environments. On this view, subjectivity is much more networked than liberal individualism generally implies. Our identities are formed in response to several social networks meaning that our 'nature' is not an essential characteristic, but rather a construction within various normative and discursive spheres.

Within critical scholarship therefore, including much (but by no means all) feminist scholarship, the concept of subjectivity has been thoroughly de-essentialised, fragmented, and pluralised. The critical understanding of subjectivity has moved well beyond the liberal individual: we are not just plural in our diversity as individuals. Rather we are plural in ourselves, in our contexts, the spaces we inhabit, the languages we speak, the discourses we channel and reconstruct. We are living interfaces for everything in our worlds, each uniquely positioned but each interconnected. Not only can we not be reduced to a universal type, the 'human condition' cannot even be adequately rendered as a specific mode of existence, beyond perhaps the barest biological facts. There are human conditions, as Hannah Arendt said, the natural and constructed things that condition us as humans (Arendt, 1958:

chapter 1),[3] but there is not *a* human condition, much less a human nature. This critique of the subject has been a politically critical project in that it has disrupted traditional norms of subjectivity by reference to foreclosed or repressed subjects – the postcolonial, the queer, the Indigenous, the female. It has also been a philosophically critical project in that it has laid bare the foundations of contemporary subjectivity. It remains of crucial significance. Despite, or perhaps because of, the fragmentation of our subjectivity, categories like 'the human' resonate *across* difference, even though we may find it difficult to give broad content to such categories.

We can speak then of contemporary critical legal theory moving or reaching 'beyond unity' in its critique of the legal subject. The idea of there being a unitary legal subject or representing all legal subjects has been challenged as has the occasional feminist dream that instead of one legal subject we could perhaps have two or more (Irigaray, 1993; 1996). The very idea that we are each separate subjective units capable of adequate representation by law has also been strongly questioned. At most, law interpellates us according to a complex array of normative inclusions and exclusions: law genders us, classes us, and attributes to us a position in its colonial regimes. But law is only one – and not necessarily the most significant – among many such normative social spheres. The hope that law could somehow correspond to or even recognise human diversity without reducing or suppressing difference seems therefore nonsensical. At the same time, the liberal positivist approach to law and its subjects is incredibly resilient and has certainly not been superseded by critical theory. The resilience of liberal thought is due to several factors, notably its rhetorical attractiveness, its adaptability in the face of changing socio-political contexts, and its undeniable usefulness (even to more radical thinkers) in many practical settings.

Are we to accept a position of compromise, which states, for example, that law necessarily does violence to people's lives by forcing complex narratives into simplified normative frames? Is the best we can hope for to minimise this violence by promoting legal norms which maximise inclusion? Strategically and practically, as many feminists have argued (Armstrong, 2004; Brown, 2000; Graycar and Morgan, 2005) compromise and negotiation are essential: we have no choice but to engage with our contexts and to try to transform them incrementally. Gayatri Spivak's much quoted characterisation of liberalism as 'that which we cannot not want' nicely encapsulates the dilemma of

---

3   As Arendt said, people are conditioned by various things, and the human products of those conditions turn into further conditions: our conditions are animated by principles of human action, rather than actions being motivated by static conditions. As the editors have pointed out to me, the conditioned nature of humanness also implicitly opens up critique of the dividing line between 'the human' and 'the animal'. Unfortunately this is a point which I can't address in detail here.

critical legal scholars. In an extended comment on the issue of liberalism's promotion of rights, Wendy Brown says:

> More generally, to the extent that rights consolidate the fiction of the sovereign individual generally, and of the naturalised identities of particular individuals, they consolidate that which the historically subordinated both need access to – sovereign individuality, which we cannot not want – and need to challenge insofar as the terms of that individuality are predicated upon a humanism that routinely conceals its gendered, racial, and sexual norms. That which we cannot not want is also that which ensnares us in terms of our domination.
>
> (Brown, 2000: 238)

To speak of liberalism, rights, and legal norms in this way responds to the practical necessity of dealing with our contemporary politico-social context. Since law is inherently incapable of responding adequately to the existence of sexual and other forms of diversity, the only possible and pragmatic approach is to pursue *at once* acceptable forms of legal change *and* the nurturing of alternative normative practices *outside or beyond the law* (Stychin, 2003: 10–11). I would like to reinforce my view that such practical responses to the discourse of positive law is essential both to feminism and to the ongoing project of enhancing the position of sexual minorities in relation to law. We cannot disengage from legal contexts, but nor can we completely give our identities over to a dominant, singular normative context such as law.

Thus the tension often identified by critical legal scholars is between the need to engage with an unsatisfactory liberal legal context, and the need to cultivate networks, communities and alternative practices not defined or determined by law. In my view, this analysis of the situation confronting feminism and queer legal theory enables the pursuit of extensive legal reform without being paralysed by critique. It is a necessary, and extremely productive, approach. At the same time, there is another, more abstract, tension which I would like to explore. That is, there is also a tension between the undeniable prevalence and force of the liberal positivist model of law, and the need/desire to crystallise from critical legal theory those moments which seem to indicate a new, more contemporary and more diversified understanding of law. This second tension does not necessarily dissolve the first but it may somewhat shift the emphasis away from the dichotomy of legal/extra-legal interventions to a more socialised concept of law where such a division is not entirely coherent. In other words, as well as arguing the need to nurture separate extra-legal spaces for alternative communities we could also be moving towards a view of law built upon alterity and inclusion, rather than sameness and exclusion. I will attempt to unpack this statement in the remainder of this chapter.

Beyond the unity of the law

On one level therefore – a pragmatic and strategic one, law for sexuality theorists and feminists is what it always has been – a state-based structure of positive rules and principles, governed by hierarchy, determined by institutional gatekeepers, and separated from community. While some have attempted to de-centre law by arguing that it is not the prime determinant of gender and sexuality-based differences of power and therefore does not hold the key to the dissolution of such differences (Smart, 1989), most theorists have not extensively questioned the *concept* of law itself as essentially a unitary and state-based institution. Law may be central or not for feminist-driven change, but 'the law' is usually assumed to be a conceptual and institutional unity.

Law is therefore normally seen as a system which, although not necessarily intrinsically or totalistically 'masculine' or 'patriarchal' or 'heterosexual', nonetheless tends to practise its various modes of exclusion on intrinsically plural women, gay and lesbian subjects, minorities, and others. The law remains somewhat male-identified, straight, and resolute in its own basic immobility, while eccentric (de Lauretis, 1990), nomadic (Braidotti, 1994), world-travelling (Lugones, 1987), performative (Butler, 1990) and cosmopolitan subjects find themselves playing around the edges of what appears to be a solid block of a concept. Subjectivity might be polyphonic, but law is still a drone. For feminists and other critical legal theorists the separateness and hierarchical nature of law is an expression of its blindness to social-based power regimes. The closed concept of law has therefore been criticised for its naïve insistence that law is conceptually separable from the social arena. Feminists have achieved a great deal in terms of decoding and exposing the foundational myths of legal discourse – in particular, the myth of separation from the social, the myth of the public/private distinction, and the myth of law's neutrality and its sub-myths of the neutrality of law's persons. However, we have rarely moved beyond that critique to ask whether the idea as well as the content of law can be imagined differently (cf. Lacey, 1998: 161–4). This is despite the fact that feminist sociology of law has provided much insight into the modes of articulation between state law and other mechanisms of social control (Petersen, 1997). On one level then, law is as it has always been for feminists, and it is important that it remain so because of the need for pragmatic engagement with law, and also because of the need to continue the critical project.

On another level, feminist and critical legal theory implies other, less monolithic, conceptions of law. The idea, practice, and discipline of law have all been undergoing profound changes for several decades. The transformation of law is not attributable to any one source, but has been driven by changing global legal practices, by immanent critiques such as deconstruction, and by socio-political critiques, especially those which, like feminism, have resisted law's role in maintaining social distributions of power and which have crossed the traditional theory–practice divide. Whether this cumulatively amounts to a new paradigm for law is yet to be seen: whether the changes are sufficiently foundational, and whether they are sufficiently cohesive to merit the name of 'paradigm' are still open questions (see generally Santos, 2002: 7–20; Ost and van de Kerchove, 2002: 13–15). As an observer and participant in jurisprudential debates, my own view is that there is undoubtedly a changing meta-discourse of law, that is, a change in the narratives, cultures, metaphors and structures of 'the legal'. At the most practical level, these transitions are illustrated by the changing contours of law's interaction with its immediate contexts: that which was once legally marginal, such as 'alternative' dispute resolution, is becoming mainstream, and that which was once legally unthinkable, such as the deployment of alternative normative orders (for instance, forms of Indigenous law) in 'legal' decision-making, is becoming at least thinkable, if not proper to law itself (McNamara, 2000; cf. Goel, 2000 for discussion of the inadequacies of circle sentencing in domestic violence cases). Indeed, I would argue that the transition in legal theory involves a movement away from any notion of law being proper to itself (self-contained, bounded) and towards a more open-ended concept (see also Santos, 2002).

One of the features of the new discourses in legal theory and socio-legal studies is that they are *anti*-paradigmatic in that they do not accommodate the possibility of a unified theory or concept of law in the way this has traditionally been assumed by legal theorists. The traditional insistence upon the closure of the concept, discipline and practice of law has been a central target of critical and socio-legal scholarship alike – one would hardly expect then a new *concept* or *theory* of law as a self-contained object to arise from this base.

Yet feminist theorists have emphasised the need to re-imagine, re-theorise or re-conceptualise law (Lacey, 1998: chapters 5 and 8; Cornell, 1993; Williams, 1987). Most of the resources for such a re-imagined law are already available in critical and socio-legal scholarship even if these have not always been articulated in a positive reconstructive mode (cf. Conaghan, 2000: 376). To me, this implies no criticism of critical legal thought: new conceptual architectures are not revealed overnight or even over the course of a few decades and, as I have said, the paradigms of positivist and liberal legalism have proven immensely resistant. Scholars should not be overly self-critical, or critical of others, for what is sometimes perceived as a failure in critique: indeed, the depth and extensiveness of change over the past two decades is only too evident. There is of course still a need for greater efforts to re-imagine the contours and the identity of law.

What are the possibilities for re-thinking law? Here I do not mean re-thinking the content of law, or re-thinking how law constructs subjects, or how it understands cultural diversity. Rather, I mean re-thinking what we understand the law to be. Accepting the need to think at once within and beyond the existing legal paradigms, several axes of the conceptualisation of law seem paramount. These may be simplified (perhaps rather grandly) as the axes of space, time, and identity, each of which consists of a number of interconnecting dimensions. In the remainder of this chapter, I want to consider each of these focal points in turn, asking specifically how feminist and critical legal thought contributes to a changing contemporary understanding of law. This should not be taken as a complete rejection of existing hierarchical and closed understandings of law: clearly these accounts have great discursive and practical purchase in the current environment, for historical and political reasons. In many contexts they can be strategically useful. However, the theoretical enterprise of re-imagining law can be seen as a theoretical 'both/and' rather than an exclusive 'either/or'. It is possible and necessary to re-imagine law while retaining a realistic understanding of what law actually is, according to present practical and theoretical conditions.

Law in space: horizontal and vertical accounts of law

Part of the feminist and critical theoretical effort to re-imagine law involves what Niki Lacey refers to as the 'horizontal' aspect of law (1998: 158–62): that is the plural social spaces and interpretive contexts within which law is constituted. In contrast to the 'vertical' and formal hierarchy of legal legitimacy, the horizontal modality of law is more 'participatory' and potentially 'transformative'. Such a reorientation of legal theory would involve a major shift in consciousness and a bringing together of the philosophical and sociological approaches to law, but it is one which, in my opinion, has been gathering strength for some time (see also Ost and van de Kerchove, 2002). In this and the next section, I briefly explore the forms of a 'horizontal' understanding of law and some of the ways in which it is already implicit in feminist and sexuality theory, for instance in alternative approaches to law reform, in the analysis of 'sexual citizenship', and in feminist-informed participatory legal practices. By way of contrast, however, I need to begin by outlining the classical vertical characterisation of law.

Legal theory has ordinarily characterised law as a pyramid, or a chain of legitimacy. The reference point for positivist legality is a hierarchically superior norm: legality flows up and down the system, through hierarchies of courts, legislators and other rule-making institutions and is hence vertical. The vertical character of law is one of the methods by which the division between law and non-law is guaranteed in positivist and semi-positivist theory: every norm internal to the system must in some way be validated by a higher reference point which is also within the system: contiguous norms or systems are not a source of legality (Kelsen, 1992; Austin, 1832; Koskenniemi, 1997) except, perhaps, where the internal space of law runs out of its own reasons for making a particular decision (see for example Dworkin, 1986).

Typically, law's unity and coherence as a system are assured by a superior principle or axiom. The result is a spatially limited symbolic domain for law. These limits circumscribe both a geographical domain and also a conceptual-discursive field of normativity.

For instance, countless examples exist of minorities and women being excluded from having their subject positions represented by law because the factors by which their 'difference' is constructed are social in character, rather than legally recognised. It is interesting to think about how such exclusions are grounded in the spatial dimensions of legal reasoning. To give just one illustration, it is well known that the common law defence of provocation has frequently been used to downgrade or partially excuse homicides committed by violent men against their female partners or (depending on jurisdiction) against a man who has made a sexual advance to another man (Howe, 1997; Tyson, 1999; Lunny, 2003). The defence is used much less frequently by women who kill, and usually in cases where the homicide was preceded by prolonged domestic assault. The subjectivity of men who react suddenly and aggressively to what they see as provocative conditions has been legally valued over that of their male and female victims and arguably over the subjectivity of women who have been assaulted for years and who end it by killing their partners (cf. VLRC, 2004: 27–30). Homophobic and patriarchal narratives of provocation have been incorporated into law and recognised by its hierarchy. They are appropriately validated and have the correct 'pedigree' to use the terminology often associated with the vertical view of law. Other experiences and perspectives – adjacent to law and not comprehended by it – have often been foreclosed. In this sense the law of provocation resembles numerous other situations where horizontal reasons and interpretive contexts are excluded from or at best marginal to formal legality (cf. Goodrich, 1986: 3).

This problem with the nature of legal reasoning and its channelling of forms of social power has been well recognised by feminist scholars. This is one reason why there has been a call for greater attention to be paid to understanding the social field rather than basing feminist interventions in existing legal categories or in critical theory allegedly detached from the core constituency of feminist politics (Conaghan, 2000). For instance, the study conducted by Jenny Morgan on homicide consciously starts with the empirical question 'who kills whom and why' rather than an examination of the legal structure of homicide (Morgan, 2002). Somewhat similarly, the Law Commission of Canada has also recognised the exclusory effects of founding our understanding of law purely on narrow legal forms. It has instead defined its research agenda around four different types of relationship: personal, social, economic and governance[4] (see generally Graycar and Morgan, 2005:

4 www.lcc.gc.ca/default-en.asp.

notes 29–36 and accompanying text; MacDonald, 2000). In these instances, the traditional vertically-defined boundaries of law do not entirely govern legal analysis and change, thus relocating law directly into the social field.

Interventions into the horizontal contexts of law do not *necessarily* disrupt fundamentally the hierarchical understanding of law. This is especially so when they are undertaken by quasi-legal institutions such as law reform agencies if the end point is merely a change in the content, not the form, of the law. Through the reform process law may appropriate new ideas, narratives, or doctrines, but this does not necessarily entail a change to law's basic technologies of exclusion. At the same time, where efforts are made to couple law reforms inspired by multidisciplinary research with new ways of conceptualising law, these modes of exclusion may begin to break down. Remarkably, the Law Commission of Canada has statutory responsibility for 'the development of new approaches to, and new concepts of, law' as well as for the 'stimulation of critical debate ... in academic and other communities'.[5] Such efforts to make a long-term intervention into the nature of law as well as its content, arguably sets this particular law reform agency apart from most others. In my view, the significant thing is not so much whether such projects do in fact succeed in reformulating law, but that they perceive the need to do so, and make an imaginative effort in that direction.

Law's horizontal dimension can therefore be understood as existing in a variety of contiguous spaces: interpretive contexts, 'extra'-legal institutions, informal practices, alternative legal systems. These spaces can be reached by empirical or theoretical investigation, or by legal practices reaching beyond the confines of the traditional legal hierarchy. Most importantly, these spaces need to be regarded as *intrinsic* to any understanding of law: while it has become common to speak of law in a social context, the vertical concept of law is really only contested when there is no absolute distinction between context and law. Affirmation of this distinction reinstates the exclusory boundaries of legal reasoning outlined above.

The horizontal can also be located in an epistemological inversion of the classical question 'What is law?' There is a deceptively simple shift here: rather than ask how the law constructs us as subjects, the question is how we, as inherently plural subjects, construct, live, and perform, an inherently plural law. Legal theory has often regarded 'law' to be a construct of a very limited group of people – 'legal officials' – legislators, lawyers, judges, and (to a limited extent) legal scholars. The contours and content of the legal field have been defined by these legal specialists and legal theory has been understood to be the theory of those who adopt this insiders' perspective. The disordered everyday fragments of people's legal experiences and the narratives they construct around those experiences are excluded from the definition of law. Also

---

5   Law Commission of Canada Act 1996, s 3. Since writing, the Conservative Canadian government has announced its intention to abolish the Commission.

excluded are law's inbuilt corruptions of neutrality such as its heteronormative symbolism and colonial fabric. Instability, flux, and contradiction are
likewise repressed in definitions of the solid institution of law. Tradition,
power, and discursive factors dictate the maintenance of this limited domain
of law. But it is nonetheless challenged by a reconsideration of *who* is
regarded as a legal insider and law-creator. Everybody, including (perhaps
especially) those who suffer any of the many forms of legal exclusion
and disciplinary techniques, experiences and interacts with the law: the
reasons for according some interactions epistemic privilege while others are
sidelined are ideological, discursive, and aesthetic, not rational (see for
example Cover, 1983).

Seeing law as a plurality of subject-based constructions and interpretations
necessarily disrupts law's traditional verticality: instead of a controlled, top-
down, structure, the idea of law becomes a bottom-up and open-ended set of
relationships, irreducible to any single form. There are certainly resonances
between what I am suggesting and feminist standpoint epistemology including 'storytelling' or outsider narrative methods or 'embodied vision' (see
for example Haraway, 1991: 183–201). The narratives derived from such
approaches are often regarded as *alternative* to law's story about itself, dis-
playing the epistemic distance between the positions of privilege and disempowerment. What I would like to see is a conception of law which harnesses
social diversity, so that we recognise the alternative stories, practices, and
experiences as intrinsic to the social understanding of law and, since the law is
only a social construct, eventually such diversity may become uppermost in
the legal understanding of law. This may appear paradoxical – essentially, I
am saying that the 'outsider' narratives about law can be reclaimed as
intrinsic to law: law itself can be reclaimed as a social project – we might then
speak of reattaching the amputated head to the body politic, but understanding the 'subject' thus recreated as intrinsically plural rather than autonomous
and self-contained.

One illustration of a transgressive and reconstructive approach to law,
which begins at the point of the subject, is to be found in contemporary
discussions of sexual citizenship. On one level, the term 'sexual citizenship'
refers primarily to the state-based modalities of recognition of lesbian and
gay subjects, which are essentially rights-focussed. However, Carl Stychin
presents a more expansive understanding of the term in his recent book
Governing Sexuality. For Stychin, sexual citizenship traverses both formal
and informal normative spheres: 'sexual citizenship articulates sexuality in
the public sphere through claims for rights and participation, while also culti-
vating (and claiming a right to) separate spaces for subcultural life' (Stychin,
2003: 17). The figure of the 'sexual citizen' suggests lesbian and gay subjects
in fluid community alliances actively reflecting upon and intervening in the
legal and social conditions of their own existences. Understood in this way,
the notion of sexual citizenship disrupts the law/non-law and public/private

dichotomies, and mobilises a dynamic and participatory understanding of legal institutions and forms. It helps to shift the balance from a purely vertical understanding of law and its rights-bearing subjects, to a more horizontal, forward looking, and inclusive approach to law.

Traditionally, law in the singular often objectifies and singularises plural subjects. In terms of legal theory, I suggest we turn this around and ask how the subject (always plural) sees and experiences law. I am not, by the way, suggesting that we should have a 'subjective' notion of law, but a notion which takes serious regard of the fact that subjects are plural.[6] Such a line of reasoning leads to the thought that it should be possible for theory to move towards a democratised or participatory understanding of law.

Law in time: prefigurative feminist politics of law

A second modality of the critical re-imagining of law is temporal, deliberately blurring the separation between law's present and its possible futures. Since Austin, positivist legal theory has distinguished 'law as it is' from 'law as it ought to be'. What law *is* for positivist theory, is strictly in the present, not in some imagined future, or in some extrinsic morality which may or may not at some point in time be incorporated into law. By definition positive law is divided from general or specific ethical imperatives.

Contemporary critical thought has challenged the is/ought distinction, emphasising in particular the 'ought' that is contained in a descriptive 'is'. Descriptions of law are not normatively neutral, they are not devoid of normative content: rather the statement that something 'is' implies a directive that we should see it as such and delimit it in a particular way. The simple temporality of the is/ought distinction, dividing the past/present from the future and the descriptive from the normative, is complicated and derailed by this insight. The point can be illustrated by reference to the genesis and reception of Austin's own work. When Austin described law 'properly so called' in terms of a command of a sovereign, habitually obeyed (etc.) he was not undertaking a pure description of law (Austin, 1954: Lecture 1).[7] The description did not capture the essence of law as it then was. It contained also

---

6   Hannah Arendt pointed out that the tradition of political philosophy tended to erase the plurality of human existence. I think this is an important point also to be made in relation to legal theory. See generally Arendt (1958).

7   Wayne Morrison says that Austin's 'knowledge claims are part of, and not antecedent to, his overall project. Austin is not a simple positivist in the sense that his knowledge claim has no pretence to anything other than the "thing-in-itself", for his image of positive law is one element of an overall project. . . . Austin's claims for jurisprudence are pragmatic in the sense that the demand for a clear jurisprudence arises to get something done, and that something is to create an image of law suitable for law to become a powerful and rational image of modernity.' (Morrison, 1997: 227)

an aspirational element: that this is how law ought to be, in particular how it ought to be understood and theorised and (therefore) how it ought to be regarded in practice (Duncanson, 1997: 138–41). Austin protested the separation of is and ought, but his theory was also instrumental in establishing the present positivity of law: by imagining and describing law as a positive phenomenon, the positivists have helped to constitute it as a legal reality.

From an analytical point of view, this may seem to be a difficult claim to justify, but it is based on two related premises: first, that an 'is' may contain an 'ought'; and second, that the concept of law is not an essence, but is performative. The first of these premises is fairly straightforward: if I say 'law has the qualities a, b, and c' that is to say that you should not regard something without those qualities as law. It is normative as well as descriptive because it lays down a rule of interpretation (Merchant, 1980: 4; Davies, 1996: 51–5).[8] If said compellingly and reiterated sufficiently often, the description prescribes the thought (law is separate from merely social norms), and the thought influences subsequent action (for instance, advice that an action is immoral, but perfectly legal, or a judgment to the same effect). To put this in the language of the philosophy of science, all observation is 'theory-dependent' and, to add a postmodernish gloss, 'theories' or world views do not just turn into frameworks for thought because they make sense, but because they are backed up by the power of reiteration through culturally prescribed pathways (cf. Cooper, 2001). Description is also discipline (Foucault, 1980). Descriptions and analyses of the law are dependent on a theory or paradigm of what law is – in most cases, legal positivism – which remains persuasive because it has become ingrained in the legal conscience. Secondly, law is performative in that its concept is derived from the repeated events which make up the law, rather than a universal essence. The performance of law as not necessarily connected with morality has made it that way for late-modern Westerners. Positivism has become the predominant paradigm – a conceptual and practical reality.

Theory which is transformative is not only descriptive, analytical, and critical, it is also idealistic, aspirational, performative, and sometimes utopian. Perhaps it will even misdescribe the present or over-emphasise certain qualities in order to bring out some transformative potential in the present. For Austin, the latent positivity of law – which has become the actual positivity of law – was an important corrective to the mysticism, religious moralities, and half-baked natural law which muddled the legal process and obstructed clarity and enlightenment in legal thought. At the present moment, it is however, the notion of positivism in law which has itself become obstructive, and the recent goal of feminist and critical theorists has been to describe other

---

8 Julius Stone refers to the 'tendency of the human mind to graft upon an actual course of conduct, a right or even a duty to observe this same course in the future' (Stone, 1966: 550).

latencies within law which may also have a transformative potential. The various forms of critical legal theory have frequently been attacked for their lack of a viable alternative model of law, but such attacks neglect two significant factors: first, that a *model* is the desired outcome of a theoretical intervention; and second (as the case of the reception of Austin's work illustrates) that conceptual change is not necessarily caused by new propositions put forward by a single theory but rather from repeated, accumulated changes in thinking across a broad spectrum of types of intervention – practical, scholarly, activist. Such changes are in all probability accelerated by changes in historical conditions (which are also, of course, themselves conditioned by cultural/discursive environments) (Teubner, 1997: 768–9).

As even the history of positivism illustrates, approaches which at once (mis)describe the present and prefigure the future existence of law can result in change. There is undoubtedly an undercurrent of such prefigurative practice running through feminist and critical legal theory (Cooper, 2001; Conaghan, 2001: 383). 'Prefigurative' is not necessarily utopian – it does not necessarily impose a general and ideal vision as a corrective to the problems raised by contemporary critiques. Rather, I understand 'prefigurative' to refer to the more practical, localised, and often tentative efforts to model new forms of legality in practice and also in theoretical debates (Cooper, 2001: 139). These are not just different legal practices or theoretical formulations but ones which specifically reach towards better ways of doing law – law practices which are more just, more flexible, and more attentive to diversity.

One could cite for example 'alternative' practices of law, such as alternative dispute resolution or Indigenous sentencing courts which introduce values of negotiation, accommodation, and recognition of the other into the broader meaning of law. Other examples might include truth and reconciliation commissions and efforts to mobilise civil society in justice initiatives, such as the Women's International War Crimes Tribunal held in Tokyo in December 2000 (Dolgopol, 2006; Chinkin, 2001). I do not mean to idealise such practices – they are often highly flawed in their attempts to equalise power and tentative in their imagining of a future justice. They are necessarily incomplete and can be confined to a terrain easily dismissed by formal law. As yet, they arguably fail to address the fundamental and constitutive ideologies of law. Where, we could ask, do we see masculine privilege in law being actively abandoned and de-constituted? Where do we see hetero-normative conventions being re-imagined as multi-sexual and variable in form? Where is the flat cultural unity of law replaced by an appreciation of depth and difference? Where do we see the property in whiteness being disowned, or a genuine effort to renounce the material and political benefits of colonialism?

Despite these rather large questions, in my view alternative imaginings of law can prefigure and test possible successor legalities in locations where theory and practice converge. Most significantly for my purposes, prefigurative legalities cross the divide between the legal present and our legal futures:

they enact possible futures in the present and leave indelible traces of what is to come on the here and now.

Conclusion: law becomes a non-identity

So far I have indicated ways in which the space and time of law's existence can be re-thought. While I have tried to summarise this re-thinking in the abstract terms of legal theory, in fact this is only a reading or crystallisation of what I believe to be tendencies in other theory (in particular, feminist and sexuality theory) and in the changing practices of social interaction with law. First, instead of thinking of law as a top-down vertical structure which ensures its identity by specified modes of inclusion and exclusion, it is possible to take more theoretical notice of the horizontal dimensions of law. The 'horizontal' itself consists of at least two interconnected modalities. In an empirical sense, it includes the social fields, interpretive contexts, and marginal/alternative practices of law which are intrinsic to the ongoing functioning of both official legality and broad social normativity. In an epistemological sense, the horizontal includes the visions of law held by ordinary, situated subjects and groups of people who participate in understanding and (therefore) creating law. Second, this dynamic illustrates the re-thinking of the temporal dimension of law and theoretically-driven legal change. Instead of focusing on law as it is in the present, legal theory must appreciate that the simple 'is' is both descriptive and prescriptive. Seeing law in a particular way, is already an intervention in the future of law: law has no identity in the present which does not also pre-empt the future of law. This opens the way for seeing prefigurative legal practices as not only extra-legal experiments, but as vital components of the ongoing dynamic of legal reconstruction. It also, conveniently, justifies quasi-utopian theoretical gestures such as this chapter.

The upshot of all of the above is, unsurprisingly, the disintegration of the concept of law as an identity with defined boundaries, specified methods of exclusion and inclusion, and a particular essence. A re-consideration of the axes of space and time in legal theory necessarily leads to a re-thinking of the axis of identity of law. Indeed it leads to a replacement of the notion of law as a defined identity with an understanding of law as a non-entity: an anti-paradigm, illimitable network, and performative set of relationships in the process of becoming.

Bibliography

Anker, K (2004) 'Law in the Present Tense: Tradition and Cultural Continuity in *Members of the Yorta Yorta Aboriginal Community v Victoria'*, *Melbourne University Law Review* 28, pp 1–27.

Arendt, H (1958) *The Human Condition*, Margaret Canovan (ed.), Chicago: University of Chicago Press.

Armstrong, S (2004) 'Is Feminist Law Reform Flawed? Abstentionists and Sceptics', *Australian Feminist Law Journal* 20, pp 43–63.

Austin, J (1954) *The Province of Jurisprudence Determined*, London: Weidenfeld and Nicholson.

Beresford, S (1998) 'The Lesbian Mother: Questions of Gender and Sexual Identity' in Moran, Monk and Beresford (eds), *Legal Queeries: Lesbian, Gay and Transgender Legal Studies*, London: Cassell, pp 57–67.

Braidotti, R (1994) *Nomadic Subjects: Embodiment and Sexual Difference in Contemporary Feminist Theory*, New York: Columbia University Press.

Brown, W (2000) 'Suffering Rights as Paradoxes', *Constellations* 2, pp 230–41.

Butler, J (1990) *Gender Trouble: Feminism and the Subversion of Identity*, New York: Routledge.

Butler, J (1993) *Bodies That Matter: On the Discursive Limits of Sex*, New York: Routledge.

Chinkin, C (2001) 'Women's International Tribunal on Japanese Military Sexual Slavery', *American Journal of International Law* 95, pp 335–41.

Conaghan, J (2000) 'Reassessing the Feminist Theoretical Project in Law', *Journal of Law and Society* 3, pp 351–85.

Cooper, D (2001) 'Against the Current: Social Pathways and the Pursuit of Enduring Change', *Feminist Legal Studies* 9, pp 119–48.

Cooper, D (2004) *Challenging Diversity: Rethinking Equality and the Value of Difference*, Cambridge: Cambridge University Press.

Cornell, D (1993) *Transformations*, New York: Routledge.

Cotterrell, R (2002) 'Subverting Orthodoxy, Making Law Central: A View of Sociolegal Studies', *Journal of Law and Society* 29, pp 632–44.

Cover, R (1983) 'Nomos and Narrative', *Harvard Law Review* 97, pp 4–68.

Dauvergne, C (2004) 'Making People Illegal', in Fitzpatrick, P and Tuitt, P (eds), *Critical Beings*, London: Ashgate, pp 83–99.

Davies, M *Delimiting the Law:'Postmodernism' and the Politics of Law*, London: Pluto.

De Lauretis, T (1990) 'Eccentric Subjects: Feminist Theory and Historical Consciousness', *Feminist Studies* 16, pp 115–50.

Derrida, J (1982) 'Différance' in *Margins of Philosophy*, Chicago: University of Chicago Press, pp 3–27.

Dolgopol, U (2006) 'Redressing Partial Justice – A Possible Role for Civil Society' in U Dolgopol and J Gardam (eds), *The Challenge of Conflict: International Law Responds*, Leiden: Martinus Nihjoff, pp 475–98.

Douzinas, C, Warrington, R and McVeigh, S (1991) *Postmodern Jurisprudence: The Law of Text in the Texts of Law*, London: Routledge.

Drakopolou, M (2000) 'The Ethic of Care, Female Subjectivity and Feminist Legal Scholarship', *Feminist Legal Studies* 8, pp 199–226.

Duncanson, I (1997) 'Cultural Studies Encounters Legal Pluralism: Certain Objects of Order, Law and Culture', *Canadian Journal of Law and Society* 12, pp 115–42.

Dworkin, R (1986) *Law's Empire*, London: Fontana.

Fitzpatrick, P and Tuitt, P (eds) (2004) *Critical Beings: Law, Nation and the Global Subject*, London: Ashgate.

Foucault, M (1980) 'Two Lectures' in Foucault *Power/Knowledge: Selected Interviews and Other Writings 1972–1977*, Brighton: Harvester Press.

Gasché, R (1986) *The Tain of the Mirror: Derrida and the Philosophy of Reflection*, Cambridge, Mass: Harvard University Press.

Goel, R (2000) 'No Women at the Center: The Use of the Canadian Sentencing Circle in Domestic Violence Cases', *Wisconsin Women's Law Journal* 15, pp 293–334.

Graycar, R and Morgan, J (2005) 'Law Reform: What's In It For Women?', *Windsor Yearbook on Access to Justice* 23, forthcoming.

Haraway, D *Simians, Cyborgs, and Women: The Reinvention of Nature*, New York: Routledge.

Harris, A (2003) 'Afterword: Bad Subjects: The Practice of Theory and the Constitution of Identity in Legal Culture', *Cardozo Women's Law Journal* 9, pp 515–25.

Howe, Adrian (1997) 'More Folk Provoke their Own Demise (Homophobic Violence and Sexed Excuses – Rejoining the Provocation Law Debate, Courtesy of the Homosexual Advance Defence)', *Sydney Law Review* 19, pp 336–65.

Irigaray, L (1993) *je, tu, nous: Toward a Culture of Difference*, A Martin trans., New York: Routledge.

Irigaray, L (1996) *i love to you: Sketch of a Possible Felicity in History*, A Martin trans., New York: Routledge.

Kapur, R (2005) *Erotic Justice: Law and the New Politics of Postcolonialism*, London: Glasshouse Press.

Kelsen, H (1992) *Introduction to the Problems of Legal Theory* (first edition of the *Reine Rechtslehre* 1934), Oxford: Clarendon Press.

Koskenniemi, M (1997) 'Hierarchy in International Law: A Sketch' *European Journal of International Law* 8, pp 566–82.

Kyambi, S (2004) 'National Identity and Refugee Law', in Fitzpatrick, P and Tuitt, P (eds) *Critical Beings*, London: Ashgate, pp 19–36.

Lacey, Nicola (1998) *Unspeakable Subjects*, Oxford: Hart Publishing.

Laclau, E (1996) *Emancipation(s)*, London: Verso.

Loader, M (2004) 'A Recipe for Recognition of Same Sex Relationships', *Australian Feminist Law Journal* 20, pp 115–26.

Lugones, M (1987) 'Playfulness, "World"-Travelling, and Loving Perception', *Hypatia* 2, pp 3–19.

Lunny, A. 'Provocation and "Homosexual" Advance: Masculinized Subjects as Threat, Masculinized Subjects Under Threat' *Social and Legal Studies* 12(3): 311–33.

MacDonald, R (2001) 'Law Reform and Its Agencies' *Canadian Bar Review* 79, pp 99–118.

McCall, L (2005) 'The Complexity of Intersectionality', *Signs: Journal of Women in Culture and Society* 30, pp 1771–1800.

McNamara, L (2000) 'The Locus of Decision-Making Authority in Circle Sentencing: The Significance of Criteria and Guidelines', *Windsor Yearbook of Access to Justice*, 18, pp 60–114.

Merchant, C (1980) *The Death of Nature: Women, Ecology and the Scientific Revolution*, San Francisco: Harper & Rowe.

Morgan, J (2002) *Who Kills Whom and Why: Looking Beyond Legal Categories*, Melbourne: Victorian Law Reform Commission.

Morrison, W (1997) *Jurisprudence: From the Greeks to Post-modernism*, London: Cavendish.

Norrie, A (2000) 'From Critical to Socio-Legal Studies: Three Dialectics in Search of a Subject', *Social and Legal Studies* 9, pp 85–113.

Nussbaum, M (2000) *Women and Human Development*, Cambridge: Cambridge University Press.

Ost, F and van de Kerchove, M (2002) *De la pyramide au reseau: Pour une théorie dialectique du droit*, Paris: Presses des Facultés Universitaires Saint Louis.

Petersen, H (1997) 'Legal Pluralism, Legal Polycentricity, Legal Culture – Their Relevance for Women's Lives and Law' in R Mehdi and F Shahid (eds), *Women's Law in Legal Education and Practice in Pakistan*, Copenhagen: New Social Science Monographs, pp 151–64.

Přibáň, J (2002) 'Sharing the Paradigms? Critical Legal Studies and the Sociology of Law' in R Banakar and M Travers (eds), *An Introduction to Law and Social Theory*, Oxford: Hart Publishing, pp 119–33.

Santos, B de Sousa (2002) *Toward a New Legal Common Sense* (2nd edn), London: Butterworths.

Smart, C (1989) *Feminism and the Power of Law*, London: Routledge.

Stone, J (1966) *Social Dimensions of Law and Justice*, Sydney: Maitland Publications.

Stychin, C (2003) *Governing Sexuality: The Changing Politics of Citizenship and Law Reform*, Oxford: Hart Publishing.

Tamanaha, B (2001) *General Jurisprudence of Law and Society*, Oxford: OUP.

Tyson, D (1999) ' "Asking for It": An Anatomy of Provocation', *Australian Feminist Law Journal* 13, pp 66–85.

Victorian Law Reform Commission (2004) *Defences to Homicide: Final Report*, Melbourne: Victorian Law Reform Commission.

Williams, P (1987) 'Alchemical notes: Reconstructing Ideals from Deconstructed Rights', *Harvard Civil Rights-Civil Liberties Law Review* 22, pp 402–33.

Chapter 8

Speaking beyond thinking

Citizenship, governance, and lesbian and gay politics*

Davina Cooper, University of Kent

Introduction

Visibility, speech and understanding, in the opportunities they offer and the limits they often reveal, have proven key tropes in modern lesbian and gay politics. Metaphors, such as the closet, exemplify for many the destructive effects secrecy and invisibility can generate for lesbian and gay life.[1] For others, by contrast, hidden and obscure spaces are cause for celebration, as invisibility and lack of surveillance make resistance and alternative ways of being possible. This position also, however, has met its counter-point, from critics who question the possibility of spaces free from power and domination; rather, they argue, it is in the very semblance and practice of freedom that the exercise of power or governance is most deeply secured.

The relationship between silence, invisibility, and unintelligibility, on the one hand, and coherence, utterances, and visibility, on the other, identifies a series of tensions that have proven central in the development of a progressive state-oriented sexual citizenship, and it is these tensions that I wish to explore in this chapter. My empirical focus is the development of lesbian and gay initiatives in British local government, between 1985 and 2000, and particularly post-1997. Drawing loosely on governmentality as a way of thinking about how governing takes place, my argument centres on local government's deployment of limited thinkability as a technology of self-care. Limited thinkability focuses on what is possible for local government given the political project it is pursuing and the power relations by which it is constituted. More particularly, it addresses the limits on what can be thought, understood and known. While limited thinkability is often aligned with a limited speakability, in the case of lesbian and gay work of the late 1990s, this ceased to be

* This chapter is based on research funded by the ESRC (project number R000 239293), 'The changing politics of lesbian and gay equality in local government, 1990–2001', carried out with Jean Carabine and Surya Monro. My thanks to Vanessa Munro and Carl Stychin for comments on an earlier draft.
1 Yet, they also suggest, according to Eve Sedgwick (1990), the central role homosexual epistemologies play in the production of modern thought.

true. Local councils went from saying nothing or little about sexual orientation to incorporating it within a slew of wider utterances about diversity,
dignity, fairness and equality. Yet, rationalities, or rather *ir*rationalities
continued to structure what was said, by whom, to whom, and where.

At the heart of my argument is the claim that the limited thinkability
surrounding lesbian and gay local government initiatives worked to contain
the effects of what was or might be said. In this way, limited thinkability
provided what I shall call a 'firewall' that worked to depress active sexual
citizenship through limiting the capacity of its agents to guide or shape governmental action. Later in this chapter, I explore the conception of active
citizenship being used here. Broadly, my aim is to disarticulate active citizenship from the individualising, consumer-oriented approach of British governmental discourse of the time, and to treat it rather as a mode of political
engagement organised around the pursuit of an agenda not yet fully (and
sometimes not even partially) captured within the currently authorised terms
of institutional discourse and practice.

In the case of lesbian and gay work, limited thinkability formed an integral
element of restricting the contagious spread of an exterior, progressive sexual
politics. But limited thinkability did not work only in this way. While it
attenuated and depressed the capacity of a non-hegemonic sexual politics to
circulate through local government, shaping its policies and practices, alone,
limited thinkability could not fully stop alternative discourses, policies and
practices from circulating. Of course, in large part, it did not have to. The
1990s witnessed a range of measures that worked to curb the active citizenship of many forces and agendas. Some curbing measures have been well
explored in other contexts, particularly those of privatisation, competitive
tendering, devolution of power, and cabinet government. In this chapter,
I close by addressing one technique that has received far less attention, but
yet is particularly important to explaining why many firewalls remained
uncontested. It concerns the emotional registers of local government as they
shifted from the mid-1980s to late-1990s.

To develop these lines of argument, I shall draw together several literatures: including those of governmentality, citizenship, sexual politics, and
local government. However, given the focus of this book, I also want to signal
the contribution feminist work makes to this area. Feminist scholarship intersects my discussion at a number of points – particularly in thinking about
citizenship, rationality, the changing character and projects of the state, and
political affectivity. While some feminist work directly tackles questions of
sexual orientation, for the most part feminist literature runs along parallel
tramlines that consequently never quite meet a smaller, more emergent, literature on the *sexualised* character of citizenship, governance and reason. In this
chapter, my methodological aim is to have these literatures speak to each
other by drawing on and interweaving both. I therefore do not treat feminist
or gay scholarship as either the problematic or as the solution, but pull them

together to better understand how local government at a particular place and time used firewalls of non-reason and depressed affect to limit the capacity of an active sexual citizenship.

To develop these lines of argument, this chapter is structured as follows. It begins by fleshing out what local government lesbian and gay work looked like between the mid-1980s and late-1990s, and then goes on to explore the new kinds of speakability brought into being. The second section addresses how these new utterances intersected a series of limits on what could be and was thought. I then pull these two strands of speakability and thinkability together in the third section to explore their relationship to local government's pursuit of self-care and its construction of firewalls against an active sexual citizenship. In the final part, I consider the place of emotional registers in enhancing or depressing the form active citizenship might take.

The lesbian and gay agenda: two generations of policy development

Lesbian and gay municipal policy development first came to public attention in the mid-1980s in a handful of mainly metropolitan authorities. While ad hoc fragmented initiatives had preceded this era, it was the rise of the new urban left within local government, and their verbal commitment to equal opportunities and anti-racism, which led to more institutionally structured developments in the lesbian and gay field. This does not mean lesbian and gay policy work in the 1980s was ubiquitous – far from it. Initiatives in the 1980s occurred in just a handful of local councils – mainly in London, Manchester, Nottingham, and Southampton. While work varied between the authorities involved, significant common ground existed. It is this common ground that is my focus here. I will briefly identify four aspects, which place in relief subsequent developments of the late 1990s (see also Lansley *et al.*, 1989; Lent, 2001).

First, lesbian and gay work was developed and delivered through distinct municipal organisational structures. Installed a few years earlier to respond to racial and gender-based inequalities, by the late 1980s these structures had begun to proliferate in response to the new inequalities recognised by local government: principally, sexual orientation, age, and disability. Structures shared a broadly common form based on formal standing committees (with council and community representatives), mini-departments known as units, and specialist officers. While the structures established generated new facilities, their aim was mainly strategic: to guide and direct officers providing public welfare provision and regulation to change their policies and practices; thus their success depended on good, effective relationships with service departments – a challenge I have discussed in some detail elsewhere (see Cooper, 1994).

Second, work aimed to remove heterosexual bias from council policies and practices. Training on homophobia and heterosexism was offered to senior and front-line council staff in line with parallel training in other equality areas. Procedures, guidelines and practices were scrutinised for covert and indirect, as well as explicit, discrimination. However, it is worth noting that developments in this area were uneven; in some services, such as education, discrimination seemed legally protected.[2] Different services also demonstrated varying levels of commitment and interest in the lesbian and gay agenda, with housing, personnel, leisure and community services proving more responsive than technical and direct labour services.

Third, work went into enhancing collective and individual capacity within lesbian and gay communities, through sector funding, symbolic initiatives, and dedicated provision. This proved, perhaps unsurprisingly, among the most controversial dimensions of the work, heightened by the media attention paid to targeted pro-gay services that involved children or recreation. Finally, governmental power was used to tackle external hostility and discrimination. Councils, if in uneven and usually very limited ways, supported protests against corporate, national and union-based homophobia in Britain and abroad, made compliance with their equal opportunities programme a condition of community group funding, and sought to use their contractual powers, particularly of procurement, to extend equality work (see Cooper, 1994, also 1999).

Lesbian and gay initiatives reached their zenith in the late 1980s. Their subsequent decline was precipitated by several factors including the long-term financial and legal consequences of a Conservative government (still in post after the 1987 general election), relentless media hostility, and a decline in the new urban left's control of local government, particularly post-1990. Initiatives did continue in various authorities, through the 1990s, if in low-key, largely ad hoc ways; still, it took the election of a Labour government in 1997 for initiatives to receive a renewed boost of energy.

Developments post-1997 resembled those of the previous decade, particularly in the continued emphasis on equality training and the elimination of discriminatory provisions. This chapter focuses on these post-1997 initiatives and practices, drawing on data from interviews with over one hundred participants (councillors, senior officers, front-line workers and community activists), and documentation from 12 local authorities in England, Scotland and Wales that were active in this field. However, alongside a re-scaling of work as more authorities introduced reform in this area, initiatives also reflected wider changes to local government, particularly the new managerialism, and marketisation (see also Creegan *et al.*, 2003); they also reflected the

---

2   Work in schools was affected by s 28 Local Government Act 1988, prohibiting the promotion of homosexuality and its 'acceptability' as a 'pretended family relationship', despite legal advice that it could not apply to decisions by teachers or school governors.

shift in governmental and community ethos towards a more gradualist and non-confrontational approach. This latter, with its emphasis on moderation and negotiation, and with its disavowal of the past, belied the extent to which the policies of the two periods were, in many respects, remarkably similar. Yet, in two respects, second-generation sexual orientation policies and structures, that is those introduced post-1997, proved different.

First, standing committees, units and posts were replaced by partnerships and multi-agency initiatives as councils externalised their work and responsibilities in this field. This shift away from specialist strategic units located at local government's organisational centre coincided with the drive for 'mainstreaming' across the 'equality' field. Mainstreaming emphasised integration, and the need to devolve equality and diversity agendas to local government departments or directorates (although many councils retained or established generic equality structures and forums). Directorates were expected to keep equality in mind across the spectrum of policies and new practices, working in partnership with external multi-agency structures.[3]

The second shift interconnected this one of organisational change. While council support for community events, such as Mardi Gras, continued, active authorities in the field placed less emphasis on 'positive' cultural initiatives. In particular, they moved away from council driven and organised gay events (although municipal facilitation of commercially successful ventures, such as urban gay villages, emerged as a significant aspect of urban councils' gay agendas, particularly by the mid-1990s (Binnie and Skeggs, 2004; Quilley, 2002)). Instead, through partnerships and inter-agency structures, involving the police, health authorities and lesbian and gay local organisations, local government oriented itself around a project based on tackling the impediments – ill health, violence, bullying, and abuse – placed on lesbian and gay civic and consumer freedom (see McGhee, 2003; also Cooper and Monro, 2003). Second-generation initiatives were also noteworthy in placing individual misconduct centre-stage. In contrast to the new urban left's contested attempts in the 1980s to use local government powers to guide, improve, and, if necessary, boycott 'bad' companies and public institutions (Cooper, 1999), by the late-1990s, local government's condemnatory gaze had shifted to private individuals, and, in contrast to an earlier feminist insistence on the domestic and intimate character of violence, particularly onto strangers.

A new speakability

Local developments in lesbian and gay policy development, especially post-1997, can be understood from several angles. My focus is the new regime

---

3 Many interviewees threw doubt on the extent to which this had occurred, particularly given local government's growing emphasis on managerial agency, municipal performance and privatisation.

of sexual 'speakability' brought into being – a term coined here to draw together, in a socially structured way, the subject's capacity and urge to speak alongside the object's ability to incite legitimate speech about itself. In the late 1990s, lesbians and gay men became a recognisable category for local government, their concerns ones local government could and should hear within a framework of diversity, social inclusion, dignity and respect (in contrast to the older discourse of equality of opportunity).

I want to explore this new speech within the context of governmentality (Dean, 1999; Rose, 1999). While this framework is not without problems, it is useful, in my view, in offering an analytical language and grammar through which the conduct and projects of government can be explored. I want to keep this discussion of the new speakability relatively brief as it is intended mainly to anchor my subsequent discussion of irrationality and municipal firewalls. Nevertheless, the following questions are particularly relevant to the issues I discuss: namely, what new modes of knowledge emerged? Who was authorised to speak and to hear? And what difficulties did the institutional context, within which this changing regime of speakability occurred, generate? My starting point is with the social problems lesbian and gay work refracted, constituted and responded to.

Rehearsing the problem

A Midlands policy officer told us: 'I would say most of it is around "tackling oppressions" rather than necessarily "promoting equality", it is very problem-focused, I think.' The general misconduct of homophobia has been extensively addressed, involving as it does utterances deemed injuries in their own right and those indicative of improper thinking (and acting); I will therefore not pursue this line of discussion further here. In the late 1990s, however, a new problem surfaced. Local government recognised it was not enough to tackle homophobia; they needed also to respond to central government's imperative that they involve lesbians and gay men more fully within the new community agenda. Coinciding, somewhat paradoxically, with 'the business case' for lesbian and gay development (with its emphasis on gay visibility), lesbians and gay men became defined as a 'hard to reach' group.[4]

While much can be made of the historic criminalisation and marginalisation of gay communities in explaining their inaccessibility, a related problem identified by interviewees – comparing lesbians and gay men to 'visible minorities' – was that of recognisability. Councils were seen as unable to say

---

4   See Home Office, *Guidance on Statutory Crime and Disorder Partnerships* (para 2.44), July 1998, Crime and Disorder Act 1998. A number of scholars, activists and officials criticised the term for placing responsibility with lesbians and gay men – as one senior police officer we interviewed declared: gay groups are not hard to reach, we have just failed to reach them.

much without lesbian and gay residents and service users saying more. While many authorities remained hesitant, as I discuss further below, to know exactly *what* an individual was, not knowing *whether* an individual was stymied progress. Yet, considerable disagreement remained as to whether and how self-declarations should operate. While some argued that lesbians and gay men, as council staff or service users, should be required to self-identify, others worried about how such utterances would be deployed, and stories were told to us, during interviews, of council managers substituting their own tactics of recognisability, such as handing out, in front of others, gay-related materials to staff assumed to be gay or lesbian.

Interfacing the problem 'out there' lay a cluster of other problems endemic to the interiority of governance (Dean, 1999). Anti-discrimination initiatives, including but not restricted to sexual orientation, drew attention to municipal self-examination – councils' identification of, and promise to remedy, internal failings. The resolve to do better permeated local government texts and utterances in this field. While such resolve co-existed, particularly pre-1997, with less public municipal utterances that refused to see the point or to understand what was required, confident, aspirational claims proved a hallmark of local authority anti-discrimination speech, especially in those speech acts constituting the council as a single, unified, hierarchical entity. *Generating* local government speech acts in this area proved hard work, but once achieved, they tended to come with an assertion that change could and would be delivered. For instance, Haringey Council's twenty-first century equal opportunities policy, *Achieving equality; respecting diversity* declares: 'The Council is committed to responding to the challenge of institutional discrimination by institutionalising an anti-discrimination ethos across the organisation – through pursuing a renewed focus on mainstreaming equalities in all core activities of the Council.'[5]

Who can speak and in what game?

Governmentality studies highlight the role played by experts in translating society into an object of government (Barry *et al.*, 1996: 131), and in guiding the conduct of citizens to make 'governing at a distance' possible through mobilising and steering subjects' freedom. In this chapter, I explore the reverse effect – the capacity of non-state forces to guide from a distance, and I discuss how such guiding worked in more detail below. However, I want to emphasise that it was facilitated and, some would argue, *co-opted* by local government's willingness to recognise the expertise of 'indigenous experts' (Rose, 1999: 189). Municipal lesbian and gay work, with its manufacture of the professional homosexual, spoke to a readjustment in the production

5   See also Glasgow City Council *Equality Policy* (also undated).

of governmental speech about sexuality, displacing the authority of experts experientially 'distant'.[6] While self-knowing may have led lesbians and gay men to govern themselves according to a liberal governmental logic (Richardson, 2005: 529), this proved a double-edged sword. In recognising that identity communities knew themselves and their situation best, and in calling on them to provide municipal training and information about their needs, lesbian and gay community politics also became the place local government went to in identifying how what should be said about sexuality should be said.[7]

Yet, this should not be taken to mean that the new speakability proved unconstrained. What local government could say remained subject to its own institutional logic and to the 'rules' of this particular 'game'. These latter were local government- rather than community-driven, and they impacted considerably on how local government spoke, how it was spoken to, and the utterances that circulated through it. The keystone, particularly between the mid-1980s and mid-1990s, was the seemingly non-negotiable claim that lesbian and gay work was controversial, unpopular within the 'broader' community, and difficult. This meant work had to be pursued with great care and tact, and developed in ways hugely mindful of the media's response – requirements that became amplified in the lead-up to local or national elections or when children or teenagers were involved.

As a consequence, the terms of speakability proved constantly in flux. Promises to support initiatives from senior officers, councillors or committees could be (and were) discarded, abandoned, ignored, or even countermanded, at any time. Speakability also became a highly nuanced business; rules governing what could and could not be said, when, where and by whom, generated complex tactics and heightened calculations on all sides. These revolved around timing, visibility, 'door-openers', 'wedges', and the deployment of discourses already in political play. For proponents, lesbian and gay work provided a means of demonstrating mastery of the municipal game. Considerable pride and status was evident among, and accorded to, those who knew the rules and could play cleverly or well. 'Dressing-up' initiatives and creating alliances could enable things to slide through without inciting 'the wrong kind of speech'. As one top-level officer of a South-East local authority commented: 'Well, the leadership were quite happy knowing that I would be very astute politically as to how it would get handled. We'd get on and deal with it; we'd earn the brownie points and we wouldn't rock the political boat.'

I have discussed the organisational and discursive constraints placed upon

6   Although some interviewees complained that local government failed to make use of community organisers' knowledge base.
7   In the 1980s, considerable stress was placed on this right, with its mandated linguistic structures: 'lesbian and gay', for example, rather than the reverse, and the prohibition, in some places, on the word, 'homosexual'.

lesbian and gay municipal work in more detail elsewhere (Cooper, 1994). What I want to highlight here, by contrast, is the new regime of homosexual speakability in place by the late 1990s. Despite the different anxieties at stake, visibility, fairness and inclusion dominated public municipal speech acts in this field. This does not mean, of course, that these things were achieved in relation to homosexuality, rather that they had come to represent norms of good governance in relation to same-sex sexual identities – now deemed benign. Yet, while more hostile or ambivalent attitudes may have become largely cleansed from direct authorised speech, they re-emerged in other forms.[8] Evidence for the existence of such hostility can be found in the tactics, strategy and calculation of second-generation proponents, who worked highly sensitised to local government's more covert underbelly, which continued to see lesbian and gay work as irrelevant and risky. However, municipal ambivalence is also uncovered when we consider not just what was said, but its relationship to what was thought. By thought, I am not trying to identify individual actors' private contemplations or psychological motivations; rather, I am interested in the reasoning derived from governmental practice. My argument is that the limited intelligibilities or rationalities apparent when we consider councils' reasoning not only worked to constrain speech, but also ensured that the progressive speech acts described would prove viable and safe.

Refusing to think

In many ways, it is unsurprising that local government's lesbian and gay programme articulated a failure to reason. Taking sex out of its 'rightful' domain – converting it into an equality issue, and placing it on the state's agenda – not surprisingly brought with it displaced anxieties. Thus, on one reading, irrationality simply followed sex out of the private domain into state policy making and practice. This is not a reading I wish to adopt. The irrationality I am concerned with – based on the limits of what could be thought by and within local government at a particular historical moment – was not implanted in local government from the outside. Feminist scholarship (for example Atherton, 1993; Lloyd, 1984; Nicholson, 1999) has very usefully displaced the set of articulations that link reason to the state and public sphere.

At the same time, to say lesbian and gay work demonstrated local government's limited thinkability does not mean it *lacked* rationality. From a Foucauldian perspective, we can see a refusal to think (or to think hard) as a non-necessary or not inevitable technology of rule, which produced a range

---

8 Kendall Thomas poses a similar argument in his discussion of the place of race within American capital punishment, see his AHRC Research Centre, annual lecture: 'If There Is Such a Thing: Race, Sex, and the Politics of Enjoyment in the Killing State', 18 March 2005.

of effects, including the consolidation of particular kinds of knowledge – about sexuality as well as about local government. The impetus for lesbian and gay initiatives emerged out of a particular political trajectory that variously combined feminist, gay, liberal and socialist traditions (Cooper, 1994). However, municipal discourse on sexual orientation became unable to deal with the different political perspectives at stake. Instead, it located second-generation work within a more widely pervasive vocabulary, set of principles and assumptions concerned with individual well-being, responsibility, governance and safety (see generally Dean, 2002: 119). We can thus read the second-generation municipal agenda, including its deployment of limited thinkability, within the broad terms of modern, Western political rationality: organised around liberty and rights, on the one hand; and order and security, on the other. In the account that follows I turn to consider three interlinked forms of limited thinkability: policy incoherence; non-reasoning or a refusal to deliberate; and a superficial intelligibility or failure to consider alternative, non-liberal perspectives.

Policy incoherence

The first dimension, I will mention briefly as the argument has been well rehearsed elsewhere. Sometimes referred to as contradictory or discontinuous rationality, it addresses the disjuncture between rationalities articulated in oral and written texts, and those forms of reasoning legible from other technologies of rule (Dean, 1999: 72; 2002: 120). In the main, despite the controversy to beset even verbal declarations of support, public utterances promised more than was delivered. But discontinuities should not be read simply as a watering down of effect from statement to policy to delivery, even leaving aside the problems with this linear model of practice (see also Cooper, 1994). Discontinuities traversed council practice at every stage, from the conflicting sexual politics of different departments, to inconsistencies of approach within departments. One community organiser described the situation in her authority:

> There are tensions about planning as one part of the council might do planning about a certain area of [the city] which impacts on another part of the council's work about, for example, public sex environments. Different parts of the council disagree about the things that impact on the LGBT community. For example, there was a situation where I wrote a web-site for the anti-homophobic bullying campaign and I contacted the information department about the council hosting it and they said 'no', they said it was an ill-thought out thing; it was [for them] about s 28, although the council as a whole does not support s 28. For example, we cannot get onto the LGBT websites as the council has a firewall, although these sites are not porn.

Inconsistencies also pervaded the subject class. So, while health programmes targeted people, usually men, who *happened* to have sex with other men, personnel policies focused on lesbian and gay *identified* employees, housing policies targeted gay *couples*, and community safety initiatives addressed those *taken to be* gay. This variance in the subject class can be read as inevitable and, indeed, necessary if the diverse ways in which sexual identity interfaces public provision are to be addressed. However, the lack of explicit elaboration or deliberation also revealed a second mode of limited thinkability.

Refusing to know

Silence, opacities, policies such as the US military's 'don't ask, don't tell', highlight the extent to which a certain kind of institutional not knowing has proved central to the management of 'moderate' gay sexualities. In British local government, not knowing can be read off from the limits of what was said. In some cases, these limits took the form of omissions and failures: for instance, the repeated exclusion of lesbian and gay issues from multidimensional equity or social justice speech and practices (particularly prior to the late 1990s). In other cases, deliberative limits were apparent from the content of utterances themselves. While governing bodies tend to present themselves as knowledgeable and authoritative – comprehensive experts of the subject in question – in some contexts, *not* knowing for a governing body – or clearly defining limits to its knowledge – has proved more productive of authority. This can be seen at specific historical junctures, such as late twentieth-century Britain, where knowing a lot about other faiths or sexual orientations became evidence for improper interests and attractions. In such contexts, it was knowledge and reason – not irrationality – that signalled affectivity, emotion and the body.

Yet, the production of not knowing does not, of course, mean a refusal to speak. While British judges marked their epistemic distance with explicit utterances regarding their own lack of knowledge (for example see Cooper and Herman, 1999), in local government, nervous and embarrassed humour offered ways of displacing and disavowing a more serious engagement. Jill Humphrey's (1999) work on lesbian and gay social workers, for example, explores how heterosexual staff used lesbian and gay colleagues to maintain their own distance from same-sex matters. Our research disclosed several similar strategies of cognitive distance and disavowal. So, councils variously refused to take ownership of, or put their name to, gay positive reports, abolished committees which had lesbian and gay issues as their purview, placed responsibility for lesbian and gay issues with officers lacking expertise and experience, and instructed officers to attend lesbian and gay forums to observe but not participate.

Externalisation of knowledge and expertise was also a marked feature of local government's lesbian and gay activities as I suggested earlier, contributing also to an institutional disavowal of knowledge. Indeed, particularly in the early 1990s, community activists, in some authorities, expressed concern that they were being used as 'unpaid advisers', saving councils' money and 'letting them off the hook' from having to do the work themselves. Use of gay experts should not lead us to discount activists' other claims that consultation was frequently inadequate, nor ignore the many occasions on which activists had to pressure authorities to recognise and utilise their expertise. Still, the general preference for freelance rather than in-house experts was not only a distinctive characteristic of second-generation initiatives, but integral to the council's overall strategy of sexual non-reasoning. Local government could combine not thinking with the development of policy, because it could access those willing to do the thinking for it. But this does not mean external experts had a free rein. In the shift from first-generation work, with its activist-driven ethos of challenging state claims head-on, to a second-generation professional-oriented training approach, consultants and advisers were expected to behave and talk appropriately, acculturated in the discourses and limits of what community talk to council staff could officially entail.

Deliberately limited understanding

The circumscribed relationship between external expertise and internal sayability raises a third dimension of local government's limited rationality: its refusal to consider different perspectives and frameworks (see Brunsson, 1986), and its almost exclusive deployment of liberal pluralist modes of intelligibility.[9] While it would be wrong to ignore the spectrum of perspectives demonstrated among authorities, by the late 1990s a particular understanding of sexuality had nonetheless come to dominate – one also articulated by central government. This was characterised by discomfort in addressing the relationship between identity and corporeality, on the one hand, and between identity and social power, on the other. To flesh this out further, I want to highlight three aspects of this limited intelligibility: mimicry, the place of sex, and the case of bisexuality.

Mimicry

From the mid-1980s onwards, local government relocated its homosexual away from the terrain of moral and practical deviance to that of social

---

9   I have explored elsewhere the spectrum of paradigms deployed in local government lesbian and gay politics through the 1980s (see Cooper, 1994).

identity, suffering its attendant problems of bias, prejudice and discrimination.[10] Sexual orientation thus became apprenticed to gender and race.
While the causes of suffering were seen to vary, suffering itself and the strategies for tackling it were identified as common across constituencies. As one
interviewee described, 'You're not actually talking about sex but harassment
due to sexual orientation.' While a policy officer elsewhere stated: 'We've kind
of taken the same views as in terms of racist harassment . . . If someone's
perceiving themselves to be harassed on account of their sexuality, then it's
recorded as such.'

Strategies of equivalence and mimicry also pervaded the co-existing discourse of need. Feminist theory has long explored the socially constructed,
discursively contested character of need (for example Fraser, 1989) – addressing how needs are produced and shaped by the politics, practices and structures of particular historical junctures. Certainly, in the context of lesbian
and gay work, groups became, if not constituted then, at least, *secured*,
through the pronouncement of their distinct needs, a process, at municipal
level, aided and contested by lesbian and gay community activists. My
own experience as a London councillor in the late 1980s was of sitting on
Haringey Council's Lesbian and Gay Sub-Committee engaged in the collective process of identifying 'our special needs'; for, given the logic of equality
politics, if distinct unmet needs could not be identified, lesbian and gay
work's survival seemed uncertain.

The problems this strategy generated were also, however, apparent. One
community organiser interviewed in our later research remarked:

> I don't want every single thing to be scrutinised by us; there isn't particu-
> larly an LGB perspective on the allocation of wheelie bins, although
> believe you me in . . . [authority] they are meeting on exactly that . . . By
> and large, whatever your sexuality, it makes no difference if the street
> lights ain't working.

The logic of special needs reflected the simultaneously assimilatory and
pluralist character of progressive liberalism. While difference was not to be
disavowed (Phelan, 2001: 145), it was framed, contained and read isomorphi-
cally.[11] Adopting a model of simple equivalence meant councils did not have

---

10 Not all homosexuals were relocated in this way, and some were left behind. This was
   particularly apparent in the way governmental support for gays was frequently articulated to
   an anti-paedophile agenda.
11 Yet, the parallels councils drew between disadvantaged constituencies were not accepted
   unequivocally. The symbolic, political and economic capital generated for community actors
   through the state's recognition of their needs caused an isomorphic model to be repeatedly
   contested. As a result, equality champions throughout the 1990s continued to oppose claims
   that the harm encountered by lesbian and gay constituencies equaled their own.

to interrogate the politics of sexuality – instead it could be seen as just another way of labeling disadvantaged people alongside gender and race. Constructing one mode of explanation and understanding thus displaced others. It also displaced the need to *think* about others. To the extent that 'rational' decision making involves evaluating different perspectives, our research reveals few instances in which different ways of understanding sexual orientation were explicitly and reflexively discussed. Some approaches seemed to be particularly organised out. These included minority and oppositional stances marked as queer and trans. However, also omitted from deliberation were an older generation of feminist and gay liberation approaches; thus sexual needs and sex-based suffering were disarticulated from a significant rethinking of the relationship between power and sexuality, the public and private, or from a new sexual ethics that might, as, Ruth Lister (1997: 166) proposed, bring the concerns of care to bear on the politics of rights.

The place of sex

The failure to link lesbian and gay work to a rethinking of the relationship between public and private intersects a second aspect of local government's liberal pluralist framework: the place of sex. Treating the body as a source of problems – of illness, offending, violence, risk – rather than of pleasures, local government sought to disentangle lesbians and gay men from sex, even as concerns about sex pervaded council discourse and utterances. So, in some authorities, public sex by gay men – as cottaging, cruising and 'rent-boy' activity – continued to receive attention (for some, too much attention) from state agencies.[12] In other cases, local government's determination to *de-sex* gay initiatives, and to publicise this de-sexing, dominated. Several interviewees referred to heterosexual council staff anxiety that gay policies would thrust graphic sexual detail upon them. In one authority, community organisations were compelled to ensure their Mardi Gras was 'family friendly': as one person put it: 'we had to demonstrate we were not a freak-show in the middle of the park'. In another case, a librarian interviewed stressed that a gay-positive ordering policy did not mean having 'magazines in the libraries with nude photos on the cover'.

De-sexing, as an instance of, and technique for achieving, a circumscribed, liberal-pluralist response to lesbian and gay needs, worked at a number of levels. It encompassed the rhetorical claim that homosexuality had no particular relationship to sex, alongside strategies aimed at disarticulating gay identity, as both empirical truth and good conduct norm, from what was seen as its too easy slide into an excessive sexuality. Yet, the enunciation of sex, in

---

12 Monro (2006) considers whether the police became in any way 'queered' through the force's new penetration of public gay life.

the same breath as homosexuality, tied gay men and lesbians to their sexual practices just as councils rhetorically sought to separate them. As I have suggested, this was not due to a failure to reason but the effect of a narrow form of reasoning that did not know what to do with the sexual supplement discourses of homosexuality invariably produced.

Domesticating bisexuality

The third example of local government's failure to reflect upon different frameworks concerns bisexuality (Monro, 2005). The treatment of bisexuality demonstrates, perhaps better than anything, the limited understanding brought to matters of sexual orientation, as well as the general reluctance of local government to turn its mind. In the 1980s, municipal categories of sexual orientation did not extend beyond lesbian and gay; but from the mid-1990s onwards many councils widened their brief to include bisexuality and, in some cases, transgender too. Despite the widespread nature of this practice, and despite the extensive, often fierce, debates within community organisations on this question, almost no deliberation took place within local government. Local councils mirrored the policy of organisations in their locality as they moved from LG to LGB and LGBT – a shift that underscores once again the extent to which expertise and authority in relation to sexual orientation was externalised. One senior Scottish councillor told us, 'We started off using "lesbian and gay", but then we changed to take on ... LGBT ... really because we were advised by the lesbian and gay people we're working with that that was the accepted wording, to take on a wider definition.' But what did this category extension mean? Did local authorities integrate the particular discrimination, status or needs of bisexual people? And what would this have entailed?

With the exception of some youth provision which sought to address the experiences and concerns of young people who did not identify unequivocally as lesbian or gay, councils added the term 'bisexual' without any visible changes to their practices. Indeed, some policy and service developments, such as adoption and fostering, maintained a – not only or always implicit – bias against bisexual applicants on the grounds that carers and adoptee parents should be in stable, monogamous, committed relationships read by some local officials as clashing with a bisexual lifestyle. One social services manager told us: 'I would struggle with any relationship which was not totally committed. It is about the needs of the child. If you are still in the process of having a number of casual relationships, are you going to meet the needs of a child?'

Bisexuality, in this way, proved the limit case for local government's project of inclusivity and equality. Added to policy texts because community organisations had added it, it nicely illustrates Pat O'Malley's (1996: 313) suggestion that governing at a distance, by appropriating indigenous forms, can lead to the incorporation of alienating and contradictory practices and assumptions which then need to be neutralised or eliminated. In this case, neutralisation occurred through a failure to address what the addition of bisexuality might mean. Yet, framing the point in this way may overstate the extent of community agency; while community groups took the lead in adding bisexuals, they too tended not to explore or integrate bisexuality's distinctive relationship to heterosexuality or homosexuality within the local government context (see also Phelan, 2001: 120). For, despite the extensive and often fierce debates within lesbian and gay organisations over extending who counted as 'in', having taken this decision, organisations largely mirrored local government in the way they incorporated bisexuals and transgender people within policy work. Our research suggests such constituencies were added with little change in the content of policies; in other words, particularly for bisexuals, their needs and interests were treated as being largely identical to those of lesbians and gay men and therefore met by a simple change in terminology to explicitly include them.[13]

The incorporation of bisexuals, in this way, on the part of local government can be seen as a pre-emptive discursive strategy that allowed councils to avoid difficult questions of desire, sexual monogamy and agency. For councils to have failed or refused to add bisexuals when community groups were doing so risked generating demands for explanation. Councils would have been pushed to come up with distinctions that would have forced them onto the terrain of sexual politics – a terrain which progressive councils, in contrast, paradoxically, to their more sexually conservative predecessors and peers, refused through their utterances to occupy.

Active citizenship and the production of firewalls

In this final section of the chapter, I want to change focus. My aim is to address how practices of speakability and limited thinkability came together in the production of municipal firewalls. To do so, I start by suggesting that a key concern of local government, particularly through the 1990s, was care of itself. Such care invoked the need for firewalls to limit, among other things, the risks ensuing from a more active sexual citizenship. Limited thinkability provided one such firewall; however, councils' unwillingness to think too much or too hard also had contradictory consequences. To the extent it also opened up pathways for a more active citizenship, limited thinkability created the need for, or, perhaps more accurately, coincided with the workings of other firewalls and brakes. The brake I shall explore briefly here, since it has tended to be ignored in the local government literature, and since it has a

---

13 For example, see *Count me in*, Brighton & Hove LGBT Community Strategy, 2001–2006, p 12, on campaigning for partnership rights to protect LGBT people's right to housing.

special relationship to gender and sexuality, is that of emotional energy or political affectivity. I have addressed local government's self-care elsewhere (see Cooper, 2006), so I will focus here on the last three parts of the argument.

Rethinking an active sexual citizenship

I want to start by elaborating a part of my argument that has remained relatively opaque to this point. It concerns the relationship between the pursuit of lesbian and gay inclusion and equality, and active citizenship. In thinking about this relationship, what comes immediately to the fore is local government's contribution, through its utterances and material practices, to the recognition, inclusion and entitlement of lesbians and gay men. In this discussion, however, because my focus is on 'active' citizenship, I shall bracket the work local government has done to achieve greater inclusivity for its gay residents. So, instead of considering how citizenship as a subject status is produced and installed from on 'high', I want to address the agentic practices of lesbian and gay actors – to explore what they do in the name of citizenship rather than what is done, in its name, to them.

Active citizenship is a term that has acquired a particular, rather individualistic resonance within modern British politics.[14] I, however, want to reclaim the term to identify here the means by which socio-political constituencies guide or imprint on governmental and institutionally established practices[15] 'from a distance'. In other words, I am interested in the 'conduct of conduct' in pursuit of a non-governmental project. In framing my objective in this way, I do not reverse so much as twist the claim that state institutions govern at a distance through relays, experts and so on (Rose, 1999). While state institutions start from the premise that governing is what they are charged with and able to do, the same is not true for oppositional social forces. Located at a distance from governmental power, or at least from its legitimate and mandated exercise, they have to find ways of exerting or having an effect.

Active citizenship is about difference and distinction. It does not signify a universalist project. Citizenship politics may entail demands in 'the name of the people' or through rereading overarching principles, such as equality, justice and dignity. However, active citizenship politics, including over sexual orientation (Bell and Binnie, 2000; Phelan, 2001; Stychin, 2003) are rooted in

14 This includes the Labour Government's programme to rescue citizens from the state (Clarke, 2005: 449), as a form of voluntary altruism in which citizens are encouraged to 'give something back' (see Kearns, 1995), and as an injunction to take responsibility for others' well-being alongside one's own, in ways aligned with – rather than intent on influencing or giving new shape to – governmental thinking (see also Chandler, 2001; Sullivan, 2001).

15 This takes account of those feminist claims that seek to trouble the distinction between public and private when it comes to citizenship practices (Beasley and Bacchi, 2000; Lister, 1997; Narayan, 1997).

the cleavages and struggles of a particular era. But while it is tempting to equate the term active citizenship with a particular constituency's struggle, what I want to centre on here in my use of the term is the project being advanced not the constituency doing the advancing. Active citizenship entails a project that seeks to impel, or that goes beyond or collides with those projects institutionally authorised. This does not mean the project pursued is necessarily coherent or unified. In the case of lesbian and gay governmental politics, several different strands were pursued simultaneously – including anti-discrimination, symbolic affirmation, gay commercial expansion, and, to a lesser degree, anti-oppression politics. However, to the extent these strands became knotted together as something other or more than local government's corporate approach, they can be seen as advancing a common active citizenship project. And to the extent that council officers and councillors, in conjunction with community activists, worked to advance this project, even as those supporters employed by and elected to the council simultaneously pursued other more *authorised* agendas, they can be identified as participants of an active citizenship.

The links between differently positioned actors highlight a second aspect of active citizenship: the capacity or at least struggle to imprint from a distance. Imprinting from a distance requires:

(i)   mediation, by which I mean establishing linkages between different governing practices;
(ii) crossing sector boundaries; and
(iii) adjusting the logic of the organisational environment so that different practices become viable, advisable, profitable and good sense.

I have discussed the third element elsewhere (see Cooper, 2004), so I shall say here something more about the first two. Controlling, guiding, or inflecting governmental and social practices may occur in open deliberative forums where different, culturally marked groups – sometimes referred to as 'communities of interest' – compete for influence over the political process. But active citizenship, importantly, also incorporates the many other ways in which influence, governance or guidance occur. Counter-normative projects exert an effect through their deployment of resources (including social capital), discipline and physical pressure, as well as through discourse. However, these latter are often paid scant regard in discussions of governance and community participation.

Impeding the pursuit of a counter-normative politics

Liberalism's emphasis on formal arenas of decision making, and on the explicit processes of negotiation, influence and overt contestation, as the spaces in which active citizenship occurs, erases the complexity of governance-based practices of power. It also undermines the importance, inscribed into the term 'guiding at a distance', of being able to cross sector boundaries so the effects of actions are felt through a range of institutional arenas and practices (see generally Somerville, 2005). This may involve pursuing a counter-hegemonic agenda through the formal, *de jure* routeways local government makes available; however, given the nature of such an agenda, it more often entails creating or working through community or council practices that establish, albeit often temporary and unstable, *de facto* connections and pathways through different institutional domains (Cooper, 2004).[16]

Central to my argument, then, is the way active citizenship is created and performed through established linkages between different – in this context, governmental – spheres. So, I am not here concerned with barriers to political entry, such as the criminalisation or cultural exclusion of gay men; rather, I am concerned with the barriers that work to cleave a multi-faceted governmental terrain. At the same time, not all practices of active citizenship seek to extend the possibilities for 'making a difference'. Active citizenship may also sometimes involve inscribing, installing, or reinterpreting boundaries or 'social walls' between spheres, for instance as a form of collective protection or empowerment. Michael Walzer (1983) famously focused on this intra-domain dimension to social justice, arguing that justice required different social goods to be distributed according to different procedures. While he recognised that no single sphere's autonomy could ever be absolute, he argued that it was wrong to be able to convert one good into another where there was no intrinsic connection between the two. For complex equality to exist, no citizen's status or position in relation to one social good should be able to be undercut or enhanced by their standing in relation to another.

Our research findings revealed occasions where inequalities were generated because some sections of the lesbian and gay community could convert capital from other domains to advance their interests within this local government one. A number of interviewees, for instance, commented on how well-funded AIDS organisations used their enhanced social and policy capital as a means of dominating lesbian and gay community organising. However, in the main, active citizenship for lesbian and gay work depended less on building walls to restrict the power of some gay community constituencies, than on breaching walls so a progressive sexual politics could circulate through local government's broad domain. Community organisers contested walls as they struggled to influence from a distance – working with both the formal and informal opportunities lesbian and gay work generated. For instance, organisers used government funding opportunities and work on community safety

---

16 While the former identifies a form of direct governing as it implicates sovereign modes of rule, the latter takes on a more indirect form.

as door wedges to enable other initiatives to be developed.[17] Council officers were also used as conduits, allowing linkages between different sectors to be forged.

In considering local government's firewalls, it is important to view them relationally. Those built to impact upon lesbian and gay work did not necessarily delimit the power of other agencies or bodies to govern at a distance. Indeed the power of central government and the corporate sector was arguably enhanced (see Tickell and Peck, 1996). Also, arguably enhanced was the ability of a 'common sense' politics to govern from a distance – a point underscoring my earlier claim that it is the project rather than identification of the actors which is crucial to thinking about active, or in the case of common sense politics, passive citizenship.

From externally generated to internal firewalls

The relationship between different state institutions in the construction of local governmental firewalls is a complex one. While a number of the measures salami-slicing political power came from central government, our research suggests that local government in the late 1990s diligently took responsibility for establishing and maintaining interior divisions and cleavages of authority in contrast to the new urban left councils of the 1980s. Indeed, some might argue that it was central government that tried, post-1997, to increase community involvement and to create strategic crosscutting partnership structures which would allow more coherent and far-reaching changes to take place (Taylor, 2000). While there is some truth to this, I want to suggest central government's facilitation of communities guiding from a distance should not be overstated for two reasons.

First, community involvement tended to take highly circumscribed forms. Several commentators have argued that central government produced a tame, devolved space with parameters so limited little real impact could be had since this required action in a terrain beyond that made available (see Newman, 2001; also Sullivan, 2001). Janet Newman and her co-authors (2004) pursue this point, drawing on interview data to suggest public dissatisfaction that only small, minor matters had been devolved to local forums, with bigger issues remaining out of reach. Several of our interviewees raised similar points, as one ex-equality officer described:

> Where you've got an officer who's got a brief and they want to reply to that brief, but the community are looking at it from a holistic point of

17 As one Welsh community activist described, 'We managed to get things done by putting them on the Crime and Disorder hook. This gave it credibility – we never would have done it otherwise.'

view and looking beyond that brief. For an example, when the lesbian and gay people are asked to give their comments upon the Crime and Disorder Audit, their response was extremely comprehensive, an A to Z of how you deal with lesbian and gay issues full stop. It went way beyond the issues that the officer was addressing.

Second, inter-agency partnerships may have allowed *some* constituencies or agencies to imprint from a distance – as the thesis of a shift to network governance suggests – and it did facilitate some lesbian and gay developments, such as community safety initiatives. However, in relation to other political projects, it not only failed to facilitate 'joined-up' action, it actively impeded it. In the discussion that follows, I explore why lesbian and gay agenda and forces were limited in their capacity to guide from a distance. My analysis focuses on two endogenous factors: limited thinkability and the production of a muted affectivity.

Limited thinkability: an ambivalent firewall

Limited thinkability impeded the attempts of lesbian and gay activists to guide or effect change at a distance in several ways. To begin with, liberal pluralist perspectives and ambivalence about the place of sex and the private domain meant initiatives could not be argued for or supported through a distinctively *sexual* politics. Local government's refusal to think about sex obliged advocates of same-sex equality initiatives to draw on their proximity to other authorised equality areas. In theory, advocates could have pursued an oppositional active citizenship strategy by introducing counter-normative sexual claims into local government. However, without any discourses or practices on which such claims could grip, the likelihood of their circulation or conversion into policy practice seemed remote.

Unwillingness on the part of councils or council departments to think about same-sex equality issues went beyond the erasure of more challenging political perspectives, to include a reluctance to think about sexual orientation at all through much of the 1990s. Municipal embarrassment, disengagement, and readiness to allow departments to ignore formal corporate policies in this area impeded the advancement of a liberal equality agenda. However, to suggest it impeded the pursuit of active citizenship is to make a different claim since I have suggested active citizenship entailed pursuing *non-authorised* or not fully authorised projects. Such projects do depend, however, on making contact. Where councils and departments refused to include gay issues in policies, funding applications or working parties, where they only talked about sexuality in joking terms, and stayed away from lesbian and gay organisations, forums and partnerships, the various opportunities in principle available for sexual orientation to enter local government as an issue of citizenship became heartily restricted. In other words, the potential for municipal circuits to be used for a counter-normative politics were significantly impeded by the failure of even a liberal sexual politics to gain access.

Yet, in other respects limited thinkability opened up spaces. Externalising knowledge allowed community politics to structure the categories for inclusion, and lesbians and gay actors to be experts of their experience and needs. The use of buffers and fragmentation allowed work to take place without having to first achieve a broad consensus across local government. Liberal pluralist discourses enabled utterances and policies that might have seemed challenging within a more reflective intelligibility, over bisexuality, for instance, to be formulated. While I have suggested that such utterances were domesticated and defused, in part through a refusal to fully consider what they implied, local government's application of limited reasoning allowed a certain, not entirely containable or controllable, sexual politics to circulate.

Closing down the flows and circuits necessary for a more radical sexual politics did not just occur through institutional structures. It also entailed active mediators. The contradictory placement of local government employees tasked with managing an equality, diversity or community agenda, and the raised expectations municipal utterances generated that council staff would facilitate active citizenship, created discontent. Janet Newman (2002) describes how officers saw themselves as performing 'emotional labour', working to contain more radical or angry voluntary sector actors. During our interviews, one similarly told us:

> When we consulted with the [anti-homophobic] forum they presented far-reaching recommendations including the adoption of a policy by the local authority for the employment of lesbian and gay teachers. We tried to put forward the view these issues needed to be taken forward on other agenda. This was seen [by them] as resistance, and tensions arose. There were no avenues for things.

The constraints imposed by muted affectivity

In this final discussion, I want to explore the part emotion or affectivity played as a brake on an active sexual citizenship.

The relationship between the state and expressive feeling is a complex and contested one. While republican traditions often emphasise the importance of passions, such as love, hate and loyalty, in political action and state building, liberal traditions tend to read the modern liberal state as a terrain outside of, and against, the circulation of affect (see also Phelan, 2001: 46). Feminist scholarship has generated a powerful body of work countering this liberal stance. Writers have expressed scepticism that passions and feelings might be banished or erased, arguing that both are and should be present. Feminist and gay work has also critically explored the kinds of emotions and passions shown by the state – underscoring the presence of cruelty, sadism and a pornographic gaze on the part both of state institutions, such as the police force and courts, and by state-building and nationalist projects (for example Moran, 1995; Smart, 1989).

In this final discussion, I want to consider the affectivities constituted by local government's lesbian and gay agenda. The circulation of affect within governmental bodies has been relatively unstudied to this point. This may change, however, given the recent explosion of interest in affectivity and emotion in a range of fields, including social movement analysis (for example see Adams, 2003; Jasper, 2002; Klatch, 2004). Political analysis and lawyers have located affectivity in the expression of an abstract will or in people's identification with a state project, such as the European Union (Gibbs, 2005; Haltern, 2003). However, I want to highlight the way affectivity can circulate *through* a governmental structure. I also want to underscore the extent to which affectivity can shift: how it can go from being a political energy that supports innovation, as it seemed to have done in the 1980s, to one that impedes it.

In making this claim about lesbian and gay local government work, I am conscious of its controversial character. Many we interviewed described the 1980s as a period of rigidity and top-down governmental control, in which feelings and attitudes were severely disciplined, and only 'politically correct' speech allowed (see also Klatch, 2004, on political conformity within social movements). While a formulaic speakability *was* evident in the 1980s, I want to suggest something different, with curious echoes of Viroli's (2005) work on the movement from an art of politics to reason of state in Renaissance Italy.

To the extent local councils were perceived as having 'gone native' in the 1980s – the state/community boundary partially breached or, at least, rendered highly permeable – we can read the passions of community politics – its enthusiasm, energy and vitality, as well as its aggression and agonisms – as having entered local government. While the affective qualities of new urban left government in the 1980s differed from the republican agenda of legal compliance, and shared or harmonised public interest which Viroli explores, similarities exist in the ostensive emphasis on virtue rather than political self-interest, active collective participation of the citizenry rather than their individual engagement as consumers, and in the privileging of justice over, rather than through, state aggrandisement.

I do not want to over-romanticise local governmental politics of the 1980s, or to overlook the presence of other, less virtuous feelings. I also want to avoid underestimating the significance of the pragmatic concerns that underpinned local councils' (and their leaderships') viability. Fatigue, anxiety, fear, scepticism and ambition were present in all the front-runner authorities pioneering lesbian and gay work. And yet, with all these caveats noted, a distinctive affectivity was present, one built around and in service of a far more utopian social imaginary than that evident by the early 1990s. As one community worker declared: 'I think that some of them [LGB activists] managed to infiltrate inside . . . there was a lot of creativity.' A council equalities officer from the period similarly remarked: 'Things were a lot more relaxed in the 1980s. There was a feeling of excitement that things were going somewhere . . . In the '80s and early '90s there was more of a sense of it being an adventure.'

The project for lesbian and gay inclusivity of the late 1990s proved a different creature; different values, shaped by nationally generated 'modernising' processes, came to the fore as increasingly hegemonic – values of management, auditing systems, prudence and performance. As one Midlands officer described: 'We've been very much a kind of big project authority . . . You know, big capital schemes . . . which has meant that we are not in a very good position to respond to this sort of [lesbian and gay] agenda.' A community activist we spoke with, looked back nostalgically to remark: 'It was more organic in the 80s and bottom-up. Now it's top-down, largely managerial. It's helpful to have the [practical] support, but it is ideologically frustrating.'

One could argue, and no doubt should, that simply a different affectivity was being expressed – more controlled, risk-averse, deferential, and accommodating. As Hoggett and Thompson argue (2002: 114): 'emotions are never not in the public sphere'. And yet, in recognising the ever-present presence of emotions, I want to underscore the power and energy generated by policy innovations that *explicitly* mobilise and activate feeling. And here I do not simply mean the emotions expressed by external community groups seeking to influence and guide local government (see generally Hoggett and Thompson, 2002; Jasper, 2002), but the energy expressed *within*. As one interviewee described: 'The only way that it works is because there's a few of us who get in there and batter our heads against a brick wall . . . We're dependent upon the passionate person [in the local authority] and at the moment . . . we ain't got them'. My own personal recollections of the 1980s similarly suggest the importance of passion. However, this was not always or necessarily an oppositional, head-butting passion. It also included a less intense, more playful version in the form of a counter-hegemonic, institutionally 'libidinal*ised* economy' (Goodwin, 1997), in which flirtation, charm and chutzpah were polyamorously, and effectively, deployed by lesbian and gay specialist staff to 'impress upon' their council (see also Ahmed, 2004).

The externalisation of lesbian and gay work through the 1990s certainly hindered the ongoing capacity of a libidinal and affective energy to structure local government's interior spaces in this area. But to what extent did this energy shift to erupt externally, for instance in inter-agency partnerships and in the utilisation of community organisational expertise? I suggested earlier that central government's approach to community involvement tended to offer a restricted, carefully stage-managed influence that was anathema to the extended circuits active citizenship requires and involves. It was anathema also to the potential for affective expression. Locating community involvement within sanitised, controlled spaces did not contribute to the generation or mobilisation of collective political energy. But responsibility here cannot entirely be placed at the door of local or central government.

Data from our project suggests several shifts within lesbian and gay activism over the 1990s towards a more mainstream, moderate and self-reliant community politics. While the 1980s treated local government as an entity that could be shaped and guided through an ideological, emotional, protest-based politics, in the later era, lesbian and gay community groups engaged with local government as a partner rather than a terrain to enter, and as a partner who, if it would respond at all, would respond to reason, evidence and community leadership.

Conclusion

In this chapter, I have explored local government's response to lesbians and gays as an emergent, politically recognisable, subject class. My focus has been the relationship between speakability and thinkability. In particular, I have argued that while new kinds of speech were brought into play in relation to a newly valorised sexually identified constituency, caution needs to be taken before reading into this valorisation the enhancement of lesbian and gay sexual citizenship. While formal equality and greater inclusivity may be apparent, this co-existed in the late 1990s with measures that countered, deliberately or otherwise, the possibilities for active citizenship. What I mean by this is that the ability of a new sexual politics to circulate through local government and to shape local government's external practices was restricted by the operation of municipal firewalls. And in considering these firewalls, I suggested limited reasoning formed a significant component. In the final part of the chapter, I argued that the blockages limited reasoning generated were underpinned and strengthened by the muting of affectivity – a process, in relation to lesbian and gay work, that coincided with a new, 'extrospective' – that is a turning outwards – of corporate local government affect as it became increasingly driven by broader imperatives of performance, technocracy and competition (Peck and Tickell, 2002).

Yet, in making this argument, one obvious counter-position arises. If local government, by the late 1990s, had demonstrated its incorporation of progressive lesbian and gay agendas, with the institution of new anti-discriminatory and recognition-based measures, does it matter if the power of a counter-normative sexual agenda had become contained? If a progressive sexual citizenship was now realised, did the diminution of an active sexual citizenship, as either a necessary or coincidental aspect of local government's sexual step forward, particularly matter? Is it oppositionalism for oppositionalism's sake to argue for the continuing importance of an *active* sexual citizenship?

Several possible responses can be given here. One is to suggest that local government has not gone anywhere near as far in practice as its rhetoric suggests; progressive sexual citizenship does not underpin local government policies and practices to any considerable extent. A second response is to suggest that politics never stands still. Without a more *active* mode of sexual citizenship, local government initiatives, however satisfactory they may currently seem, will atrophy and become quickly outdated. Both these responses have validity. However, I want to close with a slightly different response, one that goes to the heart of this book's agenda. Arguing that new forms of active citizenship continue to be necessary, it asks us to return to the question underpinning the entire project, namely, what is the point of sexual orientation initiatives? Is it just about a class who happen to be defined by who they desire and have intimate relations with, or are sexual orientation measures, and should they be, anchored in broader issues that relate to sexuality as an organising principle of power and equality, broader issues that speak in particular to questions of gender, class and race?

Adopting a broader perspective, an active sexual citizenship needs to return to a previous generation of feminist discussion and critique about the role and place of compulsory heterosexuality as a form of social practice. While heterosexuality may no longer be compulsory in the UK, it continues to work, as a socially produced orientation, to secure a gendered division of labour (in the household and beyond), and to keep women in unequal relationships. But I want to suggest this well established, if now rather marginalised, analysis needs further complicating by thinking through sexuality's relationship to class and race – to the commodification and spatialisation of desire – to how and where sex, passion and intimacy are expressed; to the substitutional processes which allow middle-class lesbians and gay men to recruit others to occupy gendered positions in the performance of services; and to the extension of child-bearing options which incorporate lesbians and, to a lesser extent gay men, within racialised, biologically reproductive kinship structures.

So, to conclude, while local government's proffered sexual inclusivity may seem to render an *active* sexual citizenship unnecessary, I want to suggest it makes it all the more important. For, without denying the benefits of incorporation and recognition to many lesbians and gay men, it is a reminder that active citizenship entails drawing new political connections, even as local government cuts through them. While the last two decades have seen lesbian and gay municipal politics increasingly located around a discrete reformist agenda of parity, recognition and inclusion, the increasing formal achievement of this agenda opens the way for other more radical possibilities to come politically to the fore.

Bibliography

Adams, J (2003) 'The bitter end: emotions at a movement's conclusion', *Sociological Inquiry* 73, pp 84–113.

Ahmed, S (2004) 'Collective feelings: or, the impressions left by others', *Theory, Culture and Society* 21, pp 25–42.

Barry, A *et al.* (1996) 'Introduction', in Barry, A *et al.* (eds), *Foucault and Political Reason*, London: UCL Press.

Beasley, C and Bacchi, C (2000) 'Citizen bodies: embodying citizens – a feminist analysis', *International Feminist Journal of Politics* 2, pp 337–58.

Bell, D and Binnie, J (2000) *The Sexual Citizen*, Cambridge: Polity.

Bell, D and Binnie, J (2004) 'Authenticating queer space: citizenship, urbanism and governance', *Urban Studies* 41, pp 1807–20.

Binnie, J and Skeggs, B (2004) 'Cosmopolitan knowledge and the production and consumption of sexualised space: Manchester's gay village', *Sociological Review* 52, pp 39–61.

Brunsson, N (1986) *The Irrational Organization: Irrationality as a Basis for Organizational Action and Change*, London: Wiley.

Chandler, D (2001) 'Active citizens and the therapeutic state: the role of democratic participation in local government reform', *Policy and Politics* 29, pp 3–14.

Clarke, J (2005) 'New Labour's citizens: activated, empowered, responsibilized, abandoned', *Critical Social Policy* 25, pp 447–63.

Cooper, D (1994) *Sexing the City: Lesbian and Gay Politics Within the Activist State*, London: Rivers Oram.

Cooper, D (1999) 'Punishing councils: political power, solidarity and the pursuit of freedom', in Millns, S and Whitty, N (eds), *Feminist Perspectives on Public Law*, London: Cavendish, pp 245–69.

Cooper, D (2004) *Challenging Diversity: Rethinking Equality and the Value of Difference*, Cambridge: CUP.

Cooper, D (2006) 'Active citizenship and the governmentality of local lesbian and gay politics', *Political Geography* 25, pp 921–43.

Cooper, D and Herman, D (1999) 'Jews and other uncertainties: race, faith and English law', *Legal Studies* 19, pp 339–66.

Cooper, D and Monro, S (2003) 'Governing from the margins: queering the state of local government', *Contemporary Politics* 9, pp 229–55.

Creegan, C *et al.* (2003) 'Race equality policies at work: employee perceptions of the "implementation gap" in a UK local authority', *Work, Employment and Society* 17, pp 617–40.

Dean, M (1999) *Governmentality*, London: Sage.

Dean, M (2002) 'Powers of life and death beyond governmentality', *Cultural Values* 6, pp 119–38.

Gibbs, N (2005) 'Examining the aesthetic dimensions of the constitutional treaty', *European Law Journal* 11, pp 326–42.

Goodwin, J (1997) 'The libidinal constitution of a high-risk social movement: affectual ties and solidarity in the Huk rebellion, 1946–1954', *American Sociological Review* 62, pp 53–69.

Haltern, U (2003) 'Pathos and patina: the failure and promise of constitutionalism in the European imagination', *European Law Journal* 9, pp 14–44.

Hoggett, P and Thompson, S (2002) 'Toward a democracy of the emotions', *Constellations* 9, pp 106–26.

Humphrey, J (1999) 'Organizing sexualities, organised inequalities: lesbians and gay men in public service occupations', *Gender, Work and Organization* 6, pp 134–51.

Jasper, J (1998) 'The emotions of protest: affective and reactive emotions in and around social movements', *Sociological Forum* 13, pp 397–424.

Kearns, A (1995) 'Active citizenship and local governance: political and geographical dimensions', *Political Geography* 14, pp 155–75.

Klatch, R (2004) 'The underside of social movements: the effects of destructive affective ties', *Qualitative Sociology* 27, pp 487–509.

Lansley, S *et al.* (1989) *Councils in Conflict: The Rise and Fall of the Municipal Left*, London: Palgrave, Macmillan.

Lent, A (2001) 'The Labour left, local authorities and new social movements in Britain in the eighties', *Contemporary Politics* 7, pp 7–25.

Lister, R (1997) 'Dialectics of citizenship', *Hypatia* 12, pp 6–26.

McGhee, D (2003) 'Joined-up government, "community safety" and lesbian, gay, bisexual and transgender "active citizens" ', *Critical Social Policy* 23, pp 345–74.

Monro, S (2005) *Gender Politics: Citizenship, Activism and Sexual Diversity*, London: Pluto.

Monro, S (2006) 'Sexualities initiatives in local government – measuring success', *Local Government Studies* 32, pp 19–39.

Moran, L (1995) 'Violence and the law: the case of sado-masochism', *Social and Legal Studies* 4, pp 225–51.

Newman, J (2001) *Modernising Governance*, London: Sage.

Newman, J (2002) 'Changing governance, changing equality? New Labour, modernization and public services', *Public Money and Management* 22, pp 7–14.

Newman, J *et al.* (2004) 'Public participation and collaborative governance', *Journal of Social Policy* 33, pp 203–23.

O'Malley, P (1996) 'Indigenous governance', *Economy and Society* 25, pp 310–26.

Peck, J and Tickell, A (2002) 'The urbanization of neoliberalism: theoretical debates neoliberalizing space', *Antipode* 34, pp 380–404.

Phelan, S (2001) *Sexual Strangers: Gays, Lesbians, and the Dilemmas of Citizenship*, Philadelphia: Temple University Press.

Quilley, S (2002) 'Entrepreneurial turns: municipal socialism and after', in Peck, J and Ward, K (eds), *City of Revolution: Restructuring Manchester*, Manchester: Manchester University Press, pp 76–94.

Richardson, D (2005) 'Desiring sameness? The rise of a neoliberal politics of normalisation', *Antipode* 37, 515–35.

Rose, N (1999) *Powers of Freedom: Reframing Political Thought*, Cambridge: Cambridge University Press.

Smart, C (1989) *Feminism and the Power of Law*, London: Routledge.

Somerville, P (2005) 'Community, governance and democracy', *Policy and Politics* 33, pp 117–44.

Stychin, C (2003) *Governing Sexuality: The Changing Politics of Citizenship and Law Reform*, Oxford: Hart.

Sullivan, H (2001) 'Modernisation, democratisation and community governance', *Local Government Studies* 27, pp 1–24.

Taylor, M (2000) 'Communities in the lead: power, organizational capacity and social capital', *Urban Studies* 37, pp 1019–35.

Tickell, A and Peck, J (1996) 'The return of the Manchester men: men's words and men's deeds in the remaking of the local state', *Transactions of the Institute of British Geographers* 21, pp 595–616.

Viroli, M (1992) *From Politics to Reason of State*, Cambridge: Cambridge University Press.

Walzer, M (1983) *Spheres of Justice*, Oxford: Basil Blackwell.

Chapter 9

Teenage pregnancies and sex education

Constructing the girl/woman subject

Daniel Monk, Birkbeck, University of London

Introduction

In contemporary Western societies, the pregnant teenager has become a powerful totem figure. Yet the phenomenon of 'concern' about her is constituted through a multiplicity of discourses.[1] Consequently, they are portrayed in ways that are often contradictory. According to Reiss they are scapegoats for social anxieties and understood to be, amongst other things:

> ... stupid sluts, as children having children, as teen rebels who flaunt their non-conformity and treat their babies as objects, as vulnerable girls whom nobody loved, as victims of abuse, as welfare moms, as dropouts and as neglectful mothers.

> (2004: 650)

Portrayed as both 'innocent victims' of ignorance, poverty and bad parenting, and, at the same time, as moral transgressors, public dependants and deficient parents, the contradictions here are clear. Similarly, the fact that they are represented as being both *reckless* juveniles and *calculating* welfare scroungers, demonstrates the crudeness in popular understandings of their motives.

What is immediately clear from these representations is the extent to which teenage pregnancy is *explicitly* a socially constructed problem. This is in contrast to the manner in which aspects of adult mothering and other issues of sexuality are frequently problematised. Indeed in many of these contexts feminist engagements have been critical in revealing the *implicit* essentialism of normative judgments. For example, women who reject their children, and female paedophiles, are often represented in legal and other narratives as 'unnatural women' (O'Donovan, 2000). Of course, pregnant teenagers may

---

1 Discourses here refer to 'practices which form the objects of which they speak' (Foucault, 1972: 49).

subsequently reject or abuse their children, but what is significant and distinct here is the fact that the 'problem' with teenage mothers is primarily their desire to become a mother (or their failure to prevent it). In other words, the critique of these behaviours has little to do with essentialist assumptions of traditional gender roles; indeed one of the ironies of the conservative demonising of teenage mothers is the fact that in their own personal narratives teenage mothers frequently reveal a remarkable commitment to traditional gender roles (Bullen, Kenway and Hey, 2001). This is not to suggest that in relation to the pregnant teenager 'nature has nothing to do with it', but, rather, to highlight the fact that the critical question here is more one of age than gender. Put simply, the boundaries and identities in question are not that of mothers and fathers or men and women but children and adults and girls and women.

The fact that the rate of teenage pregnancies in the UK is the highest in Western Europe is well known and one that the public is frequently reminded of by politicians and the media. But what is less well known, and, indeed, sometimes surprises even the most 'informed', is that the number of teenage pregnancies has decreased dramatically since the early 1970s and has stayed at a more or less the same rate since then.[2] How then to explain the iconic role of the teenage mother in political and popular discourses? The feminist academic Lynne Segal argues that:

> As funding everywhere shrinks, the working day lengthens, inequality deepens and political protect is everywhere muted, it is women and children in particular who remain at the cutting edge of the contradictions between work and welfare, markets and morality.
>
> (Segal, 1999: 8)

The heightened concern about teenage pregnancy confirms this for the issue is located precisely at the intersection of these contradictions and explains the centrality of teenage mothers to debates about poverty, 'the underclass' generally and even the 'crisis in masculinity' (Abbott and Wallace, 1992; Roseneil and Mann, 1996; Page, 1997; Monk, 1998; Carabine, 2001; Hendrick, 2003).

This chapter explores teenage pregnancy within the context of sex education, for it represents a particularly rich site for exploring the social production of sexual identities. The historian and sociologist Jeffrey Weeks argued over 20 years ago that issues concerning sexuality frequently appear to occupy a 'front-line in the battle for the future of western society' (Weeks,

---

2   The number of teenagers becoming pregnant in 1997 was 90,000; the number of under-16s becoming pregnant (i.e. those of school age and below the age of consent) was 7,700, of which only 3,700 resulted in births: Social Exclusion Unit, 1999, pp 12, 14. Between 1999 and 2005 under-18 conception rates fell by 9.8%: Department for Education and Skills, 2005: 3.

1985: 17) and this statement appears as true today as then. But sex education is about 'childhood' as much as 'sexuality' and numerous commentators have highlighted how the concerns and anxieties about childhood are uniquely indicative of the most pressing social, political and personal narratives of our time and intertwined with assessments of the economic and moral being of society (Bauman, 2003; Beck and Beck-Gersheim, 1995; Diduck, 2003; Jenks, 1996). Located then at the intersection of sexuality and childhood – it is not surprising that sex education has attracted and continues to attract fierce critics as well as staunch advocates.

Many empirical researchers in the field accept that the impact of sex education on the behaviour of young people is questionable and acknowledge the existence and significant influence of other factors on the sexual behaviour of young people (Ingham, 2005; Aggleton and Crewe, 2005). Yet, since 1986 the issue has frequently been debated in Parliament with legal reform ensuing. The debates have always been highly politicised with familiar polarised stances being taken by conservative moralists and public health and children's rights campaigners. As the historian Lesley Hall observes, sex education has always been 'intricately bound up with questions of national as well as personal health' (2004: 98) and 'a soft target for anxieties generated by wider and far less easy to influence factors in society at large, just as it has sometimes been seen as an easy fix solution' (2004: 115).

The aim here is to explore the ways in which sex education policies that target the girl/woman pupil (the potential teenage mother) reveal the broader 'social anxieties' referred to by Hall and the 'contradictions of work and welfare, markets and morality' referred to by Segal. A starting point and theoretical tool for this analysis is the premise that when children are identified and referred to in legislation and government guidance materials relating to sex education, while the focus on the surface may appear to be 'real' embodied children it is more accurate to describe these representations of children as 'semantic artefacts' (King and Piper, 1995: 63) or as 'contingent discursive constructs' (O'Donovan, 1993: 90). Reading the law critically in this way draws on post-structural perspectives that bring to the fore the socially constructed nature of the problem of teenage mothers and recognises the disjuncture between the objectified representations of (potential) teenage mothers and the embodied individual subjectivities of sexual young women. Such an approach does not, however, remove the analysis to a purely abstract level. For while this reading reveals the conflicting agendas and contradictions and tensions that inform and underlie the portrayal of children in legal discourse, this is not to suggest that law has no impact on real children. As Carrabine argues, while it is wrong to assume that:

> regulatory effects are always successful and that legal/welfare subjects are always totally submissive to the disciplinary effects of discourses . . .

this does not suggest that normative discourses do not have material consequences.

(Carabine, 2001: 310.)

This chapter takes as its starting point the Education (No 2) Act 1986. This Act was the first to refer to sex education and consequently represents a key political moment. It is important to remember, however, that prior to 1986, legal intervention had been debated on numerous occasions (Hampshire, 2005; Hampshire and Lewis, 2004). Indeed, as Hall reminds us in her review of the history of sex education in the twentieth century: 'long periods of neglect have been punctured by occasional moments of crisis and flurries of moral panic with an effect of déjà vu' (2004: 98).

Focusing on the recent history, however, provides an opportunity to interrogate the changes brought about by the much heralded 'radical' reforms introduced by the post-1997 Labour governments. As Stychin has argued in the 'adult' context of the changing politics of sexual citizenship, it is 'time to turn the glare of analysis away from the conservatives and towards the reformers' (Stychin, 2003: 26). In doing so, this chapter will argue that while the boundary between girls and women remains critical, it has become less clear, and that in the context of sex education, there is a significant shift towards recognising the agency of the sexual girl. Yet it is clear that this shift is more a response to well established fears and concerns about teenage mothers than a distinctive and principled endorsement of autonomy. What follows is effectively a history charting the representation of the traditional sexually innocent girl child to a (potentially) knowing sexual young woman; a transformation reflecting a move away from juridical prohibition to a form of self-governance by *responsible* young (sexual) citizens as opposed to autonomous subjects.

Childhood innocence/invisible sexuality 1986–97

In charting the social policy history of lone motherhood, Carabine argues that 'moralizing discourse appears to be more forcibly asserted following periods when the stigmatization of unmarried motherhood has declined' (2001: 305). This assessment has a particular resonance in the context of teenage pregnancy and sex education in the 1980s. For the 'sexual revolution' of the 1960s and 1970s and support by the Labour Government in the 1970s for innovative sex education programmes, 'failed to establish sufficient support within British society as a whole to survive the 1980s' (Meredith, 1988: 26; Hampshire, 2005); and what followed was a 'moral counter-revolution'. These developments are clearly reflected in law reform debates. For while earlier advocates for legal intervention had been progressive reformers, in the 1980s and 1990s law was successfully utilised by a powerful coalition of traditional moral conservatives and neo-liberals for whom teenage pregnancies, albeit for different reasons, were perceived as a serious problem (Monk, 1998).[3]

The Education (No 2) Act 1986 reflected both these perspectives. The Act included a back bench amendment, introduced by moral conservatives, that required governing bodies and head teachers to ensure that sex education be given 'in such a manner as to encourage pupils to have due regard to moral considerations and the value of family life' (s 46). At the same time, in keeping with the broader neo-liberal ideological shift towards market forces and 'consumerism', the Act also provided, through various measures, for greater parental accountability and a reduction of local education authority influence (Monk, 1998). Both served to restrict innovative programmes. The endeavours of health and children's rights campaigners for the recognition within schools of young people's sexuality were further marginalised by the introduction of the National Curriculum by the Education Reform Act 1988 – but this time in a far less explicit way. The National Curriculum created a distinction between the 'biological' aspects of sex education and the 'non-biological'. The former, located within the National Curriculum for Science, was now compulsory, centrally controlled by the Secretary of State for Education, and privileged in terms of time and resources. The latter was left to the discretion of individual schools. This distinction between the biological and non-biological had little to do with 'neutral scientific facts' but, rather, functioned as a powerful indicator of social and political debates about appropriate and inappropriate sexuality. The contingency of the distinction became more visible in the early 1990s as a result of heated debates in Parliament about the correct location within the curriculum for 'information about HIV/AIDS' (Monk, 1998). The result of these debates was the Education Act 1993.

The 1993 Act was groundbreaking as it made sex education compulsory in secondary schools, including the non-biological aspects.[4] This had been a long-standing demand of health campaigners, but in keeping with the history of sex education, the Act was marked by compromise. In particular, lobbying by moral conservatives ensured an explicit exclusion from the National Curriculum of any reference to HIV/AIDS and a long-fought-for right for parents to remove their children from sex education.[5] Alongside the statutory reforms, new guidance was published by the government that reasserted the emphasis on restricting access to any forms of practical information about sexual activity (DES, 1994). For example, while it stated that 'Education has

---

3   It is important to emphasise that while debates about sex education have never neatly reflected party divisions, in the 1980s the issue increasingly became 'deployed as a vehicle for right versus left wing antagonism' and at times a prominent issue in central and local government campaigns (Meredith, 1988: 17).

4   Unlike many other European countries it still remains discretionary in primary schools.

5   For a discussion of this right in more detail, see Blair (2005).

a vital part to play' in reducing the rate of teenage conceptions it did not endorse the Department of Health's objective of 'better access for *everyone* to family planning information and services' (DoH, 1992, D10; emphasis added). Instead, the guidance adopted a traditional moral programme by stating that sex education can make a 'substantial contribution' to the DoH's targets by being taught 'within a clear framework of values and an awareness of the law on sexual behaviour' (DES, para 8). While the interpretation of 'values' is of course open to debate, coupled here with a reference to the criminal law, the meaning was clear; in the context of education the solution to the problem of teenage pregnancy was 'just say no'. In effect this represented a juridical prohibition and reaffirmation of the girl/pupil as a resolutely non-sexual subject.

Conflict between the Departments of Education and Health was not new; indeed they have been a feature of policy making in this area for over a century (Hampshire, 2005). But while the *inhibitory* impact of this conflict has been much commented on, what has been less explored has been the *productive* element; in other words, the way in which the different 'truths' about child sexuality underlying the distinctive discourses of education and health inform the construction of contrasting legal identities. The distinction is particularly clear in relation to the law relating to individual advice to pupils. In the context of advice within schools the 1993 Circular stated, boldly, that 'teachers are not health professionals' and that advice on such matters as contraceptive advice 'without parental knowledge or consent would be an inappropriate exercise of a teacher's professional responsibilities' (DES, 1993, paras 39, 40).[6] At the same time, confirming the House of Lords decision in the *Gillick* case,[7] the Circular acknowledged that in the context of a patient/health professional relationship, a young person may receive practical advice on sexual matters. However, the Circular made clear that these health services should not be provided to *all* pupils but only to those who, as a result of their sexual behaviour are, 'at moral or physical risk or in breach of the law' (DES, 1993: para 40). In other words, the representation of a young person seeking contraceptive advice is not that of a 'normal' teenager but that of a problematic 'other' associated with illness, illegality and immorality. The line drawn here between 'health' and 'education' is in this way far from neutral; it does not simply delineate professional responsibilities or particular geographical locations or places but, rather, constructs conflicting spatial identities imbued with moral values.[8]

---

6   The legality of this advice was subject to stringent criticism: Bainham (1996); Blair and Furniss (1995).

7   *Gillick v West Norfolk Area Health Authority* [1986] 1 AC 122. The decision was recently confirmed in *R (Axon) v Secretary of State for Health* [2006] EWHC 37 Admin.

8   For an analysis of the significance of space in the construction of childhood see James, Jenks and Prout (1998: pp 37–58).

Locating the 'sexual girl' in the clinic, at the same time as making her invisible within the classroom, conveys a powerful message. Chris Jenks, one of the leading new sociologists of childhood, has argued in relation to the line between adulthood and childhood, that 'the system of classification stays intact by resisting the "defilement" of the abhorrent case' (Jenks, 1996: 129). This analysis was made in the very different context of the murder of Jamie Bulger by two young boys. In this infamous case the two defendants were treated by law 'as adults'; in effect the popular construction of them as 'evil' banished them from the category of childhood and law legitimised this portrayal by deeming them adults (despite the most compelling 'psychological' evidence).

The same can be seen in the context of sex education where the removal of the sexual child from the school to the adult clinic ensures that the school remains a site of childhood (sexual) innocence. The controversial practice of removing girls from school once a pregnancy becomes visible further reinforced the critical role beyond the curriculum that schooling plays in reinforcing the norm of pupilhood as non-sexual; as Kehily argues, 'teenage pregnancy becomes the irrefutable evidence of who knows what, existing as both a marker of sexual knowledge/experience and the stigma of knowing and doing' (Kehily, 2002: 179).

The distinction between education and health supports the sociologists Stainton Rogers' (1999) argument that in contemporary Western societies, child sexuality is understood through two binary constructions. The dominant discursive equation in their model is: child + sex = abuse. This denies the possibility of 'unproblematic' child sexual activity and is reflected clearly in the statements from the 1993 Circular above. The alternative, less frequent model is: child + sex = adult. Here child sexuality is acknowledged as something other than abuse, but is dependent on and made culturally acceptable by imbuing the child with the characteristics of an 'adult'; an approach that coheres closely with the approach adopted in the *Gillick* case (Moran, 1986) and by the locating of the sexual child in an adult clinic. The Stainton Rodgers' third equation in their model is: child + sex = child. Here child sexuality is not only acknowledged but accepted as a potentially unproblematic aspect of child development. These three models, and the denial and invisibility of the third, clearly cohered and helps explain the legal regulation of sex education up to 1997. The extent to which New Labour has reconfigured the sexual girl from an 'abhorrent case' or 'quasi-adult' into a 'rights'-bearing sexual citizen is explored below.

New Labour: reform and continuity

The election of the Labour Party in 1997 was welcomed by public health and children's rights campaigners who had advocated a more liberal and pragmatic approach towards sex education. The extent to which their hopes and expectations have been met is debatable, but what is beyond question is the fact that New Labour has identified sex education as a crucial and legitimate site for government intervention and investment. Indeed one of the new government's first initiatives was the commissioning of a report into teenage pregnancy (Social Exclusion Unit, 1999) and this subsequently led to significant changes in policy relating to sex education. The extent to which these initiatives represented a new direction is explored below. But the fact that sex education reform was explicitly linked with the 'problem' of teenage pregnancy represents an important sign of continuity; in other words, while the methods of reducing teenage pregnancy has changed, pregnant young women and sexual teenagers remain very much an object of public concern.

Legal reform was introduced by the Learning and Skills Act 2000[9] and subsequently, after extensive consultation, new guidance was issued by the Department for Education and Employment (DfEE, 2000). In keeping with the previous patterns both were produced in a highly politicised context and in a number of ways both attest to the continuing influence of the conservative moral lobby (Monk, 2001). For example, attempts to broaden the statutory requirement that sex education be delivered in a moral framework to include references to 'stable relationships other than marriage' and 'the importance of understanding difference' and 'preventing or removing prejudice' were defeated in the House of Lords. Similarly, children's rights campaigners object to the fact that the non-biological aspects of sex education have been kept outside of the National Curriculum (The Independent Advisory Group on Teenage Pregnancy, 2004). The new guidance has also been criticised for leaving the parental opt-out provision intact (Blair, 2005) and for failing to acknowledge the potential conflict between enhancing accountability to parents and respecting children's rights (Monk, 2001). These limitations ensure that in school the norm of the child as non-sexual is still very much in place. This is reinforced by language in two distinct ways. First, the emphasis throughout the guidance is on the negative aspects of sex, such as sexually transmitted disease and unwanted pregnancies. There is no mention of pleasure; a silence that overlooks the reason why many young people have sex (Lamb, 1997; Ingham, 2005). Secondly, wherever children's access to confidentiality or practical information about contraception is acknowledged they are referred to as 'young people', and not children. These two examples demonstrate the continuing resistance to accepting child sexuality and the Stainton Rodgers' dominant cultural models whereby

---

9   Section 148 of the Act placed a duty on schools to secure that pupils 'learn the nature of marriage and its importance for family life and the bringing up of children' and that pupils 'are protected from teaching and materials which are inappropriate having regard to the age and the religious and cultural background of the pupils concerned'. The general structure of the curriculum, however, remained unchanged.

'child + sex = abuse' (diseases and 'mistakes') or 'child + sex = adult' ('young person'). There are then important continuities between New Labour's approach and that of the previous administrations but to focus only on these limitations is to overlook an important shift.

New Labour: the emergence of young (sexual) citizenship?

Without suggesting that there has been in any sense a dramatic change in attitudes about child sexuality it is, however, possible to detect within the reforms of sex education significant shifts that enable the possibility of child sexuality and agency to be openly acknowledged within the classroom. The following three statements from the new circular reveal this; at the same time they also demonstrate explicitly the extent to which the key justification for this policy change is not an embracement of sexual autonomy but reducing teenage pregnancy.

> In England in 1998 there were over 100,000 conceptions to teenagers, of which over 8,000 were to girls under 16. This is clearly totally unacceptable ... It is *therefore appropriate* for secondary schools to provide education about contraception.
>
> (DfEE, 2000, para 2.9, emphasis added)

> Knowledge of the different types of contraception, and of access to, and availability of contraception, is a major part of the government's strategy to reduce teenage pregnancy. Effective sex and relationship education in secondary schools has an important part to play in achieving this.
>
> (Ibid., para 2.10)

> Trained staff in secondary schools should be able to give *young people* full information about different types of contraception, including emergency contraception, and their effectiveness.
>
> (Ibid., para 2.11, emphasis added)

The statement that contraception is an *appropriate* matter for education is particularly significant as it makes clear that the new statutory provisions about protecting children from 'inappropriate material', which were the result of extensive lobbying by moral conservatives, should not be used in relation to contraception. In practical terms the new guidance offers protection to schools and teachers inhibited by the previous guidance. In support of this shift, the potential for teachers' criminal liability through the principles of aiding, abetting or inciting unlawful sexual intercourse in cases where a pupil under the age of 16 is advised about contraception has been effectively removed by s 73 of the Sexual Offences Act 2003.

These developments represent an important redrawing of the health/ education boundary. Children at secondary schools are no longer constructed as sexual innocents that must be protected from sexually explicit or practical information. Knowledge and access to contraception is now endorsed for *all* secondary school pupils; as a result the sexual child is no longer simply the discursive 'aberrant other'. In this way New Labour has legitimised practical sex education and in doing so has successfully resisted the unfounded objection frequently made by conservative moralists that sex education is little more than a form of 'child abuse' that robs them of their innocence and turns them into sexual beings (Aggleton and Crewe, 2005).

A further indication of the government's apparent willingness to acknowledge the sexual agency of teenage girls is the efforts that have been made to reinforce their confidentiality rights in the context of advice (and treatment) about contraception. In 2004 the Department of Health reissued the *Best Practice Guidance for Doctors and Other Health Professionals on the Provision of Advice and Treatment to Young People under 16 on Contraception, Sexual and Reproductive Health*. This advice, the legality of which was upheld by the High Court in 2006,[10] was issued with the specific aim of protecting young people from the risks associated with avoiding treatment and advice, such as sexually transmitted diseases and late or unqualified abortions. The Government was concerned by the fact that 'young women' were unaware of their rights in this area, and conscious of the fact that over a third of all abortions on under-16-year-olds were carried out without parental knowledge. Upholding the rights of the teenage girls over their parents has not been uncontroversial, as the legal challenge to the medical guidance demonstrates. But while children's rights commentators support this approach there is an awareness of the fact that there is a degree of incoherency in the Government's attitude to parents, as Hall comments:

> At a time when the government is emphasising parents' duty to produce good moral citizens, a degree of confusion about the limits of parents' power is perhaps understandable.
>
> (Hall, 2006: 322)

The acknowledgment of the sexual activities of the young in the context of sex education is matched by a new approach towards teenage mothers more generally. Previously, teenage mothers were effectively excluded from school – often at the point when the pregnancy became visible: 'motherhood' and 'pupil-hood' represented culturally incompatible identities and their presence in schools was frequently considered a dangerous moral influence on the other girls (Dawson, 1997; Lutrell, 2003). New guidance issued by the

---

10 *R (Axon) v Secretary of State for Health* [2006] EWHC 37 Admin.

government specifically relating to school-age parents states categorically that 'pregnancy is not a reason for exclusion from school' (DfES, 2001, para 13.1). In support of this it states that there is 'no evidence that keeping a pregnant girl or school-age mother in school will encourage others to become pregnant' (para 14.7). Moreover, in keeping with the overarching aim of reducing teenage pregnancies, the guidance suggests that the presence of pregnant girls or teenage mothers in schools might, 'alert the others to the risks and realities' (para 14.7). In addition to highlighting the responsibilities of Local Education Authorities, the new guidance provides an overview of the wide range of services and support that New Labour has established to enable young mothers to not only continue their education but also to provide training and employment for those out of formal education; examples of this are the centrally funded Connexions Service and Sure Start centres and Local Authority Reintegration Officers. At present only 30 per cent of teenage mothers are in education, training or employment and the government's stated aim is to double that by 2010 (DES, 2005).

In a speech in 2003 at one of the new support centres for teenage mothers, government minister Barbara Roche said the following:

> I particularly wish to congratulate the young women who access the project. In demonstrating your desire to take responsibility for your health and well-being – and the health and well-being of your children – and in demonstrating your interest in pursuing your ambitions with regard to learning and employment, you are leading the way for others to follow.
>
> (Roche, 2003)

While, to be sure, the Minister here is not congratulating the 'young women' for becoming pregnant, the tone here and, in particular, the public endorsement of state-funded support, represents a marked shift. Under New Labour, school-age mothers are no longer only feckless teenagers and immoral scroungers, the populist scapegoats of the previous conservative governments, but, like those praised above, potentially 'young women' and responsible and good mothers. Moreover the Government's very substantive and much publicised investment in this area suggests they are no longer to be considered as 'living off the state', but as citizens receiving legitimate state support.

Locating New Labour's approach to sex education and young mothers within a discourse of rights it could be argued that the new approach goes some way to recognising that all secondary school children have a 'right' to practical sexual information and that, if a young women becomes pregnant, she has a 'right' to social support and does not forfeit her 'right' to education. For children's rights advocates there is therefore much to celebrate here for the new policies treat young people not simply as vulnerable passive objects but as subjects capable of exercising their own agency. This is a notable step;

for as Piper has observed, in tracing the origins of the dominant norm of childhood sexual innocence and its relationship with the development of welfare policies:

> There is a sense in which the price paid by children over the last 150 years for the presumed benefits of child welfare legislation and provision has been their 'de-sexing'.
>
> (Piper, 2000: 40)

However, for the reasons mentioned above it is important not to exaggerate the political embracement of children as autonomous actors, both within the classroom and beyond. In this respect it is significant that in relation to children, in contrast to parents, the language of rights is conspicuously absent both in the Government's Social Exclusion Report on Teenage Pregnancy and in their new guidance on sex education. Consequently, as Kaganas and Diduck have commented:

> . . . while giving a voice to any previously disempowered or marginalized constituency is important, and listening to children is long overdue, *we must be alert to the discourse through which that voice is heard and interpreted.*
>
> (2005: 981, emphasis added)

Kaganas and Diduck's observation is made in relation to the role of children in post-separation family disputes, but a similar caution is required in the context of teenage pregnancy and sex education. For exploring the discourses through which children voices are now being heard here reveals 'duties' and 'responsibilities' as much as 'rights'.

Childhood sexual agency: (post-) liberalism and the Third Way

> New Labour . . . is determined to integrate children into its vision of the good society, and to do that it must harmonise childhood within the uncertainties of post modernity.
>
> (Hendrick, 2003)

Sexual morality is an area where New Labour can justifiably claim to have broken with the past. Their land-slide election victory in 1997 to a certain extent represented a symbolic rejection of the traditional moral values that had been a key feature of the Conservative governments' policies in the period 1979–97. The conspicuous failure of the 'back to basics' campaign of John Major; the perception that the explicit homophobia of much of the Conservative Party had become an electoral liability, rather than a vote winner (Waites, 2000); and, similarly, the acknowledgment by Conservative modernisers that the 'scape-goating' of single mothers had led them to be perceived as 'the mean party', all represent political moments that reflect a significant shift in dominant social values. For New Labour this shift has been far less problematic. Their willingness to acknowledge the fact that alternative family forms, such as same-sex relationships and single-parent families, are realities of modern life that are not necessarily 'immoral', represents a clear break with the past that can be understood as a liberalising reconfiguration of the public/private divide. For in marked contrast to their Conservative predecessors, New Labour has explicitly rejected the idea that imposing *traditional* sexual morality and *particular* family forms is a legitimate role of the state. Sex education can be understood to be part of this overall project; indeed, the reforms in the Learning and Skills Act 2000 were explicitly linked by government ministers to the repeal of the notorious section 28 and to the equalisation of the age of consent laws (Monk, 2001). However, at the same time, it is important not to overstate this embracement of social change and, while there are parallels between policies relating to gays and lesbians and sex education and teenage mothers, there are also significant distinctions.

In relation to same-sex relations the new policies have been informed by a genuine rejection of traditional forms of homophobic prejudices. As Stychin has commented, New Labour, 'understands lesbian and gay politics through the language of equality, rights and dignity, multiculturalism and citizenship, rather than one that pathologizes the individual' (2005: 545). In the context of debates about the Civil Partnership Act the concept of equality dominated the debate and while criticisms of the laws exist within the gay and lesbian community, the reforms only came about as a result of extensive campaigning by members of the lesbian and gay community. In the context of young people and sexuality the concept of 'children's rights' has been notably absent from the Government's arguments and the well documented views of children as to what they would like to learn in sex education have been steadfastly and repeatedly ignored or marginalised (Ingham, 2005; Independent Advisory Group on Teenage Pregnancy, 2004). Moreover, as the linguistic and spatial constructions highlighted above indicate, sexual children are reconstructed as quasi-adults. In other words, the reforms in sex education are not informed by a desire to enhance equality between adults and children and in contrast to the approach towards same-sex relations, the acknowledgment of child sexual activity is highly reluctant.

The distinction between gay and lesbian law reform and the approach taken towards teenage mothers is equally revealing. Critical commentators have highlighted how the recognition of same-sex partnerships reflects more subtle modes of 'governance' and in particular the extent to which it is, 'ideologically grounded in a privatized notion of care' (Stychin, 2005: 564). The Civil Partnership Act consequently coheres with the New Labour calculation that 'stable relationships' are a social and economic good, whether between same- or opposite-sex couples. As a result, whereas two lesbians with children is now an acceptable and legally protected family unit, a single teenage heterosexual mother remains outside of New Labour's idealised vision of family life. Yet this distinction similarly reflects the 'privatisation of care', for a teenage mother's loving, stable and dependent relationship with her child does not have the economic weight to entitle it to a public state condoned celebration. And this is reinforced by benefit policies that entitle her to independent housing support only in circumstances where she is unable to live with her parents (DfES, 2001: para 11.1). Young women have 'adult' rights to contraception; but young mothers are deemed 'children' in the context of housing benefit: on the surface their position appears contradictory, but from the perspective of the state it makes coherent economic sense.

These distinctions between the approach to same-sex relations and young people and sex demonstrate the contingency of concepts such as 'rights' and 'equality' and that New Labour's reforms are as much pragmatic as principled. The approach adopted reflects social unease about child sexuality, but can also be explained by New Labour's understanding of the perceived individualism of contemporary post-modern society and the challenge that this poses for the (welfare) state. In this context the work of Anthony Giddens, the sociologist who has been identified as being a key influence on New Labour and in developing the political ideology known as the 'Third Way' is illuminative.[11]

For Giddens, the rise of individualism, by which he means not so much mindless consumerism but 'a structural phenomenon in societies breaking free from the hold of tradition and custom' (Giddens, 2001: 4) is one of the key transformations of modern society, and one that requires a new relationship between the family and the state. Recognition of the radical transformation of society by individualism highlights the *futility* of attempts to impose traditional morality. The Third Way, consequently, rejects attempts to expect young people to 'just say no' to sex in the same way that it rejects attempts to make divorce harder. At the same time, acknowledging the perceived detrimental impact of 'unbridled' individualism on society – the breakdown of traditional support systems and an increase in poverty – requires a rejection of laissez-faire Thatcherite monetarist economics and acknowledges the need for the state to develop alternative methods of support in order to create a just civil society. Consequently, while Third Way thinkers are highly critical of the traditional socialist model of the welfare state, direct government intervention is still perceived as crucial; in other words, the welfare state is to be reconstructed rather than rejected.

---

11 For an analysis of the tensions between Giddens and New Labour see Bullen, Kenway and Hay (2000).

Significantly, it is not simply the role of the state that is to be reconstructed but also that of individuals in what is described as a new social contract. This model of the welfare state reflects the much-heralded 'Third Way' slogan of 'no rights without responsibilities' (Giddens, 1988: 65, in Hendrick, 2003: 207). This belief in the *conditionality* of rights and the enforcement of *responsible* citizenship, highlights what Hendrick, the sociologist of childhood, describes as a shift away from 'Old Labour's commitment to social class towards a form of communitarianism premised upon a highly prescriptive and moral element' (Hendrick, 2003: 207). This approach was succinctly expressed by Tony Blair:

> the purpose of economic and social policy should be to extend opportunity, to remove the underlying causes of social alienation. *But it should also take tough measures to ensure that the chances that are given are taken up.*
>
> (Blair quoted in Savage and Atkinson, 2001: 10–11)

Helen Reece has analysed this reconfiguration in the context of family law reform utilising the concept of (post-) liberalism (Reece, 2003). This concept distinguishes the Third Way from conservative morality and laissez-faire liberalism: as noted above both dominant political discourses under the previous administrations that had a significant impact on the structure of sex education. What is distinct about (post-) liberalism is that it represents a far more invasive form of governance; to the extent that it imposes on individuals a demanding model of 'responsibility'. In contrast to traditional socialism it emphasises the role of the individual over the collective, while in contrast to traditional conservatism it demands that the individual *internalise* responsibility rather than simply conform to juridical commands.

A pertinent example of this is the statement made by the government minister Roche quoted above. Addressing teenage mothers who had 'taken up' places on a government training scheme she referred to, '. . . *your desire* to take responsibility . . .'. While the women on the scheme may indeed have chosen to take part, to the extent that they are not coerced into doing so, the Minister's statement masks the very limited choices of young mothers and the fact that the 'support and encouragement' to stay in education or undertake training sometimes takes the forms of inducements. For example, the *Care to Learn* programme launched in 2003 provides financial and non-financial support for young mothers who 'want to learn' and the Activity Agreements and Activity Allowances scheme (currently being piloted) that increases benefits to encourage 'disengaged 16 and 17 year olds back into education' (DES, 2005: paras 4.3 and 4.5). The language used by the Minister also reflects the extent to which, in a (post) liberal society, 'psychological norms have replaced social norms, and therapeutic correctness has become the new standard of good behaviour' (Reece, 2003: 217). In this context the consequence is that the young mothers who do not take up the opportunities to act responsibly are perceived as having the wrong 'desires'. As Bullen *et al.* argue, there is a marked degree of continuity here with past agendas as, 'the vocabulary of New Labour (like that of the old radical Right) is emblematic of the search for a rhetoric of moral civility that will waylay and reinvent the wayward' (2000: 445).

In the context of family law Reece argues that a (post-) liberal approach replaces the moral code of marriage/good versus divorce/bad with good responsible/divorce versus bad/irresponsible divorce. The same shift in relation to divorce can be seen in relation to child sexuality. Like divorce, a child that is sexual is something to be regretted and certainly not encouraged or celebrated but, at the same time, it is acknowledged as a reality of modern life. And there is now a good 'responsible' way for a child to be sexual and it takes two forms. First, 'she' must not get pregnant. Secondly, failing the first, she must continue in education and training. Both are explored below.

The Social Exclusion Unit's report into Teenage Pregnancy, stated that 'young men are half the problem and half the solution' (SEU, 1999, para 11.12) and this statement has been reiterated since then in numerous government documents (DES, 2004, para 4.23). But despite increased efforts within sex and relationship education to focus on boys' sexual responsibilities, in meeting the Government's targets to reduce teenage pregnancy, the emphasis is predominantly on girls; it is 'she' who must not get pregnant. Young men may be 'half the problem', but in the very lengthy policy documents where this truism is stated, boys are only referred to explicitly in one or two paragraphs. It is not that young men are absent from the New Labour project overall, rather, the gendered focus reflects the old (unattributed) adage that 'boys get in trouble with crime and girls get in trouble with boys'. Moreover, in the context of education, boys are the objects of popular concern primarily when statistics demonstrate that they are 'falling behind' girls. The assumption that it is girls who must take responsibility for pregnancy and the fact that their relative educational attainments are not praised attests to the enduring extent to which, as Carabine argues, 'the moral hazard produced in women is more often than not sexual' (2001: 306). Where fathers, young or otherwise, are deemed 'irresponsible', it is in relation to their failing to fulfill financial responsibilities.[12] This emphasis coheres with the reconfiguring of the welfare state and an increased privatising of care. At the same time it also reinforces the traditional role of the father as breadwinner. Ironically, however, the traditional women's role is not condoned or encouraged for teenage (or single) mothers. As Bullen *et al.* argue, the result is:

12 At the same time, however, it is notable that unmarried and single fathers have in recent years successfully utilised a discourse of victimhood in order to challenge the working of the Child Support Act and in debates relating to contact disputes.

a double standard in which the drive to get young lone mothers into education, training and employment denies them the rights and choices extended to mothers in traditional family units.

(2000: 449)

The absence of the political use of the concept of 'equality' between single and unmarried mothers, and those in 'traditional' units, once again demonstrates its contingency on economic calculations. For where a teenage mother becomes pregnant, the Third Way social contract expects her to take advantage of the services provided to enable her to continue her education in order that she might subsequently be employed and financially independent. As Latham, one of the leading exponents of the Third Way argued:

A revitalised welfare state has just two purposes – to move people into work or into new skills. Government needs to fund active citizenship not pander to the inactive. Unless welfare recipients are willing to take responsibility for improving themselves and the society in which they live, they have no right to permanently live off society.

(Latham in Hendrick, 2003: 208)

Work, together with education (education, education) and pragmatic, 'responsible' individualism are central tenets of the Third Way and New Labour's reconstruction of the sexual girl as a young woman with 'agency' can only be explained and the contradictions made sense of by 'being listened to' through these discourses.

Conclusion

Locating the investment the Government has made in relation to the sexual girl and the potential teenage mother within the discourses of the Third Way, reveals the extent to which the initiatives are informed, less by shifts in understandings of sexual morality, but predominantly by notions of civic responsibility, work and education. In what might appear an ironic twist this New Labour stance fully acknowledges the traditional feminist slogan that 'the personal is political'. Yet in many respects this shift away from an explicit concern with *sexual* morality towards a concern with the economic consequences of sex is not new, rather, it represents a return to an earlier era at the beginning of the nineteenth century. As Carrabine states, in relation to the 1834 New Poor Laws, it was 'social policy about poverty . . . that played a constitutive and normalizing role in relation to ideas about appropriate and acceptable sexuality' (2001: 295). Similarly, Weeks, commenting on the same period, argues that, 'what mattered more to a community was the potential economic burden of illegitimate children rather than the issue of "immorality" of pre-marital sex' (1989: 22). These observations reveal a consistency of public concern about the reproductive habits of working-class women, but the particular resonance with the recent developments is the fact that sex itself is not the problem or driving force behind either government intervention or popular concerns, rather it is one of the consequences of sex, teenage pregnancy, that is the problem. This is not to suggest that child sexuality is now *unproblematic*. But, more tentatively, that in the contexts of policy reform new possibilities now exist for speaking of, and framing laws about, what has for over a century been 'unspeakable'. That it is 'only' a century or so is a fact that is often forgotten. Indeed what is striking is that this 'new' reconfiguration of child sexuality has a similar resonance with the beginning of the nineteenth century. Hendrick argues that, '[T]he concept of childhood in 1800 was not that in 1900. In 1800 its meaning was ambiguous; nor was there a popular demand for an unproblematic conception' (quoted in Piper, 2000: 26). In the context of sex education the changes over the last 20 years demonstrate a movement away from a fixed notion of the girl child as non-sexual, the dominant Victorian innocent child, towards a more complex and indeed ambiguous conception. She is now very much part of the (adult) project of sexual citizenship. But while the sexually innocent child was, indeed, an oppressive construct, 'sexual liberation' as adult feminists know only too well, is hard to define both in practice and theory.

Bibliography

Abbott, P and Wallace, C (1992) *The Family and the New Right*, London: Pluto Press.

Aggleton, P and Crewe, M (2005) 'Effects and effectiveness in sex and relationship education', *Sex Education* 5(4): 305–6.

Allen, I (1987) *Education in Sex and Personal Relationships*, London: Policy Studies Institute.

Atkinson, R and Savage, S (eds) (2001) *Public Policy under Blair*, Basingstoke: Palgrave.

Bainham, A (1996) 'Sex Education: A Family Lawyer's Perspective' in Harris, N (ed.) *Sex Education and the Law*, London: Sex Education Forum, pp 24–44.

Bauman, Z (2003) *Liquid Love*, Cambridge: Polity.

Beck, U and Beck-Gersheim, E (1995) *The Normal Chaos of Love*, Cambridge: Polity.

Blair, A (2005) 'Calculating the Risk of Teenage Pregnancy: Sex Education, Public Health, the Individual and the Law' in Harris, N and Meredith, P (eds) *Children, Education and Health: International Perspectives on Law and policy*, Aldershot: Ashgate.

Blair, A and Furniss, C (1995) 'Sex, Lies and DfE circular 5/94: the Legal Limits of Sex Education', *Education and the Law* 7, pp 197–202.

Bullen, E, Kenway, J and Hey, V (2001) 'New Labour, Social Exclusion and

Educational Risk Management: the Case of the "Gymslip" Mums', *British Educational Research Journal*, 26(4): 441–56.

Carabine, J (2001) 'Constituting sexuality through social policy: the case of lone motherhood 1834 and today', *Social and Legal Studies* 10(3): 291–314.

Dawson, N (1997) 'The Provision of Education and Opportunities for Future Employment for Pregnant Schoolgirls and Schoolgirl Mothers in the UK', *Children and Society* 11, pp 252–63.

Department of Education and Science (1994) *Education Act 1993: Sex Education in Schools*, Circular 5/94, London, HMSO.

Department for Education and Employment (2000) *Sex and Relationship Education Guidance*, Circular 0116/2000, London, DfEE.

Department for Education and Skills (2001) *Guidance on the Education of School Age Parents*, Circular 0629/2001, London, DfES.

Department for Education and Skills (2005) *Government Response to the Third Annual Report of the Independent Advisory Group on Teenage Pregnancy*, London, DES.

Diduck, A (2003) *Law's Families*, London: LexisNexis, Butterworths.

Foucault, M (1972): 49 *Archaeology of Knowledge* trans. Alan Sheridan, London: Tavistock, originally published 1969.

Freeman, M (1996) 'Children's Education: A Test Case for Best Interests and Autonomy' in Davie, R and Galloway, D (eds), *Listening to Children in Education*, London: David Fulton Publishers, pp 29–48.

Giddens, A (2001) Introduction in Giddens, A (ed.) *The Global Third Way*, Cambridge: Polity Press, pp 1–21.

Hall, L A (2004) 'Birds, bees, and general embarrassment: sex education in Britain from social purity to section 28', in Aldrich, R (ed.) *Public or Private Education?* London: Woburn Press, pp 98–115.

Hall, L A (2006) 'Children's rights, parents' wishes and the state: the medical treatment of children' April [2006] *Family Law*, pp 317–22.

Hampshire, J (2005) 'The Politics of School Sex Education Policy in England and Wales from the 1940s to the 1960s', *The Social History of Medicine* 18, pp 87–105.

Hampshire, J and Lewis, J (2004) 'The Ravages of Permissiveness: Sex Education and the Permissive Society', *Twentieth Century British History* 15(3): 290–312.

Hendrick, H (2003) *Child Welfare: historical dimensions, contemporary debate* Bristol: Policy Press.

Independent Advisory Group on Teenage Pregnancy (2004) *Annual Report 2003/04*, London: Department for Education and Skills.

Ingham, R (2005) ' "We didn't cover that at school": education against pleasure or education for pleasure?' *Sex Education* 5(4): 375–88.

James, A, Jenks, C and Prout, A (1998) *Theorising Childhood*, Cambridge: Polity Press.

Jenks, C (1996) *Childhood*, London: Routledge.

Kaganas, F and Diduck, A (2004) 'Incomplete citizens: changing images of post-separation children', *Modern Law Review* 67(6): 959–81.

Kehily, M J (2002) *Sexuality, Gender and Schooling*, London: RoutledgeFalmer.

King, M and Piper, C (1995, 2nd edn) *How Law Thinks About Children*, Aldershot: Arena.

Lamb, S (1997) 'Sex education as moral education: teaching for pleasure, about fantasy, and against abuse', *Journal of Moral Education* 26, pp 301–16.

Lutrell, W (2003) *Pregnant bodies, fertile minds: gender, race, and the schooling of pregnant teens*, New York and London: Routledge.

Meredith, P (1988) *Sex Education. Political Issues in Britain and Europe*, London: Routledge.

Monk, D (1998) 'Sex Education and the Problematisation of Teenage Pregnancies: a genealogy of law and governance', *Social and Legal Studies* 7(2): 241–61.

Monk, D (2001) 'New Guidance/Old Problems: Recent Developments in Sex Education', *Journal of Social Welfare and Family Law* 23, pp 271–91.

Monk, D (2002) 'Children's rights in education: making sense of contradictions', *Child and Family Law Quarterly* 14(1): 45–56.

Moran, L (1986) 'A reading in Sexual Politics and the Law', *Liverpool Law Review* VIII(1): 83–94.

O'Donovan, K (1993) *Family Law Matters*, London: Pluto Press.

O'Donovan, K (2000) 'Constructions of maternity and motherhood in stories of lost children', in Bridgeman, J and Monk, D (eds), *Feminist Perspectives on Child Law*, London: Cavendish, pp 67–84.

Page, R (1997) 'Young single mothers', in Jones, H (ed.), *Towards a classless society?* London: Routledge, pp 151–78.

Pilcher, J (2004) 'Sex in health education: Official guidance for schools in England 1922–1977', *Journal of Historical Sociology* 17, pp 185–208.

Piper, C (2000) 'Historical Constructions of Childhood Innocence: Removing Sexuality', in Heinze, E (ed.), *Of Innocence and Autonomy: Children, sex and human rights*, Dartmouth: Ashgate, pp 26–45.

Phoenix, A (1991) *Young Mothers*, Cambridge: Polity.

Reece, H (2003) *Divorcing Responsibly*, Oxford: Hart.

Reiss, M (2004) 'Review Symposium', *British Journal of Sociology of Education* 25(5): 650–53.

Roche, B (2003) http://www.socialexclusion.gov.uk/news.asp?id=396 (accessed 2 July 2006).

Roseneil, S and Mann, K (1996) 'Unpalatable Choices and Inadequate Families: Lone Mothers and the Underclass Debate', in Bortolaia Silva, E (ed.), *Good Enough Mothering? Feminist Perspectives on Lone Mothering*, London: Routledge, pp 191–210.

Segal, L (1999) *Why Feminism?* Cambridge: Polity Press.

Social Exclusion Unit (1999) *Teenage Pregnancy*, London: HMSO.

Stainton Rogers, W and R (1999) 'What is good and bad sex for children?' in King, M (ed.), *Moral Agendas for Children's Welfare*, London: Routledge.

Stychin, C F (2003) *Governing Sexuality: the changing politics of citizenship and law reform*, Oxford: Hart.

Stychin, C F (2005) 'Couplings: civil partnership in the United Kingdom', *New York City Law Review* 8(2): 543–72.

Thomson, R (1997) 'Diversity, values and social change: renegotiating a consensus on sex education', *Journal of Moral Education* 26, pp 257–71.

Waites, M (2000) 'Homosexuality and the New Right: The Legacy of the 1980s for

New Delineations of Homophobia', *Sociological Research Online*, 5(1), May, www.socresonline.org.uk/.

Weeks, J (1985) *Sexuality and its Discontents*, London: Routledge.

Weeks, J (1989) *Sex, Politics and Society* (2nd edn), Harlow: Longman.

Chapter 10

'Faith' and the 'good' liberal

The construction of female sexual subjectivity in anti-trafficking legal discourse

Ratna Kapur, Centre for Feminist Legal Research, New Delhi

> From the internal colonialisms of the sixteenth and seventeenth centuries, to the overseas colonialism of the late eighteenth through the nineteenth centuries, this fully evolved [Western concept of law] . . . was the gift of civilization to be brought to others; as an incomparable vehicle for establishing peace and order, it was simultaneously the vehicle through which the forces of violence and disordering were legitimated.
>
> (Rosemary Coombe, 'Contingent Articulations: A Critical Cultural Studies of Law' in *Law and the Domains of Culture*, Sarat, A and Kearns, T (eds) 1998, Ann Arbor: University of Michigan, 27)

> In the global South and East, victims of the sex trade are often young women and girls who are desperately poor in cultures where females are expected to sacrifice themselves for the well being of their families and communities.
>
> (Dorchen Leidhold, Co-Director, Coalition Against the Trafficking in Women, (CATW), 1999[1])

> We want bread! We also want Roses!
>
> (Slogan of the International Sex Workers Rights Poster produced for the International Sex Workers Carnival, Calcutta, India, 3–6 March, 2001)

This chapter emerges from a concern about the ways in which issues of sex and sexuality are taken up in and through international and national legal discourses of 'prostitution' and trafficking. It is written at a time when notions of reaffirming sexual purity, cultural cohesion, and national security, are sweeping through public discourse and entering the courts and the legislative arena. The battle over the labelling of certain desires, pleasures, sexed bodies, and sexual acts as either illicit or licit has always been contentious.

---

1 'Position paper for the CATW' available at www.uri.edu/artsci/wms/hughes/catw, 4.

But it has been particularly contentious in the current moment, when sexual transgressions are being coupled with cultural 'Othering' and rendering the transnational female migrant subject as a threat to the very constitution of the nation-state and normative sexuality. Intersecting with emerging discourses of the religious and conservative right, as well as the focus of some feminists on issues of sexual violence, rather than on sexual rights, sexual migrations are becoming a favourite target for majoritarian surveillance and discipline sanctioned by law. Legal interventions focussed on criminality, surveillance and border controls, are producing clandestine migrant mobility regimes that facilitate the movements of transnational sexual subjects.

In this chapter I explore the contours of female sexual subjectivity as constituted in and through anti-trafficking interventions in law by both the conservative or religious right, as well as by some feminist and human rights scholars and advocates. I do not conduct an evaluation of the anti-trafficking laws, but focus in particular on the ways in which the contemporary laws constitute female sexual subjectivity and the implications of this construction for women in the post-colonial world and progressive politics. I argue that these interventions frequently constitute female sexual subjectivity in ways that are reminiscent of the colonial encounter. In the course of this analysis, I illustrate how these representations of female sexual subjectivity intersect with other non-legal, non-state forms of governance. I focus on three documentaries that portend to deal with the issue of trafficking and female sexual subjectivity in a post-colonial setting: Zana Briski's 2005 Oscar-winning documentary 'Born into Brothels', Andrew Levine's 'The Day My God Died' and Shohini Ghosh's 'The Tale of the Nightfairies'. I explore what each film reveals about female sexual subjectivity as well as trafficking in a post-colonial context and how such representations intersect with legal discourse in ways that produce meanings and constitute subjects. I argue that Briski's and Levine's representations reproduce the 'oriental fantasy' of the female sexual subject as passive, devoid of sexual subjectivity, and in need of rescue by a 'civilized West'. Such representations combine with anti-trafficking legal discourse to erase the complexities of human trafficking and marginalise the layered and intricate subjectivities of victims of trafficking. In contrast, Ghosh's film focuses on the complex subjectivities of the female sex worker in post-colonial India, bringing into sharp relief the technologies of power and strategies of resistance that lap at the shores of anti-trafficking interventions and their focus on 'prostitution', threatening to both undo or unmake, as well as remake the very core of the agenda.[2]

---

2   I use the term 'prostitute' or 'prostitution' when it is the preferred term of particular groups or political ideology. In the context of trafficking, the term 'prostitute' or 'prostitution' is invariably used by those who conflate these two issues under the heading of 'sex trafficking' – that is, they consider prostitution as equal to trafficking. In all other instances, I use the terms 'sex work' or 'sex worker'.

The emergence of anti-trafficking discourse

'Sex trafficking' has become the primary concern of women's human rights struggles in the contemporary period. It has appeared on the agendas of right-wing, conservative groups, as well as human rights groups, feminists and other well-intentioned social justice movements worldwide. The issue is represented in alarming terms, citing statistics that are invariably anecdotal (Laczko *et al.*, 2002; Sung, 2001; Botti, 2000), and presenting scenarios that reduce trafficking to one of brutal and violent organised criminal networks, raping and abusing innocent, thoroughly victimised women and dragging or duping them into prostitution or sexual slavery (Smith, 2000). There now exists a 'discursive verbosity' in the area of trafficking that emanates from the very different and even opposing political and ideological positions[3] (Foucault quoted in Stoler, 1995: 180; Berman, 2003). The concern has led to a startling proliferation of laws and policies at the domestic and international level.

The issue of human trafficking, especially trafficking in women, is neither new nor unfamiliar. The legal regulation of trafficking has been developing over the course of the past century. The issue of sex and violence, evil traffickers and innocent victims, have appealed to the religious right, conservatives and human rights activists alike since the early 1900s when the issue of 'white slavery' was first addressed by the international community.[4] Invariably, the legal responses were based on tales of abuse of young women, taken to foreign lands by force, fraud or false promises, and used for immoral purposes (Doezema, 1999; Demleitner, 1994: 165–7; GAATW, 2001: 26; Roberts, 1992; Walkowitz, 1982). The early responses to trafficking grew out of the anti-prostitution movement which focussed primarily on the trafficking of white women and children for the purpose of prostitution or sexual exploitation.[5]

---

3   See for example Prepared Remarks of Attorney General John Ashcroft, National Conference on Human Trafficking, Tampa, Florida delivered on 16 July, 2004, available at http://www.usdoj.gov/trafficking.htm#reporting (last visited 21 September, 2005) and also Jennifer Block discussing the interest of evangelicals in the issue of trafficking and the odd coalition developing between feminists and faith groups on this issue: Block (2004); Human Rights Watch (1995: 1–2); Statements by feminist activist Janice Raymond (2005).

4   See International Agreement for the Suppression of the White Slave Traffic, UN Sales No 1950.IV.1 (1904) (hereinafter IASWST); International Convention for the Suppression of the White Slave Traffic at Final Protocol, United Nations Sales No 1450.IV.2 (1910) (hereinafter ICSWST, Final Protocol). See also International Convention to Suppress the Slave Trade and Slavery, 25 September 1926, 46 Stat 2183, 60 LNTS 253, available at http://www1.umn.edu/humanrts/instree/f1sc.htm (last visited 14 September 2005); International Labour Organization Convention Concerning Forced or Compulsory Labour (No 29), 28 June 1930, 39 UNTS 55 (hereinafter ILO Forced Labour Convention (No 29)).

5   See IASWST id, art 2 (that provides 'effective protection' to women and girls against the white slave traffic and calls on governments to monitor ports for persons in charge of 'women and girls destined for an immoral life'); See also International Convention for the Suppression of the Traffic in Women and Children, 30 September 1921, 53 UNTS 39,

Little attention was given to issues of forced labour or keeping workers in slavery-like conditions. The early legal responses had weak enforcement mechanisms, focussing on warning possible victims, restricting or discouraging migration, emphasising law enforcement and criminalising the conduct of traffickers, and international co-operation. However, there was essentially no discussion of the rights, needs, or interests of the trafficked women themselves or of trafficked men.

In the contemporary period, there has been a refocus on the issue of trafficking as a result of the numbers involved and the enormous profits that it generates. In the area of anti-trafficking legislation, the United Nations Trafficking Protocol epitomises how the trafficked subject is conceived and addressed.[6] While the definition of trafficking in the UN Trafficking Protocol extends beyond the specific issue of prostitution, it retains its focus on prostitution and violence against women in the broader public arena.[7] States throughout the world are enacting legislation pursuant to the anti-trafficking campaign that invariably lapse into moral surveillance techniques over women as well as a visceral concern over border security that neither advance women's rights nor solves the problem of trafficking.

The definition of trafficking under the UN Trafficking Protocol is intended to cover instances such as the case of a woman from a developing country who ends up enslaved at a garment factory in the United States; or a man smuggled from a North African country into Europe and then forced to harvest crops under threat of beatings or death; or a Nepali woman who is taken across the Indian border and held against her will to work as a prostitute. However, in popular discourse trafficking has invariably been conflated with women who are duped, forced or deceived with legitimate jobs, kidnapped, and then sold into prostitution. Unfortunately, the broad array of situations of abuse and exploitation that constitute trafficking have been overshadowed by a focus on 'sex trafficking'. Claims of sex trafficking are presented as being the overwhelming problem by nearly all players in the human rights arena.

(hereinafter ICST), art 7 (that requires member states to draw up regulations 'for the protection of women and children travelling on emigrant ships').

6   United Nations Protocol on Trafficking Protocol to Prevent, Suppress, and Punish Trafficking in Persons, Especially in Women and Children, (GARes 55/25, UN GAOR, Annex II, Supp No 49, at 60, UN Doc A/45/49 (2001)) 2000 (hereinafter 'UN Trafficking Protocol').

7   The UN Trafficking Protocol defines 'trafficking in persons' as:

> [T]he recruitment, transportation, transfer, harbouring or receipt of persons, by means of the threat or use of force or other forms of coercion, of abduction, of fraud, of deception, of the abuse of power or of a position of vulnerability, or of the giving or receiving of payments or benefits, to achieve the consent of a person having control over another person, for the purpose of exploitation. Exploitation shall include, at a minimum, the exploitation of the prostitution of others or other forms of sexual exploitation, forced labour or services, slavery or practices similar to slavery, servitude or the removal of organs.

This focus is produced through constant and repeated reference to over-whelming and alarming statistics,[8] a sensationalised rhetoric that speaks in terms of 'supply of flesh', 'duped women' and horrifying journeys, as well as the reiteration of the victim's innocence and vulnerability. The issue is presented simultaneously as an issue of protecting women's rights while also securing the destination country from contamination through sexual immorality or threats of criminality. While it needs to be stressed that cases of trickery, fraud and forced sex work do take place, unfortunately many of the legal interventions have done little to protect women's rights (Global Alliance Against Traffic in Women, 2001). In fact, these issues have often served as a metonym for using the criminal law to intensify border security, lobby for the abolition of sex work, and view gendered migrations primarily in terms of victimisation and violence. The complex processes of migration and constitution of subjectivity, including sexual subjectivity, are flattened and replaced with simplistic, linear narratives about 'sex trafficking' and women's subjectivity.

The current responses to human trafficking continue to be informed by a focus on 'innocent victims', especially from the 'Third World', and playing on fears of migrant hoards flooding the country as well as immorality through sex work. Legal discourse all too often collapses concerns over violent crimes committed against women with the complex phenomenon of migration in the current period of globalisation (ILO, 2001). It further conflates distinctions between trafficking and sex work, despite evidence that trafficking exists in ways that are completely disconnected from sex work. The contemporary legal responses to trafficking continue to reproduce the flaws of earlier legal responses, focussing on the victimisation of the trafficked person, linking traf-ficking to sex work, and reinforcing the biases towards the 'Other' that have resonance with the colonial encounter (Kapur, 2005: 142–50).

Female 'others' and the oriental fantasy

To the Women of Hindu India: 'Your culture, it is true, is under no necessity to satisfy our Western judgment. But until it satisfies that judg-ment in what we consider essential points of common humanity, it must do without our respect. Until you change the facts, therefore, the verdict [on a cruel and barbaric culture] cannot be different. ... The

8 There are no reliable statistics that substantiate this claim, which is invariably based on figures that are outdated and anecdotal. The US State Department, in 2002, estimated that 700,000 to 4 million persons who were trafficked, were 'mostly women and children'. It has subsequently revised its estimates to between 600,000 to 800,000 people – mostly women and children – being trafficked annually across national borders. The Department has not published its methodology for collecting these statistics nor explained why these figures were so substantially revised; see also Pheterson (1996:30–6).

liberty afforded to American women for example, is as great as your thralldom.'

(Katherine Mayo, *Slave of the Gods*, London: Jonathan Cape, 1929: 212)

In 1927 Katherine Mayo, an American feminist, visited India to write about the condition of Indian women. Her views were published in *Mother India*, a furious invective against the unhappy condition of Indian women. The text is primarily an inventory of the brutishness of Indian men, horrors of different cultural practices, such as child marriages, the treatment of widows, as well as the unsanitary habits of the Indian (Sinha, 2000; Albinia, 2005). Women were presented as atavistic slaves to their husbands' whims and fancies (Liddle and Rai, 1998). The text served as both an exoneration of, as well as justification for the continuation of, Imperial rule, and the view that these appalling conditions were not the consequences of Empire, but of native backwardness and barbarism. It was designed to subvert the national agitation for self-rule, claiming that given the condition and treatment of women in the subcontinent, Indians were unfit for self-rule.

While Mayo considered herself a far-sighted liberal feminist, her arguments set the stage for a vitriolic attack on her writings by prominent male Indian nationalists (Ranga Iyer, 1928; Mukherji, 1928; Lajpat Rai, 1985, reprint). Many commentators dismissed Mayo's analysis as foreign, inapplicable to the Indian context, and also demonised Western feminism. This nationalist trepidation of feminism continues in the current period. They also resorted to cultural authenticity arguments – that the emancipation of Indian women had to be sought in indigenous practices and idioms. Mother India was regarded as suspiciously imperialistic and provoked an indigenous or relativist response, which served merely to polarise positions around women's rights. It is nevertheless a representation that has continued to resonate in the work of 'First World' as well as post-colonial feminists. [9]

Mayo's work epitomises how the 'Other' was an entity that was central to the logic and project of Orientalism (Said, 1979: 3). While a full mapping of Orientalism is beyond the scope of this chapter, I highlight its major attributes as set out in Said's work. He argued that Orientalism was a 'Western

---

9   Elizabeth Bumiller, for example, dismisses the Indian critique of Mayo and also applauds to some extent the work of Mary Daly, whose arguments were reminiscent of those made by Mayo. Bumiller states that 'Indians still revile Katherine Mayo, although, interestingly, there has been an American radical feminist interpretation of her work. Mary Daly, in her 1978 book, *Gyn/Ecology* wrote that Mayo 'shows an understanding of the situation which more famous scholars entirely lack. Her work is, in the precise sense of the word, exceptional.' 'Mayo, in her own way was a feminist . . . Katherine Mayo, egregious as her views were, held a certain fascination for me. She had done, after all, what I was trying to do.' (Bumiller, 1990: 20–2)

style for dominating, restructuring, and having authority over the Orient' (ibid.). It was grounded on an ontological and epistemological distinction between the 'Orient' and the 'Occident' (ibid.: 2). While Orientalist discourse lacked any correlation with 'reality' and was concerned primarily with the making of the West and locating it in a position of superiority to the 'Rest', it remained internally consistent and highly attractive (ibid.: 5–7). It was a discourse that influenced scholars both in the West and in the 'Orient' itself, though through the work of Indian historiography, the Orient no longer remained an 'inert object', but was active and participating.[10]

The theories of gender and racial identity were also heavily influenced by scientific theories, especially those of Darwin that were predominant in the late nineteenth century. All women were associated with the faculties of 'the lower races . . . and of a past and lower state of civilization' (Darwin, 1871: 275). The actual brain size of women was considered smaller to that of men, and used to assert that men and women belonged to two different species and that the female skull resembled that of an infant, and to a greater degree, that of the lower races (Stott, 1989: 76–7). Like the 'darker races', women were unreliable, irrational, passive and inferior to the white man. In addition, the lower races were perceived as sexually deviant (Sander, 1985). White women were still more civilised and morally pure than their darker racial counterparts (Burton, 1994). At the same time, these assumptions about women fused with those about the lower races were used to reinforce the argument than neither women nor the colonial subject were capable of self-rule, whether in the home or in politics, and needed to be constantly subject to the control and governance of the white man. The gender identity was further displaced onto religious and regional dichotomies. Thus, Hindus were considered superior in intelligence, but simultaneously as effeminate and lacking in manliness, while the Muslims were regarded as lustful and aggressive (Sinha, 1995). At the same time, the Indian was also constructed as being obsessed with sex – sex that was vile, ritualistic and even sadistic. The presence of female and male sexual symbols, sexual sculptures and erotic temples, worship of dark erotic goddesses, together with the practice in some parts of the continent of child marriage, rendered the Indian as lewd and lascivious, and evidence of the native's depravity (Oman, 1973: 246).

This fantasy was reinforced in the context of interrelations between 'native' women and the coloniser, which were often sexual in nature. The native woman was initially, essentially regarded as a sexed subject. While the system of concubinage was prevalent until the middle of the nineteenth century, from the 1860s onward there was a marked shift in preference for a

---

10 While Indian historiography was meant as a corrective to Orientalism, it continued to rely on certain practices of Orientalism such as mapping or fixing boundaries and identities (Prakash, 2000: 60).

self-contained English type of society and family arrangement (Sen, 2002: 44–5). Sexual liaisons with native women were regarded as a matter of shame and disapproval. The major cause of the shift was the 1857 Mutiny that brought about a rift between the races as well as the subsequent consolidation of a distinct imperial identity that required distance from the local natives. The distance was enforced through an increased policing of interracial sex (Strobel, 1992: 6–7). At the same time, the 'natives' sought to control the sexuality of their women through confinement in zenanas, where they were sequestered away from the colonial gaze. The colonial power regarded such a practice as an example of the backwardness of the native subject, and sought to bring women into the open through the eradication of the system of confinement. The native woman's body became the site of contest over the meaning of culture and identity, and played out most significantly over the controversy surrounding the Age of Consent Act 1891 (Sarkar, 1993; Sarkar, 1996; Chandra, 1998).

From the middle of the nineteenth century onwards, the focus of the colonial power in the area of social reform was the 'upliftment' of the native woman and elimination of social practices that were identified as oppressive and barbaric. These included the oppression of widows, female infanticide, child marriage, and the practice of veiling or purdah. Their responses were cast as chivalric, while those of native men were regarded as degrading and oppressive. Yet their ultimate objective was not to produce a free, strong-minded, liberated, fully active native woman. It was to endorse the ideals of self-denial and the idea of a gentle subservient wife (Sen, 2002: 65–7). The native man was constituted by the colonial power in terms of his opposition to women's equality. At the same time, the colonial interventions retained the assumption that women were different from men, and needed to be protected from men. The discourse of equality was invoked at one and the same time to reinforce the idea that all women are, or should be, the same (Indian women should be treated the same as English women), as well as the idea that women are not and should not be the same as men. Thus the colonial power was able to delegitimise the recognition of cultural differences without challenging the assertion of natural gender difference. It was at best a form of intervention that would bring about the 'Victorianisation' of the Indian woman (Sen, 2002: 70).

Social reformers in the nineteenth century sought legal changes from the colonial administration to improve the status of Indian women. The women's question was raised as part of a broader agenda of social and political reform. Social reformers sought to eliminate a host of social practices, from sati, to the prohibition on widow remarriage, to child marriage. The position of women within Hindu tradition was symbolically deployed by the British to legitimise colonial rule. Attention was directed at the most extreme of cultural practices as evidence of the 'barbarity' of Indian society and of its resulting need for foreign rule. Social reformers, in turn, sought to eliminate these cultural practices, and improve the position of women.

At one level, law was a site on which competing visions of Hindu tradition and custom were fought out. Social reformers sought to reform this tradition and custom, while simultaneously seeking support for this reform in Hindu scriptures. In the last decades of the nineteenth century, the contradictions of engaging on this terrain came to the fore, as Hindu nationalists entered the fray, and sought to undermine the very authority of this terrain (Sarkar, 2002; Chandra, 1998; Kapur and Cossman, 1996: 43–50). In these debates, law was again a site on which the much broader visions of the social reformers and the Hindu nationalists were fought out. In this contest, the very legitimacy of law was at issue. While the social reformers were successful in so far as their demand to raise the age of consent was passed into law, the Hindu nationalists were enormously successful in their efforts to rearticulate the domestic sphere as beyond the reach of the colonial intervention.

The strategies of the social reformers, much like that of the colonial power, were informed by a form of protectionism. Women were not assumed to be equal to men; indeed, the discourse of equality was strikingly absent from the debates, as were the voices of women themselves (Kosambi, 2000: 54; Sinha, 1995: 33–68). Social reformers sought to eliminate customs and practices that they considered to be evils perpetrated on women. They sought protective forms of legislation, prohibiting these practices. The discourse within which these legal reforms were sought was heavily embedded with familialism. As Meera Kosambi has argued, '[t]he patriarchal image of the ideal woman, as the ideal wife and mother, was generally accepted and propagated even by progressive social reformers' (ibid.). Women were assumed to be wives and mothers by nature, and the social evils had to be eradicated in order to protect women in these roles. Even the campaigns for women's education, which gathered support from the mid-nineteenth century, and which would bring women out from the confines of the family, were justified in the name of the family (Roy, 2005). Educated women would be stronger in their roles as wives and mothers.

The role of law was in effect contradictory. While legislation was ultimately passed to raise the age of consent for child marriage, for example, the controversy succeeded in mobilising a resistant discourse that insisted on non-intervention in the realm of the private sphere (Bannerjee, 1998). The legislation condemned the practice of child marriage by further raising the age of consent, but the outcome of the discursive struggle was to mobilise the Hindu nationalists very effectively and undermine the legitimacy of the efforts of the social reform movement in seeking legislative change from the colonial state. Tanika Sarkar has argued that what was at stake in the age of consent controversy was no less than the definition of conjugality, which was in her view 'at the very heart of the formative moment for militant nationalism in Bengal' (Sarkar, 1993: 1970). The Hindu nationalists sought to redefine Hindu conjugality, and renegotiate the public/private, the domestic realm of the family, the home, as beyond the reach of colonial intervention. The family was reconstituted as a 'pure space' of Hindu culture and tradition, uncontaminated by colonial intervention. Women who occupied this space, in turn, came to represent all that was pure and untouched by colonialism. Social reformers, who were attempting to redefine Hindu tradition to exclude child marriage, were thereby trying to introduce change into the very sphere that, in the eyes of the Hindu nationalists, was most representative of Hindu culture and tradition. The contest between the social reformers and the Hindu nationalists was not simply over the legitimacy of engaging with the colonial state, but was also a contest over the power and authority to define Hindu culture and tradition and the constitution of women's sexuality (Roy, 2005).

The representation of the native woman as incapable of decision making, whose body is a site of contest over the meaning of cultural and national identity, continues to haunt contemporary discourse of both the conservative and religious right, as well as the discourse of some human rights and feminist scholars and activists in the anti-trafficking debate.

'Sex trafficking', female morality, and the religious right

I use the term 'religious right' to refer very generally to groups in different countries who use orthodox, conservative or even deeply fundamentalist visions of their religion and defend a very strict understanding of family and women's roles within that unit. In this chapter, I refer specifically to two such organisations or networks – the Christian Evangelicals in the United States and the Hindu right-wing nationalists in India.[11] These groups have a

---

11 The term 'Christian Right' has been used by some scholars to include a broad range of American organisations: Buss and Herman, 2003: xviii–xxi. I use the term to refer quite specifically to evangelical Protestantism, which is a biblically literalist Protestantism that is more widespread in the United States than anywhere else, and US Catholicism, which is closer to Irish Catholicism in its doctrinal strictness than to less stringent western and southern European Catholicism. The evangelicals currently exert a considerable influence on the Bush White House, including its human rights agenda.

The Hindu Right refers to a religious right-wing and nationalist movement in India, informed by the ideology of Hindutva (not Hinduism) that is dedicated to the establishment of a Hindu State. It has effectively pursued issues of sexuality in and through a liberal rights discourse and been remarkably successful in advancing their agenda. I use the term Hindu Right to refer to the central organisations and movements of the current phase of Hindu communalism in India – the triumvirate of the Bharatiya Janata Party (BJP – The Indian Peoples Party), the Rashtra Sevika Sangh (RSS – Association of Nationalist Volunteers), and Vishwa Hindu Parishad (VHP – World Hindu Council), collectively known as the Sangh Parivar (the bonded family): Cossman and Kapur (2001: 6–15).

The Christian evangelicals and the Hindu Right recognise women's rights, but within the confines of dominant familial and sexual ideology. The difference between them for the

specific international agenda of supporting women's equality with men, but in a way that either promotes 'harmony' in the family or supports women's formal rights to equality. Thus, they can and do support women's right to work or to be educated, while simultaneously recognising and celebrating women's natural differences from men, including their role as caregivers, in the interests of preserving the family (Buss, 1998; Kapur and Cossman, 1996: 234–48).

Over the course of the past five years, the Christian evangelicals in the United States have exercised considerable influence on the human rights agenda of one of the most religious White Houses in US history. They have been responsible for the extensive remarks made by George Bush on sex trafficking in 2003 and 2004 at the UN General Assembly meetings.[12] On 12 March 2004, International Women's Day, George Bush spoke about 'sex slavery'. He extolled the work of Sharon Cohn, director of Anti-Trafficking Operations for the International Justice Mission (IJM), a Christian organisation. Bush, went on to state that the IJM was 'working to end sex slavery' and that the US government would stand with them. 'We abhor – we abhor – the practice of sex slavery, and we will do all we can to help you. Support for human rights is the cornerstone of American foreign policy' (Block, 2004; Nathan, 2005).[13]

Such human rights issues appeal to the white evangelical base of the Bush White House, who historically belong to denominations such as the Southern Baptists and the Assemblies of God. The evangelicals believe that the Bible is the Truth, that members have a duty to proselytise and convert and that the only way to salvation is through Jesus Christ. The embracing of human rights by Christian evangelicals produces an interesting alliance with liberals and human rights groups. Although human rights groups work on a broad range of issues on which they disagree with the evangelicals, such as abortion, school prayer or homosexuality, on the issue of 'sex trafficking' they appear

---

purposes of this chapter is that the evangelicals usually have a conservative and scripturally oriented position on women's roles and rights and the family, while the Hindu Right is a nationalist movement which may have a less conservative position on women, though they are still shaped by dominant familial ideology. Their enemies are Muslims, and their primary concern is to highlight the gender-egalitarianism of Hindus in contrast to the Muslims (Keddie, 1998).

12 See the Recommendations for the conference on 'Pathbreaking Strategies in the Global Fight Against Sex-Trafficking' from 23–26 February 2003, organised by the Department of State in alliance with non-governmental 'War Against Trafficking Alliance', available at http://www.state.gov/g/tip/rls/rpt/20834.htm (last visited 2 September 2005). See also latest Victims of Trafficking and Violence Protection Act of 2000: Trafficking in Persons Report, 2005 Report.

13 The administration has dedicated over 150 million dollars in two years towards eradicating sex-trafficking.

content to forge alliances with the orthodox right which is so closely aligned with power at the White House.[14]

In 2000, Richard Cizik, vice president for government affairs of the National Association of Evangelicals, forged together a coalition of groups, that included representatives from Equality Now, Ms Magazine as well as B'nai B'rith, to lobby for the enactment of the US Victims of Trafficking and Violence Protection Act 2000 (hereinafter the 'US Act, 2000'). A primary concern was the trafficking of women from the 'Third World' to industrialised countries, through force or coercion.[15] The focus on 'Third World' women resonates with the 'charitable' instincts of evangelicals and their do-good notions of saving the 'wretched of the earth'. Although this instinct is not to be derided, it is the deeper political agenda of the evangelicals that is a cause for alarm. This includes their views on sexual integrity and the role of women in the family. Sex for them must be non-commercial, preserved exclusively within marriage, and only between a man and a woman. Woman's primary role is in the home, as a caregiver and domestic provider.

While the US Act 2000, was intended to concentrate on labour abuses across all industries, such as debt-bondage and force, it was drafted as part of a package against violence against women. Conservatives supported the Bill as it did not threaten their business constituencies. The Bill was also consistent with the evangelicals' concern over moral turpitude and sex, as well as the positions of one segment of the feminist lobby, which was determined to link prostitution with trafficking and violence in the law (Freeman, 1996). In practice, the US Act 2000 has placed undue emphasis on commercial sex work, rather than focussing on exploitation in a broad range of jobs and industries. The Act was reauthorised in 2003 and amended, calling for increased co-operation between governments, assistance for the family members of victims of trafficking, as well as enhanced prosecution of traffickers. The amendments permitted victims to sue their perpetrators in criminal court and for the government to terminate contracts with companies or individuals who are found to be engaged in trafficking. The Act was reauthorised again in 2005, seeking to combat trafficking by addressing the needs of victims of

---

14 *New York Times* columnist Nicholas Kristof epitomises this liberal/human rights voice, arguing that such groups can work with the orthodox right on the issue of trafficking, never addressing the serious consequences for the women who are ostensibly the recipients of such well-intentioned interventions. See for example 'Hidden in Brothels: Slavery by Another Name' *New York Times*, 1 June 2006, A25; 'Bush Takes on the Brothels' *New York Times*, 9 May 2006, A27; 'Hitting Brothel Owners Where it Hurts' *New York Times*, 24 January 2006, A21; 'Sex Slaves? Lock up the Pimps', *New York Times*, 29 January 2005, A19.

15 I use the term 'Third World' when it is the preferred term invoked by particular groups or political ideologies. Otherwise, I use the term 'post-colonial context' or 'post-colonial world' to refer to a theoretical position which analyses the ways in which the historical processes produced during the period of the colonial encounter, continue to discursively inform the post-colonial present (Marks, 2003: 451; Said, 1995; Said, 1979).

trafficking in post-conflict settings, as well as to address domestic trafficking for the first time. It further expands the US criminal jurisdiction for felonies committed by US government personnel or contractors abroad to ensure they are held accountable if they are involved in human trafficking. Despite these amendments, the Act authorises programmes which are primarily geared toward reducing the demand for prostitution in the United States and thus continues to conflate trafficking with prostitution or sexual wrongs. And an appeal to faith-based groups is central to this pursuit. After signing the 2005 reauthorisation of the Act, George Bush stated:

> We're attacking this problem aggressively. Over the past four years, the Department of Homeland Security has taken new measures to protect children from sexual predators, as well as pornography and prostitution rings. The Department of Health and Human Services has partnered with faith-based and community organisations to form anti-trafficking coalitions in 17 major cities across our country.[16]

For feminist organisations such as the Coalition Against Trafficking in Women, (CATW) there is no such thing as consent to sex work and every woman who has crossed borders to work in prostitution is a victim of trafficking. And their concerns are pursued in and through the discourse of human rights. Janice Raymond, a member of CATW, wrote, 'Opposing sex trafficking, the system of prostitution and the sex industry doesn't make you a conservative, a moralist, or an apologist for some political party or group. It helps make you a feminist and a human rights advocate' (Raymond, 2005). Raymond and CATW do not represent the views of all feminists on the issue of trafficking. In fact, as Kempadoo argues, there is a growing body of literature that is beginning to understand and analyse the impact of the colonial encounter on contemporary feminist conceptions of sex work, including trafficking:

> Nevertheless the need for feminist theory to engage with racialised sexual subjectivities in tandem with the historical weight of imperialism, colonialism and racist constructions of power has only been raised recently in the context of this feminist theorizing on prostitution.
>
> (Kempadoo, 1998: 13)

The views of Raymond and others of her ilk have overwhelmingly come to inform the position of faith-based organisations, orthodox groups, US policy, and legal interventions on issues of trafficking around the world. The

---

16 Available at http://www.whitehouse.gov/news/releases/2006/01/20060110–3.html, 10 January 2006.

troubling alliance of some feminists with the Christian evangelicals has been reconciled by one former anti-porn activist, Laura Lederer, and appointee to the US State Department's anti-trafficking office, who stated that faith-based groups have brought 'a fresh perspective and a biblical mandate to the women's movement. Women's groups don't understand that the partnership on this issue has strengthened them, because they would not be getting attention internationally otherwise'[17] (Crago, 2005).

This image of the battered sexual subject, especially in the post-colonial world, and the missionary zeal of religious and some feminist interventionists was portrayed in 'Born into Brothels', directed by Ross Kaufman and Zara Briski. The film was awarded the Oscar for the best documentary film at the 77th Academy Awards in 2005. While documenting the experiences of sex workers in Sonagachi, the red-light district of Calcutta, Briski offered children in the area a chance to record their own lives. The children were provided with cameras to present a portrait of the realities of their world. Although it is not made evident in the film, not all the children are those of sex workers, and are simply poor children excited about participating in a project that is both fun and one in which they can take charge. The children click away happily, though it is evident that not all those who are represented in the portraits are consenting to the activity.[18] In the end, the film centres more on Briski than the children or the situation of the sex workers. Briski becomes the heroine in the film, who takes on the Indian bureaucracy, teaches the children photography, tries to get them into missionary schools, tests them for HIV and also takes them to the zoo. 'Aunty' Zara, who has a master's degree in theology and religious studies, endeavours to save the children from 'dead-end' lives, where the boys have limited prospects and the girls are merely being groomed to 'go onto the line' as prostitutes. In contrast to the representation of Briski as the 'Great White Saviour', the sex workers themselves are mostly represented in the documentary as cruel and uncaring parents. While Briski promised not to screen the film in India, after having won the Oscar, the lives of these women and their families has become a part of global public consumption.

Briski's film was awarded the Gender Lens Award by the White House

---

17 Laura Lederer was editor of the feminist anti-pornography anthology *Take Back the Night* (1980).

18 The sex workers of Sonagachi protested against this film partly on the grounds that Briski refused to submit her work and idea to the Sex Workers Ethics Committee. See 'Calcutta sex workers respond to Born into Brothels', a letter published in *The Telegraph*, 15 March 2005. Swapna Gayen, secretary of Durbar Mahila Samanwaya Committee, (The Unstoppable Movement of Women) Calcutta, (the committee which represents the membership of 60,000 sex workers of West Bengal, in western India) states: 'In this age, when it is the norm to respect ethical considerations while making documentaries, the film used hidden cameras to shoot intimate moments in the lives of sex-workers and their work zones.'

Project.[19] The film reinforces the position of faith-based groups as well as their influence on the trafficking agenda in the international arena. These groups have worked with the Bush administration to aggressively link issues of sexuality to morality, using law and rights discourse to advance this link. In January 2003, the United States' international aid agency (USAID) issued a notice that it would provide no more funding for projects against trafficking in people to 'organisations advocating prostitution as an employment choice or which advocate or support the legalisation of prostitution.'[20] The directive is part of the broader US funding policy to cut funding to projects perceived as supporting trafficking of women and girls, legalisation of drugs, injecting drug use, and abortion. Some feminists have celebrated the move as a way in which to finally deal with the issue of prostitution and to rescue women and girls who are in the trade. As Donna Hughes from CATW stated, 'The challenge now is to implement these landmark [anti-prostitution] policies in order to free women and children from enslavement' (Crago, 2005).

In a similar vein, the religious right in other democratic countries have advanced anti-trafficking agendas in and through rights discourse. For example, in post-colonial India, the Hindu Nationalists have pursued a women's rights agenda that includes domestic violence, sexual harassment as well as anti-trafficking laws. The issue of sexuality is integral to the definition of the post-colonial nation and informed by the politics of the colonial encounter. Restoring masculinity and clearly defined borders has been an overriding definition of the Hindu male and the Hindu Nation in the agenda of the Hindu Right. Hindu nationalism is based on the articulation of a right-wing stance on Indian politics, culture, race, gender and sexuality and the naturalisation of difference (Breckenridge and Van der Veer, 1993). A key to the construction of Hindu Nationalist identity is the role of women. The Hindu Right's official position on women is filled with commitments to

---

19 http://www.thewhitehouseproject.org/about/boardofdirectors.html (last visited 3 October 2005).

20 The amendment ensures that no taxpayer funds designated for HIV/AIDS prevention may be used to promote or advocate the legalisation of prostitution or sex trafficking, and that no funds may be given to any group or organisation that does not have a policy explicitly opposing prostitution and sex trafficking. See Public Law 108–25, the US Leadership Against HIV/AIDS, Tuberculosis, and Malaria Act of 2003, s 301(e) and (f) Assistance to Combat HIV/AIDS, available at http://thomas.loc.gov/cgi-bin/query/C?c108:./temp/~c108tyosT9. Two US district courts have struck down the provisions as unconstitutional and violative of the free speech clause, *Alliance for Open Society Inc et al. v United States Agency for International Development et al.*, United States District Court Southern District of New York, dated 9 May 2006, available at http://brennancenter.org/programs/pov/AOSI%20v%20USAID%20Decision.pdf, and *DKT International Inc v United States Agency for International Development et al.*, United States District Court for the District of Colombia, order dated 18 May 2006 available at http://www.dcd.uscourts.gov/Opinions/2006/Sullivan/2005-CV–1604~9:33:28~5–18–2006-a.pdf.

equality, which involves a pledge to restore women to the position of equality with men that the Indian tradition proposed and accepted (Sarkar, 2001; Bacchetta, 2004). The policy on women often focusses on the roles in the family that have traditionally been allocated to women according to the sexual division of labour. For example, healthcare, particularly maternal and natal care, is taken up, as are sanitation facilities for poor, rural, and slum women. Policies that reinforce women's roles in the family as mothers and wives are supported as part of women's equality rights. In so doing, the Hindu Right reinforces the assumption of natural and essential differences between women and men. Women are mothers and wives – they are different, and these differences must be honoured and protected.

A central discursive component of the Hindu Rights agenda on women's rights is informed by a 'modern but not Western' position. While emphasising the need for women to attain equality, and to work outside of the home, modernisation is posited in opposition to Westernisation[21] (Basu, 1993: 85). Women can work, but must also guard against losing their cultural traditions and identity. This message is directed specifically to women's roles in the family. Women are thus identified not only as biological reproducers, but as cultural reproducers, with the special responsibility of transmitting 'the rich heritage of ethnic symbols and ways of life to the other members of the ethnic group, especially the young' (Yuval-Davis and Anthias, 1989: 9). It is in their roles as wives and mothers, as guardians of the tradition to be passed on to younger generations, that women of the Hindu Right must guard against encroaching Westernisation. She is modern, but remains 'the new Indian woman', 'perennially and transcendently wife, mother and homemaker, who saves the project of modernisation – without Westernisation' (Sunder Rajan, 1995: 133). This argument is deployed in opposition to the West, to distinguish the Hindu national identity and Indian culture from the West, while at the same time to portray it as advanced. The Hindu Right argues that the battle for equality cannot be fulfilled 'by blind imitations of the modes and techniques of struggles adopted by the so-called liberated women of the West' (Sinha, 1985: 5). A more extreme position is that 'the position of women is better in India than anywhere else in the world, and "women libbers" as the worst enemies of woman kind' (Malkani, 1980: 172).

The Hindu Right is attempting to reconstitute an identity for women that firmly reinscribes their roles within the family, while embracing the demands of contemporary consumer capitalism and global economic restructuring (Nanda, 2003). This new identity of 'modern but not Western', of the new Hindu woman as strong wife and mother, is all the more useful in the context of the renegotiation of the public and private spheres engendered by the new

---

21 'The Hindu Woman Rises' *Organiser* (22 May 1994: 1) quoting Uma Bharti, a virulent exponent of Hindu Right politics, and prominent female member of the BJP.

economic policies. The Hindu Right's discourse on women is an effort to ensure that neither the mass politicisation of women, nor their increasing integration into the labour market, undermine the patriarchal family, nor women's roles as wives and mothers therein. Unlike the revivalist discourse of the nineteenth century, women's identities are being reconstituted to explicitly include their roles within the public sphere (Sarkar, 2001; Kapur, 2005: 43–50). The Hindu Right's discourse on women and equality can be seen as an effort to contain the challenge that this renegotiation presents to the traditional patriarchal family. Within this discourse, women remain the repositories of tradition and culture, and the primary site for performing the role of cultural progenitor remains the family. Familial and revivalist discourse become the terms on which women are permitted to move beyond the confines of the private sphere. It is the discourse through which women's new political and economic roles are being negotiated and articulated.

The issue of trafficking needs to be understood against this backdrop of how women's subjectivity and sexuality is conceived and constructed within the discourse of the Hindu Right. While the issue of migration is indeed critical in terms of the foreign remittances that are returned to the sending country, women's conduct should not exceed the normative prescriptions that have been accorded to them. It is possible to understand the government's support for the South Asian Association for Region Co-operation convention on Preventing and Combating Trafficking in Women and Children for Prostitution 2002 (SAARC Convention), and its definition of trafficking, which not only reproduces the conflations between trafficking and prostitution, it also addresses women and girls together and excludes any reference to young boys or to sites of exploitation other than sexual exploitation.[22] Yet the SAARC Convention is consistent with the normative prescriptions regarding women's sexual and moral behaviour. It is a position that advances Indian women's distinction from Western women, preserves the country's national integrity, and reinforces the conflation between trafficking and prostitution. Women's migration is viewed through the lens of coercion and national identity and can be neatly articulated in terms of human rights violations. While this position does little to advance women's choice to move, or complicate the factors that influence female migration, the Hindu Right is able to use the modern, universal discourse of liberal rights, rather than deploy cultural relativist arguments, to restrict both her movement, reproduce conservative sexual morality, and also subject her to moral surveillance.[23]

22 SAARC Convention art 1(3); for a commentary on the human rights implications and limitations of the SAARC Convention, see Coomaraswamy (2001: para 39).
23 While the Hindu Right's political wing, the BJP, lost power at the centre in the 2005 general elections, there was no radical shift from the position of the BJP and the new Congress-led government in which the left parties hold the balance of power. Armed with well-intentioned liberal credentials and claiming to be devoid of the ideological baggage of the Hindu

For the Christian Right and the Hindu Right, the most appropriate response to the issue of trafficking in discursive terms is to prevent the violation of the sovereign state as well as women's bodies. In practical terms, this entails strengthening border controls, punishing those who engage in trafficking for the purposes of prostitution, criminalising pimps and brothel owners and increasing moral surveillance on women who seek to cross borders. While the agenda of the religious right-wing forces is rarely concealed, what becomes a matter of concern is how the liberal response to trafficking is increasingly difficult to distinguish from that of right-wing agendas.

The liberal response

The Public Broadcast System channel in the United States gave considerable air-time to the screening of a film entitled 'The Day My God Died', directed by Andrew Levine, a young independent film-maker.[24] It documents the lives of several Nepali women and girls who were trafficked into the sex trade, from Kathmandu into Calcutta and Bombay. The director also entered the brothels of Bombay and filmed the conditions in the brothels and those who work there using a hidden spy camera. The film makes the case for those who seek to rescue and rehabilitate women in the sex trade as well as abolitionists, who want to see the trade abolished. The film is replete with images of victimisation, abuse and subordination of Nepali women and children. The International Justice Mission, a law enforcement and faith-based organisation in Washington DC, praised for its work by the Bush White House, and local non-governmental organisations such as Maiti Nepal in Kathmandu and Sanlaap in Calcutta, are represented as the 'crusaders', the 'real heroes' and saviours of these women. They work with the police to conduct raids on brothels, which lead to the incarceration of women into protective homes, separated from their children who are sent either to shelters, juvenile centres or inadequate government facilities.

Levine's film constitutes part of a well-intentioned liberal initiative to address the issue of trafficking and goad the international community to respond to the issue. It converges with the efforts of the human rights community which has been enthusiastically pursuing the anti-trafficking agenda. These efforts are reflected partly in the successful lobbying of anti-trafficking initiatives domestically, regionally and globally at an extraordinary rate over the past four years. This flurry of activity has promoted a sense that something is being done, that a well-intentioned social justice project is being pursued. Yet, well-intentioned liberal and feminist interventions directed at

Nationalists, the government nevertheless continues to pursue a paternalistic attitude in the area of women's rights.

24 Screened 1 January 2004 on the Public Broadcasting System.

women's oppression in the non-Western or post-colonial world are frequently reminiscent of the imperial moment. Campaigns on violence against women, for example, operate within a similar logic – that the women are victims of a culturally barbaric, monolithically oppressive and backward context, who need to be rescued and rehabilitated (Akram, 2000). These interventions invariably involve an appeal to a liberal, secular, and Western standpoint as a means for resisting such violence.

And women's bodies remain the terrain for shifting discourses about the 'Third World Woman' and Western women's agency. It is a discourse that fails to critically examine the ways in which the state and community invoke women's bodies and ultimately reduces women to their bodies. The responses to gender essentialist interventions are equally problematic as they rely on cultural stereotypes (Narayan, 2000). As Narayan argues, cultural responses are invoked as a way in which to 'avoid the "Scylla of Sameness" ', often resulting 'in moves that leave one foundering on the "Charybdis of Difference" ' (Narayan, 2000: 83).

Anti-trafficking interventions propelled by well-intentioned human rights advocates also sometimes suffer from similar limitations. They fail to engage with how the colonial encounter, together with its assumptions about the sexuality of the 'Other', has shaped the liberal project. When the colonial encounter is placed at the centre of the analysis the comfort zone of the 'do-good' notions of some well-intentioned human rights campaigners, or of those who believe that they are engaged in a transformative project, lies fully exposed. While the liberal project in its human rights guise seeks to liberate the 'wretched of the earth', it simultaneously results in producing a racist and culturally essentialist construction that is displaced onto a 'First World'/'Third World' divide, here and there, us and them.

In the arena of anti-trafficking laws, Levine's film exemplifies how the colonial past continues to discursively influence the post-colonial present, even in the liberal response. The proliferating discourses on sexuality were not simply present in Europe or the West, they were integral to the sustaining of the imperial project (Stoler, 2002: 78–9). The sexual identity of the European self was contingent on the racialised, sexualised 'Other'. Sexuality remained a site of contest between the colonial power and the ruled and the central struggle over the constitution of national and cultural identity. The legal interventions on issues of trafficking and their focus on prostitution, render this history invisible. As a result, the interventions of liberal activists can at times be as problematic or troublesome as those devised by the conservative or religious right.

Some human rights groups are also responsible for reinforcing these divisions and feeding into the moralistic and patronising responses of governments to the issue of sex work. For example, Human Rights Watch has recommended that the South Asian Association for Regional Co-operation should co-operate with Interpol to stem the increase in trafficking in women between India and Nepal (Human Rights Watch, 1995: 90). Many of the recommendations in the report are directed towards the curtailment and restriction of rights rather than their facilitation. For example, the report criticises the open border policy, which permits people to pass freely between the two countries without a passport, visa, or residential permit. Instead of contextualising the strengths and limits of an open border policy in a region closed and isolated from its neighbours, Human Rights Watch states that the policy 'makes it extremely difficult for border police to check illegal activity. Traffickers and their victims move easily across the border and the onus is on individual police officers to stop and question suspicious-looking travellers' (Human Rights Watch, 1995b: 12). The report thus recommends that Nepal and India should establish a system for strictly monitoring the border to 'guard against the trafficking in women and girls, including the inspection of vehicles'. The suggestion to tighten borders as a way to control trafficking has been enthusiastically adopted by many governments around the world, especially First World governments that fear the spectre of the immigrant (Munro, 2005).

Although Human Rights Watch claims not to take a stand on prostitution or sex work in the report, it favours the criminalisation and punishment of owners of brothels, pimps, and traffickers (Human Rights Watch, 1995: 86). It also strongly condemns 'laws and official policies and practices that fail to distinguish between prostitutes and victims of forced trafficking, treating the latter as criminals rather than as persons who deserve "temporary care and maintenance" in accordance with international human rights standards'. It further opposes 'laws and policies that punish women who engage in prostitution, but not the men who operate and profit from prostitution rings and who patronise prostitutes: such policies are discriminatory on the basis of sex' (Human Rights Watch, 1995: 198). This statement demonstrates a concern for the human rights of victims of forced trafficking, while refusing to advocate in favour of the human rights of those engaged in sex work. In making a distinction between the two categories of women, Human Rights Watch makes human rights contingent on the subject's victim status.

In a similar report on cross-border trafficking between Burma and Thailand, Human Rights Watch requested donors to ensure that loans for the construction of roads and other infrastructure projects near the border take into consideration the effect of such a project on the trafficking in women (Women's Rights Project, 1993: 159). The extraordinary assumption implicit in this recommendation is that withholding assistance for the construction of basic infrastructure will help stop cross-border traffic. Indeed, it will curtail, if not entirely stop, border crossings, both legal and illegal.

The focus on the victim subject and violence invites remedies and responses from states that have little to do with promoting women's rights. Thus, a related concern is that the victim subject position has invited protectionist, and even conservative, responses from states. The construction of women exclusively through the lens of violence has triggered a spate of domestic and international reforms focussed on the criminal law, which are used to justify state restrictions on women's rights – for the protection of women. The anti-trafficking campaign, with its focus on violence and victimisation, is but one example. It spawned initiatives in the 1990s by states such as Bangladesh and Nepal which imposed minimum age limits for women workers going abroad for employment. In 1998, Bangladesh banned women from going abroad as domestic workers. Although Bangladesh is reconsidering the ban, it still remains in effect. In a similar vein, although not entirely prohibiting migration by women, the Nepal Foreign Employment Act 1985 prohibits issuance to women of an employment licence to work overseas without the consent of the woman's husband or male guardian (Sanghera and Kapur, 2001: 24). Similarly, the government of Burma, reacting to a publication of a report by Human Rights Watch about the trafficking of Burmese women and girls into Thailand's sex industry, imposed rules prohibiting all women in this area between the ages of 16 and 25 from travelling without a legal guardian (Belak, 2003). Such measures conflate women's movement or migration with trafficking, where even women moving (legally or illegally) to seek higher-wage work are suspected of being trafficked. There is no mandatory require-ment to provide any services or protect the rights of the victim under these documents, as states are reluctant to provide support for non-nationals. Such interventions reinforce women's victim status and resort to a protectionist and conservative discourse that early feminist interventions struggled to move away from through anti-discrimination discourse. At the same time, the graphic, violent and often titillating accounts of women's abuse marginalises any understanding of the circumstances that lead women to move and rely on traffickers or smugglers to facilitate their movement. For example, the Levine film completely fails to address the context of poverty, the lack of jobs and education, as well as a booming Indian economy, that lead adult women and young girls to migrate voluntarily into India to work as domestic workers, sex workers, as well as in the construction and textile industry. The dominant representation of the women in the film is that they are forced or kidnapped. It corresponds to the image as well as paternalistic responses that some feminists have adopted to the issue of 'sex' trafficking.

Contemporary feminist responses to trafficking

Some of the current feminist scholarship on trafficking and sex work that takes place in the post-colonial world evokes the imagery of the abject victim subject, whose sexuality is understood almost exclusively through the lens of violence and coercion. It is an image which also happens to coincide with the position of the religious right. Kathleen Barry, Catharine MacKinnon and Gloria Steinmen have all been involved in the new anti-trafficking crusades that continue to perpetuate the victim image of women especially from the

'Third World'. These feminists regard sex as a primary tool of abuse of women by men and view prostitution *per se* as the denial of a woman's humanity and ultimate expression of female objectification by men (MacKinnon, 1993). For some scholars, the legalisation of prostitution simply 'normalizes domination, torture, cruel, inhuman and degrading treatment' and violates a range of human rights norms and conventions (Marcovich, 1999).

Kathleen Barry's work on trafficking, which has been extremely influential in this debate, recreates this colonial imagery (Barry, 1995; Barry, 1979). She argues that prostitution is violence against women and that it reduces all women to sex and argues in favour of some form of heroic interventions by feminists on behalf of sex workers (and women generally) to save them from violence, abuse and degradation. She states that prostitution is *per se* a violation of women's human rights. Any woman who migrates for prostitution or to work in the sex trade is also a victim of human rights violations. Barry is a co-founder of CATW, which exerts considerable influence on the strategies against trafficking being developed at the international level. Her work, and that of CATW, has been subjected, however, to a considerable amount of critique for their colonialist representation of women in the developing world and the imperialist character of the interventions they recommend, especially rescue and rehabilitation (Kempadoo, 2001; Kempadoo, 1998: 11–12; Doezema, 2001).

Barry locates trafficking of women in pre-industrial and feudal societies, where women are excluded from the public sphere, and contrasts them with post-industrial, developed societies, where women have been economically independent and prostitution is normalised. The consequence of this kind of argument is that women in the Third World and non-Western world are represented as ignorant, illiterate, tradition-bound, domesticated, and victimised. As feminist scholar Kamla Kempadoo states, 'Barry's representation of the "Third World" woman leaves her not yet a "whole or developed" person; instead, she resembles a minor needing guidance, assistance, and help' (Kempadoo, 1998: 11). The image that is produced is that of a truncated 'Third World' woman who is sexually constrained, tradition-bound, incarcerated in the home, illiterate, and poor. It is an image that is strikingly reminiscent of the colonial construction of the Eastern woman (Mani, 1990; Chaudhuri and Strobel, 1992). In striking contrast to this emaciated image stands the image of the emancipated Western woman; she has 'control over her income, her body and her sexuality'. The analysis is structured along the contours of colonial thought: the assumption being that women in the Third World are infantile, civilisationally backward, and incapable of self-determination or autonomy.

Similar assumptions justified incursions into the lives of the native and the colony. Empire would assist in the development of the civilisation until it reached a point at which it was capable of self-determination (Mehta, 1999). Civilisational achievement was a necessary pre-condition for realising progress, and the stage of civilisation was the marker for determining if progressive possibilities would be within the reach of a community at any given point of time. Infantilising women in the post-colonial world reproduces the colonialist rationale for intervening in the lives of the native subject (to save those incapable of self-determination) in order to justify the rescue operations advocated by Barry and others.

Contemporary international feminist legal politics has reproduced the subject of colonial discourse in its articulation of the exploited sex worker in the post-colonial world. The woman's subjectivity is erased and she is produced in legal discourse as an object – a body which is vulnerable, coerced and easily accessible to traffickers. She is immobilised in terms of her agency and decision-making ability in the course of crossing borders. Legal interventions have produced a victimised subject, based on assumptions of the female 'Other' as incapable of self-determination, justifying rescue and rehabilitation operations, which are strikingly reminiscent of the British justification for colonisation and the establishment of Empire. The victimised subject completely ignores the lived reality of the lives of sex workers in these other parts of the world. As Kempadoo points out, African and Caribbean countries 'where one can speak of a continuum of sexual relations from monogamy to multiple sexual partners, and where sex may be considered as a valuable asset for woman to trade', are completely ignored in this analysis 'in favour of specific Western ideologies and moralities regarding sexual relations' (Kempadoo, 1998: 12). And the victimised subject has consequences on the legal strategies being formulated in the international arena and 'First World' countries that have little to do with the rights of 'victims'.

The issue of trafficking is linked to organised crime, an understanding that encourages a punitive approach to human trafficking for sexual exploitation. The emphasis is on the purpose of the movement, rather than on the violence experienced by women in the course of being transported, migrating, or moving (Chuang, 1998). While women are increasingly encouraged to avail themselves of opportunities outside the confining domestic familial arrangement, these new approaches send a strong message. Women who move are invariably regarded as 'victims' of trafficking, conflating migration (legal or clandestine) with trafficking, lending to the notion that the solution lay, in part, in directing governments to draft legislation to keep their people at home. In the name of protecting women's rights, these initiatives are invariably based on assumptions about women's sexuality, especially about women from the post-colonial world, as victims, infantile and incapable of decision making (Lyons, 1999). These assumptions have invited highly protectionist legislation and at times even justified protective detention and intervention strategies that further reinforce gender and cultural stereotypes.

The oriental fantasy of the native woman as oppressed, subordinated and thoroughly victimised, is reproduced in some contemporary human rights and feminist discourse in the area of trafficking. It is a strategy used to justify interventions by Western feminists to secure the rights of the female 'Other'. Feminist and human rights discourse triggers an orientalist response because it is in informed by culturally monolithic assumptions about the 'Other' as oppressive and backward, especially in its treatment of women. By appealing to a liberal, secular, humanist discourse as a means for resisting that violence, such interventions also simultaneously erase or marginalise the history of exclusion that has been associated with these values and are therefore unable to effectively address the oppression with which they are concerned. The liberal values of equality, liberty and freedom have a history that is intertwined with the history of the colonial encounter and its exclusionary impact (Mehta, 1999; Kapur, 2005: Chapter 1).

Similarly, the interventions of Indian feminists, like their Western counterparts, also collude with nineteenth-century Orientalism, cultural orthodoxies and a 'neo-Orientalist' human rights discourse (Bacchetta, 2002). While many Indian feminists might challenge the persecutory and violent representations of Indian culture by Western feminists and Western human rights advocates, some of them are deeply implicated in reproducing the same gaze when intervening in the lives of women from minority religious communities and even sexual minorities. In the case of sex workers, for example, the language of some Indian feminists engaged in anti-trafficking interventions speak in the language of the 'Other' – as fallen women, or helpless, victimised subjects.

For example, some leftist women's groups in India are accusing the government of promoting 'prostitution' through its commitment to address the problem of AIDS in the country. Their position is framed as a cultural defence argument.[25] In a letter to the former Indian Prime Minister, Atal Bihari Vajpayee, over 50 women's groups alleged that the government had violated constitutional and legal norms by directing World Bank money and other bilateral aid to intervene in the behaviour of 'high risk groups' and promote condom use. The letter states that:

> . . . [w]e write to communicate our anguish and horror at recent State-led developments. Instead of strong measures to remedy age-old malpractices and curb trends derogatory to the dignity of women, we are witnessing in this, the 51st year of our Independence – State acquiescence to the gross violation of the Constitution and the laws of the land aimed at prevention of Immoral Traffic [*sic*]. . . . There is now the beginning of State co-operation for a *permissive environment* within which there is acceptance of the woman's body as a commodity for sale together with abdication of State responsibility to rescue and rehabilitate the poor

25 Letter from the Joint Action Forum to the Prime Minister of India, dated 11 November 2000 (on file with author).

women caught in a vicious vice trap as non-feasible/not-cost effective! This will perpetuate sexual abuse and exploitation; and, *constitutes degradation of the dignity and human rights of Indian womanhood itself.*

(Emphasis added)

The victim status conferred on the sex worker is essential to the survival and the purity of the nation and the preservation of Indian womanhood. This statement is at some level even more restricting of the rights of sex workers as it seeks to deny them information on how to practise safe sex. The signatories seek 'culturally sound' and 'legally correct efforts' to address the problem, including a stringent application of existing laws.

The sexual stereotypes invented during the colonial period remain present in the contemporary period, constantly reproduced in images both on screen and off screen. These representations persist especially in relation to women in the post-colonial world, and continue to inform the legal regulations of trafficking, and the idea that women are victims of a horrific culture, that is mechanical, timeless, and immutable. These ahistorical narratives about the sexual and cultural 'Other' lie at the centre of the critique of scholarship on 'Third World' women by US and European scholars. In brief, this critique maintains that the continuing political and economic domination by 'First World' countries of former colonies informs Western feminist discourse on the 'status of women' in other societies and keeps it focussed on the cultural nature of women's oppression. This position generates a static image of an oppressed woman in the post-colonial context, devoid of any economic, political or historical analysis – a somewhat mindless universalism. This analysis illustrates how it is impossible to address issues of sexuality outside a complex web of shifting, multiple relations, made up of race, ethnicity and Empire, that continue to discursively inform the post-colonial present (Liddle and Rai, 1998: 497–8). Law plays an integral role in constituting sexual subjectivity, and the complexities and contradictions that are exposed in the process of subject constitution.

Women's sexuality remains a contested site for fixing competing discourses. They are fixed with an unproblematic identity that is inscribed in culturally materialist practices and institutionalised structures. The female body enables the discourse of curtailment and containment (Campbell, 1992: 79). The production of this stable identity requires the casting of certain elements of the body, such as sexuality, into a 'defiling otherness' (Butler, 1990: 133–4). Such a move enables the body to become naturalised and immobilised. Yet as Butler argues, the body is performative, and gender 'tenuously constituted in time' and constituted through the process of repetition (ibid.: 140–1). At the same time, resistance is produced at the very point where relations of power are exercised (Foucault, 1980: 142).

The female 'other' responds

> ... there are no relations of power without resistances; the latter are all
> the more real and effective because they are formed right at the point
> where relations of power are exercised.
>
> (Foucault, 1980: 142)

> Like many other occupations, sex work is also an occupation ... we
> systematically find ourselves to be targets of moralising impulses of dom-
> inant social groups, through missions of cleansing and sanitising, both
> materially and symbolically. If and when we figure in political or devel-
> opmental agendas, we are enmeshed in discursive practices and practical
> projects which aim to rescue, rehabilitate, improve, discipline, control or
> police us. Charity organisations are prone to rescue us and put us in 'safe'
> homes, developmental organisations are likely to 'rehabilitate' us through
> meagre income generation activities, and the police seem bent upon to
> regularly raid our quarters in the name of controlling 'immoral' traffick-
> ing. Even when we are inscribed less negatively or even sympathetically
> within dominant discourses we are not exempt from stigmatisation or
> social exclusion. As powerless, abused victims with no resources, we are
> seen as objects of pity.
>
> (Durban Mahila Samanwaya Committee, 1997: 2–3)

In the arena of law, the sexed body is constituted in myriad forms – as
criminal, delinquent, procreative, but rarely ever as erotic or pleasurable. Law,
born of violence and projected as force, operates along trajectories of regulations, prohibitions, and penalties, designed to monitor, deter and punish. In
the context of sexuality, these prohibitions operate along the fault-lines of
normative sexuality – marital, non-commercial, and heterosexual. Yet legal
prohibitions, as expressions of power, are productive in contradictory ways.
These very attempts to contain have set the staging for the resistive subject,
the subject who has been rendered visible and active partly because of the
impact of the mechanisms that are designed to specifically exclude her. While
the body of the sex worker remains a site of regulation and discipline, it
also produces resistive practices that move beyond the focus of disciplinary
surveillance. As a result, legal prohibitions can, among other things, eroticise
the very practices they seek to outlaw. By enumerating a set of sexual practices that are prohibited, or sexed subjects who are designated as deviant,
delinquent or criminal, law brings such practices and subjects into the
public domain and invests them with erotic potential, through the very acts
of prohibition and punishment.

The debate on sex trafficking is frequently displaced on to a 'First World'
and 'Third World' divide, where the sex workers in the latter are deemed to
be the primary targets of coercion while those in the 'First World' are deemed

to have some rights as well as choices. This dichotomy denies women in the post-colonial world the right to self-determination. As Kempadoo argues, the struggle for sex workers rights in the post-colonial world is not essentially Western. Sex workers have historically struggled for rights and against discrimination in the post-colonial world, and they have been involved in insurgent activities outside of their own needs and demands. Veena Oldenburg's work on the Lucknow courtesans provides an important example of how these women occupied multiple spaces of resistance and power simultaneously (Oldenburg, 1990). In 1976, Oldenburg was examining the civic tax ledgers of 1857–77 and related records in the Municipal Corporation office in Lucknow, a large city in Northern India. Much to her surprise, she discovered in these ledgers the presence of the Lucknow courtesans, the famous dancing and singing girls of the city who also performed sexual services. She was not only surprised to find them present in the tax records, but they were in the highest tax bracket, with the largest individual incomes of any in the city. Their names were also on lists of property confiscated by the British from these women for their involvement with the rebellion against the British in 1857. Apparently, they were penalised for instigating, as well as providing, pecuniary assistance to the rebels. Their struggle was anti-colonial as much as it was pro-courtesans' rights. As Kempadoo states, '[s]ex workers struggles are thus neither a creation of a Western prostitutes' rights movement nor the privilege of the past three decades' (Kempadoo, 1998: 21).

In the contemporary period, sex workers, migrants, some post-colonial feminists as well as some regional groups, such as the Global Alliance Against the Trafficking in Women, working on issues of trafficking in Asia, have begun to question the sudden focus on the issue of trafficking and the laws being enacted in many countries ostensibly to curb the problem. The US Act 2000 has come in for specific criticism as being designed to curb migration of a certain class of people, namely 'nannies, maids, dancers, factory workers, restaurant workers, sales clerks, [and] models', rather than to stop the abuse, and violence that takes place in the course of trafficking. They are challenging feminist and orthodox groups, who oppose sex work, and supported this legislation without concern for the fact that it targets migration and migrants from the post-colonial world to the North and is not directed at the problems of abuse and harm that women may experience in the course of transportation or movement.

The intensification of the repressive move to further regulate the lives of sex workers has been challenged by the sex workers themselves. AIDS intervention strategies have intensified mobilisation among sex workers to lobby for their basic human rights, as well as to articulate their concerns in related areas, such as the rights of their children, support in their old age, and better working conditions. They are contesting the underlying assumption that economic necessity drives women into sex work. She is a 'speaking' and 'animated' subject who can and does make choices for economic empowerment, which includes migration. She is an unbounded subject who exists outside the supervision of the family. This intensifies concerns about the threat to the family as well as to the purity of the nation. The movement of the sex worker outside national boundaries, where moral panics have been erupting with increasing frequency, is leading to repressive measures that contain women within national boundaries. Her movement challenges the anti-trafficking regime being advocated as the new international regulatory mechanism for ostensibly protecting the human rights of women. She exposes how this new regime curtails mobility and economic opportunities for women and other migrants, and intensifies the moral surveillance of women's sexual conduct. It is a regime that does not necessarily restrict the number of women who are moving or migrating, but simply makes it more dangerous for women to cross borders. It is not directed towards protecting the rights of women who are in the sex industry or who migrate, albeit clandestinely, for purposes other than sex work.

The sex worker brings about several disruptions. Her claims to rights as a parent, entertainer, worker, and sexual subject disrupt dominant sexual and familial norms. Her repeated performances also challenge and alter dominant cultural norms. From her peripheral location, the sex worker brings about a normative challenge by negotiating her disclaimed or margina-lised identity within more stable and dominant discourses, that is, the way in which the intersection of the dominant sexual, familial, and market ideolo-gies structure her experience of the world. By renegotiating and occupying dominant sexual, familial, and cultural norms, she brings out the ambiva-lence of these norms. She simultaneously creates the potential for a more inclusive politics, opening up a space for subjects who have remained unad-dressed in the women's human rights politics as it has emerged, such as single parents, other sexual minorities, and religious and cultural minorities.

The idea that the post-colonial sexual subaltern subject can consent to sex work, and that she may consent to move or enter into a consensual arrange-ment with someone who arranges her transport from one port to another, free from coercion or violence, is also challenging at a normative level. Women from the post-colonial world can and do consent to commercial sex, and thus challenge sexual and cultural normativity, as well as the imperialist representations of women from the post-colonial context that have come to inform certain aspects of the international women's rights agenda as well as some of the policy responses of 'First World' governments. Women cross borders to engage in sex work and other practices, such a domestic labour, thus challenging the dominant assumptions that inform both the contempor-ary international legal regime as well as feminist legal politics which assumes that she is dragged, beaten, forced, kidnapped, or abducted into this work. Women can and do choose to move and work in the sex industry, and even find clandestine means by which to enter into another country searching for economic opportunities if legal ones are not open to them. She is a market actor who understands the economic and other opportunities available to her in other parts of the world. As a market actor, she challenges the over simplistic and patronising assumption that women in the post-colonial world enter the sex trade because of conditions of poverty, which belies the question why all poor women do not opt for sex work (Chuang, 1998: 84–5). They can choose to cross borders in search of better economic opportunities as do, for example, educated middle-class graduates from developing countries.

The subjectivity of the sex worker in the post-colonial context is captured in the 'Tales of the Night Fairies', directed by Shohini Ghosh, a reader in Media Studies in New Delhi, India, who produced a documentary about the lives of sex workers in Sonagachi in Calcutta. The film stands in stark contrast to the representations projected by Briski and Levine. It depicts how these women have organised themselves into a movement of over 60,000 members. With help from activists, social workers and medical practitioners, the Sonagachi woman have organised to reduce the rate of HIV infection among sex workers to below 5% (as compared to 80% in Bombay, where the sex workers remain unorganised), a dimension of their lives that is afforded no recognition in Briski's film, nor is the movement ever acknowledged in the Levine documentary. They have also set up financial institutions to organise loans for sex workers and the local community, health clinics, sex education, schools and blood banks throughout the Sonagachi area. 'Tales of the Night Fairies' is a film shot with the informed consent of all those who feature in the documentary and their active participation. The women are the real heroes in this representation. The story of these women and their families speaks to their choices, struggle, agency and also opposition to the anti-trafficking strategies that have become such a significant component of the women's human rights agenda over the past decade.

The fact that women cross borders, and ought to be able to cross borders, has been conflated with the purpose of their journey, rather than with the conditions under which they cross borders. Some of the recent literature in the area of international human rights continues to invoke the trope of poor, 'Third World', women's bodies, that is, the body of the 'Third World' subject exclusively as a victim, reinforcing arguments against sex work *per se* as inherently exploitative, rather than supporting the rights of these women to move or envisioning the possibility of a more complex subjectivity than the flattened, cardboard cut-outs to which their subjectivity has been reduced. Little attention is given to the coercive and abusive practices that women may be subjected to in the course of movement, including a lack of interrogation of the racist, sexist, and 'neo-colonial' anti-trafficking laws being advocated by 'First World' governments (and reproduced in some feminist literature). These initiatives harm more women than they help and reinforce stereotypes of the 'Third World' as barbaric in the treatment of its women.

Conclusion

Drawing on the insights of postmodern, post-colonial and social constructionist theory, sex and sexuality as represented in law must be understood
within the matrix of power, knowledge and resistance. The subject is constituted along the fault-lines between operations of power and manoeuvres
of resistance. In the legal regulation of the sex and sexuality, the subject
remains amenable to discipline. Yet there is an excess, the excluded aspects of
sexuality, that carries the potential for the emergence of an alternative sexual
subject; a resistive subject who produces counter-knowledge that challenges
dominant meanings and constructions of sexuality (Kapur, 2004). Through
engagements with the power of the law, alternative sexual subjects and sexual
practices produce bodies that are attributed different meanings. And these
different meanings shape the materiality and lived reality of the body.
Thus, the homosexual may have been cast as a pathologised body through
dominant medical and legal discourses, but through the process of resistance
and the simultaneous production of knowledge, the shapes and contours of
this body altered. It was no longer a body that was delinquent, diseased or
deviant, but human, imbued with rights, rather than one that ought to be
isolated, incarcerated or eliminated. This process of mapping and codifica-
tion of the lives and reality of resistive or differently sexed others, is con-
tinuous and constantly disrupts and re-fashions dominant sexual, familial,
cultural and legal paradigms.

Through resistance, another space, marked for exclusion, is rendered visible and insistent on inclusion. Sex and sexuality is thus a site of complexity
and contradiction. It is not exclusively defined and shaped by power, but is
produced both through the exercise of power, in particular the process of
exclusion, but also by resistance, in particular by insistent visibility. When
the sex worker, for instance, defines herself as a worker, a solicitor of sex, a
mother and parent, she transgresses every boundary established for sexed
subjects and produced through sexual normativity. She challenges the definition of 'productive labour', the borders of dominant familial ideology, and
renders visible the intersection of consent and compulsion, obscured by
liberalism's assumption about the location of labour in the free market. By
insisting on making visible her exclusion from sexual normativity, she
exposes its translucency and thus also renders the norm vulnerable. It is a
form of discursive resistance that is produced through dissonant statements
and a challenge to the determined boundaries of sexuality as well as female
subjectivity.

The three documentaries discussed in this chapter reflect the different sides
of an ever-increasing divide over the way in which women in the post-colonial
world, and in particular, the female 'Other', have come to be represented.
These representations epitomise the different ways in which women's subjectivity, especially of the 'poor', 'Third-World' subject, is conceived and

constructed. In Briski's narrative, the children are victims and her missionary based interventions presented as an effort to rescue them from the misery and desperation of their lives. The children are happiest with their cameras and this moment stands in stark contrast to the emptiness of their daily lives. They are imagined as disposable, deficient victim subjects, an image that is starkly familiar, given its dominant presence in media and celluloid in the global north. At the same time it is Briski's struggle that is centred in the film, giving the impression that no one in India is concerned with or wants to improve the squalid situation of the children, and the mothers are either violent or just do not care. In the second image, Levine is the well-intentioned liberal, who intends his film to represent the human rights violations occurring in a place he 'deeply cares about'. Once again, the young women are represented as utterly victimised, where the local human rights organisation allied with the (Christian) International Justice Mission, seek to rescue and rehabilitate the girls to live 'more productive' and fulfilling lives, one option being marriage. In the third representation, Ghosh attempts to foreground the subjectivity of the sex workers, and complex layering of their lives. They are constantly exercising choices, claiming their identities as sex workers, while also resisting the abuse, sexual exploitation and violence that they may experience, by demanding rights. While the film maker remains largely in the margins, the struggle of the women is central to the narrative. There are moments when they are infantilised, prancing around chairs at a carnival, in a version of musical chairs. Yet largely, they are depicted as resistive subjects, who are not seeking rescue and rehabilitation, but respect and a space from which to assert their rights and subjectivity.

The legal responses to trafficking largely reinforce the representations put forth by Briski and Levine, of trafficked women, which is mediated through the nexus of gender, racialised innocence and criminality. She is usually a young innocent victim and invariably trapped into prostitution. The victim subject and the focus on violence invite remedies and responses from states that have little to do with promoting women's rights. Instead they have triggered a spate of domestic and international reforms focussed on the criminal law, which are used to justify state restrictions on women's rights – for the protection of women as well as to reinforce sexual, cultural and racial stereotypes. The legal regulation of trafficking in the international arena is largely focussed on the point of crossing borders. It is at this point that the women's subject identity is rendered unstable. While women cross as mothers, wives, tourists, professionals or migrants, the law intervenes to potentially disrupt, if not derail, these subjectivities in order to render her victimised, as well as illicit and immoral, by the reassignment of her subjectivity through trafficking discourse. All agency is retained by the trafficker, and the focus on criminality enables states to strengthen laws to curb trafficking as well as increase the punishment for trafficking.

The images inspired by 'Born into Brothels' and 'The Day My God Died' echoed in the work of evangelicals, liberals and some feminists (both here and there) alike need to be seriously questioned. The patronising and protectionist responses of liberals through human rights co-joined with the 'crusading' zeal of orthodox groups and evangelicals, reveals a lack of sensitivity to the ways in which women live in the post-colonial world despite their situations of disadvantage. In this well-meaning stereotype there can be no 'Bandit Queen' or 'Nightfairies' or the sexual humour, songs and dances of the Sonagachi women in the post-colonial world. They shatter the neatly sculpted image of the post-colonial subject and the representation of women as existing always and exclusively as poor, unhappy and unfortunate victims, devoid of sexual agency. A challenge to these images might create the possibility for more genuine alliances that are forged on the basis of respect, regardless of the material and social conditions in which women may exist.

Bibliography

Akram, S (2000) 'Orientalism Revisited in Asylum and Refugee Claims', *International Journal of Refugee Law* 12(1): 7.

Albinia, A (2005) 'Womanhood Laid Bare: How Katherine Mayo and Manoda Devi Challenged Indian Public Morality' in Narula, M, Sengupta, S, Bagchi, J, Lovink, G, *Sarai Reader*, pp 428–35.

Bacchetta, P (2004) *The Nation and the RSS: Gendered Discourse, Gendered Action*, New Delhi: Kali for Women.

Bannerjee, H (1998) 'Age of Consent and Hegemonic Social Reform' in Midgley, C, *Gender and Imperialism*, Manchester: Manchester University Press.

Barry, K (1979) *Female Sexual Slavery*, New York: Avon.

Barry, K (1995) *The Prostitution of Sexuality: The Global Exploitation of Women*, New York: New York University Press.

Basu, T, Datta, P, Sarkar, S, Sarkar, T, and Sen, S (1993) *Khaki Shorts, Saffron Flags: A Critque of the Hindu Right*, Delhi: Orient Longman.

Belak, B (2003) 'Migration and Trafficking of Women and Girls', in *Gathering Strength: Women from Burma and Their Rights*, Thailand: Images Asia online available at http://www.ibiblio.org/obl/docs/GS12.migration-and-trafficking.pdf.

Block, J (2004) 'Sex Trafficking: Why Faith is interested in the Sex Trade', Conscience, available at http://www.catholicsforchoice.org/conscience/archived/SexTrafficking.htm.

Botti, A (2000) 'The Trade in Human Beings is a Worldwide Scourge', *International Herald Tribune*, 1 June 2000.

Breckenridge, C and Van der Veer, P (eds) (1993), *Orientalism and the post-colonial Predicament: perspectives on South Asia*, Philadelphia: University of Pennsylvania Press.

Bumiller, E (1990) *May you be the mother of a hundred sons: A Journey Among the Women of India*, New York: Random House.

Burton, A (1994) *Burdens of History: British Feminists, Indian Women and Imperial Culture, 1865–1915*, Chapel Hill: University of North Carolina Press.

Buss, D and Herman, D (2003) *Globalizing Family Values: The Christian Right in International Politics*, Minneapolis, London: University of Minnesota Press.

Butler, K (1997) 'Shame of EU over 500,000 Sex Slaves', *The Independent*, 28 April 1997.

Campbell, D (1992) *Writing Security: United States foreign policy and the politics of identity*, Minneapolis: University of Minnesota.

Chandra, S (1998) *Enslaved Daughters: Colonialism, Law and Women's Rights*, New Delhi: Oxford University Press.

Chuang, J (1998) 'Redirecting the Debate Over Trafficking in Women: Directions, Paradigms, and Context', *Harvard Human Rights Journal* 11, pp 65–107.

Coalition Against the Trafficking in Women (CATW) (2000) 'Victory in Vienna' http://www.uri.edu/artsci/sms/hughes/catw/posit1.htm.

Coomaraswamy, R (2001) Report of the Special Rapporteur on Violence Against Women, its Causes and Consequences: Mission to Bangladesh, Nepal and India on the Issue of Trafficking of Women and Girls (28 October–15 November 2000), United Nations Office of the High Commissioner for Human Rights, E/CN.4/2001/73/Add.2, New York.

Cossman, B, and Kapur, R (2001) *Secularism's Last Sigh? Hindutva and the (Mis)Rule of Law*, reprint, Delhi: Oxford University Press.

Crago, A 'Unholy Collaboration: Feminists and the Christian Right are in bed together' available at http://quebec.indymedia.org/en/node.php?id=11966.

Darwin, C (1971) *The Descent of Man and Selection in Relation to Sex, (1871)*, Limited Editions Club edition, Adelaide: The Griffins Press.

Demleitner, N (1994) 'Forced Prostitution: Naming an International Offense', *Fordham International Law Journal* 18, pp 163–197.

Doezema, J (1998) 'Forced to Choose: Beyond the Voluntary v Forced Prostitution Dichotomy', in Kempadoo, K and Doezema, J (eds), *Global Sex Workers' Rights*, New York: Routledge, pp 34–50.

Doezema, J (1999) 'Loose Women or Lost Women: The Re-emergence of the Myth of White Slavery in Contemporary Discourses of Trafficking in Women' (paper presented at the 40th Annual Convention of the International Studies Association, 16–20 February), available at http:// www.ciaonet.org/isa/doj01/doj01.html.

Doezema, J (2001) ' "Ouch!" Western feminists wounded attachment to the "third world prostitute" ' *Feminist Review* 67, pp 16–38.

Doezema, J (2005) 'Now You See Her, Now You Don't: Sex Workers at the UN Trafficking Protocol Negotiation, *Social and Legal Studies* 14 (1), pp 61–89.

Durbar Mahila Samanwaya Committee (1997) 'Sex Worker's Manifesto', First National Conference of Sex Workers in India, 14–16 November, Calcutta, at www.walnet.org/nswp.

Engels, D (1989) 'The Limits of Gender Ideology: Bengali Women, the Colonial State and the Private Sphere, 1890–1930', *Women's Studies International Forum* 12(4): 425–37.

Foucault, M (1980) *Power/Knowledge: Selected Interviews and Other Writings 1972–1977*, Gordon, C (ed.) New York: Pantheon Books.

Freeman, J (1996) 'The Feminist Debate over Prostitution Reform' in Weisburg, K D (ed.), *Applications of Feminist Legal Theory to Women's Lives: Sex, Violence and Reproduction*, pp 237–49.

Global Alliance Against Trafficking in Women (2001), *Human Rights and Trafficking in Persons: A Handbook*, Bangkok, Thailand.

Human Rights Watch (1995a), *Global Report on Women's Human Rights*, New York: Human Rights Watch.

Human Rights Watch (1995b), *Rape for Profit: Trafficking of Nepali Girls and Women to India's Brothels*, New York: Human Rights Watch.

International Labour Organisation (2001), *Stopping Forced Labour: Global report under the follow–up to the ILO Declaration on Fundamental Principles and Rights at Work*, Geneva: ILO.

Kapur, R (2005) *Erotic Justice: Law and the New Politics of Postcolonialism*, London: Cavendish.

Kapur, R and Cossman, B (1996) *Subversive Sites: Feminist Engagements with Law in India*, New Delhi, London, Thousand Oaks: Sage.

Keddie, N (1998) 'The New Religious Politics and Women Worldwide: A Comparative Study' *Journal of Women's History* 10(4): 11–34.

Kempadoo, K (1998) 'Introduction: Globalising Sex Workers' Rights', in Kempadoo, K and Doezema, J (eds) *Global Sex Workers' Rights*, New York: Routledge, pp 1–33.

Kempadoo, K (2001) 'Women of Color and the Global Sex Trade: Transnational Feminist Perspectives' *Meridians: Feminism, Race, Transnationalism* 1, pp 28–51.

Kosambi, M (2000) 'Motherhood in the East–West Encounter: Pandit Ramabai's Negotiation of "Daughterhood" and Motherhood', *Feminist Review* 65(1): 49–67.

Laczko, F, Klekowski von Koppenfels, A, Barthel, J (2002) 'Trafficking in Women from Central and Eastern Europe: A Review of Statistical Data', *Migration Challenges in Central and Eastern Europe*, Geneva: IOM.

Lajpat Rai, L (1985) *Unhappy India*, reprint Delhi: Anmol Publication.

Lewis, R (1996) *Gendering Orientalism: Race, Femininity, and Representation*, London and New York: Routledge.

Liddle, J and Rai, S (1998) 'Feminism, Imperialism and Orientalism: the challenge of the "Indian woman" ' *Women's History Review* 7(4): 495–520.

Lyons, H D (1999) 'The Representation of Trafficking in Persons in Asia: Orientalism and Other Perils' *Re/productions* 2 (online journal) at www.hsph.harvard.edu/Organizations/healthnet/SAsia/repro2/.

McClintock, A (1995) *Imperial Leather: Race, Gender and Sexuality in the Colonial. Contest*, New York: Routledge.

MacKinnon, C (1993) 'Prostitution and Civil Rights', *Michigan Journal of Gender & Law* 1, pp 13–32.

Malkani, K R (1980) *The RSS Story*, New Delhi: Impex India.

Marcovich, M (1999) 'Human Rights – A European Challenge?' in Hughes, D and Roche, C (eds) *Making the Harm Visible Global Sexual Exploitation of Women and Girls, Speaking Out and Providing Services*, available at http://www.uri.edu/artsci/wms/hughes/mhvtoc.htm (last visited 29 July 2006).

Marks, S (2003) 'Empire's Law' *Indiana Journal of Global Legal Studies* 10(1): 449–65.

Melman, B (1992) *Women's Orients: English Women and the Middle East, 1718–1918*, Ann Arbor: University of Michigan Press.

Mehta, U S (1999) *Liberalism and Empire: A Study in Nineteenth Century British Liberal Thought*, Chicago: University of Chicago Press.

Mukherji, D G (1928) *A Son of Mother India Answers*, New York: E P Dutton.

Munro, V (2005) 'A Tale of Two Servitudes: Defining and Implementing a Domestic Response to Trafficking of Women for Prostitution in the UK and Australia' *Social and Legal Studies* 12(1): 91–114.

Nanda, M (2003) *Prophets Facing Backwards: Postmodernism, Science and Hindu Nationalism*, Rutgers: Rutgers University Press.

Nathan, D (2005) 'Oversexed', *The Nation*, 11 August 2005.

Narayan, U (2000) 'Essence of Culture and a Sense of History: A Feminist Critique of Cultural Essentialism', in Narayan, U and Harding, S (eds), *Decentering the Center: Philosophy for a Multicultural, Post-colonial, and Feminist World*, Bloomington: Indiana University Press, pp 80–100.

Oldenburg, V T (1990) 'Lifestyle as Resistance: The Case of the Courtesans of Lucknow, India' *Feminist Studies* 16, pp 259–87.

Oldenburg, V T (2002) *Dowry Murder: The Imperial Origins of a Cultural Crime*, New York: Oxford University Press.

Oman, J C (1973) *The Brahmans, Theists and Muslim of India: Studies of Goddess Worship in Bengal*, reprint, Delhi: Heritage Publishers.

Pheterson, G (1996) *The Prostitution Prism*, Amsterdam: Amsterdam University Press.

Prakash, G (2000) 'Writing Post-Orientalist Histories of the Third World: Perspectives from Indian Historiography', in Chaturvedi, V (ed) *Mapping Subaltern Studies and the Postcolonial*, New York: Verso, pp 163–90.

Ranga Iyer, C S (1928) *Father India: A Reply to Mother India*, New York: Lewis Carrier & Co.

Raymond, J G (2005) 'Sex Trafficking is not "Sex Work" ', *Conscience* 26 (1) available at http://action.web.ca/home/catw/readingroom.shtml?x=74355.

Roberts, N (1992) *Whores in History: Prostitution in Western Society*, London: HarperCollins.

Roy, A (2005) *Gendered Citizenship: Historical and Conceptual Exploration*, New Delhi: Orient Longman.

Said, E (1979) *Orientalism*, New York: Vintage Books.

Said, E (1993) *Culture and Imperialism*, London: Chatto & Windlus.

Sander, L G (1985) 'Black bodies, White bodies: Towards an Iconography of Female Sexuality in Late Nineteenth-Century Art, Medicine, and Literature', in Gates, H L (ed.) *Race, Writing and Difference*, Chicago: Chicago University Press.

Sanghera, J and Kapur, R (2001) *Report on Trafficking in Nepal: Policy Analysis – An Assessment of Laws and Policies for the Prevention and Control of Trafficking in Nepal*, New Delhi: Population Council.

Sarkar, T (1996) 'Colonial Lawmaking and Lives/Deaths of Indian Women: Different Readings of Law and Community', in Kapur, R (ed.) *Feminist Terrains In Legal Domains: Interdisciplinary Essays on Woman and Law*, New Delhi: Kali for Women, pp 210–38.

Sarkar, T (2001) *Hindu Wife and Hindu Nation*, New Delhi: Permanent Black.

Sen, I (2002) *Women and Empire*, New Delhi: Orient Longman.

Sinha, M (1985) 'Women's Equality – Miles to March' (1 September 1985) *Organiser*.

Sinha, M (1995) *Colonial Masculinity: The 'Manly' Englishman' and the 'Effeminate*

Bengali' in the Late Nineteenth Century, Manchester: Manchester University Press.

Sinha, M (ed.) (2000) *Katherine Mayo: Mother India: Selection From the Controversial 1927 Text*, Ann Arbor: University of Michigan Press.

Smith, R J (2000) 'Sex Trade Enslaving East Europeans: A Survivor's Brutal Tale', *International Herald Tribune*, 26 July 2000.

Stoler, A (1995) *Race and the Education of Desire: Foucault's History of Sexuality and the Colonial Order of Things*, Durham & London: Duke University Press.

Stoler, A (2002) *Carnal Knowledge and Imperial Power: Race and the Intimate in Colonial Rule*, Berkeley: University of California Press.

Strobel, M (1993) *Gender, Sex and Empire*, Washington DC: American History Association.

Sung, G (2001) 'Europe to Deal a Blow to Human Trafficking', *The Straits Times* (Singapore) 6 December 2001.

Sunder Rajan, R (1995) *Real or Imagined Women: Post-colonialism, Gender and Culture*, London, New York: Routledge.

Volpp, L (1994) '(Mis)Identifying Culture: Asian Women and the "Cultural Defenses" ' *Harvard Women's Law Journal* 17, pp 57–101.

Walkowitz, Judith (1982) *Prostitution and Victorian Society: Women, Class, and the State*, New York: Cambridge University Press.

Yuval-Davis, N and Anthias, R (eds) (1989) *Woman–Nation–State*, New York: St Martin's Press.

Chapter 11

Making sense of zero tolerance policies in peacekeeping sexual economies

Dianne Otto, The University of Melbourne *

Faela [not her real name] is 13 and her son Joseph is just under six months old. Sitting on the dusty ground in Bunia's largest camp for Internally Displaced People [in eastern Democratic Republic of the Congo], with Joseph in her arms, she talks about how she ensures that she and her son are fed. 'If I go and see the soldiers at night and sleep with them then they sometimes give me food, maybe a banana or a cake,' she explains. 'I have to do it with them because there is nobody to care, nobody else to protect Joseph except me. He is all I have and I must look after him.'

(Holt, BBC News, 2004)

Yvette [14] and her friends ... loiter outside the camps of UN peace-keepers, hoping to sell their bodies for a mug of milk, a cold soda or – best of all – a single dollar. 'I am sad about it. But I needed the dollars. I can't go farm because of the militias. Who will feed me?' asked Yvette.

(Wax, Washington Post Foreign Service, 2005)

Chantal, 17, stood sullenly outside a Moroccan troop camp [in Bunia] one recent evening ... 'To us they are the town's best employer', she said with a shrug. 'I know everyone is saying it's bad. But why don't they come and give us jobs? Tell me, who will feed me?'

(Wax, Washington Post Foreign Service, 2005)

On 9 October 2003, the United Nations (UN) Secretary-General instituted a zero tolerance policy that banned UN peacekeeping personnel from engaging in a broad range of sexual activities, including the 'survival sex' that Faela, Yvette and Chantal rely on (Secretary-General, 2003). The ban on 'sexual exploitation and sexual abuse' was widely welcomed, after years of institutional inertia in the face of allegations of rape and other forms

---

* Thanks to Alice Miller for long conversations about this project, to Carole Vance for her close reading of the text, and to Joan Nestle for her words.

of sexual violence by UN 'peacekeepers',[1] as a shift away from the prevailing culture which dismissed such behaviour as an inevitable by-product of military masculinities. While I too applaud the Secretary-General for his efforts to take seriously the problems faced by women and girls who are too often the silent and stigmatised victims of sexual crimes, I am troubled by many aspects of his response, particularly the over-inclusiveness of its broad definitions of 'sexual exploitation' and 'sexual abuse', which include consensual sex between peacekeepers and local people. Also troubling are a number of other aspects of the Bulletin's approach: the invocation of protective representations of women, the conflation of women and children, the adoption of 18 as the age of consent, the imperial dimensions of the 'anti-fraternisation' policies that have been adopted in the Bulletin's implementation, and the presumption of hetero-normativity that the Bulletin confirms, even as it bans the activity itself. The repressiveness of the Secretary-General's zero tolerance approach to sex can work to conceal the many productive effects of the new rules as a form of power (Foucault, 1990). My contentions about the productivity of the new code are first, that taking an approach that is so out of step with the promotion of women's and children's rights sets back both of those projects by giving a new legitimacy to conservative hierarchies of gender and sexuality and, second, that the Bulletin's primary motivation is institutional survival rather than securing the human rights of the 'vulnerable' populations it purports to be protecting.

My discussion is concerned with the particular set of practices known colloquially as 'obligation' or 'survival' sex, which are a form of livelihood for the 'vulnerable' participant and, often, through a web of obligations, for members of their extended family as well. Survival sex generates income or leads to access to privileges and resources that are necessary for everyday material survival. Economies of survival sex arise from conditions of poverty and are made possible by large disparities in wealth, which are present in most peacekeeping contexts. As former head of the office to address sexual abuse allegations in the UN Mission in the Democratic Republic of the Congo (MONUC), Nicole Dahrendorf, comments, '[i]t's extraordinary how much money is bandied about here [in Kinshasa] by UN personnel and how poor the local population is' (Reuters Alertnet, 2006). She describes peacekeepers with $100 bills to spend while most people in the local population are desperate to find the $20 that will pay the rent for a month. Although survival sex is the result of economic decision making in highly invidious circumstances, it nevertheless involves a level of agency and negotiation that distinguishes it from sexual offences like rape, sexual assault, forced

---

1   I use the term 'peacekeeper' to include all categories of peacekeeping personnel associated with peace support operations including humanitarian workers and private military contractors.

prostitution and sexual slavery, where consent is absent. While coercion, agency and survival form a 'complex matrix' (Miller, 2004: 39), drawing distinctions on the basis of consent, no matter how fine they may turn out to be, is critical to respecting the dignity of the young 'victims', which subsists despite considerable differences in power and economic status.

While survival sex is a form of sex work, I do not discuss prostitution more generally in this chapter, although its inclusion in the Bulletin's ban is also deeply troubling and many of the arguments that I make about survival sex apply equally to other forms of sex work. My argument is that zero tolerance is the wrong response to the complex set of circumstances that give rise to survival sex economies because it is driven by 'sexual negativity' (Rubin, 1984: 278),[2] rather than by the desire to address the underlying human rights and social justice issues. This approach has frequently been promoted by women's human rights activism, which has emphasised, often for strategic reasons in the face of denial and indifference, that sexual harm is the 'worst abuse' that can happen to a woman (Miller, 2004: 19). Zero tolerance does not address the grinding poverty or the poorly resourced charity-based models of aid that produce economies of survival sex. Instead, giving centre stage to the repressive politics of the body serves to divert attention from the politics of social justice and save the UN's humanitarianism from scandal. It makes the survival of the 'victims' it claims to protect even more precarious.

The problem of 'survival sex'

Since the end of the Cold War, at the same time as the Security Council's ambitions for its peacekeeping missions expanded dramatically from monitoring ceasefire agreements to building the institutional and legal infrastructures that might sustain post-conflict societies (Boutros-Ghali, 1992; 1995), concerns about the complex sexual economies that are produced by UN peacekeeping missions have surfaced. As early as 1992, anxiety was expressed about the rise in prostitution that accompanied the UN Mission in Cambodia (UNTAC) (Serey Phal, 1995; Mackay, 2001) and, in 1993, there were reports of UN military personnel in Mozambique (ONUMOZ) buying sex from hundreds of girls between the ages of 12 and 18 (Orford, 1996: 379; Machel, 2001: 58). There followed other reports condemning the sexual activities of UN peacekeepers in, for example, Somalia (Lupi, 1998), Bosnia-Herzegovina (Human Rights Watch, 2002; Mendelson, 2005),

---

2   Rubin uses this term to describe the prevalence of the idea that sex is a 'dangerous, destructive, negative force', unless performed pursuant to a narrow set of socially approved 'excuses', like 'marriage, reproduction and love'. She limits her observations to 'Western cultures', and blames 'most Christian traditions' for originating the idea. However, it is clear that sexual negativity characterises many non-Western traditions as well, although it will be manifested through historically and culturally specific social practices.

Eritrea (Barth, 2004: 13–14) and Timor-Leste (East Timor Institute for Reconstruction Monitoring and Analysis, 2001; Charlesworth and Wood, 2002: 331).

The allegations, and the investigations that followed, have not been limited to criminal sexual activities involving coercion or violence, but have also censured many consensual sexual exchanges as if they were of the same ilk. In fact, over a decade of discussion of peacekeeping sexual economies is notable for its lack of interest in distinguishing between coerced and voluntary sexual activities, between forced prostitution and sex work, and between those 'trafficked' women who are seeking to migrate and those who are forced to move. The result is that diverse sexual activities are conflated by a culture of sexual negativity into a single problematic of sexual injury or harm. In this process, stereotyped assumptions about the sexual vulnerability of women and girls in the face of sexually predatory military men are uncritically reproduced, and there is no space for conceptualising sex as labour, as survival, and/or as pleasure. The idea that heterosexual sex, even when it is consensual, can be harmful for women has firm roots in some feminist thinking. Catharine MacKinnon, for example, has long argued that heterosexuality, practised under conditions of women's inequality, is the eroticisation of male dominance and women's subordination (MacKinnon, 1987: 29; MacKinnon, 2006: 247–58). This paradigm pushes sexual negativity to a new extreme because it suggests women may never be able to experience (hetero)sex as pleasure, and adamantly rejects sex as labour or survival because women's inequality makes all sex harmful (MacKinnon, 1987: 85–92).

When it comes to the complex realities of women's everyday lives, treating sexual harassment, pornography, domestic violence, prostitution, rape, survival sex and heterosexual sex under conditions of gender inequality, as all instances of a unitary idea of sexual harm is not only alarmingly broad, but also sexually repressive. Sex itself becomes the harm, the total harm, divorced from the material conditions under which it takes place (Miller, 2004: 19). Such over-determined sexual and gender stereotypes provide ready fodder for 'sexual panics', which can serve to displace other fears and anxieties onto sexual activity (Vance, 1984: 434; Rubin, 1984: 297). Sexual panics not only divert attention from underlying problems, but also make it relatively easy for the state, or the international community of states, to enact new 'protective' laws that extend its power to regulate erotic behaviour (Franke, 2004). Thus, many of the reports about peacekeeping and sex radiate a crusading urgency; there are 'innocents' who must be saved, female honour that must be protected, and an evil scourge that must be eradicated.[3] The crusading

---

3   See, for example, NewsMax.com, 'UN Slammed for Refugee Sex Scandal', 8 March 2002; 'UN Finally Forced to Probe its Paedophilia Scandal', 7 May 2002.

fervour erases the agency of the purported victims and the material and social realities of their lives. It also makes it impossible for the 'perpetrators' to 'speak', despite the likelihood that at least some of them may believe they are doing something beneficial for the 'victims' (Barth, 2004: 15).

The muddied thinking that treats diverse sexual activities as synonymous with sexual harm could perhaps account for the reluctance of the UN military-diplomatic establishment to establish effective mechanisms to address the criminal (coercive) sexual activities that have been associated with peacekeeping missions. However, this explanation is belied by the official lack of interest in questioning the underlying assumptions that have enabled such conflations. For many years, the official response to allegations of sexual violence was a mixture of denial, on the one hand, and a 'boys will be boys' dismissal, on the other (Orford, 1996: 378),[4] which has served to legitimate the stereotype of sexually predatory peacekeeping men who cannot control themselves (Connell, 2001). Some peacekeepers and journalists have even felt pressured not to speak out or pursue investigations (Holt, 2005). Yet because reports continued to surface, and many women's and children's NGOs persisted in demanding accountability, some steps were eventually taken towards at least being seen to be addressing some of the problems. More emphasis was put on codes of conduct banning sex with minors, services and repatriation were offered to some trafficked women in Bosnia-Herzegovenia, and there were increased efforts at building gender awareness into the training of peacekeeping forces, but these efforts did little, if anything, to stem the steady flow of allegations.

Eventually, it was a study, published in early 2002 by the UN High Commissioner for Refugees (UNHCR) and Save the Children-UK (UNHCR/ STC-UK, 2002), which galvanised the Secretariat into stronger action. The result was a zero tolerance response promulgated in the form of a Secretary-General's Bulletin, which, following MacKinnon, conceptualised the main harm as (hetero)sex. The Bulletin treats (almost) all sex as coercive, and completely ignores the other components of the complex matrix concerned with agency and survival. While I agree that the study's findings demanded a determined response, my argument is that the Bulletin wrongly constructs the main problem as sex. By taking this approach, attention is diverted away from the distributional injustices of the international economic order that come to be reflected in the day-to-day realities of post-conflict societies and exacerbated by UN humanitarianism which is, itself, in crisis because it does not address these injustices.

---

4   The most senior UN official in Cambodia, Under-Secretary General Yashushi Akashi, infamously dismissed allegations of sexual abuse of girls by Bulgarian peacekeepers in Cambodia in the early 1990s by saying that he was not a puritan and that '18-year-old, hot-blooded soldiers' have a right to chase 'young beautiful beings of the opposite sex'.

The West African researchers based their findings on discussions and interviews with refugee and internally displaced communities, including children, in the Mano River countries of Western Africa: Guinea, Liberia and Sierra Leone. They organised their findings into two categories of sexual activity with children (defined as everyone under 18), 'sexual exploitation' and 'sexual violence', distinguishing between the two in terms of consent – the former involving consent that is not fully informed, and the latter defined by the absence of consent (UNHCR/STC-UK, 2002: 83–4). When it came to 'sexual exploitation', they found the worst offenders were humanitarian workers, from local and international NGOs as well as from UN agencies, who exchanged humanitarian aid for sexual services, particularly from girls between the ages of 13 and 18. In some places these practices were 'chronic and entrenched' (UNHCR/STC-UK, 2002: 43). Although the study mostly reflected the experience of refugee and displaced children, the limited contact the researchers had with host nation children indicated these issues were just as pertinent to them (UNHCR/STC-UK, 2002: 26). They found a wide range of other actors were also implicated in these practices, notably international and regional security and military forces, school teachers, refugee leaders in the camps, and other influential people including religious leaders and small businessmen; in short, people in the community with power and money – mostly men (UNHCR/STC-UK, 2002: 42–52). While the majority of the allegations concerned men having sex with teenage girls and a few involved women sexually exploiting boys, the researchers were concerned at the complete silence about sexual exploitation of boys by men, which they attributed to entrenched homophobia (UNHCR/STC-UK, 2002: 41, 69). However, they did find that it was common for boys' (non-sexual) labour to be exploited in exchange for humanitarian goods and services (UNHCR/STC-UK, 2002: 41).

The researchers found that 'sexual violence' (where consent is absent) was less widespread, but affected much younger children, including babies (UNHCR/STC-UK, 2002: 75). They were concerned that the high prevalence of sexual exploitation, which was more or less tolerated, had distorted community perceptions of sexual violence, dramatically diminishing the assessment of its seriousness if some form of monetary or material exchange had accompanied it (UNHCR/STC-UK, 2002: 71). Yet the researchers are surely not in a position to make a judgment about the morality of community perceptions about where the line between acceptable and unacceptable sexual conduct is to be drawn. Sex is constituted in historically and socially specific circumstances and the politics of sex changes with changing social conditions (Foucault, 1990). In the context of post-conflict displacement and the dire poverty of the subjects of the study, it is extremely important to give credence to local perceptions, rather than dismiss them as morally suspect.

In her study of the sexual interactions between Filipina entertainers and men from US military bases in South Korea, Sealing Cheng goes against the

grain of sexual negativity in feminist thinking, which has equated prostitution, where military men are the main customers, with war crimes and sexual
slavery (Enloe, 1989; 2000; Harrison, 2003). She emphasises the importance
of looking at the everyday interactions between military men and those who
provide them with sexual services, in order to question the assumption of
women's inevitable victimhood. Despite being often portrayed as 'trafficked',
she found that the women she interviewed were legal migrants who saw
themselves as 'autonomous agents exercising control over their bodies and
sexuality' (Cheng, 2005: 7). In defence of her methodology she says, '[w]here
there is little space for political organising or collective actions, it is all the
more important to attend to the mundane aspects of life to understand
[women's] social and cultural agency' (Cheng, 2005: 2).

In my reading of the West African research, the young women involved in
the study are unlikely to see themselves as the victims of 'sexual exploitation',
but rather as acting to ensure their own survival and, often, the survival of
their families. Indeed, to its credit, the West African report provides a great
deal of information about the everyday matters that motivate many of the
young women who engage in 'sexually exploitative' relationships. As is also
evident from the stories of Faela, Yvette and Chantal with which I began, the
researchers acknowledge that these relationships are 'survival and coping
mechanisms', not only for the young women involved, but also for their
families and communities (UNHCR/STC-UK, 2002: 40). They accept that
for most refugees and displaced people, it is the only way to access money
(UNHCR/STC-UK, 2002: 55). They find that most girls and their parents
consider such relationships to be a 'privilege' because of the resulting conferral
of advantages (UNHCR/STC-UK, 2002: 45) and that for many young
women such relationships are a means of gaining parental respect (UNHCR/
STC-UK, 2002: 54), which hints at the family pressure that gender inequalities
can generate, but also suggests there may be a sense of self-worth that flows
from fulfilling familial and communal obligations. Other young women were
seeking greater independence, traveling vast distances to earn money by
providing sexual services to comparatively wealthy peacekeeping personnel,
without regard for the security situation, and in the hope of a better life
(UNHCR/STC-UK, 2002: 49).

Yet the researchers also found the 'exchange rate' for sexual services was
frequently meagre. If payment was in the form of money, it was often not
even enough to buy a full meal. If, as was more common, the exchange was in
kind rather than cash, it might constitute a few biscuits, a bar of soap, a
plastic sheet, clothes, shoes, school books and pencils (UNHCR/STC-UK,
2002: 43), and there was always the risk that no payment at all would be
forthcoming (UNHCR/STC-UK, 2002: 46). They found that the girls and
young women had little or no power to negotiate the rate or to determine the
kind of sexual exchange that took place, including whether safe sex was
practised (UNHCR/STC-UK, 2002: 68). It could be argued that this makes

the tag 'survival sex' something of a misnomer because of the relative powerlessness of the young women and girls, the paltry returns for their efforts, and the high risk of pregnancy and transmission of potentially fatal sexually transmitted diseases. While all these elements are undoubtedly present, it is also important to understand how the young women perceive what is happening, and on what basis they are engaging in sex with peacekeeping personnel. Their stories offer an opportunity to question over-determined representations of powerlessness and to respect the rational calculations they are making, shaped by hierarchies of gender, family obligations and poverty: a complex mix of coercion, agency and survival indeed; but it is poverty that is the main harm, not sex.

The West African study did identify poverty as the primary underlying cause of the high rates of 'sexual exploitation', including shortages of the most basic items essential for survival, including food, and the lack of alternative means of livelihood (UNHCR/STC-UK, 2002: 11). They also found the management practices of humanitarian operations to be a contributing factor, including poor monitoring of the implementation of programmes and lack of retribution for staff who abuse their positions of power. The two other causes identified were the inadequate protection provided by national laws and legal systems, and a 'breakdown of community values and lack of communal sense of responsibility' evidenced, in their view, by the widespread acceptance of sex as a trading commodity (UNHCR/STC-UK, 2002: 11–12). With respect to the latter, the researchers again fall into the trap of sexual negativity, which prevents them from analysing sex as a form of exchange necessary for survival, and from formulating recommendations that might flow from this premise. What is also missing from their analysis is the recognition that entrenched systems of gender inequality also play a causal role, predicating unsafe working conditions and inadequate recompense for sexual services, as well as shaping gendered family expectations and obligations. While the researchers are attentive to the different experiences of girls and boys, they fail to account for those differences as resulting from gender inequalities. This repeats a common problem with the implementation of gender mainstreaming in the UN system, where gender analysis is limited to taking gender differences into account, instead of questioning the hierarchies and stereotypes that the differences represent, which divests gender mainstreaming of its transformative potential and does nothing towards the end goal of achieving gender equality (Otto, 2007; Whitworth, 2004: 124–7). Another absence in the study is discussion of the racial and neo-imperial dimensions of the problems it identifies. Paul Highgate is one commentator who has not been so reticent, describing a 'colonial disposition' displayed by peacekeepers towards host populations, which feeds off the extremes of financial (and I would add gender) inequalities in peacekeeping economies (Highgate, 2003: 7).

The West African researchers make wide-ranging recommendations, starting with measures to ensure basic levels of humanitarian assistance, create alternative employment options, and provide sufficient assistance to girls at risk to cover basic needs (UNHCR/STC-UK, 2002: 15–17), which reflect their view that poverty is the primary causal factor. They also recommend increased consultation with local communities, including children, about policies and programme development, in order to 'foster initiative rather than dependency' (UNHCR/STC-UK, 2002: 17). In this proactive context, they propose a blanket prohibition on sex between humanitarian workers and beneficiaries who are under 18 (UNHCR/STC-UK, 2002: 22).

The approach of the Secretary-General's Bulletin

Given the pervasive culture of sexual negativity in the West African research, and in other discussions of peacekeeping sex, it is perhaps hardly surprising that the Secretary-General's Bulletin only picks up on its prohibitionist recommendations. However, the Bulletin does not stop at children, but bans sex between peacekeepers and adult beneficiaries as well, allowing few exceptions. Although it legally binds only those who are employees of the UN, the Bulletin purports to also apply to all forces conducting operations under UN command and control (Secretary-General, 2003: s 2.2) and non-UN entities that have entered co-operative arrangements with the UN (Secretary-General, 2003: ss 6.1 and 6.2). Cases of sexual exploitation and sexual abuse are to be treated as 'serious misconduct' meriting disciplinary measures, including summary dismissal (Secretary-General, 2003: s 3.2(a)), and a system of mandatory reporting is instituted where UN staff members are expected to report any 'concerns or suspicions' about fellow workers (Secretary-General, 2003: s 3.2(e)).

Despite the Secretary-General's claim that he is simply reiterating existing international legal norms and prohibitions already included in UN Staff Rules and Regulations (Secretary-General, 2003: s 3.1), my reading of the Bulletin is that it serves the sexually conservative agendas of the present US Administration and many fundamentalist states, and thereby sets back the projects of realising women's and children's human rights. The first plank in the Bulletin's repressiveness is the three broad categories of sexual activity that it prohibits. The first is sexual activity with children under the age of 18, regardless of the local age of consent (Secretary-General, 2003: s 3.2(b)).[5] The second prohibited category is the '[e]xchange of money, employment, goods or services for sex, including sexual favours or other forms of humiliating, degrading or exploitative behaviour' (Secretary-General, 2003: s 3.2(c)). The third 'strongly discourage[s]' sexual relationships between UN staff and

---

5   Mistaken belief in age is no defence. Further, s 4.4 makes an exception in the case of legal marriage to someone under 18, provided they are not under the age of consent in their country of citizenship.

beneficiaries of assistance, 'since they are based on inherently unequal power dynamics, [and] undermine the credibility and integrity of the work of the United Nations' (Secretary-General, 2003: s 3.2(d)).[6] It must be asked why the Bulletin did not confine itself to the prohibition of sex with children, as recommended by the West African researchers. What is the justification for prohibiting consensual adult sexual exchanges, including all forms of sex work? Why set the age of consent at 18, which is out of step with the vast majority of national laws and practices? Why deem sexual relationships between UN staff and local people as 'inherently unequal', making them all automatically suspect? The extremity of the Bulletin's response raises many more questions than it answers.

A second plank in the Bulletin's repressive approach is the over-inclusiveness of its definitions of 'sexual exploitation' and 'sexual abuse' (Secretary-General, 2003: s 1). There is considerable overlap between the two definitions, primarily because consent is not relevant to either one, not as a subjective aspect of the 'victim's' experience or as a facet of the awareness of the 'perpetrator'. The objectivity of the definitions drains agency from both people involved, completely blurring the distinction between consensual and non-consensual forms of sex. This is an approach that has been adopted in some criminal law jurisdictions in an attempt to overcome the problems associated with proving the absence of consent beyond reasonable doubt in rape cases. One alternative has been to require that 'coercive circumstances' be proved, instead of lack of consent, as applied in the Michigan Criminal Code.[7] In the Bulletin's adaption of this model, the effect is to reduce consent to a 'privilege' that can be enjoyed only by those who engage in sexual conduct that is officially condoned (Rubin, 1984: 305–6). The Bulletin authorises peacekeeping sex in only two situations: where the local woman/man is legally married to the peacekeeper (Secretary-General, 2003: s 4.4) and where the relationship has been given a special dispensation by the Head of Mission because 'the circumstances of the case justify an exception' (Secretary-General, 2003: s 4.5). All other sex between peacekeeping personnel and local residents is suspect. While the borderline between consensual and forced sex is highly contested, among feminists as well as in popular political and cultural discourse, drawing the line so over-inclusively – effectively failing to draw it at all – completely denies women's agency in matters of sexuality.

A further problem lies in the vagueness of the concept of 'sexual exploitation', which potentially captures a very broad range of activities. Although

---

6   Note further, s 4.5, which gives the Head of a Mission the power to use his or her discretion in applying s 3.2(d) where the beneficiary is over 18 and 'the circumstances of the case justify an exception'.

7   Michigan Criminal Sexual Conduct Statute (1974).

the term has frequently been used in anti-trafficking and human rights instruments, there has never been agreement as to its scope. In particular, there is disagreement about whether sex work is exploitative *per se*, or whether only forced or coercive prostitution is exploitative. The UN Anti-Trafficking Protocol, adopted in December 2000, is the most recent international instrument to use the language of 'exploitation' in relation to sexual conduct.[8] Despite a year-long debate about the meaning of the term during the drafting process, it was ultimately left undefined, although a majority of states' delegates and the NGO Human Rights Caucus[9] agreed that voluntary, non-coerced participation by adults in sex work is not exploitative (Jordan, 2002: 4). The Protocol is concerned with crime control and law enforcement, rather than with the human rights of trafficked sex workers, an approach that has also pervaded human rights treaties. Even the Convention on the Elimination of All Forms of Discrimination Against Women (CEDAW) focuses on criminalising those who 'exploit' the prostitution of women rather than on protecting the rights of women as sex workers or economic migrants.[10] The Convention on the Rights of the Child (CRC) takes a similar approach, promoting measures that curb and punish the activities of those who sexually exploit children,[11] without any reference to the emerging sexual rights and agency of children and young people. The CEDAW Committee has long taken the same view as the majority of those involved in drafting the Anti-Trafficking Protocol, indicating that it does not consider sex work to be inherently exploitative – not a form of discrimination against women *per se* – but that it is the marginal status of prostitutes which makes them vulnerable to violence and exploitation.[12] However, this is not the approach adopted by Prince Zeid, the Secretary-General's adviser on addressing the problem of sexual exploitation and abuse by UN peacekeeping personnel, in his report of March 2005, where he equates prostitution with sexual exploitation (Zeid, 2005: para 6). He too ignores the crucial difference between voluntariness and coercion, which should mark the boundary between sexual

---

8 Protocol to Prevent, Suppress and Punish Trafficking in Persons, Especially Women and Children (2000), art 3, 'Exploitation shall include, at a minimum, the exploitation of the prostitution of others or other forms of sexual exploitation, forced labour or services, slavery or practices similar to slavery, servitude or the removal of organs'.

9 Members of the Human Rights Caucus: Global Rights (formerly International Human Rights Law Group) were Foundation Against Trafficking in Women, Global Alliance Against Traffic in Women, Asian Women's Human Rights Council, La Strada, Ban-Ying, Fundacion Esperanza, Foundation for Women, KOK-NGO Network Against Trafficking in Women, Women's Consortium of Nigeria, and Women, Law and Development in Africa (Nigeria).

10 Convention on the Elimination of All Forms of Discrimination Against Women (1980), art 6.

11 Convention on the Rights of the Child (1989), arts 19, 34.

12 Committee on the Elimination of Discrimination Against Women, 'Violence Against Women', General Recommendation No 19 (1992), para 15.

conduct that is criminal, and that which lies in the realm of sexual freedom, which should be protected by privacy and sexuality rights.

Returning to the definitions in the Bulletin, there seems to be little, if any, difference between the circumstances of 'differential power' that define 'sexual exploitation' and 'unequal circumstances' that define 'sexual abuse'. Indeed, all (hetero)sexual conduct under conditions of women's inequality is potentially caught by these definitions. Thus the Bulletin uncritically embraces the sexual negativity of those feminists and conservatives who view almost all heterosexual sex as injurious to women. In the context of international law, sexual negativity also repeats the moralism of the 'civilising mission' of many earlier feminist efforts (Midgley, 2001) by promulgating a conservative sexual morality in societies emerging from conflict. Furthermore, in the implementation of the Bulletin, these definitions are showing a propensity to expand to cover even broader notions of 'sexual misconduct', as in the peacekeeping Code of Conduct adopted in the DRC which enlarges the definitions of sexual exploitation and abuse to include 'any sexual misconduct that has a detrimental effect on the image, credibility, impartiality or integrity of the UN' (OIOS, 2005: para 21). This casts an alarmingly wide net, conceivably catching sexual speech like providing birth control or HIV-AIDS information, and wearing clothing that some might consider being sexually provocative. The figures speak for themselves. Prince Zeid reports that of the 105 investigations undertaken by the Department of Peacekeeping Operations (DPKO) in 2004, only 18 per cent concerned sexual offences (rape and sexual assault), while 45 per cent involved sex with people under 18, 31 per cent involved adult sex with prostitutes, and the remaining 6 per cent involved other forms of sexual exploitation and abuse (Zeid, 2005: para 9). Paradoxically, the emphasis is on the contested category of 'sexual exploitation' rather than on 'sexual offences', about which there is no disagreement.

A further problem with the Bulletin's approach is its reliance on protective representations of women that have long been recognised as inconsistent with the realisation of women's equality and human rights (Hevener, 1978; Otto, 2005). In characterising sex between peacekeepers and beneficiaries as almost always sexual harm, sexual power and agency is located with men and the stereotype of sexually vulnerable women and girls needing protection is reinforced. Protective representations also allow the conflation of women and children, as seen in the Bulletin (Secretary-General, 2003: paras 2.2 and 3.2), which is reminiscent of early international legal texts before women enjoyed independent legal personality. Protectionism resonates with conservative sexual ideologies and revives imperial ideas about Third World women, as victims, in need of rescue from 'uncivilised' traditions and practices (Kapur, 2005: 114–20). Protective frameworks promote protective responses, like 'rescue' and 'rehabilitation', which reinforce women's lack of agency rather than treating them as bearers of human rights. This can be seen in the Bulletin, which is so preoccupied with its rescue mission that it fails altogether to identify the inequality of women as an underlying cause of the problems it is seeking to address. Two of the young women that I quote at the beginning of this chapter, Faela and Yvette, had been raped previously by militias and were, as a consequence, considered 'worthless' by their communities (Holt, 2004; Wax, 2005), which plays a major role in shaping their economic choices and decision making. By ignoring the significance of entrenched gender inequalities in the construction of economies of survival sex, the Bulletin not only denies women's sexual agency but also thwarts the larger project of realising women's human rights.

While protecting women recalls an era when they were denied full legal subjectivity, protecting children may often be appropriate, but the scope of protective measures allowed under the CRC is not without limits. While the CRC sets the general age of majority at 18, it recognises that domestic laws may well set the age lower.[13] Further, a child is to enjoy her/his rights 'in a manner consistent with the[ir] evolving capacities'.[14] In the Mano River countries, the law sets the age of marriage for girls at 14 in Sierra Leone, 16 in Liberia and is silent on this matter in Guinea (UNHCR/STC-UK, 2002: 11–12). Culturally, the definition of a child is determined more by custom than formal law, which generally allows young women to marry at 14. While the West African researchers were well aware of these legal and cultural norms, they adopted 18 as the age of consent, which makes their claim that they were following the CRC rather disingenuous (UNHCR/STC-UK, 2002: 36). While the Committee on the Rights of the Child has been actively encouraging states parties to set the minimum age for marriage at 18 because of concern about the negative impacts of early marriage and pregnancy on young women,[15] it has also emphasised the importance of recognising the evolving capacities of adolescents so that they are able to progressively exercise their rights, including in relation to their sexual and reproductive maturation before marriage.[16] The Committee recognises that adolescents may be particularly susceptible to pressure to adopt risky behaviour, which may be magnified in the context of armed conflict. However, while the Committee emphasises the importance of enacting and enforcing laws that prohibit all forms of 'sexual exploitation' and related trafficking, it emphasises preventative measures and the rights of adolescents, not prohibitionism.[17] Further, as the majority of those involved in survival sex are

---

13 Convention on the Rights of the Child (1989), art 1.
14 Above, art 5 in general, art 12(1) with regard to freedom of expression, and art 14(2) with regard to freedom of thought, conscience and religion.
15 Committee on the Rights of the Child, 'Adolescent health and development in the context of the Convention on the Rights of the Child', General Comment 4 (2003), CRC/GC/2003/4, para 20.
16 Above, paras 1, 2 and 8.
17 Above, paras 36 and 37.

aged 13–18, it would have been more appropriate for the researchers to follow the practice of the CRC Committee and refer to them as 'young women' or 'adolescents', instead of 'children'. The language of 'children' in the context of sexuality is highly emotive, and the researchers' choice to use it throughout their study, to refer to all those up to and including the age of 18, helps to create an atmosphere of sexual panic. The Bulletin perpetuates this hype by setting the age of consent at 18, pushing the protective category of childhood beyond its legal and cultural limits. This erodes the already tenuous social status of young women engaging in survival sex and thwarts the project of children's and young people's rights, especially in the area of sexual expression and self-determination.

Setting the age of consent at 18 also has imperial dimensions because it treats those young people who are in receipt of the UN's beneficence, situated primarily in the developing world, differently from young people in the west, who generally enjoy an age of consent of 16. Extending Kapur's analysis, this represents young women in post-colonial societies as more sexually vulnerable, and more in need of protection, than their counterparts in the 'civilised' countries of the north. The Bulletin further reinforces this imperial hierarchy by deeming sex between those who have come to 'rescue' and those who need to be 'saved' to be inherently unequal. This view has justified the adoption of non-fraternisation policies, which prohibit peacekeeping personnel from mixing socially with local residents and declare certain areas in local towns off-limits (Deen, 2005).[18] Such policies have a negative impact on the local economy and reinforce hierarchies of status, power and race between peacekeeping personnel and 'beneficiaries', already pronounced by stark inequalities in income and resources. Why, instead, is more integration with the local population not encouraged, with the aim of breaking down divisions and spreading some of the economic opportunities that peace-keeping missions create? Maintaining parallel societies, one of relative wealth and the other of abject poverty, constructs new imperial hierarchies.

While I do not want to suggest that the Bulletin's broad prohibitions should be extended to same-sex sexual activity, it is problematic that the Bulletin repeats the cultural silencing of homosexual activity that the West African researchers found to be of concern because it lends support to the shame and opprobrium that all too commonly attaches to homosexuality. The UN is described as having 'a particular duty of care towards women and children' and the 'vulnerable populations' that the Bulletin sets out to protect are described as 'especially women and girls' (Secretary-General, 2003: ss 2.2 and 3.2). Further, one of the two situations in which sex between peacekeeping personnel and someone in the local population is not considered to be

18 The DPKO listed premises and areas that are out of bounds to all UN personnel in Côte d'Ivoire, Liberia, Democratic Republic of the Congo, Ethiopia, Kosovo, and Timor-Leste.

exploitative or abusive is where they are 'legally married' which, while excessively narrow for heterosexual couples, completely excludes homosexuals and other sexual minorities in most countries. The discretionary power granted to the Head of Mission to exempt sexual relationships from the Bulletin's coverage is not explicitly limited to heterosexual relationships, but this provides little comfort in a world where sex remains presumptively hetero-sexual. In short, the Bulletin's conservative sexual code repeats, rather than challenges, the sexual hierarchies that have been responsible for so much human suffering over the centuries, and continue to make sexuality a matter of life and death for many today (HRW, 2004).

Despite the promulgation of the Bulletin, reports of 'sexual exploitation and abuse' perpetrated by UN peacekeepers have continued unabated. Allegations concerning MONUC led to a full investigation by the UN Office of Internal Oversight Services (OIOS), which released its findings in early 2005 (OIOS, 2005).[19] The findings were similar to those of the West African study: many young women, aged mostly between 13 and 18, had regular sexual contact with peacekeeping personnel and 'for most of them, having sex with the peacekeepers was a means of getting food and sometimes small sums of money' (OIOS, 2005: para 11). In addition, boys and young men who facilitated the sexual encounters sometimes received food as payment for their services (OIOS, 2005: para 11). Also, like the West African researchers, the OIOS investigations identified poverty, and specifically hunger, as a major cause of children and young people making contact with MONUC troops (OIOS, 2005: para 31). The report gives little space to the 'voices' of the young women involved in survival sex, but it does include six brief case studies which reveal the exercise of a measure of agency by the young women, despite their desperate circumstances. For example, V046A, who was 14 years old, gave evidence that she had refused to have sex on a second occasion with MONUC soldier PK2 because he did not have money or food for her (OIOS, 2005: para 14). Another 14-year-old, V030A, said that a MONUC soldier had given her food on four occasions before, on the fifth occasion, he requested sex with her in exchange for food, and 'she agreed' (OIOS, 2005: para 15). This might well be described as 'exploit[ing] the dire needs of vulnerable children', as the OIOS report contends (OIOS, 2005: para 22), but placing a ban on such exchanges without addressing the underlying causes of poverty and gender inequality undermines the survival strategies and decision making of these young women, as I have argued. Elsewhere, since the adoption of the Bulletin, allegations of sexual exploitation and abuse

---

19 A total of 72 allegations were investigated, but more than half were closed because the victims and/or witnesses could not be identified or traced. Ultimately, 19 cases involving military personnel were sufficiently substantiated to be referred by the DPKO to the relevant troop-contributing countries, although in none of these cases did the peacekeeper admit to the alleged conduct.

have come from Haiti (Refugees International, 2005b), Côte d'Ivoire (IRIN, 2005), Eritrea (Deutsche Presse Agentur, 2005), Burundi (UN News, 2005a), Liberia (Refugees International, 2004; Hoge, 2005), DRC (UN News, 2005b) and Sierra Leone (IRIN, 2006). Refugees International reported, in 2005, that peacekeepers in Haiti and Liberia thought of the 'zero-contact rule' as 'a rule that makes no sense' (Martin, 2005: 16). Recent research in Liberia suggests that survival sex with young women may be becoming more commonplace and more culturally acceptable because many families have come to depend on the food or money generated (Save the Children UK, 2006).

The Bulletin's lack of impact illustrates a final problem with attempts to prohibit sexual economies, which is that they are notoriously unsuccessful. Even in less desperate circumstances than post-conflict societies, prohibitionism drives sexual economies underground and makes participation more dangerous and exploitative. The West African researchers recount a story where the local chief had banned young women from going to the nearby peacekeeping compound, which led to some of them going via a back route in a canoe. The canoe capsized and all ten of the young women drowned (UNHCR/STC-UK, 2002: 48). They observe, later in the study, that '[t]he need to hold on to the only activity that brings in an income is so important that the person concerned would do just about anything just to keep it going' (UNHCR/STC-UK, 2002: 60). They found instances where, if the young person failed to bring money home when it was expected of them, they would be severely beaten (UNHCR/STC-UK, 2002: 61). Zero tolerance reinforces the low social status of women and girls. It makes collective organisation for the purposes of reproductive health, safety and adequate remuneration impossible, and it further decreases the likelihood that an individual would report any sexual abuse that may occur in the sexual economy of peacekeeping missions. Why then is such an approach pursued in the Secretary General's Bulletin and in the follow-up work of Prince Zeid? It is to this question that I now turn.

The productive effects of the Bulletin

In order to understand why the Secretary-General has promoted zero tolerance as the solution to peacekeeping survival sex economies, it is useful to analyse the Bulletin as a form of power, as Foucault would suggest, looking beyond its apparent repressiveness to its many productive effects. I have already identified some of these effects, including thwarting the projects of women's and children's rights by reinforcing neo-imperial sexual and gender relations, and giving a new legitimacy to conservative hierarchies of sexuality. However, there are two other productive effects that help to more fully account for the Bulletin's approach: it deflects attention from the responsibilities of the international community to address the unequal distribution of global wealth, as reflected in the local economies of UN peacekeeping missions; and it avoids confronting deep problems with the concept of UN humanitarianism as it is currently practised (Rieff, 2002).

Despite the many problems with the Secretary-General's Bulletin that I have outlined, it has been widely embraced. Prince Zeid's report, released in March 2005, sets out a 'comprehensive strategy' that promises to eliminate future sexual exploitation and abuse in UN peacekeeping operations. The strategy not only fully endorses zero tolerance and the Bulletin's broad definitions of sexual exploitation and abuse, but seeks to have them more widely applied. Zeid recommends that urgent measures be taken so that the new rules are made to apply to all categories of personnel in peacekeeping operations (Zeid, 2005: paras 15–19), and that troop-contributing countries be obliged to make those rules binding on members of their military contingents (Zeid, 2005: paras 23–5). He also recommends the establishment of a permanent independent mechanism with the authority and expertise to investigate cases of sexual exploitation and abuse in peacekeeping operations and that troop-contributing countries conduct on-site court marshals when serious criminal offences have occurred (Zeid, 2005: paras 31–6). His report extends the discipline-and-order approach of the Bulletin, defining the issue narrowly as a problem of sexual harm that will be solved by prohibiting sex, still without addressing the underlying causes of poverty and women's inequality. Indeed, he dismisses contributing factors like high levels of extreme poverty, lack of income-generation possibilities and discrimination against women and girls as 'factors external to the Mission' (Zeid, 2005: para 13).

Prince Zeid's report has received widespread support from the NGO community (Refugees International, 2005a) and enthusiastic institutional endorsement. The Security Council welcomed it, expressing its concern that the 'distinguished and honourable record of accomplishment in UN peacekeeping' was being 'tarnished by the acts of a few individuals', and urging the Secretary-General and troop-contributing countries to implement the recommendations without delay.[20] At the same time, the Under-Secretary-General for Peacekeeping Operations announced that the DPKO was treating the issue as a matter of the highest priority and that a network of focal points on sexual exploitation and abuse was being established in all missions to facilitate the receipt of allegations.[21] A number of states announced that they had taken disciplinary action against some of their peacekeepers, including France, Morocco, Nepal, Pakistan, Tunisia and South Africa (Jordan, 2005). The General Assembly expressed its support in June 2005[22] and, by early

---

20 Presidential Statement, S/PRST/2005/21, 31 May 2005, presented by Security Council President Ellen Margrethe Løj.
21 Briefing to the Security Council, Under-Secretary-General for Peacekeeping Operations, Jean-Marie Guéhenno, 31 May 2005.
22 GA Res 59/300, 30 June 2005.

August, eight missions had established 'Conduct and Discipline Units', charged with ensuring compliance with the Bulletin (UN News Centre, 2005). Individual missions have developed even more stringent codes of conduct by introducing curfews, requiring troops to wear uniform at all times, listing off-limits establishments and setting up telephone hot-lines to report abuse (UN News Centre, 2005). The UN Deputy Secretary-General, Louise Fréchette, has visited many peacekeeping missions to promote the zero tolerance policy (UNAMSIL, 2005; UN News, 2005c). While all this activity may mean that the culture of impunity for sexual offences committed by peacekeeping personnel is changing, it also means that peacekeepers are losing their jobs for having sex with sex workers (BBC, 2005).

The hyperbole about sexual exploitation, and all the activity it has generated, stands in striking contrast to the silence about the scandalous shortage of humanitarian resources available to peacekeeping missions, which tarnishes the UN's 'distinguished and honourable record' much more fundamentally. Where is the outrage at the global inequalities in wealth that are reflected in peacekeeping missions; at the lack of employment opportunities in post-conflict societies; at the insufficient clean water and food rations available to international aid agencies to meet human needs in a world of plenty; and at the poverty that creates a market for survival sex? The sexual panic has enabled the repressive politics of the body to trump the politics of social justice. By characterising the harm in survival sex as sexual rather than economic, attention has been deflected from the responsibilities of international economic institutions to address poverty in post-conflict societies. Also unacknowledged are the obligations of states to co-operate internationally to ensure that everyone enjoys economic and social rights[23] and promote development that is equitable and sustainable.[24] By the same token, the disgraceful level of arrears of many wealthy countries in their assessed financial contributions to peacekeeping, among which the US is the most recalcitrant (Deen, 2004), has also not been taken up as a causative issue. No one is outraged at the fact that developing states, which provide most of the on-the-ground peacekeeping troops, are effectively subsidising UN peacekeeping operations because they are not reimbursed in a timely fashion. As Miller aptly observes, 'sexual exploitation' is the only form of exploitation that appears to be generating policy responses (Miller, 2004: 31–2).

A second underlying cause, from which the focus on sex manages to deflect attention, is the imperial, charity-based model of humanitarian assistance practiced by the UN. Although the West African study identified the (mis)-management of humanitarian operations as, following poverty, the second most significant underlying cause of 'sexual exploitation', their analysis did

---

23 International Covenant on Economic, Social and Cultural Rights (1966), art 2(1).
24 Declaration on the Right to Development, GA Res.41/128, 4 December 1986.

not question the model itself, unlike Barbara Harrell-Bond, in her study of the treatment of refugees receiving services from the UNHCR and their implementing partners in East Africa (Harrell-Bond 2002). She concludes that the altruistic model of humanitarian assistance makes it almost inevitable that inhumane behaviour in its delivery becomes normative, arguing that the hierarchies created by altruism give humanitarian workers the power to decide who is 'deserving' of the gift of aid and require the recipients to cede power and become dependent on the giver because there is no possibility of reciprocation. This dynamic produces the stereotype of helpless refugees who need assistance from outsiders, which not only legitimises the authority of the helper vis à vis the aid recipient, but also provides the justification for international assistance to be controlled and organised by expert outsiders rather than by the refugees themselves. The whole system depends on the understanding that deserving refugees are helpless and vulnerable, and the distributional relationships created by aid as charity require that refugees perform their client status. The result is that ingratiating yourself to humanitarian workers becomes a survival strategy.

Curiously, Harrell-Bond does not use any sexual examples in her many descriptions of inhumane treatment by humanitarian workers, and nor does she engage gender or sexuality as analytical categories. However, it is easy to see how the system, as she describes it, comes to incorporate 'sexual ingratiation' as a key component, and how the protective stereotypes of helpless refugees would attach particularly to women and children. Further, much of her critique of humanitarianism is applicable to the broader context of peacekeeping missions which are essentially 'protective' rather than 'empowering' in their conception (Otto, 1999). Unlike the West African researchers, Harrell-Bond dismisses the idea that inhumane behaviour of humanitarians can be explained by the scarcity of resources (Harrell-Bond, 2002: 69–70). Instead, she attributes it primarily to the dysfunctional organisational structure of humanitarian organisations, which are a product of workers' psychological struggles to cope with the stress of their jobs, particularly the impossibility of significantly improving the lives of the beneficiaries of humanitarianism. If this is so, that participants in post-conflict peacebuilding missions have to confront the impossibility of making a difference, it raises fundamental questions about the humanitarian efforts of the UN in the post-Cold War era. It suggests that the UN and its partners urgently need to re-examine their modus operandi. However, such a re-examination poses enormous institutional risks, and it is easy to see how the 'quick fix' of a ban on survival sex can become irresistible to policy makers preoccupied with concerns about the reputation and longevity of their organisations and institutions.

There is certainly some evidence that the underlying motivation for the policy of sexual zero tolerance is, in fact, institutional survival, although I am not suggesting that this is a deliberate or conscious move. Prince Zeid is preoccupied with the idea that the image and credibility of UN peacekeeping may have been irreparably damaged (Zeid, 2005: para 10), while the Security Council has been concerned to limit the problem to the acts 'of a few individuals', even as it relies on the perception of scandal to justify the far-reaching ban.[25] The Under-Secretary General for Peacekeeping Operations, Jean-Marie Guéhenno, expressed concern that the reputation of UN peacekeeping has been 'tarnished' and that the 'national honour' of troop-contributing countries was at stake.[26] Recall too, the elasticity of 'sexual misconduct' which now includes conduct that 'has a detrimental effect on the image, credibility, impartiality or integrity of the UN'. It would seem that the institution's own survival strategies have necessitated diverting attention away from the underlying causes of survival sex economies, which include poverty, gender discrimination, social injustice and a deeply flawed model of humanitarianism. Sadly, the result is to make fragile lives even more so.

Conclusion

The Secretary-General's Bulletin responds to disturbing revelations, including the widespread misuse of humanitarian aid and a pattern of abuse of power by aid workers against those who depend on them for protection and assistance in rebuilding their lives. Because of gender inequalities, it is women and girl children who bear the brunt of the negative consequences of such failures of humanitarianism, and it is they who also suffer the costs of heavy-handed attempts at solutions driven by a culture of sexual negativity. The Bulletin does not respond to the endemic poverty and desperate material circumstances of its female objects, which drives the market for the survival sex it is primarily concerned with. Instead, in the name of protecting women and children, the UN Secretary-General has chosen zero tolerance over the nuanced recognition of the myriad ways that peacekeepers can influence the economies of survival with which they interact. Rather than acknowledging the complexities of the economic decision making that constitute the practices of survival sex, the sweeping sexual prohibitions make the Bulletin a blunt and dangerously over-inclusive instrument, which leaves no intellectual, legal, cultural, or personal space for listening and responding to the material circumstances in which survival sex is negotiated.

By focussing on sex as the problem, the Bulletin is an example of the disproportionate explanatory power that can be attached to sex, particularly where sexuality can be perceived as transgressing cultural and generational boundaries. It institutes a repressive sexual code that undermines the projects

---

25 Above, Presidential Statement, 2005.
26 Report of Security Council 5379th meeting to consider sexual exploitation and abuse in United Nations Peacekeeping Operations, SC/8649, 23 February 2006.

of realising women's and children's rights, and reinforces conservative hierarchies of gender and sexuality and imperial hierarchies of status and wealth. The productive effect of the Bulletin's focus on sex is to divert attention away from the obligations of the international community to co-operate to address global inequalities in wealth and opportunity, and ensure that humanitarian assistance leads to tangible and sustainable improvements in the lives of its recipients.

Instead of responding with the bluntness of discipline-and-order, the international community needs to work more closely and co-operatively with local communities, thinking of them not as 'beneficiaries' dependent on the largesse of donors and states, but as bearers of human rights, including economic and social rights, which peacekeeping missions are there to help realise. While rights relating to sexual agency and expression are almost everywhere contested, particularly when it comes to women, children and sexual minorities, the propensity for this contestation to be hijacked by conservative forces and turned into sexual panics and scandals needs to be strongly resisted. We need to always be suspicious of projects aimed at regulating sexuality because their sweeping edicts can provide cover for the pursuit of larger and less 'popular' agendas, like propping up the inequitable international economic order and the charity ethic of humanitarianism, which cause and feed off survival sex economies, even when sex is banned.

Bibliography

Barth, E (2004) 'The United Nations Mission in Eritrea/Ethiopia: Gender(ed) Effects', in Olsson, L, Skjelsba, I, Barth, E F and Hostens, K (eds), *Gender Aspects of Conflict Interventions: Intended and Unintended Consequences*, Oslo: International Peace Research Institute, pp 9–24.

BBC (2005) 'UN Sex Abuse Sackings in Burundi', 19 July.

Boutros-Ghali, B (1992) *An Agenda for Peace*, New York: UN.

Boutros-Ghali, B (1995) Supplement to *An Agenda for Peace*, UN Doc A/50/60–S/1995/1.

Cain, K, Postlewait, H and Thomson, A (2004) *Emergency Sex (and other desperate measures)*, London: Ebury Press.

Charlesworth, H and Wood, M (2002) 'Women and Human Rights in the Rebuilding of East Timor', *Nordic Journal of International Law* 71, pp 325–48.

Cheng, S (2005) 'Romancing the Club: Love Dynamics between Filipina Entertainers and GIs in Military Camp Towns in South Korea', pp 1–21, unpublished paper.

Connell, B (2001) 'Masculinities, Violence and Peacemaking', Peace News 2443, http://www.peacenews.info/issues/2443/index.php.

Deen, T (2004) 'UN: Bullies and Beggars', International Press Service, 28 May 2004.

Deutsche Presse Agentur (2005) 'UN Investigates Alleged Sexual Abuse by Peacekeepers in Eritrea', 14 April.

Deen, T (2005) ' "No Go" Zones to Prevent Sex Abuse by UN Peacekeepers', International Press Service, 4 April.

East Timor Institute for Reconstruction Monitoring and Analysis (2001) 'Commentary: International Security Forces and Sexual Misconduct', *The La'o Hamutuk Bulletin* 2 (5), p 7.

Enloe, C (1989) *Bananas, Beaches and Bases: Making Feminist Sense of International Politics*, London: Pandora.

Enloe, C (2000) *Manoeuvres: The International Politics of Militarising Women's Lives*, Berkeley: University of California Press.

Foucault, M (1990) *The History of Sexuality: An Introduction, Volume I*, first published in 1976, translated from the French by Robert Hurley, London: Penguin.

Franke, K M (2004) 'Sexual Tensions of Post-Empire', *Columbia Law School Public Law and Legal Theory Working Paper*, pp 1–44.

Harrell-Bond, B (2002) 'Can Humanitarian Work with Refugees be Humane?' *Human Rights Quarterly* 24, pp 51–85.

Harrison, D (2003) 'Violence in the Military Community', in Highgate, P (ed.), *Military Masculinities*, Westport Conn: Praeger, pp 71–90.

Higate, P (2003) *Case Studies: The Democratic Republic of the Congo and Sierra Leone*, Pretoria: Gender and Peacekeeping, Institute for Security Studies (ISS), Monograph Series no 91.

Hoge, W (2005) 'Report finds UN isn't moving the end sex abuse by peacekeepers', *The New York Times*, 19 October.

Holt, K (2004) 'DR Congo's Shameful Sex Secret: Young Refugees Sell their Bodies to UN Peacekeepers' BBC News, 3 June.

Holt, K (2005) 'How the UN was Forced to Tackle the Stain on its Integrity', *The Independent*, 11 February.

Human Rights Watch (2002), *Hopes Betrayed: Trafficking of Women and Girls to Post-Conflict Bosnia and Herzegovenia for Forced Prostitution*, New York: HRW, vol 14, no 9(D).

Human Rights Watch (2004), 'Sierra Leone: Lesbian Rights Activist Brutally Murdered', New York: HRW Press Release, 5 October.

IRIN (Integrated Regional Information Networks) (2005) 'French Peacekeeping Force Opens Inquiry into Sex Abuse Claims', 20 May.

IRIN (2006) UN Peacekeeping – Working Towards a No-Tolerance Environment, IRIN Web Special on violence against women and girls during and after armed conflict.

Jordan, A D (2002) *Annotated Guide to the Complete UN Trafficking Protocol*, Washington DC: Global Rights.

Jordan, M J (2005) 'UN Tackles Sex Abuse by Troops', *Christian Science Monitor*, 21 June.

Hevener, N K (1978) 'International Law and the Status of Women: An Analysis of International Legal Instruments Related to the Treatment of Women', *Harvard Women's Law Journal* 1, pp 131–56.

Kapur, R (2005) *Erotic Justice: Law and the New Politics of Postcolonialism*, London: Glasshouse Press.

Kien Serey Phal (1995) 'The Lessons of the UNTAC experience and the ongoing responsibilities of the international community in Cambodia', *Pacifica Review* 2(7): 129–33.

Lupi, N (1998) 'Report by the enquiry commission on the behaviour of Italian

Peacekeeping troops in Somalia', *Yearbook of International Humanitarian Law* 1, pp 375–9.

Machel, G (2001) *The Impact of War on Children*, London: Hurst and Young for UNICEF and UNIFEM.

Mackay, A (2001) 'Sex and the Peacekeeping Soldier: The New UN Resolution', *Peace News* 2443, http://www.peacenews.info/issues/2443/index.php.

MacKinnon, C A (1987) *Feminism Unmodified: Discourses on Life and Law*, Cambridge: Harvard University Press.

MacKinnon, C A (2006) *Are Women Human? And other international dialogues*, Cambridge: Harvard University Press.

Martin, S (2005) *Must Boys be Boys? Ending Sexual Exploitation and Abuse in Peacekeeping Missions*, Washington DC: Refugees International.

Mendelson, S E (2005) *Barracks and Brothels: Peacekeepers and Human Trafficking in the Balkans*, Washington DC: Centre for Strategic and International Studies.

Midgley, C (2001) 'British Empire, Women's Rights and Empire, 1790–1850', in Grimshaw, P, Holmes, K and Lake, M (eds), *Women's Rights and Human Rights: International Historical Perspectives*, New York: Palgrave.

Miller, A M (2004) 'Sexuality, Violence Against Women, and Human Rights', *Health and Human Rights* 7, pp 16–47.

Office of Internal Oversight Services (OIOS) (2005) Investigation by the OIOS into allegations of sexual exploitation and abuse in the UN Organisation Mission in the Democratic Republic of the Congo, A/59/661, 5 January.

Orford, A (1996) 'The Politics of Collective Security', *Michigan Journal of International Law* 17, pp 373–410.

Otto, D (1999) 'Whose Security? Re-imagining Post-Cold War Peacekeeping from a Feminist Perspective', in Patman, R G (ed.), *Security in a Post-Cold War World*, London: Macmillan Press and St Martins Press, pp 65–86.

Otto, D (2005) 'Disconcerting "Masculinities": Reinventing the Gendered Subject(s) of International Human Rights Law', in Buss, D and Manji, A (eds), *International Law: Modern Feminist Approaches*, Oxford and Portland: Hart, pp 105–29.

Otto, D (2006) 'A Sign of "Weakness"? Disrupting Gender certainties in the Implementation of Security Council Resolution 1325', *Michigan Journal of Gender and Law* 13, pp 113–75.

Refugees International (2004), 'Sexual Exploitation in Liberia: Are the conditions ripe for another scandal?', Press Release, 20 April.

Refugees International (2005a), 'Refugees International Welcomes Far-Reaching UN Report on Eliminating Sexual Exploitation in Peacekeeping Operations', Press Release, 25 March.

Refugees International (2005b), 'Haiti: Sexual Exploitation by Peacekeepers Likely to be a Problem', RI Bulletin, 7 March.

Reiff, D (2002) *A Bed for the Night: Humanitarianism in Crisis*, London: Vintage, Random House.

Reuters Alertnet (2006) 'DRC: UN investigations into allegations of sexual offences by peacekeepers', 26 January.

Rubin, G (1984) 'Thinking Sex: Notes for a Radical Theory of the Politics of Sexuality', in Vance, C S (ed.), *Pleasure and Danger: Exploring Female Sexuality*, Boston: Routledge & Kegan Paul, pp 267–319.

Save the Children UK (2006), From Camp to Community: Liberia study on exploitation of children, Discussion Paper, 8 May.

Secretary-General (2003), 'Special measures for protection from sexual exploitation and abuse', Secretary-General's Bulletin, ST/SGB/2003/13, 9 October.

UNAMSIL (United Nations Mission in Sierra Leone) (2005) 'Deputy Secretary-General on Completion of Mission to Sierra Leone Says UN to Reform its Approach to Sexual Exploitation and Abuse Issues', Press Release, 4 March.

United Nations High Commissioner for Refugees and Save the Children UK (UNHCR/STC-UK) (2002) Sexual Violence and Exploitation: The Experience of Refugee Children in Liberia, Guinea and Sierra Leone, Report of assessment mission carried out from 22 October to 30 November 2001.

UN News (2005a) 'UN Conducts Inquiry into Alleged Abuse by Peacekeepers in Burundi', 11 March.

UN News (2005b) 'UN Mission Probes Possible Breaches of Zero-Tolerance Policy on Sexual Exploitation', 12 April.

UN News (2005c) 'Fréchette to Visit Kosovo as Part of Tour to Eliminate Sexual Abuse in Peacekeeping', 3 June.

UN News Centre (2005) 'UN Establishes Disciplinary Units to Eliminate Sexual Abuse by Peacekeepers', 4 August.

Vance, C S (1984) 'Epilogue', in Vance, C S (ed.), *Pleasure and Danger: Exploring Female Sexuality*, Boston: Routledge & Kegan Paul, pp 431–9.

Wax, E (2005) 'Congo's Desperate "One-Dollar UN Girls" ', *Washington Post Foreign Service*, 21 March.

Whitworth, S (2004) *Men, Militarism and UN Peacekeeping*, Boulder: Lynne Rienner Publishers.

Prince Zeid Ra'ad Zeid Al-Hussein (2005), A Comprehensive Strategy to Eliminate Future Sexual Exploitation and Abuse in the United Nations Peacekeeping Operations, study undertaken for the Secretary-General by the Permanent Representative of Jordan, A/59/710, 24 March.

Chapter 12

Wives and whores

Prospects for a feminist theory of redistribution

Prabha Kotiswaran, School of Oriental and African Studies, University of London

Introduction

In 2004, upon hearing that the mayor of Kolkata had promised to issue licences to sex workers, Seema Nandy, a Kolkata housewife, wrote the following letter to the editor of a Bengali newspaper:

> During the last thirty-three years of my married life, bereft of any recognition from the biological father and from the father-in-law, I could not understand throughout the whole of my life where do I belong, where is my home. Till date, I cry pretending that the tears were caused by smoke. Now if our Mayor considers the case of innumerable housewives like me, by conferring upon us the status of 'worker', then we shall be highly obliged. I am a housewife. I have pleased/entertained all the members and relatives of my in-laws, through domestic labour, for the last thirty-three years. I have tried to raise my children as good citizens. That apart, I had to do bone-crushing work day in and day out, while trying to divine the psychological conditions and needs of almost everyone. Even then there were no escape from numerous humiliations and insults. Parents told me that after marriage the house of the in-laws became my own home. Yet my husband-deity tells me on any slim pretext, 'I shall throw you out of the house' (Do mothers sometimes resort to female feticide because they swallow so much insult?) When the body revolts after the toils of a long working day from dawn to night, one has to endure the caresses of the husband, like a corpse enduring the beaks and claws of a swooping vulture.

> My request, sir, if you show a little sympathy towards these housemaids-cum-sex workers 'packaged as housewives', then at the end of our sleep-less nights we shall no more be constrained to think that, 'at the end of the day, the sacrificial fire of dejection has turned everything into ashes'. My slogan on behalf of the housewives:

'We labour, that is why we eat,
A licence is what we need'.

Seema Nandy, Kolkata 700 092[1]

The articulate Seema Nandy notwithstanding, the housewife's envy of the militant sex worker is far from paradigmatic of the complex material, cultural and attitudinal equations between wives and whores. If anything, the more familiar scripts of engagement between wives and whores in circulation include the sex worker's claim that her commercial sexual labour alone protects women, including wives, from the irrepressible sexual urge of the male; or the reverse envy of the sex worker who constantly aspires to ultimately leave life in the 'line' and lead a married life outside the red-light area; or the resentment that sex workers harbour towards relieved wives whose husbands do not visit sex workers during periods of religiously sanctioned sexual abstinence.

These scripts, however, presume the distinct institutional spheres of the family and the sex industry and the mutually exclusive existence of social actors therein. This delineation of the sex affective and sex productive realms is not always borne out empirically and renders invisible the material locations of wives and sex workers within marriage and sex work. Note, for example, the fact that 73 per cent of the sex workers in Kolkata's biggest and oldest red-light area, Sonagachi, irrespective of their class profile, have been married before entering sex work (Third Follow-Up Survey of Sonagachi Project, 1998: 18). Even though this statistic may be taken to reflect the failures of marriage as an institution, sex workers in their relationships with male lovers both conform to, and routinely challenge the boundaries of heterosexual monogamous marriage. Specifically, their affective relationships with men, not unlike marriage, often involve a complex combination of affective and material considerations. At the affective end of the spectrum of relationships, some sex workers will formally marry their male lovers or enter into marriage-like relationships with them by maintaining a marital household in the red-light area and bearing children with them. Others become concubines of male lovers, and at the most productive end of the spectrum, sex workers enter into ongoing relationships with several men who are colloquially referred to as 'fixed' customers.

Meanwhile, just as sex workers engage with the institution of marriage, wives participate in the sex industry. My preliminary study of the sex industries in two Indian cities indicated that the participation of housewives in

1   This letter appeared in the letters to the editor section of the Anandabazar Patrika on 6 April 2004, in response to the Kolkata mayor's election promise on 11 March 2004, that he would consider issuing licences to sex workers after the parliamentary elections were over. I am very grateful to Pradip Baksi for drawing my attention to this letter and for translating it from Bengali to English.

sex work was substantial and that local sex industries in fact designated housewives as 'flying' sex workers (in Kolkata) or 'secret' sex workers (in Tirupati). In fact, sex workers residential in Sonagachi in particular, complained about how flying sex workers had depressed the price of sex in the red-light area although their resentment towards flying sex workers was cultural as well. An older sex worker from the Bowbazar red-light area in Central Kolkata, for instance, noted:

> My mind has been filled with resentment and anger – not only towards men, but also towards some women and housewives. Some women who live in families as wives come here on the sly and make money. This part of their life is hidden from society. Some of them are caught red-handed, even college girls have been found here. But all the contempt of society is directed towards us. Why? Why can't we have a decent place in society? Why do people marry our children knowing fully well about their parentage and later abuse them? What steps does society take against such oppressions?
>
> (Interview with Arati Barman, 2004)

The blurred boundaries, or the adjacency at any rate, between the institutions of marriage and the sex industry are perhaps best illustrated lexically, for the most common expressions that non-sex-worker wives in a study were said to use for sex were *kaam* that is, work and *dhandha* or business, suggesting that women view sex more as a chore or involving contractual and impersonal exchange relations rather than a pleasurable activity which is the basis for a companionate marriage (Kakar, 1989). Note that *dhandha* is also a term that sex workers in North India use routinely to refer to their sex work.

This chapter stems out of an intense desire to make feminist legal sense of the continuities between and the specificities of the institutions of marriage and sex work, as well as of the traffic *of* and *by* women between these institutions with a view to interrogating their implications for the regulation of sex work.[2] In the first part of my chapter, I assess the existing feminist theorising on the relationship between marriage and sex work. Given that much more has been written about the ideological dimensions of this relationship than its material aspects, I focus in particular on feminist scholarship that theorises the materiality of female sexual labour in marriage and sex work, while acknowledging that the ideological reinforces the material and vice versa. Based on this analysis, in the second part of the chapter, I argue for the need in feminist debates on sex work and trafficking to *explicitly centre* once again, a distributive (read materialist) analysis of the economies of female sexual

---

2   Although the initial social setting for charting the relationship between sex work and marriage is Indian, I suspect that the normative discussion in the following pages will have some resonance in Western settings.

labour in marriage and sex work, which resists the exceptionalist treatment of sex work. My goal in doing so is not to flatten sex work and marriage, and normalise, much less advocate, the legalisation of sex work as conventionally understood, merely because marriage is an apparently legitimate institution. Nor do I suggest that women who enter into marriage are affected by false consciousness in their inability to view marriage as effectively amounting to sex work. Instead, I forgo an attempt at normative closure and instead synthesise the insights of feminist theory on sex work and marriage to outline a tentative regulatory project that plots the varied and differential stakes that wives and whores have in the regulation of marriage and sex work.

Wives and whores: some schema for analysis

Broadly, I see three frameworks used by feminists to theorise the relationship between marriage and sex work. The first approach (which I term the 'Overlap' approach) is where the overlap between sex work and marriage is thought to be significant. In other words, marriage is understood to approximate sex work or vice versa. The second approach (which I term the 'Continuum' approach) is keenly focussed on the continuum along which women provide sex for consideration, with marriage at one end of the continuum and sex work at the other, and how the two institutions sustain and reinforce each other in the service of patriarchy. The third approach (which I term the 'Bargaining' approach) takes on more directly the conflicting interests of women in these two institutions and uses a strategic lens to explore the bargains struck between wives and whores. I proceed to elaborate on each of these approaches, which far from being mutually exclusive, in fact, have much in common. However, I present a sharp delineation between these 'ideal' types purely for heuristic purposes.

Marriage and sex work as overlapping

In this approach, feminists theorise the overlap between marriage and sex work as being considerable. This overlap can be articulated in several ways:

(1) Definitional Overlap: here, an expansive definition of prostitution is presented under which bourgeois marriage is subsumed.
(2) Functional Overlap: here, we find in the practice of sex work, that is, a certain mode of organisation of sex work, a configuration of female labour that mimics marriage. One example is the *malaya* form of sex work in Nairobi around the time of World War II, where a certain class of sex workers sold, in addition to sexual services, a short-term rental of the woman's room and domestic services such as 'bed space, cleaning, cooking, bath water, companionship, hot meals, cold meals and tea' (White, 1986: 256) for the period of the customer's stay. This led White to

conclude that 'prostitution in Nairobi, as elsewhere, is domestic labor. In addition to sexual intercourse, prostitutes sold individual domestic tasks, or sets of tasks, that literally reproduced male labor' (White, 1986: 256). Sex tour packages in present day Thailand present another example. Alternatively, female labour in marriage could incorporate aspects of sex work. For example, Hindu Brahminical texts prescribed that a 'good wife's *dharma* was to be a servant at work, a mother at mealtimes, and a prostitute in love making' (Sangari, 1999: 358).[3]

(3) Agential Overlap: although feminist theorising has tended not to theorise this overlap,[4] agential overlap is where an actor within the institution of marriage, namely, the wife, or the female members of a family, routinely engages in sex work, or where a sex worker procreates and socially reproduces members of her own family household.

I will focus in this section on Definitional Overlap, since it exemplifies a certain mode of and moment in theorising within the canon of socialist feminism. Specifically, I use Alexandra Kollontai's writings on sex work to elaborate on this approach.

Definitional Overlap: classical socialist feminism

The socialist feminist Alexandra Kollontai attributed the existence of sex work to the stark economic reality of women under capitalism and a culture whereby women expected to be supported in return for sexual favors instead of in return for their labour (Kollontai, 1977: 265). She defined prostitutes[5] as 'women who sell their bodies for material benefit' (ibid.: 262) which included exchanging sex for food, luxury items, or favours in business and promotions at work (ibid.: 270–1). She also defined prostitutes as 'all those who avoid the necessity of working by giving themselves to man, either on a temporary basis or for life' (ibid.: 262). Thus, a housewife was also a prostitute. Given this expansive understanding of prostitution, Kollontai advocated for a pro-active role of the state, instead of waiting for communism to ameliorate conditions of poverty which led women to take up sex work. Yet when the

---

3   The overlap of marital/familial, non-marketised sexual services and marketised sex work is also visible in the Kamasutra, Vatsyayana Mallanaga (c. 3rd century CE), *Kamasutra* (trans by Wendy Doniger and Sudhir Kakar), Delhi: Oxford University Press, 2002, see Introduction lxviii and Book Six 131–59.

4   Several representations are, however, to be found in popular culture. See Ramamirtammal (1936), where the daughter of a *dasi* refuses to become a *dasi* and instead chooses to get married, but when she is abandoned by her mother, mother-in-law and husband, is forced to leave her daughter with a *dasi*. See chapter titled Vivekavathi's Plight, at 170.

5   Kollontai used the terms 'prostitution' and 'prostitute', but I use the term sex worker to refer to women who perform sex work outside marriage.

Russian interdepartmental commission for the campaign against prostitution considered the criminalisation of all parties engaged in and benefiting from sex work, the people's organisations[6] eventually decided against the criminalisation of prostitution. Neither sex workers nor their customers would be criminally prosecuted. Instead, full-time sex workers would be treated as labour deserters. Similarly, a woman who was otherwise employed but engaged in part-time sex work for supplemental income could not be criminally prosecuted. In other words, 'A prostitute is not a special case; as with other categories of deserter, she is only sent to do forced labour if she repeatedly avoids work' (Kollontai, 1977: 272). Similarly, all third parties benefiting from sex work were to be prosecuted for living off other people's earnings rather than their own labour. Customers were, however, not held guilty of labour desertion although by visiting sex workers, they were arguably violating the communist spirit of treating women as equals and with respect and possibly being less productive themselves.

Thus, even at the height of the socialist experiment and the founding of the first labour republic, sex work was sought to be eradicated. The sex worker was a signifier for the labour deserter, the corrupter of communist ideals and the impoverished condition of the woman, whether in marriage or in sex work and contrary to academic impression (Baldwin, 1992: 102), sex work was in fact viewed as the very antithesis of work.

The Overlap approach evaluated

The Overlap approach is vital in countering the current influence of radical feminist analyses of sex work which treats sex work essentially as sexual violence. For one, by asking the provocative question of whether there is any difference between sex work and marriage, it displaces the exceptionalism with which sex work is currently treated in the discursive and policy realms. Secondly, the Overlap approach as evident in Kollontai's writings was indifferent to the various forms of sexual relationships, with no underlying preference for marriage or family.[7] For Kollontai, 'a relationship is harmful and alien to the collective only *if material bargaining between the sexes is involved, only when worldly calculations* are a substitute for mutual attraction' (1977: 271). Hence 'where passion and attraction begin, prostitution ends' (ibid.: 275). So Kollontai rejected the bourgeoisie definition of sex work as rendering sexual services for payment. Instead, for her, sex work was a trope for all

---

6   These were the post-revolution years, and the governmental status of the agencies mentioned in Kollontai's speech, such as the interdepartmental commission, the Central Department, the Commissariat of Justice, etc is unclear. Hence I refer to them as the people's organisations.

7   Kollontai is in fact critical of even politically aware communists who are reluctant to acknowledge weakening family ties across Russia and who cling on to so called sacred family ties (Kollontai, 1977: 274).

sex tainted by material considerations, be it in the form of bourgeois marriage (where women sold themselves to their husbands) or the more conventional understanding of sex work that is, selling sex on a transactional basis. This then meant that the people's organisations could not find a logical reason for prosecuting sex workers while not prosecuting housewives. If sex workers were labour deserters, so were most housewives. Similarly, the people's organisations could not punish customers, for they would then have to punish most husbands. Thus, sex work had to be viewed merely as a problem of labour desertion and exploitation. Thus, Kollontai's version of socialist feminism demonstrates how a normative theory of sex, that does not distinguish between marital and non-marital sex, can only flounder when called upon to penalise non-marital sex, as opposed to radical feminism, which privileges marital sex over non-marital sex by calling for the criminalisation (even if partial, that is directed at the customer) of sex work. In the process, Kollontai brings marriage back into the debate on sex work which is in contrast to currently influential radical feminist analyses of sex work, particularly, its activist version expressed by the Coalition Against the Trafficking of Women, which view sex work as nothing but sexual violence, while ignoring the exploitation inherent in marriage unless it assumes the form of domestic violence.

Despite these insights of the Overlap approach, it has serious drawbacks. Although the Overlap approach demonstrates that no conversation on sex work is possible without debating marriage, it adopts a strong moral posture against the exchange of sex for material considerations although Kollontai acknowledged the impossibility of ascertaining whether a relationship was based on mutual attraction or material bargaining when she asked:

> Can we really persuade a couple to admit whether or not there is an element of calculation in their relationship? Would such a law be workable, particularly in view of the fact that at the present time a great variety of relationships are practiced among working people and ideas on sexual morality are in constant flux? Where does prostitution end and the marriage of convenience begin?
>
> (Kollontai, 1977: 272)

In effect then, the Overlap approach privileges uncommodified sex over commodified sex and this sustains the lingering hope that a sex affective realm unpolluted by material considerations is possible and desirable. Setting up this ideal, however, means that we are unlikely to acknowledge the vastly differential socio-economic and cultural valences of marriage and sex work and can indeed comprehend the aspirations, roles and stakes of wives and whores within these institutions solely through the flattening device of false consciousness. In the process, the materiality of female labour in both marriage and sex work, but particularly in sex work, is erased. Finally, the Overlap approach exemplified by Kollontai offers a simplistic theory of causation for sex work, namely, the poor economic status of women, the inadequacy of which has been demonstrated by the experience of erstwhile socialist states where governments undertook to rehabilitate and find alternate employment of sex workers.[8]

Marriage and sex work on a continuum

Feminist theorists have articulated different aspects of the Continuum approach in relation to varied socio-economic and historical contexts. Feminists asserting the Continuum approach repeatedly caution against collapsing marriage and sex work into each other and argue that sex work and marriage indeed form two ends of the continuum along which women provide sex for consideration. In other words, 'prostitution certain[ly] exists, . . . on a continuum with other ways of socially organising and transacting sexual relationships where relationships are already mediated by a logic of profit and loss' (Singer, 1993: 50). In some cases such as marriage, the currency used is love, romance and social legitimacy, whereas in sex work, it is money (Singer, 1993: 50). At the heart of the Continuum approach is a theory of reproductive labour, the main components of which are 'biological sex (procreation and bodily pleasure) and social maintenance services' (Truong, 1990: 194). The relationship between the sexual and social aspects of such reproductive labour is not static and uniform and hence its social, economic and political effects on women are varied. Having recognised that both wives and sex workers perform sexual labour, Truong is quick to caution against equating a housewife with a sex worker on the basis of female poverty and wagelessness since not all sex workers are poor, and not all poor housewives enter sex work (Truong, 1990: 53).

Similarly, she resists the simplistic extension of the wages-for-housework campaign of the 1970s and 1980s to wages for sex work because the consequences of wages for female reproductive labour would have highly varied consequences for wives and sex workers.

Theorists of the Continuum approach argue that patriarchy and capitalism appropriate the reproductive labour of women in both marriage (sexual and social labour) and sex work (sexual labour). The agential role of capitalism is particularly heightened in the work of Truong and Singer. For instance, Truong argues that although commercial sex pre-dated the emergence of capitalism, capitalism and the wage labour process in particular led to the

---

8   See Waters (1989) 'Restructuring the "Woman Question": *Perestroika* and Prostitution', *Feminist Review* 33, p 3 for a detailed analysis of the Russian experience.

incorporation of women's reproductive labour under exchange relations, resulting in the extraction of surpluses both by the state as well as by economic agents (Truong, 1990: 197). Further, in both their works, capitalism operates according to an inner logic which they seek to unearth. In Truong's study of the development of the Thai sex industry for instance, relating the entry of leisure into the international division of labour, Truong highlights the peripheral role that certain countries play by providing social infrastructure and facilities, but which have limited control over the processes of production and distribution, producing in effect a version of feminist dependency theory (Truong, 1990: 198).

Yet, the emergence of sex package tours has exposed contradictions in the international reach of capitalism because despite its initial role in the fragmentation and commodification of reproductive labour, it was now responsible for the re-integration of these elements of reproductive labour (Truong, 1990: 199). Similarly, Linda Singer in her study of sexual economies, in the context of the HIV epidemic, observes that a central feature of a sexual economy under late capitalism is that it forms a unitary system, which for its survival, necessarily involves a binary system of regulation. Hence, 'although the logic of late capitalism would demand an enlargement of erotic and reproductive commodities, this logic does not operate seamlessly but finds its limits regarding an oppositional profit logic in terms of which sexual labour, reproductive and erotic, must also remain the only form of labour which is unpaid and uncompensated' (Singer, 1993: 49). The value obtained from this oppositional logic is undoubtedly economic, for the invisibility of sex work as a form of labour only enhances capitalist accumulation while legitimating the use of force to discipline sex workers and increase their productivity (Truong, 1990: 197). The oppositional logic, however, also has an ideological function since all forms of uncompensated sexual exchanges are hegemonised and naturalised to sustain dominant class and gender interests (Singer, 1993: 49).

The ability to optimise the appropriation of women's sexual labour is not limited to capitalism. Sangari, writing on reforms in female domestic labour markets in the nineteenth and early twentieth century in India, notes that patriarchy appropriates female labour through its material organisation both within the household and the market (Sangari, 1999: 300), assisted by 'the consensual construction of binary oppositions between procreative and nonprocreative sexuality-good wives and "others" such as widows or prostitutes – creating a hierarchical differentiation of labour and services' (Sangari, 1999: 300). In other words, on the one hand, sex work is delinked from labour and the entry of women into sex work explained in terms of sexual gratification (Sangari, 1999: 358). On the other hand, despite the affective qualities of domestic labour, the loss of wifely status in the joint family through widowhood immediately translated into an increased load of domestic labour and reduced consumption (Sangari, 1999: 354), which then paved the way for the widow's entry into the market for domestic labour or sexual labour.

Although not adequately theorised, the Continuum approach also provides for the notion of the traffic of, and by, women between the institutions of marriage and sex work. For example, both sex workers and widows represented the potential slide from the domestic economy of labour to the market economy of labour (Sangari, 1999: 358). Ultimately, proponents of the Continuum approach argue that, by appropriating and optimising women's reproductive labour, the institutions of marriage and sex work reinforce each other in complicated ways. Effectively then, 'both marriage and prostitution unilaterally guaranteed the availability of many women to one man, along a range of fluctuating monetary arrangements' (Sangari, 1999: 359).

The Continuum approach evaluated

The Continuum approach furthers a feminist politics of redistribution in relation to sex work in important ways. To begin with, the materiality of female reproductive labour, including sexual labour, is forefronted within the Continuum approach. Further, the Continuum approach keeps both sex work and marriage in the conversation by highlighting their differential institutional co-ordinates for female sexual labour without collapsing them into each other or articulating a hidden preference for one over the other. To that extent, the Continuum approach does not treat sex work as exceptional. This appears to offer a discursive space for debating sex work in a way that the radical feminist analytic of sex work does not, concerned as it is with sexual violence rather than sexual labour.

Despite the strengths of the Continuum approach, its perspective on the regulation of sex work warrants closer examination. Singer, for example, while acknowledging the differential legal regulation of marriage and sex work is against the legalisation of sex work. She is sceptical that the exploitation in sex work can be eliminated through legalisation when legality and selective exploitation co-exist in marriage and employment (Singer, 1993: 56). In making this argument, however, she explicitly draws on the radical feminist analytic of sex work which either negates the possibility of any choice on the part of the sex worker or understands its existence as false consciousness. Hence, when sex workers argue that they are superior to wives because they can negotiate the substantive and temporal aspects of paid transactional sex rather than committing to life-long unpaid sex on demand, Singer views them as labouring under false consciousness (Singer, 1993: 54). After all, for one who has demonstrated that the power of capital lurks everywhere, it is ironic that monetary mediation should be articulated in terms of personal autonomy (Singer, 1993: 48).

Similarly, Truong acknowledges that the recognition of the sex workers' labour would help in their organisation. However, according to her, given the inexorable surge of capital in developed and developing countries, its prolific commodification of pleasure and eroticism and the sexual subordination of women that leads to the availability in sexual labour to begin with is 'to stop judging prostitution is one thing, but to cease imposing ethical boundaries on the use of sexual labour is quite another' (Truong, 1990: 202). In other words, treating sex work as legitimate work would be ethically problematic. There are certainly many valid reasons for not wanting to treat sex work as a form of legitimate work. As I suggested earlier, the goal of this chapter is not to argue that since sex work involves a component of reproductive labour which most women perform, namely, sexual labour, it should be treated as a form of legitimate work, to be regulated in turn by currently available models of legalisation. Instead I am interested in examining the modes of argumentation which feminists employ in dismissing any move to alter the sex work–marriage continuum by making sex work legal – a status that marriage already enjoys. The legality of marriage is far from being a sufficient condition for the elimination of the exploitation of wives. However, it is not clear from this deficiency of legality why it should be withheld from sex work at the very threshold. In my view, despite the nuanced analysis of the sex work–marriage continuum, the stumbling block to legalising sex work (whether that means simply making it legal, that is decriminalising it or legalising it by regulating it) comes from a certain understanding of the powers of global capitalism. To the extent that Singer treats any indication of sex worker agency in the face of late capitalism as symptomatic of false consciousness and Truong feels compelled to impose ethical boundaries on the expansionist forays of capitalism in markets for women's sexual labour (suggesting that it is otherwise without boundary), one might argue that the Continuum approach is informed by a theory of power, which like radical feminism, shares many of the features of what Kennedy calls paranoid structuralism.[9]

---

9   Paranoid structuralism teaches us that it is part of our modern social and individual psychological condition that we are playthings of forces whose existence and true relationships the 'normal' discourse of our world denies, thereby helping to reproduce the denied condition. The forces have a 'logic' we can master, to some extent, but only if we overcome the denial ... The paranoid structuralist asks how unwanted things get reproduced, rather than how the organism sustains itself through time. The answer is paranoid because it emphasises that 'out there' forces or people or structures operate behind our backs, insinuating themselves into our very being to make us feel that we are freely choosing what is bad for us. The result is that we can't trust ourselves or anyone else, unless and until ... we have undergone enlightenment.

(Kennedy, 2001: 1169.)

Kennedy characterises radical feminists as using the template of paranoid structuralism (Kennedy, 2001: 1173–4).

As Kennedy has observed, 'even as an explanatory device, the abstract notion of "men's interests" or the "interests of capital" and in the case of post-colonial dependency theory, an intersection of both, suppresses too many particularities to be useful in understanding the problem at hand' (Kennedy, 1993: 150). Since the purpose of this chapter is not to enter a social theoretical debate on structuralism, I will limit myself to two cautionary notes.

The first cautionary note relates to the exemplary powers of explanation that theorists of the Continuum approach attribute to capitalism. This I think has the potential to detract from contextual studies of the political economies of sex industries. For example, Indian feminists often argue that if the state were ever to decriminalise sex work, India would become another Thailand. This is despite the fact that although urban Indian sex industries may have originated in the wake of the expansionist projects of colonial capital, they are structured as informal labour markets whose links to tourism-driven global capital are tenuous. Convenient analogies thus come at the cost of a more precise accounting for the histories of capital in these two national contexts. It does not help either that feminist theory at this historical juncture presents disincentives to the study of the economics of sex industries. Note, for example, how when the ILO attempted to study the sex industry as an 'economic sector' in South East Asia in 1998, radical feminists accused the International Labour Organisation of advocating a laissez faire approach to sex work and supporting legalisation. Against the backdrop of such disciplining measures, one has to be particularly wary of theoretical projects which overstate the power of capital.

The second cautionary note relates to the propensity of the Continuum approach for being used more generally to support the abolition of sex work. In other words, a theory of reproductive labour and the consequent recognition of the sexual labour inherent in sex work is no guarantee that calls to abolition will not persist, based on the claim that sex work as a form of labour is inherently harmful like child labour and should be abolished (D'Cunha, 1997: 230). This in some ways rehearses prior debates within feminism on the foundational status of sex work, albeit on the register of women's labour (that is, is sex work slavery or wage labour?). This suggests that the Continuum approach may continue to be used to selectively target sex work but not marriage itself.

The bargain between marriage and sex work – left liberal law and economics

The Bargaining approach, or the understanding that wives and sex workers have explicitly conflicting stakes in the regulation of sex work, is arguably the most intuitive one in fathoming the relationship between marriage and sex work. Cultural expressions of the routine bargains struck between sex workers and wives abound.[10] Colonial texts make mention of aristocratic British women in colonial India who insisted that the colonial government provide lower class British soldiers with native prostitutes so that they did not molest decent British women (Andrew and Bushnell, 1899: 13–14). Sex worker narratives repeatedly suggest that it is sex workers' labour that keeps potential rapists off the street and marriages intact. How does feminist theory make sense of such bargains struck between sex workers and wives on the streets, in brothels and bedrooms, every day and every night and everywhere, other than symptomatic of false consciousness?

Linda Hirshman and Jane Larson, applying a bargaining model of law and economics to understand the bargains between wives and whores, argue that sex workers and wives have historically never been able to adopt a united stance on sex work because sex workers in the short run, bid down the price of heterosexual access and where anti-sex work efforts by non-sex workers could be thought of as 'collective bargaining', sex workers could be understood as 'strikebreakers' (Hirshman and Larson, 1998: 287). Hence, while non-sex workers may collectively act to raise the price of sexual access for men to all women (whether wives or sex workers) by strengthening rape law, or requiring an implied contract of concubinage in the case of sex work, non-sex workers are known to use anti-sex work criminal laws to close off avenues through which men gain access to defectors from collective bargaining efforts (Hirshman and Larson, 1998: 291). In reality, however, anti-sex work laws drive up the price of sexual access and affect the availability of sex workers (Hirshman and Larson, 1998: 260). Hirshman and Larson view anti-sex work laws as hypocritical and the lack of consent and the commodification of sex as inadequate defences for criminalising sex work, especially given the perceived beneficial effect of decriminalisation on sex workers. They therefore argue for placing sex work within the purview of labour law and outside of criminal law, but view selling sex as an illegal labour contract, subject to the same penalties as those attending socially unacceptable and undesirable forms of labour such as sweatshop labour or child labour. For this, they cite the special nature of sex (Hirshman and Larson, 1998: 291) and the exceptional harm of sex work which cannot be reduced by legalisation to levels of domestic violence in marriage.

10 For example, there is the nod and the wink that Chameli (played by Kareena Kapoor) directs towards Aman Kapoor (played by Rahul Bose) in the Hindi movie *Chameli* (only '*ghar ka khana*' (or home cooked food)?, she asks rhetorically) or the triumphant revenge of abolitionist wives in the novel, *Web of Deceit* who assume the guise of a *dasi* (courtesan) to win their husbands back, only to go on to reform the *dasis* through marriage (*Web of Deceit*, 2003); the novel is replete with several instances of robust 'bargaining' of the part of both *dasis* and wives over money and male affection, respectively.

The Bargaining approach evaluated

On the one hand, the Bargaining approach problematises the category of woman which much feminist theory takes for granted. For this reason, it demonstrates the vastly varying stakes that at least two different groups of women, namely, wives and sex workers have in the regulation of sex work, without, in my view, forsaking a feminist project. For instance, it is plausible that even assuming that sex workers reduce the bargaining power of all women, amendments to the rape law, requiring a contract of concubinage as Hirschman and Larson themselves suggest, or using the strategies of organised labour, could substantially increase the rights of the weaker workers so that the interests of both stronger workers (wives), as Larson and Hirschman characterise them, and the weaker workers (sex workers) are protected. However, treating sex as special leads Hirschman and Larson to invoke a politics of harm and injury to argue that while for pragmatist reasons, sex work should be decriminalised, it should not be recognised as a form of labour. It is then highly unclear how, as Hirschman and Larson suggest, 'prostitutes could demand payment for work performed under an illegal contract, protest harsh working conditions, or unionise without suffering legal penalty, even though their employment would remain illegal' (Hirshman and Larson, 1998: 289). In other words, is the regulatory model that Hirshman and Larson suggest, substantially different from the current criminalisation of sex work, harboring as it does an aspiration for abolition? Does the game theoretic modelling of the Bargaining approach then simply amount to setting the baseline for negotiation by non-sex workers while paying lip service to the interests of sex workers by producing a utilitarian result in favour of stronger players, namely wives?

Feminist theorising on sex work revisited

So far, I have outlined the Overlap, Continuum and Bargaining approaches on the relationship between marriage and sex work. In this section, I situate these approaches in relation to the broader debate within feminism on sex work. For this, I briefly summarise the state of the debate as I view it before going on to articulate how I think a politics of redistribution, inspired by insights from the three approaches outlined above, might present a critical intervention in this debate. It is now fair to say that in the wake of the sex wars of the 1980s, feminist theorising around sex work and trafficking occupied two major feminist camps, that of the individualists and structuralists. Crudely put, structuralist feminists are against the commodification of sex; they view sex work as coercion, violence, and bad sex and view sex workers as victims who lack agency and are slaves to institutionalised violence. Individualist feminists, on the other hand, are agnostic to the commodification of sex; they understand sex work in terms of choice and work and view sex workers as agents who can negotiate within institutions as individuals. Both camps have institutional power, most recently evidenced in the role they played in the passage of the UN Protocol against trafficking[11] (Doezema, 2005; Halley *et al.*, 2006).

While feminist legal projects of regulation are arguably more amenable to such polarised presentations, feminist theorising is far more nuanced and sophisticated than these ideal typical formulations of the feminist position of sex work and trafficking suggest. Indeed, feminists are always mindful of the fractious nature of the feminist debates on sex work and negotiate their ways around them even if this means simply acknowledging the need for breaking out of the impasse in light of the limitations of both approaches. For that matter, even structuralist feminists will acknowledge that sex workers have some agency, some of the time, and that the commodification of sex may be permissible on pragmatic grounds,[12] while individualist feminists will recognise that sex workers choose to do sex work out of a highly restricted set of livelihood options and experience violence in sex work. Most feminists however, unable to resolve the originating fundamental dilemma over the terms of this debate – is sex work a form of work or violence, is it chosen or coerced, are sex workers agents or victims? – belie an uneasy truce between the ideal types of the structuralist analysis offered by radical feminists, on the one hand, and the individualist analysis offered by sex radicals and sex workers, on the other. In other words, in between these two apparently extreme feminist camps lies a continuum of feminist positions of a structuralist or individualist persuasion.

A sub-set of these feminists are motivated by an impulse to hybridise these opposing feminist camps and set out to make peace (Lucas, 1998: 432; Sunder Rajan, 2003: 142; Van der Veen, 2001) between the feminists who occupy the two extreme ends of the continuum. They articulate a mode of argumentation whereby they support the rights of sex workers but not the right to sex work (Overall, 1992: 723–4; D'Cunha, 1997: 252); they support empowering practices of individual sex workers within the sex industry but are against the institution of prostitution itself (Overall, 1992: 723; Sullivan, 1997: 165; Sunder Rajan, 2003: 146); and acknowledge the agency of sex workers but interrogate why sex work should be viewed as work (Sunder Rajan, 2003: 138–40). I call such feminism middle-ground feminism. Specifically, when confronted by sex workers' demands for workers' rights, middle-ground feminism is able to respond only in the language of harm and injury and reject proposals for workers' rights for sex workers because sex work causes

11 Protocol to Prevent, Suppress and Punish Trafficking in Persons, Especially Women and Children, Supplementing the United Nations Convention Against Transnational Organized Crime, GA Res 25, Annex II, UN GAOR, 55th Sess, Supp No 49, at 60, UN Doc A/45/49 (Vol I) (2001).
12 See generally Radin (1996).

'harm with a capital H' to both sex workers and non-sex workers. This harm with a capital H can be further broken down into four harms (Millett, 1971; Barry, 1979; Barry, 1995; Jeffreys, 1997).[13] The first most obvious harm being the physical, emotional and mental harm and exploitation resulting directly from sex work itself; the second harm being the harm arising from the object-ification and commodification of women in sex work (Radin, 1996); the third harm being its gendered reality and its consequent feminisation; and the fourth harm being the harm done to all women because sex work reinforces stereotypes of female availability, exacerbates gender inequality and is a form of sex discrimination (Satz, 1995: 64; Shrage, 1989: 349, 352; Overall, 1992: 721; Hirshman and Larson, 1998: 291). The feminist resistance to considering sex work as a form of legitimate work is despite the fact that these harms (even with a capital H) are not unique to sex work, so while they cannot be ignored, invoking them does not constitute a compelling argument for not conceptualising sex work as a form of labour or legitimate work or for abol-ishing sex work. Again, I am not arguing here that sex work should be a form of work, only that the vocabulary of harm and injury in relation to sex work has a propensity to obliterate the fact that many women, whether wives or whores, perform sexual labour in vastly varied contexts. A case in point is where middle-ground feminism calls upon sex workers who demand workers' rights to explain to feminism the nature of the labour involved in sex work and why it should be recognised as work (Sunder Rajan, 2003: 140).

It is in light of the above feminist theorising of sex work that we need to recollect the normative inputs of the Overlap, Continuum and Bargaining approaches in propelling it from a politics of harm and injury towards a politics of redistribution. It is fair to say that socialist feminist analyses of sex work, which informs much of the three approaches I have outlined, have for a range of historical, political and otherwise unfathomable reasons in the feminist debates on sex work, been overshadowed and even mischaracterised as supporting sex work as a form of legitimate work (Baldwin, 1999: 102). Of course, one might argue that at the end of the day, the 'result' in policy terms of the socialist and radical feminist analyses of sex work would not have differed too much. After all, even in the labour republic, sex work was viewed as the very antithesis of work. Still the modes of argumentation of these two strands of feminist theorising have significant differences, the most pertinent one being, in my view, the socialist feminist insights into the relationship between sex work and marriage. This is consistently true for the socialist feminists who I have considered in this chapter irrespective of whether they adopt the Overlap approach, the Continuum approach or the Bargaining approach. This is in contrast to the legacy of the radical feminist analytic on sex work which effectively privileges marriage over sex work. The result is that

---

13 But see Nussbaum, 1999: 288–97, for a detailed response to these harm-based arguments.

the contemporary feminist debate on sex work has largely dropped marriage out of the debate by treating sex work as an exceptional condition. Even where feminists ostensibly keep marriage in the debate by highlighting social practices like mail-order brides, the marriage contract is treated as a corrupted form of marriage which is merely another form of sex work without problematising marriage more generally or keeping in view the differences between mail-order brides and sex workers.[14] In this sense, despite the short-comings of the Overlap, Continuum and Bargaining approaches, they are valuable to a feminist politics of redistribution in relation to sex work.

In lieu of a conclusion: implications for legal projects of redistribution

In this concluding section, I briefly contemplate how feminist frameworks for theorising the relationship between marriage and sex work as exemplified by the Overlap, Continuum and Bargaining approaches could inform the regulatory debates surrounding sex work. In particular, I am interested in how these approaches might both deepen and widen an understanding of the distributional consequences of anti-sex-work laws so as to ultimately expand the rather limited regulatory repertories to be found in the current feminist discourse on sex work. An attempt at such distributional legal analysis might more generally signal towards the scope of the project of rendering sex work less exceptional, the substantive possibilities it offers and the methodological challenges it poses.

In attempting distributional legal analysis I assume the plurality of social actors within the institutions of marriage and sex work, their institutional locations and the relational dynamics between them. I draw on legal realism to assert that the legal playing field in any given situation consists not only of the legal rules at hand but also legal rules that structure the alternatives to remaining in the bargaining situation (Kennedy, 1993: 87). Further, I assume that the legal system does not ordain any one set of outcomes, that social actors differentially endowed by the rule network routinely enter into bargains with each other and that these bargains can in turn be plotted to assess the distributional outcomes of any given set of rules (Kennedy, 2002: 80).

Although an extensive cataloguing of social actors is possible based on the Overlap, Continuum and Bargaining approaches, I will confine myself to three sets of actors. Drawing on the Overlap approach is the housewife who does sex work secretly to support her family. Similarly, drawing on the notion of the traffic *of and by* women between the institutions of marriage and sex work within the Continuum approach, we have the wife who due to the

14 Note, for instance, the lack of any serious consideration of women's sexual labour in marriage in an article exhorting the adoption of a labour paradigm on sex work (Hernandez-Truyol and Larson, 2006).

failure of her marriage either voluntarily enters sex work under force of circumstance or is trafficked into sex work by a trafficker. Finally, drawing on the Bargaining approach, we could assume the existence of two sets of heterosexual married couples, one in which the husband visits a sex worker and the other in which the husband does not visit a sex worker.

The most obvious set of legal rules that affects sex work are anti-sex-work laws. Rules that structure the alternative to being in the bargaining situation, in this case marriage, are family law rules. Let us assume for the moment then that the rules regulating sex work criminalise all activities necessary in order to do sex work. Let us assume also that family law rules which typically determine the terms of entry into marriage, the conditions of marriage and exit from marriage, in the current context, do not provide for the remuneration of reproductive labour performed by wives within the home. In this first legal scenario, one may hypothesise that the wife who does sex work secretly resorts to sex work because her reproductive labour is not remunerated and her only option to support her family is by selling her sexual labour in the market. Similarly, we have the wife who, upon the failure of her marriage, is unable to claim any remuneration for the years of reproductive labour that she has rendered to her family and who gets trafficked into sex work because the criminalisation of sex work makes it lucrative for traffickers to do so.

As for heterosexual married couples where the husband visits a sex worker, the wife has limited bargaining power, not in the least, because her position in the marriage is vulnerable and should she exit, she will have no means of subsistence or reward for her reproductive labour. Finally, even seemingly disinterested parties like wives and their husbands who do not visit sex workers have stakes in this status quo. Anti-sex-work laws that criminalise sex work benefit husbands who are not customers of sex workers because anti-sex work laws terrorise wives should they contemplate exit from marriage. Wives may also benefit, albeit to a lesser extent than husbands, from such laws, since the risk of arrest must have some deterrent effect on the husband. Overall, however, heterosexual married couples will benefit from anti-sex work laws to the extent that the law privileges marital, procreative and affective sex.[15] From this foregoing discussion, the vastly differential stakes of wives, sex workers and husbands in the regulation of marriage and sex work are already evident.

Let us now consider a second legal scenario where there is no change in family law rules and that reproductive labour within the home continues to be unpaid. Let us also assume that the rules pertaining to sex work have changed; that sex work is no longer criminalised and is instead regulated by the state so as to render sex work less violent, more safe and conducive to the

---

15 I base this on the idea of the tolerated residuum; see Kennedy (1997: 155, 159–60).

empowerment of sex workers. What then are the implications of these rule changes for the social actors that I have identified? Although the legalisation of sex work may, on the face of it, appear to be beneficial for the wife who does sex work secretly, the increased regulation of sex work in fact risks the exposure of her identity. Hence the new set of legal rules will in fact compel her to stop doing sex work, which in turn means that her bargaining power within the marriage is reduced. In effect then, she will be worse off due to the change in anti-sex work laws. As for the wife who enters sex work because of the breakdown of her marriage, the legalisation of sex work may mean that she now enters sex work under force of circumstance but relatively voluntarily, that she is less likely to be trafficked and that she views sex work purely as a short-term work option.

As for the heterosexual married couple where the husband visits sex workers, the legalisation of sex work could have varying results. If the legalisation of sex work and the attendant improvement in working conditions leads to an influx of women into the sex industry, thereby depressing the price per sex-work transaction, the husband will continue to visit sex workers and may in fact visit them more often. In the absence of any changes in the family law rules, the bargaining power of the wife in this marriage will weaken. If however, despite the lower price per sex-work transaction, the increased regulation of sex work leads to a loss of pleasure, then assuming that the husband has no access to other sexual economies, such as say, extra-marital unpaid sex, the bargaining power of the wife in this marriage will increase. Finally, in the case of the heterosexual married couple where the husband does not visit sex workers, the legalisation of sex work could mean that wives enjoy a psychic benefit because sex work is now less terrific. A few wives may even contemplate exiting marriage and entering sex work. Where the legalisation of sex work leads to a lower price per sex-work transaction, or the lifting of prior social sanction, husbands may begin to visit sex workers thereby reducing the bargaining power of wives who continue to stay in the marriage.

The limited distributional legal analysis that I have attempted above is by no means exhaustive or conclusive. Indeed it is possible to contemplate a model with several other scenarios, involving a larger sub-set of social actors, legal rules (for example, labour laws) and sexual economies (for example, sex harassment, pornography, sexy dressing, erotic dancing, adultery, consensual non-marital sex, cohabitation and so on).

It does however suggest that if we were to forefront marriage in the debates on sex work, that we will find that the categories of sex worker and wife are by no means unitary or mutually exclusive, that a range of social actors other than sex workers and their customers have vastly differential stakes in the legal regulation of sex work and marriage, that any change in one set of background rules relating to either sex work or marriage will produce varied distributional consequences for these stakeholders, and that these consequences cannot be predicted *a priori*. Most importantly, the distributional consequences of any set of legal rules regulating sex work cannot be assessed without mapping the consequences that this would have for wives and vice versa. This I suggest will further a politics of redistribution both for wives and whores.

Bibliography

Andrew, E and Bushnell, K C (1899) *The Queen's Daughters in India*, London: Morgan and Scott.

Baldwin, M (1992) 'Split at the Root: Prostitution and Feminist Discourses of Law Reform', *Yale Journal of Law & Feminism* 5, pp 47–120.

Barry, K (1979) *Female Sexual Slavery*, Englewoods Cliffs: Prentice Hall.

Barry, K (1995) *The Prostitution of Sexuality*, New York: New York University Press.

D'Cunha, J (1997) 'Prostitution The Contemporary Feminist Discourse', in Thapan, M (ed.), *Embodiment: Essays on gender and identity*, Delhi: Oxford University Press, pp 230–51.

Department of Epidemiology All India Institute of Hygiene and Public Health, Calcutta & Family Health International, Report of the Third Follow-Up Survey of Sonagachi Project 18 (April-June 1998).

DMSC-TAAH Research Project, Interview with Arati Barman 8 (2004).

Doezema, J (2005) 'Now You See Her, Now You Don't: Sex Workers at the UN Trafficking Protocol Negotiations', *Social & Legal Studies* 14(1): 61–89.

Frug, M J (1992) 'A Postmodern Feminist Legal Manifesto, (An Unfinished Draft)', *Harvard Law Review* 105, pp 1045–75.

Halley, J, Kotiswaran, P, Shamir, H and Thomas, C, (2006) 'From the International to the Local in Feminist Legal Responses to Rape, Prostitution/Sex Work, and Sex Trafficking', *Harvard Journal of Law & Gender* 29(2): 335–422.

Hernandez-Truyol, B and Larson, J (2006) 'Sexual Labor and Human Rights', *Columbia Human Rights Law Review* 37, pp 391–445.

Hirshman, L and Larson, J (1998) *Hard Bargains: The Politics of Sex*, New York: Oxford University Press.

Jeffreys, S (1997) *The Idea of Prostitution*, North Melbourne: Spinifex Press.

Kakar, S (1989) Intimate Relations Exploring Indian Sexuality, Delhi: Oxford University Press.

Kamasutra (trans by Wendy Doniger and Sudhir Kakar) (2002), Delhi: Oxford University Press.

Kennedy, D (1993) *Sexy Dressing Etc: Essays on the Power and Politics of Cultural Identity*, Cambridge: Harvard University Press.

Kennedy, D (2001) 'A Semiotics of Critique', *Cardozo Law Review* 22, pp 1147–89.

Kennedy, D, (2002) 'Legal Economics of US Low Incomes Markets in Light of "Informality" Analysis', *The Journal of Law in Society* 4, pp 71–98.

Kollontai, A (trans from Russian by Alix Holt) (1977) *Selected Writings of Alexandra Kollontai*, London: Allison and Busby.

Lucas, A (1998), 'The Dis(-)ease of Being a Woman: Rethinking Prostitution and Subordination', unpublished PhD thesis, University of California, Berkeley.

Millett, K (1971) *The Prostitution Papers*, New York: Ballantine Books.

Nussbaum, M (1999) *Sex & Social Justice*, New York: Oxford University Press.

Overall, C (1992) 'What's Wrong with Prostitution? Evaluating Sex Work', *Signs* 17, pp 705–24.

Protocol to Prevent, Suppress and Punish Trafficking in Persons, Especially Women and Children, Supplementing the United Nations Convention Against Transnational Organized Crime, GA Res 25, Annex II, UN GAOR, 55th Sess, Supp No 49, at 60, UN Doc A/45/49 (Vol.I) (2001).

Radin, M (1996) *Contested Commodities*, Cambridge: Harvard University Press.

Ramamirtammal, M (1936) *Web of Deceit* (trans by Kalpana Kannabiran and Vasanth Kannabiran, 2003), Delhi: Kali for Women.

Sangari, K (1999) *Politics of the Possible: Essays on Gender, History, Narratives, Colonial English*, Delhi: Tulika.

Satz, D (1995) 'Markets in Women's Sexual Labor', *Ethics* 106, pp 63–85.

Shrage, L (1989) 'Should Feminists Oppose Prostitution', *Ethics* 99, pp 347–61.

Singer, L (1993) *Erotic Welfare, Sexual Theory and Politics in the Age of Epidemic*, Butler, J and MacGrogan, M (ed.), New York: Routledge.

Sullivan, B (1997) *The Politics of Sex: Prostitution and Pornography in Australia Since 1945*, Cambridge: Cambridge University Press.

Sunder Rajan, R (2003) *The Scandal of the State: Women, Law and Citizenship in Postcolonial India*, Durham: Duke University Press.

Truong, T (1990) *Sex, money and morality: prostitution and tourism in southeast Asia*, London: Zed Books.

Van der Veen, M (2001) 'Rethinking Commodification and Prostitution: An Effort at Peacemaking in the Battles over Prostitution', *Rethinking Marxism* 13, pp 30–51.

White, L (1986) 'Prostitution, Identity, and Consciousness in Nairobi during World War II', *Signs* 11(2): 255–73.

Index